The Paradox of Church and World

The Paradox of Church and World

Selected Writings of H. Richard Niebuhr

Jon Diefenthaler

Fortress Press
Minneapolis

THE PARADOX OF CHURCH AND WORLD

Selected Writings of H. Richard Niebuhr

Copyright © 2015 Fortress Press. All rights reserved. Except for brief quotations in critical articles or reviews, no part of this book may be reproduced in any manner without prior written permission from the publisher. Visit http://www.augsburgfortress.org/copyrights/ or write to Permissions, Augsburg Fortress, Box 1209, Minneapolis, MN 55440.

Images in this book are in the public domain and are provided courtesy of: Special Collections, Yale Divinity School Library; Eden Theological Seminary Archives; William G. Chrystal.

Cover image: American theologian Dr Helmut Richard Niebuhr (1894 – 1962) at Yale Divinity School, New Haven, Connecticut, 4th October 1955. Photo by Alfred Eisenstaedt/The LIFE Picture Collection/Getty Images

Cover design: Tory Herman

Library of Congress Cataloging-in-Publication Data

Print ISBN: 978-1-4514-9414-3

eBook ISBN: 978-1-5064-0261-1

The paper used in this publication meets the minimum requirements of American National Standard for Information Sciences — Permanence of Paper for Printed Library Materials, ANSI Z329.48-1984.

Manufactured in the U.S.A.

This book was produced using PressBooks.com, and PDF rendering was done by PrinceXML.

In memory of
Marlin George Diefenthaler
(1914–2002)

Contents

Acknowledgments	ix
General Introduction: Reexamining H. Richard Niebuhr	xi

Part I. Formative Years in the Evangelical Synod

1.	The Evangelical Synod and the New World of America	3
2.	Addressing the World of the Roaring Twenties	33
3.	Worldly Impediments to Churchly Integrity	85
4.	First Prescriptions for Church Revitalization	127
	Plates	171

Part II. The Crucible of the Great Depression

5.	The Church in a World of Social Upheaval	177
6.	Reconsidering Worldly Issues from an Orthodox Christian Standpoint	219
7.	Back to the Future Of Cultural Engagement	261

Plates *299*

Part III. Challenges of War and Peace

8. The Church and a World Again at War *305*
9. The Peacetime Church and the Threat of World Communism *357*
10. Reclaiming the Church's Reformation Heritage *425*

Epilogue: Niebuhr and Post-Church America *499*
Index of Names and Subjects *523*

Acknowledgments

My wife Vivi is a woman of deep personal piety and prayer. Almost nothing for her is off-limits when it comes to seeing the hand of God. For this reason, she is thoroughly convinced that there are no accidents in life. Work on this book, from beginning to end, has made Vivi's perspective more credible for me. When I sat down with Will Bergkamp of Fortress Press in the faculty lounge on a spring afternoon at Concordia Seminary in St. Louis, my highest hope was to gain the advice of a seasoned religious book editor on whether an effort to bring together some of the writings of H. Richard Niebuhr was worth pursuing. That conversation immediately led to the proposal that in a relatively short time eventuated in the manuscript that Fortress has now seen fit to publish.

Along the way, there have been several others who have made significant contributions to the process, whom I must acknowledge with deep gratitude. First and foremost, there is Matthew Borrasso, a student in one of my classes at Concordia who is now serving as parish pastor in The Lutheran Church—Missouri Synod in Parkton, Maryland. This bright young man immediately took an interest in this project and since then has accompanied me at every step toward its completion, serving as a regular conversation partner and preparing the entire manuscript according to the publisher's specifications. Matt's interest in Niebuhr and his assisting role in assembling the contents of this book have made it plain to me that there may be a very promising future for him as a religious scholar.

I must also acknowledge with great thanks the assistance of Gustav Niebuhr, who is honoring his grandfather's legacy with distinction in the academic world at Syracuse University, for granting permission to include many of the published and unpublished documents that appear on the pages that follow. Recognition must be given as well to two seminary presidents in the St. Louis area. Dale Meyer of Concordia made it possible for me to join his seminary faculty as an adjunct professor, and David Greenhaw of Niebuhr's Eden Seminary not only gave me his enthusiastic support but graciously allowed the publication of the articles connected with Niebuhr's years in the Evangelical Synod of North America. I am grateful as well for those who read at least some portions of the manuscript and shared their comments, especially William Chrystal, John Nunes, James Burkee, Anthony Cook, Robert Kolb, and my long-time friend and seminary classmate, Richard Lischer. Not to be overlooked are the Fortress staff assigned to this book, Esther Diley, Lisa Gruenisen, and Layne Meyer. All performed their important roles with great care and attention to detail.

The dedication of this book is to my late father, Marlin George Diefenthaler, not only because his father's denominational ancestry was the same as that of the Niebuhr family, but because he, more than anyone else in my life, showed me what it means to be a truly "evangelical" Christian.

Jon Diefenthaler
June 2015

General Introduction: Reexamining H. Richard Niebuhr

The ancient Christian paradox of church and world is one with which Helmut Richard Niebuhr (1894–1962) wrestled deeply, and often profoundly, over the course of his career as a prominent twentieth-century American theologian. Long before him, St. Luke demonstrated his awareness of it in his two-volume New Testament account of the life of Jesus and the early Christian church. More specific insights surfaced in the second-century *Epistle to Diognetus,* which asserted that "nowhere" do Christians "live in cities of their own" or "practice an eccentric way of life"[1] because, as the church father Tertullian (155–240) put it in addressing the provincial governors of the Roman Empire, they "sojourn with you in the world, abjuring neither forum, nor shambles, nor bath, nor booth, nor workshop, nor inn, nor weekly market, nor any other places of commerce."[2] Perhaps the best source for this paradox, however, has always been the Gospel of St. John, where Jesus prays to his Father

---

1. "The Epistle to Diognetus," in *The Apostolic Fathers in English,* 3rd ed., trans. and ed. Michael W. Holmes (Grand Rapids: Baker Academic, 2006), 288–301.
2. Tertullian, "The Apology," in *Latin Christianity: Its Founder, Tertullian,* The Ante-Nicene Fathers 3, ed. Alexander Roberts, James Donaldson, and Arthur Cleveland Coxe (New York: Cosimo Classics, 2007), 17–60.

on behalf of his disciples, "They do not belong to the world, just as I do not belong to the world. Sanctify them in the truth; your word is truth. As you have sent me into the world, so I have sent them into the world" (John 17:16-18 NRSV). On the basis of this text, Christians have tended to believe that as the Son of God, Jesus, who was not of the world, came into the world to reveal the truth about God. While here, he called disciples out of the world they were in, only to send them back into it for the purpose of carrying on the same saving mission for which he had come.

As the body of Christ, the church, therefore, is always to be *in* but not *of* the world. While the steps in this process of reasoning are logical ones, the concluding idea that it yields is not. To be *in* the world and at the same time not *of* the world are seemingly contradictory notions. Yet because both are in fact true, they form a paradox, two truths about the church that must be dynamically kept in tension with each other as it engages the world into which its Lord continues to send it.

H. Richard Niebuhr's insights into this paradox are reflected in the three major works for which he is still remembered. The first was published in 1929 as *The Social Sources of Denominationalism*. While it employed sociological analysis in order to explain the multitude of denominational divisions in American Protestantism, this book was also an exposé of a church that had repeatedly become *of* the world into which it had been sent. To him, it made no difference whether one looked at denominations in terms of class, region, nation, immigrant origins, or racial identity. All of them of were guilty of worldly accommodation.

His second major work, which came off the press in 1937, put greater emphasis on the opposite side of the paradoxical relationship between church and world. In *The Kingdom of God in America*, he combed through the records of America's religious past in search of places where faith in God as Father, Son, and Holy Spirit had altered the surrounding world in which its churches had been at work. In the process, the book succeeded not only in bringing the Puritans, Jonathan Edwards, and the later evangelical revivalists out of the dark cellar to which secular historians had relegated them, but in helping encourage a subsequent generation of religious historians to give more extensive attention to the role of their theology in the shaping of American culture. Here he also chose to depict the church's relationship to the world as a "dialectical movement" that was expressed "in the direction toward God and the direction toward the world which is loved in God, in the pilgrimage toward the eternal kingdom and in the desire to make his will real on earth."[3]

Appearing in 1951, his book *Christ and Culture* outlined five distinct Christian attitudes toward the world. Between the two extremes of worldly (Christ *of* culture) and separatist (Christ *against* culture) types of behavior on the part of the church, he placed three mediating varieties, all of which sought to keep the church in its "in-but-not-of" relationship with the world. The synthesist type (Christ *above* culture) commended the world for its civilized achievements, but still needed the church to point it to a godly center of value. The dualist type (Christ and culture *in paradox*) vested Christians with a double citizenship and called upon them to give allegiance to the church and to the state in each of these "two kingdoms." For the conversionist type (Christ *the transformer of* culture), the entire world, while corrupted by human sinfulness, remained the one sphere of divine activity, and for this reason proponents saw the church's mission as one aiding of its redemption by calling upon societies as well as individuals to turn away from their idolatries and to make God the focus of their faith. Frequent references to one or more

---

3. H. Richard Niebuhr, *The Kingdom of God in America* (New York: Harper & Row, 1937), xiv–xv.

of these same five categories on the part of contemporary church leaders and scholars seeking to explain the Christianity's present or past relationship to a particular society clearly attest to the enduring value of this important book.

My own interest in this important feature of H. Richard Niebuhr's thinking exceeds the span of a church career that has taken me from seminary teaching to two parish pastorates, to a judicatory leadership position, and then back to adjunct teaching in another seminary setting. In the historiography course my graduate school program required me to take, the professor called upon me to write a paper comparing the work of Ernst Troeltsch and Niebuhr. I am still grateful for this assignment because it set the table for a doctoral dissertation that involved me in a closer examination of those features of Niebuhr's life that helped to shape his interpretations of America's religious history. My own religious upbringing served to pique my interest in researching his early years in the Evangelical Synod of North America, a small church body similar to my own Midwestern Lutheran denomination in terms of its German immigrant origins. Along the way, I even discovered that the religious lineage of my paternal grandfather, George W. Diefenthaler, was in fact German "Evangelical." The fact that he was born on July 4, 1878 and given the middle name "Washington" by his parents, moreover, has led me to believe that my grandfather's family was as eager as Niebuhr's to embrace the new world of America that had become their home. In my dissertation, I argued that over the course of his career, Niebuhr explored all five of the church-world relationship types that he ultimately set forth in *Christ and Culture*. With the assistance of Professor Timothy Smith and a postdoctoral fellowship at Johns Hopkins University, this work was transformed into *H. Richard Niebuhr: A Lifetime of Reflections on the Church and the World*, published by Mercer University Press.

Since then, controversy has erupted among scholars over the enduring value of Niebuhr's typology. The first salvo came in 1989 from Stanley Hauerwas and Will Willimon in their book *Resident Aliens*. As they provocatively put it, "We have come to believe that few books have been a greater hindrance to an accurate assessment of our situation than *Christ and Culture*."[4] The "situation" on their minds was the post-Constantinian world to which Christians had been awakened and in which churches were already struggling to find their bearings. While Niebuhr in fact shared the conviction of these authors that "God, not the nations, rules the world," and stated this at many points throughout his writings, they viewed him as a prime example of the Christendom, first brought into being by the Emperor Constantine in 313 CE, in which the church had consistently sought to make its faith credible to the prevailing culture in order to retain its position of privilege. In the last days of Christendom in America that followed World War II, Niebuhr could be just as critical as they were of the fusion of Christianity with right- and left-wing political agendas. And yet these two well-respected theologians pictured his Christ-the-transformer-of-culture model as the church that "liberal, mainline, American Protestantism aspired to be," one that "busied itself with making America a better place in which to live" and sought to transform "society into something of which Jesus might approve."[5]

In taking this position they shared the thinking of John Howard Yoder, one of the sharpest critics of Niebuhr's typology. Yoder had in fact stated his objections well before Hauerwas and Willimon but did not publish them until 1996, in an essay entitled "How H. Richard Niebuhr Reasoned." Put off by the weaknesses of his own Anabaptist

---

4. Stanley Hauerwas and William H. Willimon, *Resident Aliens: Life in the Christian Colony* (Nashville: Abingdon, 1989), 40.
5. Ibid., 39–43.

tradition highlighted in *Christ and Culture,* Yoder targeted Niebuhr's implicit assumptions, the criteria he employed for evaluating each of his types, and the logic of his presentation, all of which he was ready to regard as "demonic" because they deceptively predisposed readers to see the "superiority of the fifth position."[6] In addition, Yoder took issue with Niebuhr's "monolithic" view of culture, which in his estimation blinded Niebuhr to the diversity of cultural attitudes most any group might exhibit, and he chided him for failing to put Christ into the context of the robust New Testament confession of him as "Lord." Having said all of this, however, he provided no cogent reason to reject the conversionist model he accused Niebuhr of favoring, and his apologetic call for the church, out of obedience to its Lord, to set itself apart as an alternative culture in order to join Christ in liberating the world from the grip of demonic principalities and powers only seemed to confirm rather than repudiate Niebuhr's assessment of the separatist model.[7]

Yoder also seconded Hauerwas and Willimon's criticism of *Christ and Culture* "as a prime example of repressive tolerance."[8] Niebuhr insisted that the relative nature of everyone's intellectual constructs not only ruled out the possibility of making any of his five types the "last word," but kept all the others in play when it came to assessing church-world relationships in ever-changing contexts. To think otherwise would be usurping a position that belonged to God alone. "Tolerant equiprobabilism" was the derisive term Yoder coined for such thinking. To him, Niebuhr's appeal to God as only source of absolute certainty was a "diversionary" tactic he was using in order to avoid affirming any definite plan of action.[9] In the

---

6. John Howard Yoder, "How H. Richard Niebuhr Reasoned: A Critique of *Christ and Culture*," in *Authentic Transformation: A New Vision of Christ and Culture* (Nashville: Abingdon, 1996), 42–55.
7. Ibid., 71–76.
8. Hauerwas and Willimon, *Resident Aliens*, 41.

"Concluding Unscientific Postscript" to his book, Niebuhr had in fact stated that his understanding of God as the ultimate reality to whom persons of faith might look for guidance kept his thinking from becoming "relativistic." It required one to stand within a larger human community and to enter into dialogue with other present and past interpreters of church-world relationships. It also encouraged the making of specific decisions, albeit humbly and as a confession of one's own faith.[10] Yet Yoder remained bold enough to charge Niebuhr with thinking that he had found "a way to eat his cake and have it too." In keeping with the tolerant, inclusive, and pluralistic outlook of his "Ivy League graduate school culture," his use of "divine transcendence" to forbid anyone else's claim to the truth actually served to put himself in a better position to have the "last word."[11]

At about the same time, Glen H. Stassen and D. M. Yeager served to moderate Yoder's hefty barrage of criticisms. Both sought to interpret the meaning of Niebuhr's conversionist model in light of some of his other writings on the subject of church and world. Their major criticism was that Niebuhr was reluctant to spell out a "specific" set of ethical principles or "concrete" courses of action that might flow from this model. Yeager in particular upbraided him for his failure to prophetically address instances of oppression, violence, and abuse of power during the years following the publication of *Christ and Culture*.[12] In an article in 1946, Niebuhr had stated that the "mind of Christ" was the church's "norm," one that it set forth as a confession of its faith and expressed in codes of conduct. But when the church "substitutes for the person of Christ some set of

---

9. Yoder, "How H. Richard Niebuhr Reasoned," 81.
10. H. Richard Niebuhr, *Christ and Culture* (New York: Harper & Row, 1951), 230–56.
11. Yoder, "How H. Richard Niebuhr Reasoned," 82.
12. See D. M. Yeager, "The Social Self in the Pilgrim Church," and Glen H. Stassen, "Concrete Christological Norms for Transformation," in *Authentic Transformation: A New Vision of Christ and Culture* (Nashville: Abingdon, 1996), 91–126, 127–89.

metaphysical or legal propositions," to him it had "begun to lose its character as church and to become a dogmatic or legal society."[13] Nevertheless, Stassen saw this as a deficiency in need of correction. Taking his cue from Yoder, he proceeded to list seven "bedrock normative practices" for the church to follow in order to bring the incarnate reality of Christ to the attention of the world.[14]

In 1999, on the fiftieth anniversary of the lectures at Austin Presbyterian Seminary on which Niebuhr based *Christ and Culture*, the American religious historian George Marsden stated somewhat provocatively that Niebuhr's "analysis in its present form could be near the end of its usefulness." In his assessment of Niebuhr, however, he sought to provide a positive answer to the question embedded in the original title of his lecture, "Can These Categories Be Saved?" For one thing, he pointed out that Niebuhr's book had appeared during the period immediately following World War II; in the midst of the debates then taking place over the future of Western civilization, he was attempting to counter those "secularists" who viewed Christianity as a foe rather than a friend in the shaping of a better future for the world. In answer to the "multiculturalist" objections to the book, he also stressed that Niebuhr was writing in the "consensus" era of American history, when "building a healthy and unified mainstream culture" was the chief objective. In response to critics who emphasized that Niebuhr's categories were "historically inadequate," moreover, Marsden stated his belief that they could be salvaged if they were not seen as mutually exclusive. "Virtually every Christian and every Christian group expresses in one way or

---

13. H. Richard Niebuhr, "The Norm of the Church," *The Journal of Religious Thought* 4 (Autumn–Winter 1946–1947): 10–11.
14. Stassen, "Concrete Christological Norms," 164–67. His list of "bedrock practices" include: 1) not judging, but forgiving, healing, and breaking down barriers that marginalize or exclude; 2) delivering justice; 3) evangelism, preaching the gospel and calling for repentance and discipleship; 4) nonviolent transforming initiatives; 5) love of enemy; 6) mutual servanthood; and 7) prayer.

another," as he put it, "all five of the motifs." Furthermore, he felt that adding more categories to the celebrated typology was unnecessary because the five Niebuhr had originally proposed remained "extremely useful analytical tools" as long as one recognized the "complexity of any real historical subjects."[15]

When the fiftieth anniversary of *Christ and Culture* in 2001 became the occasion for the publication of a new edition of the book, other scholars weighed in on the side of Niebuhr. In his foreword, Martin Marty lauded the book as a "classic"—not only because one could not go back to a thought world that existed prior to Niebuhr without confronting his typology and recognizing the marks it had left but also because the circle of persons finding it useful for evaluating the relationship between religion and society had been broadened to include scholars of other world religions and the growing number of self-identified Christians not connected with any church. He also stated that instead of "imposing straitjackets, building silos, or hermetically sealed containers" in order to confine and define the Christian writers whom he selected to support each of his types, Niebuhr had in fact created five "zones" designed to illustrate how Christians wrestle with a dominant culture.[16]

In his preface, subtitled "An Appreciative Interpretation," James Gustafson—a student, colleague, and friend of Niebuhr—took more direct aim at the critics. His chief target was Marsden, who, in attempting to "save" Niebuhr's categories, had in Gustafson's estimation retained the same wrong assumptions as those who were trying to discount their value. Gustafson argued that judgments about the "historical adequacy" of Niebuhr's work were beside the point because it was never Niebuhr's intention to write a history of

---

15. George Marsden, "Transforming Niebuhr's Categories," *Insights: Faculty Journal of Austin Seminary* 115, no. 1 (Fall 1999): 4–15.
16. Martin E. Marty, "Foreword," in H. Richard Niebuhr, *Christ and Culture* (San Francisco: HarperSanFrancisco, 2001), xiii–xix.

Christian theological ethics. His "ideal types" were in fact "heuristic devices to enable readers to understand materials and issues to which they refer." Gustafson, moreover, saw Niebuhr as a teacher who wanted to show the readers of the book, as he did his students, *how* rather than *what* to think about church-world relationships by encouraging them to thoughtfully compare various historical options. In addition, he asserted that Niebuhr's "undogmatic mind" remained one that "after careful consideration, could persuasively but undramatically articulate his theological and ethical judgments." According to Gustafson, when Niebuhr's real purpose was properly understood, the book could also enable one to locate the church-world positions of vocal critics such as Hauerwas and Yoder and consider the possible implications in light of the other types.[17]

More recently, conservative evangelical scholar D. A. Carson put forth his evaluation of the Niebuhr typology in his *Christ and Culture Revisited*. Rather than launching a frontal assault, he found reasons to side with earlier critics in viewing Niebuhr's types as "mutually-exclusive choices" that pointed to "Christ-the-transformer of culture" as the one Niebuhr intended to prescribe. Like Yoder, he deemed Niebuhr's *Christ* to be "sub-biblical" and his concept of *culture* to be in need of sharper definition. He also shared Hauerwas and Willimon's contempt for the "intolerance of tolerance," which the relativism that governed Niebuhr's thinking about them could easily reinforce. In place of Niebuhr's fivefold paradigm, moreover, Carson proposed a single "holistic" model for assessing church-world relationships grounded in what he regarded as the "great turning points in redemptive history" as these were set forth on the pages of the Old and New Testaments.[18] Niebuhr would have probably

---

17. James M. Gustafson, "Preface: An Appreciative Interpretation," in H. Richard Niebuhr, *Christ and Culture* (San Francisco: HarperSanFrancisco, 2001), xxi–xxxv.
18. D. A. Carson, *Christ and Culture Revisited* (Grand Rapids: Eerdmans, 2008), 1–58.

flagged Carson's paradigm as a form of biblicism because it made a book rather than God the object of faith. To Niebuhr, the Bible functioned as a "dictionary" that enabled one to interpret more precisely the ways in which God was continuing to reveal himself in the public and private experiences of contemporary life.[19] Carson acknowledged that different features of his biblical paradigm might receive greater emphasis in certain historical and cultural contexts. Nevertheless, for him all of his "turning points" remained "non-negotiables."[20]

Other participants in this debate over the value of Niebuhr's *Christ and Culture* could be cited, but the ones I have highlighted appear to be of three types: critics (Hauerwas and Willimon, Yoder, and Stassen), defenders (Marty and Gustafson), and fixers (Marsden and Carson). Like Niebuhr, I am mindful of the hazards of constructing typologies and acknowledge that some of his analysts might fit in more than one category. But it is their differing perspectives on Niebuhr and their lively discussion of his ideal types that serve to confirm the enduring quality of his work. The debate has prompted me to assemble this collection in order to give Niebuhr more of a chance to speak for himself. Most of the aforementioned scholars, despite their differences, recognize the need to investigate the larger corpus of Niebuhr's thoughts in order to achieve a more complete picture of his approach to church-world relationships. While some have attempted to do this, all have tended to ignore his formative years as a budding scholar and church leader in the Evangelical Synod of North America. With this book, I am hoping to help correct this deficiency.

---

19. See, for example, H. Richard Niebuhr, "Reformation: Continuing Imperative," *The Christian Century* 77 (March 2, 1960): 250.
20. Carson, *Christ and Culture Revisited*, 59–65.

THE PARADOX OF CHURCH AND WORLD

In 1929, well before the appointment to the Yale Divinity School faculty that would give him a platform for addressing all of mainline American Protestantism, Niebuhr told members of his German-immigrant church body that "ultimately the problem of church and world involves us in a paradox; unless the church accommodates itself to the world it becomes sterile inwardly and outwardly; unless it transcends the world it becomes indistinguishable from the world and loses its effectiveness no less surely." The relationship between the two was one he also chose to depict in dynamic terms: "The rhythm of approach and withdrawal need not be like the swinging of the pendulum, mere repetition without progress; it may be more like the rhythm of the waves that wash upon the beach; each succeeding wave advances a little farther into the world with its cleansing gospel before that gospel becomes sullied with the earth."[21] As his first two books, *The Social Sources of Denominationalism* and *The Kingdom of God in America*, more clearly demonstrate, Niebuhr understood that the church was inevitably shaped by the world it set out to shape, and in some cases even succeed in shaping. Many of America's religious historians continue to employ this hermeneutic in order to adumbrate our past and thereby help us identify a preferred pathway into the future.[22]

Over the course of his career, the terminology Niebuhr employed to describe this paradox became progressively more nuanced. Already in *Social Sources*, he recognized that from a sociological standpoint the church could become as worldly as the world into which it was being sent. Subsequently, in *Kingdom of God*, he drew a distinction between Christianity as movement and as institution, stating that the

---

21. H. Richard Niebuhr, "The Church in the Modern World," *The Keryx* 20 (May 1929): 10, 29.
22. See, for example, Nathan O. Hatch, *The Democratization of American Christianity* (New Haven, CT: Yale University Press, 1989); Mark A. Noll, *America's God: From Jonathan Edwards to Abraham Lincoln* (New York: Oxford University Press, 2002); and Grant Wacker, *America's Pastor: Billy Graham and the Shaping of a Nation* (Cambridge, MA: Belknap, 2014).

"true church is not an organization but the organic movement of those who have been 'called out' and 'sent.'"[23] By the time he wrote *Christ and Culture*, he had abandoned this terminology altogether. For *world*, he substituted *culture*, which he defined as the realm of human activity. Despite its godless ways, the *world* to him was still God's creation and the object of his redemption. Furthermore, the term *Christ* permitted him to separate more clearly those features of the *church* that made it as corruptible as its culture from the gospel message it was called to bring to that culture's attention.[24] In spite of Niebuhr's change in terminology, I have chosen to use the terms *church* and *world* on all the pages that follow, as I am principally interested in keeping the focus on his profound understanding of the paradoxical nature of their relationship.

The existential character of so much of what Niebuhr said about church-world relationships also motivates this book. His deep faith in a transcendent God, whom he believed was also omnipresent in the world, made every event potentially revelatory. Therefore, it is helpful to examine at least some of his responses to key events in the world and the church during his lifetime. Niebuhr did not see himself as a professional historian. Instead, he brought his considerable historical knowledge to bear on his assessments of contemporary developments. Nor did he fit the "ivory tower" academic stereotype. Niebuhr's chief commitment was always to the church of his day. Hence, I have purposely selected writings in which he was addressing church members, both lay and clergy.

I also need to say a word about the process of choosing documents for this collection. To keep the book within the established

---

23. Niebuhr, *Kingdom of God in America*, xiv.
24. On the basis of his other writings, Niebuhr would acknowledge that human understanding of Christ and the gospel are also subject to corruption, and that for this reason, these same truths must remain subject to correction. See H. Richard Niebuhr, *Christ and Culture*, 11–39.

parameters, I needed to make some hard choices. There were also theological gems that I would like to have included but did not because they have been published or republished elsewhere. I direct the attention of all interested parties to William Stacy Johnson's fine collection of chiefly unpublished Niebuhr documents, *H. Richard Niebuhr: Theology, History, and Culture,* and to Kristine A. Culp's *"The Responsibility of the Church For Society" and Other Essays by H. Richard Niebuhr.* In addition, two other criteria drove my choices. One was that I wanted to present documents that illustrate the context in which aspects of Niebuhr's church-world thinking developed in each of the three major periods in his adult life: formative years in the Evangelical Synod (1914–1929), the decade of the Great Depression (1930–1940), and World War II and its aftermath (1941–1962). The other was that I wanted to inject an element of variety into the selection of Niebuhr's writings in terms of their theological density.

Finally, I respectfully disagree with Hauerwas and Willimon's assessment of Niebuhr, and more particularly his book *Christ and Culture,* as a relic of the Christendom era that has now passed away. The writings of H. Richard Niebuhr I have chosen will demonstrate to readers that in some ways, he was a Christian thinker who was ahead of his time with respect to the applicability of the age-old paradox of church and world. Not only that, but in the epilogue I will make a case for inviting him to the table for conversations about the challenges facing the post-Constantinian church in the twenty-first-century world of North America.

PART I

Formative Years in the Evangelical Synod

1

The Evangelical Synod and the New World of America

H. Richard Niebuhr was a "cradle" member of the Evangelical Synod of North America. His father, Gustav Niebuhr, had emigrated from Germany as a young man, attended the Synod's Eden Theological Seminary in St. Louis, and served as a parish pastor in San Francisco, Wright City and Saint Charles, Missouri, and Lincoln, Illinois. His mother, Lydia Hosto Niebuhr, was the American-born daughter of the Evangelical pastor with whom Gustav worked in the first of his charges, as well as an unflagging source of support as her husband carried out his ministry. Like his brother Reinhold, born two years before him, Richard followed the prescribed path to ministry in the Evangelical Synod by leaving home as a teenager to attend Elmhurst College, the denomination's preparatory school near Chicago, and going on to seminary at Eden.

For the decade and a half after his seminary graduation, Niebuhr pursued a career of distinguished service to the Evangelical Synod.

Following his ordination in 1916, he served as the pastor of Walnut Park Evangelical Church in north St. Louis. In 1919, he was appointed to the Eden Seminary faculty. Then, after a two-year leave to complete both his Bachelor of Divinity and PhD at Yale Divinity School, he became president of his alma mater, Elmhurst College, in 1924. He returned to Eden Seminary in 1927, this time as academic dean, a position he held until he went back to Yale in 1931, this time to join the divinity school faculty. During this same period, he also chaired the committee conducting the negotiations that eventually led to the merger of the Evangelical Synod with the German Reformed Church in 1934.

Unlike the other German immigrants that by 1840 had started coming in greater numbers to the Midwest, especially the Lutherans, those who were drawn to the Evangelical Synod had no serious objections to a union church identity. In fact, congregations chose to retain the *Evangelische* name of the German state churches composed of Lutheran and Reformed elements, resulting from a union the Prussian King Friedrich Wilhelm III had first initiated in 1817. "In so far as they agree," the Augsburg Confession, Luther's Small Catechism, and the Reformed Heidelberg Catechism formed their confession of faith. Disagreements were relegated to the light the Holy Scriptures might shed on them and to liberty of conscience.[1]

In addition, the warm concern for the physical as well as the spiritual welfare of both the individual and society that the *Innere-Mission* (Home Mission) movement championed among German Evangelicals was just as evident in the New World denomination. Gustav Niebuhr, for example, vigorously supported the Synod's Emmaus Homes for the care of epileptics. Also, while serving his parish in Lincoln, Illinois, he not only oversaw the work of a newly

---

1. Carl E. Schneider, *History of the Theological Seminary of the Evangelical Church* (St. Louis: Eden, 1925), 12, 39–43.

constructed Deaconess Hospital, but took an active interest in the budding deaconess movement for women desiring to do this kind of church work.[2]

Despite this ecumenical frame of mind and heart, the Evangelical Synod was slow in adapting to its New World context. Niebuhr's brother Reinhold remembered it as a "little Germany": congregations continued to use their native tongue in worship and confirmation classes and to operate their own parochial schools. Little or no knowledge of English was necessary for most of their clergy to function. More than four decades after its founding, Eden Seminary petitioned the Synod for permission to add a faculty member to teach classes in English; this request was turned down because the Synod's board of directors feared that this might deprive vacant German-speaking congregations of the kind of pastor they needed. Hence, some American-born ministerial students who began their preparation at Elmhurst College were forced to learn to improve their German. When they arrived at Eden, they were the only ones on campus capable of conducting classes in America's official tongue.[3] Until World War I, the Synod also kept close ties with the union church in Germany. Eden Seminary in particular took from it not only its academic standards, but most of its faculty and nearly half of its students. Since he was an American-trained pastor, therefore, Gustav Niebuhr was denied an appointment to its faculty.[4]

Like their father, Richard and Reinhold believed it was time for their Synod to "come out of her shell" and enter the mainstream of America's culture.[5] At Eden, the brothers found in Samuel D. Press a mentor who was willing to listen to their kind of voice. While he

---

2. William G. Chrystal, *Niebuhr Studies* (Reno: Empire for Liberty), 31–34.
3. Ibid., 79.
4. Ibid., 32.
5. Gustav Niebuhr, "Die Zunkunft der Deutschen Evang. Synode von N.A.," *Der Evangelishce Diakonissen Herold* 7, no. 3 (February, 1913): 8.

had studied theology in Germany, Press did not disavow his native-born American roots. He not only became the first professor to teach his seminary classes in English; he freely introduced his students to the theological contributions of Americans like Jonathan Edwards and Mark Hopkins. In his course on the Old Testament prophets, moreover, he repeatedly drew his students' attention to the utterances of Amos as a model in addressing contemporary social problems.[6]

At the same time, it took the cataclysm of a world war to shake the Evangelical Synod out of its ethnic isolation. The outbreak of conflict on the European scene in 1914 created a loyalty issue for pastors and members of their congregations. Pro-German sentiments were natural and common enough to motivate another Niebuhr brother, Walter, to serve briefly as a war correspondent accompanying the Kaiser's armies on the battlefields of eastern Europe. Like him, Richard soon questioned the tremendous sacrifice of human life on all sides that warfare entailed. In addition, Reinhold chose to cite "disloyalty" as a "suspicion" that German-Americans had brought upon themselves.[7] For Richard, it became another reason for making English the primary language for worship in the north St. Louis congregation he was serving.

Once America entered the war in 1917, Richard Niebuhr joined his brothers in endorsing the Allied cause. When Reinhold became the executive secretary of the Synod's "War Welfare Commission," Richard stepped forward to take care of its business and correspondence in the St. Louis area. He also enlisted as an army chaplain, though he never served troops in combat because orders for him to report for chaplaincy schooling did not come until the summer of 1918. As William Chrystal has pointed out, these patriotic gestures became a "matter of necessity" for the Niebuhr family and

---

6. Chrystal, *Niebuhr Studies*, 49–75.
7. Reinhold Niebuhr, "Failure of German-Americanism," *Atlantic Monthly* (July 1916): 13–18.

their Evangelical Synod. Despite what they said and did to the contrary, German immigrant ties still made Reinhold subject to government investigation, and Walter resigned from the Creel Commission because he was suspected of being a "Kaiserite" and a "fifth columnist." Furthermore, wartime patriotism, which Reinhold in particular had grounded in President Woodrow Wilson's plans for a more lasting peace, quickly gave way to disillusionment on the part of the entire Niebuhr family when the Treaty of Versailles brought most of those same plans to naught.[8]

Nevertheless, World War I was a catalyst for the Americanization of the Evangelical Synod. For Richard, reform of its education system for preparing church workers was the place to begin. He and Reinhold believed that the programs at Elmhurst and Eden, patterned as they were on German models of higher education, had given them insufficient exposure to the social and physical sciences and had failed to challenge them when it came to researching primary sources. He not only called for more attention to the need for graduate scholarships, but became something of a consumer of graduate-level classes himself. Besides the work he did for his doctorate at Yale, Niebuhr enrolled at Washington University in St. Louis, Columbia University and Union Theological Seminary in New York, the University of Michigan, and the University of Chicago. In addition, he advocated for equally sweeping revisions in congregational educational programming.

The Synod positions Niebuhr assumed during the 1920s provided him with a golden opportunity to make changes in his church body's educational system. During his three-year tenure as president of Elmhurst College, the initiatives he advocated included accreditation, curriculum revision, reorganization of the faculty into eight

---

8. Chrystal, *Niebuhr Studies*, 111.

departments, a faculty ranking system, a salary scale, and a program of sabbatical leaves. He also drew up a set of ambitious plans to create a school endowment, expand the campus facilities, and open Elmhurst's doors to students interested in careers other than church work, to women, and to the community at large. The creation of a federation of several small Protestant colleges in the Chicago area was also part of his vision.

H. Richard Niebuhr scholars tend to overlook these years of his life. I have chosen the writings that follow not only to illustrate the formative influence on him of the Evangelical Synod, but to demonstrate the beginnings of his strong determination to help this immigrant church become a denomination that would more fully take up its role in the world of America to which its members had been coming for nearly three-quarters of a century.

Youth

Written toward the end of H. Richard Niebuhr's second year as a student at Eden Seminary, this poem expresses the heady optimism of a young idealist. World War I, which began later that year, was a crushing blow. At this point, Niebuhr had no inkling of the difficult days that were to come for the church in which his spiritual formation was taking place. On the other hand, the poem provides evidence of his lifelong sense of being a participant in the history of the whole Christian church on earth and of God being present in every moment of its unfolding story.

Source: *The Keryx* 4, no. 3 (June 1914): 1.

My life is strong with the strength of years
    That were and are to be;

My soul is bold with the vanquished fears
    And the victories I shall see;

My thoughts are the gleam of a prophet's dream,
    The light for men unborn—

The heritage of death is mine,

To give the living a right divine,
    And to put the wrong to scorn.

My hands are filled with deeds of fame
    Of soldier, saint and sage;

My heart has brought the martyr's flame
    A fire to burn and rage;

THE PARADOX OF CHURCH AND WORLD

The sacrament of their blood is spent,
    To hallow and make me true—

Their faith, their strength are mine to share,

Mine is the blessing of their prayer,
    I'll be the answer, too!

I am both yesterday and to-day,
    And to-morrow is mine to choose,

Mine is the victory in the fray,
    And mine the blame, to lose.

But I am a son of the Mighty one,—
    I battle in His name:—

His strength is mine to do the right,

My arm is His to win the fight—
    Should I be put to shame?

THE EVANGELICAL SYNOD AND THE NEW WORLD

The Hope of the World/Eden and the War

During his last year at Eden Seminary, Niebuhr served as the editor of its student publication, The Keryx. *These two brief editorials demonstrate how deeply affected he was, and would be throughout his life, by the human toll of modern, industrialized warfare. While he shared the sympathy many members of his Evangelical Synod felt for the German cause, he also saw America as a nation that stood in the vanguard of world progress. Already in 1914, moreover, he was placing his hope, as he would in subsequent world conflicts, in a divine purpose that transcended victory by either side—a purpose that would serve to further God's kingdom on earth.*

Sources: *The Keryx* 4, no. 4 (September 1914), 13–14; *The Keryx* 4, no. 5 (December 1914), 13.

The Hope of the World

The heavy pall of death lies on the whole wide world. Destruction grins with hideous malice from the blackened devastation of ruined cities, that once lifted their proud domes and spires to the eternal blue. Gaunt misery stalks over trampled fields where golden grain, that was to nourish men, lies trodden in the dust; stalks stealthily into the huts of peasants, into the silent cities, where the noisy wheels of industry are stilled. Famished women shriek to feel its cold breath, cold as from a tomb; palsied men cannot drive its ominous presence from their doors, and wondering, wide-eyed children begin too soon to understand the woe of life, that is the woe of death.

The cold rain drizzles on marred faces of the dead, staring with blank eyes up to a dismal heaven. The shambles reek with blood—blood, and death as far as the eye can see. But even the bitterness of dying seems sweeter than the agony of living, living in blood of comrade and of foe.

Men have unlocked the doors of hell and mankind lies crushed beneath its iron terror.

The clutch of death is at the throat of humanity. And we, far from its awful presence, feel the breath of the world choking and sobbing, the terror of death beating in its heart. Overpowered by the inutterable [sic] woe of brother-men, we are so weakly helpless to alleviate their pain. We would share their agony if it might thereby be lessened. We would gladly give our lives if death might thereby be satiated. But there is naught to do.

Naught to do? Nay, there is much to do, new life to give, a new world to build, a new heaven to raise. In the heart of America beats now the life of the world. The burden of man's progress rests in its hands. America must be strong to bear the burden onward and upward. America must not fail in the crisis.

Death shall not be victorious! Oh, America, you are the womb of life today. Pray to your God, that your child may be a man-child, strong unto peace, strong to bear the sorrows of a world, to dry its tears and bring a new life, a new hope to those in the shadow of death.

Eden and the War

We at Eden have a most eager interest in the progress of the European war, especially because of the fact that several of our comrades have friends and relatives in the struggle. One of Cramer's brothers was killed in an engagement in France, while the other lies wounded in a hospital. Many others have relatives for whom they fear—so Jersak, whose parents reside upon the battle-fields of the Russo-German conflict. Beccken, Bergstraesser and Stange have had news of the death or wounding of persons very close to them.

The greater part of us can happily and with a good, clear conscience place our sympathies on the side of German. Not only because we trace our descent from Germany, or because our education is under direct German influence, but because we have the conviction that under all the diplomatic sugar-coated statements, there is some truth and justice to Germany's claims.

Nor are we at Eden men among those who pray for an unconditional peace at any price. Although our hearts yearn for Germany victorious, our prayer has been and will be that peace may come only when it shall be to the furthering and strengthening of the kingdom of God in the belligerent nations as well as for the world. Not a peace based upon sentimentality, but a peace bringing a moral victory to all nations is our prayer. We know that suffering has furthered the kingdom of God heretofore on earth, and we know that this terrible scourge of war can and will be used by the Omnipotent for humanity's uplift and for the extension of the kingdom of heaven.

The Purposes of Catechetical Instruction

An often-overlooked biographical detail is the fact that in 1919 Niebuhr served as the Evangelical Synod's Sunday School Executive, a position that gave him the opportunity to actualize some of his hopes for educational reform in his church body. Confirmation was the equivalent of believer's baptism in the Synod, a rite of passage that was preceded by a period of intensive catechetical instruction. The experience was a source of great pride among the Synod's congregations and their families. In this essay, therefore, Niebuhr took a bold step by calling for the modification of this tradition. Yet he was convinced that religious education involved not just inculcating abstract truths through memorization but also preparing young people for real-life situations in the world.

Source: *Religious Education in the Evangelical Synod, 1920–1923: Official Report of the Third National Convention of the Evangelical Sunday Schools, St. Louis, Missouri, June 28–July 3, 1923* (Board of Religious Education of the Evangelical Synod of North America), 235–42.

May I begin by making a change in my announced subject: There are two words in it to which exception may be taken: catechetical and instruction. They are both good words but they do not deserve to be exalted too much. I should like to substitute the terms: The Purposes of the Pastor's Class in Christian Education. It would be carrying coals to Newcastle were I to try to show how necessary it is to have a purpose in mind—a real purpose—in our work as educators; yet it is evident that frequently our teaching is being carried on without a definite purpose in mind—often because we have so many purposes that we cannot center upon one. The purposes which are presented to us by tradition and modern education theory—all claiming to be the only purposes which deserve any kind of consideration—need to be criticized by every individual teacher, certain ones need to be eliminated, certain ones put into a subordinate position, and the right, guiding purpose so established.

The first purpose which we may eliminate as a *purpose* but may reintroduce as a *means* is represented by that word "instruction." Instruction has been the traditional aim of the pastor's class, and for that reason the catechism has been the main handbook also. Our work must not be conceived as instruction for several reasons: First of all because the Christian religion is not a system of doctrines which can be taught as a set of propositions. We have inherited from the reformation and even more from the eighteenth century an intellectualistic idea of Christianity which is quite in contrast to its true genius. The catechisms, in general, were written at a time when Christianity was looked upon as essentially a system of right beliefs. The purpose of the catechetical class was to give the children a system of right beliefs about God, about Jesus, about man, sin, immorality, the church, etc.

Now it is apparent that Christianity as the religion of Jesus Christ and of Paul, and as the religion which you and I seek to cultivate, is not primarily a matter of right beliefs at all, but primarily a matter of right attitudes—of right sentiments and right thoughts—but of a right direction of the will primarily. Christianity is spirit life. And we are very far today from believing that right belief alone is a guide to right action. Yet it is evident, I think, that while Christianity is not primarily intellectual, it contains a large intellectual element and that there is need for theology in Christian education. But theology is not the primary thing, and the teaching of theology is not our purpose.

Secondly, instruction is not our aim because the child is not primarily intellectual. The idea behind our catechism and behind much of our teaching is that the child is a little adult, and a very intellectual little adult at that. Most adults are not intellectual enough to be touched deeply by our catechetical instruction. Men, modern psychology has amply demonstrated, are not primarily thinking, but primarily *acting* beings. When we speak to them in intellectual terms only we are speaking over their heads the large part of the time. Add to this the fact that the truths which Protestantism is concerned about are abstract truths, or truths which can be clothed only in very abstract language, and the fallacy of an intellectual aim in "catechetical instruction" becomes even more apparent. [Otto] Baumgarten in that excellent little book *Neue Bahnen*, writes; "A fundamental law of all newer pedagogy demands consideration of child nature and its naivete. 'When I was a child, I spoke as a child, I understood as a child, I thought as a child.'" But how do we usually speak with our children? As if they were interested in the inner life, as if they stood in constant inner conflict with themselves, as if they lived under the oppressive sense of sin, as if they yearned for salvation! As if there were any continuity in a child's thinking upon inner questions; as if it of its own accord, without being forced, reflected upon an unseen world, or upon its self! But all instruction in Christianity turns about the hidden man of the heart, about the concern for the eternity of the inner world. And especially Lutheran Christianity is completely dependent upon Paul, who not only put off all that was childish but who was as unchildlike as ever any one was, who constantly looked upon the state of childhood from the viewpoint of its incompleteness and weakness." Protestantism, Baumgarten goes on to say, is much more in danger than Catholicism of being ineffective in its instruction because of this inner character of the religion which it teaches. The child thinks only in concrete terms, but in instruction we must use abstract terms. Yet we need not do so nearly to the extent to which we do. For instance, it is possible to teach concretely about the life of Jesus, but only abstractly about the nature of the exalted Christ. But our catechetical instruction takes the exalted Christ into consideration a great deal more than the Jesus of the synoptic Gospels.

Again instruction is not a correct purpose because the primary principle of education is that we learn by doing, by expression, by activity. But we are too often concerned merely with impressions when we conceive our aim to be instruction. Impressions which are not expressed cannot stay in the mind; they almost literally pass into one ear and out of the other. The kind of truths which we place our emphasis upon in instruction can never be expressed, except intellectually.

Furthermore, instruction is not a correct aim because it emphasizes the amount of the material. We must get through the catechism we say, and we are very glad if we finish the book a few weeks before Palm Sunday and so have ample time for review. In the long run it makes very little difference whether we get through the book or not. If the child is not led into the right attitude to God and man learning the whole of the book doesn't do any good. And if half of the book serves that purpose we may let the other half go. Being a Christian is never a completed process. All that we can hope to attain in catechetical instruction is to start the child upon the right track. If we do, we must trust him to acquire the deeper insights for himself. If we do not, we shall not be able to attain anything by getting through a certain amount of material. But again, it is evident that there is a certain system of Christian truth and that this system in its essentials ought to be made a part of our instruction. The primary point here is this; the catechism which we use no longer embodies what we conceive today to be the essential elements of the Christian religion. It may contain them but it doesn't emphasize them, and it emphasizes much which no longer seems important to a great number of Christians today.

Another false aim of catechetical instruction is represented by the method of memorization. If our object is the memorization by the children of a certain number of definitions and statements we shall be wasting our precious time upon an effort which will bear little fruit. But I think that it is so evident to all of us that it is hardly necessary to dwell upon the point. Memorization we all know is not learning, and a memorized definition may be far from having any real effect on Christian life. At the same time a certain amount of memorization is decidedly useful and necessary—the memorization of the great creeds, of Bible verses, of great hymns, which will serve to make articulate the inarticulate religion of the great mass. One might mention any number of other aims which are more or less incorrect—and all of them the conscious or unconscious purposes of much of our work as teachers. Preparing for church membership may be a very false aim if our idea of the church is that of an ecclesiastical institution whose function is solely the preaching of the word of God and the administration of the sacraments. Preparing the child to receive the sacraments may become a purely external and unmeaning process. Again education may be looked upon as a process intended to save the child's soul and its main means thought to be the stirring of the feeling of sin and repentance. Undoubtedly the sense of sin is an essential part of the Christian life, but not as primary as it is often made out to be. Psychological studies of the religious feelings of adolescents indicate that the sense of sin is frequently much more physiological than psychological and more psychological than religious. The sense of the absolute holiness of God and of the profaneness of human nature, is to be nurtured of course, but the negative sense of sin ought to be only the reflex of the positive sense of the holiness of God. From God to sin, not from sin to God is the actual course of the religious life. As in the case of Isaiah the vision of God comes first and then the outcry: "Woe is me, I am undone, for I am a man of unclean lips and dwell among a people of unclean lips." Or as in the case of Job. "I had heard of thee by the hearing of the ear, but now mine eye seeth thee and I repent in dust and ashes." The souls of many children are unnecessarily tortured by much teaching about sin. Adolescence inclines anyway to be gloomy and the disillusionments which come to children in our confirmation classes are often teaching enough about sin. Let us speak of sin in a straight-forward and honest way, but let us not try to nurture an emotional crisis in the lives of children by speaking vaguely about sin as a general thing. There at least should be emphasized: the feeling of sin which we find in our boys and girls in the confirmation classes is connected to a very large extent with the fact of adolescence, with the growing of the sex life, and what is needed by the child there is not only the strong emphasis upon the divine demand of purity but also a fatherly helpfulness on the part of the teacher in assisting him to face this crisis in his life without unnecessary qualms.

Another purpose which is frequently advanced as the true aim of religious education is that of unfoldment of the child's religious capacities. This also contains a large measure of truth but religion is not an instinct which can be developed by encouraging free self-expression. It is a way of life which must be acquired. Religion is probably less an individual than a social matter, though of course it is both. At all events it is not enough to say that education must unfold latent qualities in the child. Some latent qualities it must suppress, some it must encourage, others it must supplement. Man's native inheritance is not enough to make him a Christian.

And finally it is necessary to criticize the aim of education which we find advanced so much today and which has been referred to as a necessary partial aim or means to keep in mind—the aim of producing the right behavior in the child. Religion is much more than mere activity. It is a matter of sentiments, attitudes, as well as of actions, and the culture of the right sentiments and attitudes is a necessary part of education as well as training in a certain kind of life.

The aim of the catechetical class must fall in line with the general aim of all religious education. And for this it is difficult to name a single formula. As a matter of fact despite all of our theories we usually have a number of aims in religious education. We have almost all of those which were criticized previously. The harm results when we exalt any one of these aims into the whole purpose and forget the wider nature of the child and the wider spirit of our religion. What, let us ask first of all, is the religious life? Some say it is the adoption and maintenance of a definite attitude toward the highest social values—it is love of the neighbor as of the self, in the case of the Christianity. It is the desire to give and conserve for the neighbor all of the values which we should like to have for ourselves. Others maintain religion is primarily the adoption and maintenance of a definite attitude toward God, it is loving God with all the heart and soul and mind; it is, in Schleiermacher's phrase, the feeling of dependence upon God. It seems to be impossible to reduce these two characteristics of the religious life to one. There are some who maintain that right love of the neighbor brings love to God, others that love of God is necessarily followed by love to the neighbor. But the facts are against both theories. There are many lovers of God in the religions of the world who are very little concerned about their neighbors and there are lovers of men who have no attitude of dependence upon and love toward God. Christianity, as Ritschl has pointed out, is not a circle with a single center, but an ellipse with two foci: the love of God and the love of the neighbor. Christianity is both religious in the narrow sense and ethical. Drop either one of these foci, try to combine one with the other, try to draw a circle with a single center and you distort Christianity. Not that the two foci are unrelated; they are the foci of one ellipse, but they are two nevertheless.

The result of this understanding of the nature of Christianity for education is that I believe: religious education has no single aim but a double one. They are not very far apart from each other. They do not mean that the child must change this direction to seek now the one, now the other aim, but they do involve a change of attention. A man who attends only to God is in danger of becoming a mystic, who is not concerned about his brother men. A man who attends only to right living with his fellowmen is in danger of becoming a moralist without the optimism which the love of God brings without the energy which religion produces and without the inner glow of communion with God. Our minds are so constructed that we can attend to only one thing at a time, but while we attend to the one thing another one may be in the fringe of consciousness and color our whole mental attitude. A Christian is a man who approaches God with the idea of his sentiment of love for his brother men in the fringe of consciousness, and who approaches his brother men with the idea of God and the love of God as the immediate background of his attending consciousness.

Now what we are concerned about in religious education is the culture of the attitude of love to God and of love to man. It will not do to say that we are concerned with the culture of the sentiment and attitude of love. Love always has an object. There is love of the world, love of persons, love of gold, love of definite comforts, but is there such a thing as love in general? And what we are concerned about is the attitude of love in respect of two definite objects, God and men. It follows however also that love of men is too general a term. Let us say, love of neighbor, always of definite men, each definite man with whom the child comes into contact love also of course of the societies of men, the church, the state, above all of the ideal society, the Kingdom of God. We might use this term Kingdom of God as inclusive of both God and man and say with [George Albert] Coe that the aim of religious education is "growth of the young toward and into mature and efficient devotion to the democracy of God, and happy self-realization therein," if the term Kingdom of God or democracy of God, is not explained in a onesided [*sic*] fashion, as meaning only the rule of God, or as meaning only the society of men. The peril of having two aims, united in the constant living reality of an individual active mind which passes from one to the other, is to be preferred to the danger of losing either aim out of account by seeking simplicity of statement.

The aim of religious education then, perhaps, can be stated as follows: The aim of Christian education is the guidance of the growth of the young into the relationship of love to God and love to men. If we want to use the language of Paul: it is the nurture of the mind of Christ in each individual.

It is guidance of growth, not instruction, not inculcation, not training, because the relationship of love cannot be imparted by instruction, it cannot be inculcated by methods of memorization, it cannot be trained as habits are trained. It has a natural basis in human instincts and in the human situation in the world. The instincts of parental love, the tender emotion, the instinct of subordination, the instinct of wonder, the emotion of awe, these are probably innate patterns in the individual mind and they are all involved in the characteristic religious response to a religious object. Furthermore, the human situation in the world of nature and of men nurtures the feeling of dependence, the attitude of loyalty and devotion, feelings and attitudes which we seek to connect with a religious object, with God. It is not our task to create these attitudes but to bring them in connection with two definite objects: God and fellow-men. We must guide the growth of these innate tendencies. Furthermore, the task of religious education is the guidance of the growth of the other tendencies in the young life, tendencies which are either instinctive or acquired from the social environment. Sin it has been rightly pointed out is largely atavism, the use of the instincts in primitive situations to which they are no longer applicable. To guide the growth of the instinct of anger so as to turn it against evil, of the instinct of love, of the instinct of fear, is the task of religious education. Insofar we are dealing primarily with the nature of the child and not with a book or a system.

Guidance involves another element, however. The relationship of love between men and God is not merely an emotional relationship. It is not a matter of living in the constant presence of God and constant awareness of the needs of fellowmen. The relationship of love in human life means reliance in and trust in man; it means constant interaction between men. It means being in the right adjustment to a fellow-being so as to receive from the fellow-being all that he has to give to us for the enrichment of our own life and through us to the lives of others. The right adjustment we call love. We cannot receive love until we give love. What we are concerned in, in the case of religious education, is the knowledge and adoption of this right religious adjustment of the child to God and to men. We want to guide the child so that it will constantly make this adjustment to God and to its fellows. One ought to define that adjustment more definitely but limitation of time prevents. It is the adjustment which Jesus made to God and men. Its essential characteristics are: complete trust in God, but also in man, obedience to moral law, as the will of God and the law of human welfare, willingness to go all the way with that law. Negatively it is defined by the sense of unworthiness and incompleteness without God, and by the counting of each better than the self, that is by humility.

Now we are concerned in all our education with the adoption on the part of the child of this right religious adjustment. Its adoption involves: 1) the creation of habits of right adjustment, and the right adjustment in prayer, as well as in social intercourse may largely prepared by training in right habits. 2) The connection of the instincts and sentiments, as indicated above, with the religious and the social object in the sense of Jesus Christ. 3) The knowledge of the nature of God and of men. If the child is to know God and to be in such constant adjustment to him that he will receive the benefit of Divine Companionship he must not only have an instinctive and habitual attitude toward a mysterious entity in the world, and not only have certain sentiments about the religious object, but he [sic] must *know* eventually also where God is to be found. Hence our instruction must include theology, Natural theology and Christian theology. We are to teach a Christian world-view, in contrast to the materialistic world-view which will so often come to the child's attention. Such a world-view [sic] will not be in contrast to science, on the contrary it ought to use science as a revelation of God in the universe. We are to teach secondly a theology, leading the child to an appreciation for the Divine Element in Jesus Christ, and the Divine Element in Christian history. Such an appreciation will not be fostered by our abstract definitions as to the person and work of Jesus Christ, but by the study of his life. In the third place we are to teach Christian social ethics, the foundation of the right adjustment to men. The best sources of those ethics are, of course, the Sermon on the Mount and the epistles of Paul.

This is the general aim of all education and the aim of the catechetical class does not differ from it. In a way it ought to be a culmination of all that has preceded. Only we cannot count a great deal upon the religious instruction that has preceded. We are teaching then not with the rite of confirmation in mind any more than the high school teacher teaches with graduation in mind. Perhaps it would be well if the rite of confirmation came somewhere else than at the end of the period of instruction so that the child might not be encouraged in the idea that this is the end of his Christian training. It is a great and noble rite and has tremendous educational value. But it also has its great drawbacks if it is thought of as the close of instruction and education in Christian faith.

The Evangelical Church has a wonderful opportunity to excel in religious education just because it has the catechetical class. We have the possibility offered to us giving the children a real religious education. But are we not in danger of missing the opportunity if we stress confirmation and not the education, and if we make the hours given us to spend with the children, hours of formal instruction in definitions, hours of intolerable word-definition, hours of drill in memorization? Would it not be a help if we had a text-book which would serve the purpose of guiding the growth of the child into the relationship of love to God and to men rather than a book of theological definitions? But whatever text-book we use, let us keep in mind that our purpose is not the acquisition of certain dogmas, nor the memorization of certain verses, but the culture of his religious and social attitudes, after the pattern of Jesus Christ, that the mind may be in him which was also in Christ Jesus.

The Larger Educational Program of the Evangelical Church

In 1925, members of the Evangelical Synod had reason to feel good about the state of their denomination's educational institutions. Eden Seminary had just moved out of the urban congestion of St. Louis into comfortable new quarters in suburban Webster Groves. At Elmhurst College, Niebuhr was developing plans to upgrade both the school's programs and its facilities. Yet like his brother Reinhold, he still believed that their denomination lagged far behind others in higher education. This report not only documents some of the specific improvements he aimed to make at Elmhurst, but more importantly, it also shows that he was proposing them in order to put his Synod into a more competitive position and to offer more of its young people the benefits of a college education—all for the sake of a world in need of their Christian influence.

Source: *Report of the Third National Convention of the Evangelical Women's Union, Cleveland, Ohio, July 14–17, 1925,* 170–74.

The educational program of the Evangelical Synod must grow out of its apprehension and vision of its task. Programs cannot be made but must grow as the needs of the various departments of the educational enterprise become apparent; and the educational program of the Evangelical Church has been growing recently as it come [*sic*] to a realization of its duties toward its children.

The educational task of the church is an exceedingly broad one, for education is a tremendous enterprise, not a single, formal course of instruction. Like religion, education is one of those large generic terms which it is difficult to define because it covers so many different aspects of activity. There is cultural education and vocational education and religious education; there is the education of the home and the education offered by the playground and neighborhood and the education of the school; there is the unconscious education which comes to us through social agencies of various sorts, through public opinion, through social ideals and through social standards. All of these must be considered by the church when it seeks to envisage its educational task, for they are all important in molding the character and the mind of the youth. We cannot concern ourselves only with the formal instruction offered in the school rooms but must take into account the often much more influential forces which operate through the social agencies which do not seem to be directly educational.

The chief educational agency of all men still is the home and no church is fulfilling its educational task which does not bend all of its effort toward the conservation and the development of the Christian home. Such conservation and development cannot be achieved by the passage of laws—though laws may help—but only through the constant and unrelenting insistence of Christians upon the maintenance of Christian ideals in sex relationships and in the relationship of parents and children. It is necessary, furthermore, if Christian education is to succeed, that the church seek to infuse all social agencies, public opinion and group thought, with the principles and ideals of Christ. We seek in our schools and Sunday schools, in our churches and colleges to set before the youth of the land the high ideals of Jesus and bid the young men and young women follow him. But the silent voice of social thought, the multitudinous voices of the market-place, of political life and of social morality suggest to them that the only worth-while ideal is the ideal of material success. We are all affected by the current social standards and infected with the virus of materialism. The larger educational task of the church consists in the Christianization of public and social life, so that things which we never speak about, the things that are taken for granted, the social standards which remain the more powerful because they are unobserved and silent, may be Christian through and through. Our effort to develop high ideals in our schools and colleges will remain futile to a large extent so long as the education of society to Christianity in its political, industrial and national activities remains incomplete.

We are accustomed, however, to think of education in narrower terms. Primarily education means for us the formal education of childhood and youth in school and college and professional school. The task of the Evangelical Synod, so far as it is educational from this point of view, may be divided into three parts; there is first of all the task of the religious education of childhood, secondly there is the task of providing adequate facilities for higher education for our young people of college age and, thirdly, there is the task of preparing pastors for their calling through the work of the theological seminary.

We well recognize the importance of the first of these tasks. It is evident that the state is both unwilling and incompetent to provide religious education for the childhood of America. Public education in religion, under the direction of the state, has been tried in European countries without much success while the clash of denominations in America makes it impossible, as it is undesirable, that religion be taught under state auspices. We have made great strides in recent years in developing the work of religious education but far more than has been done remains to be accomplished. A large part of the youth of America is spiritually illiterate and we must be aware of the fact that our religious education must be developed far beyond its present standards before it can hope to be effective.

Much as needs to be done for the religious education of childhoods, more must be done for the higher education of our youth. There is no department of our church activity in which we fall so far behind the other religious denominations of America as we do in higher education. Our foreign missionary work can be compared with that done by other churches; our home mission work can be set alongside of that done by other denominations; our Sunday school work is as effective as that of others; but we cannot compare our work in education with that of the other religious bodies. We are far behind them all. The Congregationalists are larger than we are; they have about three times as many members as we have and are about six times as strong financially, but in higher education they are forty-one times as strong. The Methodists of the north have some twelve times as many members as the Evangelical Synod, but they have forty-four times as many colleges. The Presbyterians have six times as many members, they raise fifteen times as much money, but they have fifty-six colleges to our one. When we take the smaller churches into consideration we find the same situation. The Seventh Day Adventists have only one-fourth as many members as we but they have six colleges where we have one; the German Baptists, the Dunkers, are but one-third our size but they have nine colleges. The Reformed in the U.S. are about our size in every way, but in higher education they excel by far in that they have six colleges—one of them a women's school—and in addition support two academies and three seminaries. When we compare ourselves with the Lutherans we find the same situation to exist. The United Lutherans are about three times as strong as we in membership and in other respects but they are eleven times as strong in higher education. The Missouri Lutherans are two to three times as strong in membership and finances but they have fourteen colleges to our one besides having two seminaries, one of them the largest theological school in the United States. The Iowa Synod is much smaller than our Synod but it has built five colleges and seminaries while the Wisconsin Synod, also less than half as strong as ours, supports two colleges and two seminaries. It is evident that we have failed to do our duty to the youth of our church and to our nation in our failure to provide for higher education.

We have failed in our duty to our nation because the nation must look to the churches for an important part of its educational work. The great universities of our country were founded and nurtured by the churches. Congregationalists built Harvard and Yale; the Episcopalians founded Columbia; the Presbyterians sponsored Princeton; and the Baptists gave us Chicago University. Among the colleges of the country many of the best are church schools—Oberlin, Beloit, Knox, Wesleyan and others. If the church colleges were taken out of our country it would be impossible to replace them with any agencies which could take their place. Out of them have come and still come the cultural leaders of the nation. It is the small college which is still producing the teachers and the preachers, the authors and the journalists, the poets and political idealists of America. The great state universities excel in the education of men for the trades and technical professions, but the small college which is concerned not only with the education of the head but also with the promotion of high ideals and noble appreciations is producing the real leaders of America, the men who make up the soul of the nation. The Evangelical Synod has failed to do its duty in providing for this sort of education. Perhaps it was unable to do what it wanted to do in the past but it can no longer shirk its responsibility for the education of American youth.

We have not only failed to do our duty to our nation but also have failed to do our duty toward our children. There are from six hundred to one thousand evangelical young men and women in the colleges of the country. They are not studying in Evangelical schools but in schools founded and supported by Presbyterians, Congregationalists, Baptists, and Methodists. This does them no harm, but we are letting other churches carry our burden and the time ought to come when we can reciprocate and invite the children of these churches to share the education we provide for our children. The membership of our church is beginning to send its children to college in increasing numbers every year. High school enrollments throughout the country have increased tremendously during the last five years and college enrollments are continuing to rise with celerity. We may expect thousands of Evangelical young people to be attending colleges in the next years and we will need to make some haste if we want to be ready to take care of at least a part of them.

Because the Seminary Board of our Synod has envisaged its task in this way it has decided to adopt a four year and a ten year program for the development of Elmhurst College. One of our first needs is the establishment of an endowment fund of $400,000 which we must have before we can gain recognition as an accredited senior college. We need a gymnasium in order that the physical education of our students may not be neglected and we need a further dormitory as well as a service building. These things are to be provided in the four year program, while the ten year program looks forward to a school of four to five hundred students with an endowment of a million dollars. Another step in the development of Elmhurst was taken the other day when the Seminary Board decided to recommend to the General Conference that it convert Elmhurst College into a coeducational school. That decision was reached after it became evident that there are many young women in our churches who would like to attend college but must either attend some non-Evangelical school or otherwise give up the plan. We need a school for girls. It is evident that we cannot afford at the present time to build up a college for girls. If we wanted a first class, recognized school—and no one wants any other—we should need to duplicate all of Elmhurst [sic] equipment upon another campus; we should need to raise another endowment fund of not less than $400,000; we should need to employ another faculty of not less than eight men with good standing as college teachers, we should need to provide laboratories and libraries. It is possible, however, to take care of a large number of additional students at Elmhurst without a similar expenditure. We have the equipment and the faculty and we can provide for the education of the young women of the Synod with little additional cost to us.

We ought not to think of Elmhurst's development as the final part of our educational task. When we have completed the work at Elmhurst we will want to go on to Oakwood to build up a first class school there; then on to Robinson, perhaps, eventually, on to Dunkirk. Since the Evangelical Synod undertook to build a New Eden and carried through its program there with such splendid success, we have all taken new courage and have received new inspiration to take hold of the work before us with a will. We can do what others have done, what we must do if we would do our duty, what our young men and our young women may expect us to do for them. Let us build schools for them where they will learn to seek and find the truth and where they will be introduced to men's finest dreams and noblest aspirations.

2

Addressing the World of the Roaring Twenties

In the 1920s, the majority of Americans may have desired the "return to normalcy" that presidential candidate Warren G. Harding offered them. Instead, they found themselves swept by unprecedented industrial growth into a new consumer-oriented society that provided almost every middle-class home with electricity, a telephone, and a radio, as well as an automobile and easy access to movies and other mass forms of entertainment. For the first time, more Americans lived in cities than in rural areas. Social divisions sharpened in the wake of these trends, and as opposition from businesses and government leaders stiffened, the labor movement began to decline. Mass migration of African-Americans from the South to northern cities helped to quicken the pace of urbanization, but it also exacerbated racial prejudice among white Americans. The homeward trajectory of the nation's foreign policy, moreover, only served to strengthen similar attitudes toward populations of other nations, especially newer immigrants aspiring to become American citizens.

For this reason, toward the end of his tenure as president of Elmhurst College H. Richard Niebuhr held a three-day "service conference" on campus. "Modern problems were presented and discussed as to their relation to college men and to people as whole,"[1] the school's newspaper reported. "It brought to our minds new realizations and caused us to form new convictions as to the complex problems which our age is facing."[2] Niebuhr's brother Reinhold was among the featured speakers. He presented lectures on "An Industrial Civilization and the Kingdom of God" and "The Challenge of Race to Christian Conscience." Other topics included "The Effect of the Metropolitan Region on Human Personality" and "Christianity versus Nationalism." Not only did all students at Elmhurst participate through their attendance at this conference, there were also delegates from Eden Seminary as well as DeKalb and other neighboring colleges. Niebuhr's hope in the spring of 1927 was that this conference, whose focus was the world in which he wanted his church to play a much larger role than it had before, would become "the single greatest event in Elmhurst history."[3]

Niebuhr was seeking to build on the heritage the Evangelical Synod had bequeathed to him. As a union church of Reformed and Lutheran constituents, the Synod's theology included John Calvin's conviction that Christian efforts at conversion must be directed not only at individuals but also at their society. Thus, despite its ethnic isolationist tendencies, the Synod saw fit to join the Federal Council of Churches. Leaders of the Social Gospel movement like Washington Gladden and Walter Rauschenbusch were also invited

---

1. "Service Conference Successful," *Elm Bark* 7, no. 24 (April 2, 1927): 1.
2. "The Elmhurst Service Conference," *The Evangelical Herald* 26 (April 21, 1927): 327.
3. Ibid., 344–45.

to lecture at its Eden Seminary. Shortly before his untimely death in 1913, the family patriarch, Gustav Niebuhr, had published a two-part article in one of the Synod's periodicals entitled, "In What Way and to What Extent Should the Church Exercise Influence on Social and Political Conditions?" He chided the members of his denomination for letting their "bickerings" with each other and the "business" of their congregations take precedence over "remedying municipal and social evils of any kind."[4] The "Christian standard of righteousness," he argued, required the "decided concerted action of all."[5]

In addition, Samuel D. Press, the mentor of the Niebuhr brothers as students at Eden, offered a course on social service that gave students an opportunity to canvass St. Louis neighborhoods to determine those needs that could be met by a settlement house Press had helped to found.[6] Both of the brothers followed in their mentor's footsteps in this regard: Reinhold served as the pastor of an Evangelical congregation near the front line of the rapidly developing auto industry in Detroit, and Richard not only took graduate courses in sociology but also offered his own classes on the subject when he joined the Eden faculty.

The 1920s also featured upheaval within the Protestant establishment. The moment that received the greatest attention was the 1925 Scopes Trial in Dayton, Tennessee, where a local high school science teacher named John Scopes had been indicted for teaching evolution in his classes. Three-time presidential candidate William Jennings Bryan and high-profile criminal lawyer Clarence Darrow squared off over the literal approach to interpreting the Bible. While Scopes was convicted of the charge, the publicity put fundamentalist Christians in a less-than-favorable light. Fiercer battle

---

4. Gustav Niebuhr, "In What Way and to What Extent Should the Church Exercise Influence on Social and Political Conditions?" *The Messenger of Peace* 12 (May 15, 1913): 2.
5. Ibid. (June 1, 1913): 1–2.
6. William G. Chrystal, *Niebuhr Studies* (Reno: Empire for Liberty, 2012), 59.

lines were drawn in Baptist and Presbyterian denominational families. In 1923, for example, J. Gresham Machen, a professor at Princeton Theological Seminary, stirred up considerable controversy with *Christianity and Liberalism,* a book in which he contended that given the naturalistic presuppositions with which they had chosen to undergird their theology, liberals among Presbyterians and elsewhere had in fact left the Christian fold. When his church's General Assembly failed to support him, Machen and his followers left and eventually formed their own church, the Presbyterian Church of America (later renamed the Orthodox Presbyterian Church).

The Fundamentalist-Modernist controversy had been brewing for more than five decades among American Protestants. Following the Civil War, Darwinism's enthroning of natural forces at work in the environment over time precipitated a paradigm shift not only among biologists and other scientists but also in other realms of the academic community. In theology, the Bible was placed under the lens of higher criticism, subjecting it to the same kind of analysis that other literary and historical experts were employing. While liberals embraced these new developments, traditionalists were placed on the defensive. Prior to Machen at Princeton, B. B. Warfield and A. A. Hodge had sought to shore up confidence in the Bible by applying the doctrine of inerrancy to all scientific, historical, and geographical details set forth on its pages. Others sought refuge in a more supernatural view of history and the future of humankind, choosing to adopt John Nelson Darby's dispensational version of premillennialism. Between 1910 and 1915, moreover, a twelve-volume series called *The Fundamentals* was published in order to defend those features of orthodox Christianity that the authors perceived to be under assault from modern philosophy and liberal theology.[7]

No such controversy erupted during this period in the Evangelical Synod, though Niebuhr did receive conservative pushback from several members of his denomination. One was a pastor who, at a conference in Chicago in 1927, took issue with Niebuhr's effort in his presentation to update the Christian concept of a personal devil, asserting that persons with such liberal convictions should not be allowed to teach in the Synod's schools. A more serious flap came in 1929 when a colleague on the Eden faculty, Manfred Manrodt, charged that Niebuhr believed that the Bible only "contains" rather than "is" the word of God, and that he was misleading students by teaching them that salvation included reform of the social order. The Eden board of directors quickly extinguished the fire, however, by releasing Manrodt from his position and indicating to the Synod that this was an administrative decision that needed to be made in view of curriculum changes at the seminary.[8]

In any event, Niebuhr showed little sympathy for fundamentalism in his writings. His first book, *The Social Sources of Denominationalism*, attributed fundamentalism's rise to rural Protestant churches' resistance to urbanization.[9] In *Christ and Culture*, he identified the movement as a type of cultural Christianity that differed from its liberal rival only in that it sought to conserve the "cosmological and biological notions of older cultures," that it turned acceptance of these notions into a "loyalty test," and that it fused "obedience to Jesus Christ" with "early American social organization."[10] In *The Purpose of the Church and Its Ministry*, published in 1956, he criticized the fundamentalist emphasis on the

---

7. See George M. Marsden, *Understanding Fundamentalism and Evangelicalism* (Grand Rapids: Eerdmans, 1991), 9–61.
8. Jon Diefenthaler, *H. Richard Niebuhr: A Lifetime of Reflections on the Church and the World* (Macon, GA: Mercer University Press, 1986), 35–36.
9. H. Richard Niebuhr, *The Social Sources of Denominationalism* (New York: Henry Holt, 1929), 184.
10. H. Richard Niebuhr, *Christ and Culture* (New York: Harper & Row, 1951), 102.

inerrancy of the Bible by asserting that the syllogisms with which participants in the movement sought to defend this doctrine made them guilty of bibliolatry.[11]

Niebuhr found the liberal side of the controversy to be more compatible with his own outlook. Like his father before him, he viewed the kind of research into the biblical documents associated with higher criticism as an aid rather than a threat to the illumination of the Christian faith.[12] During his graduate work at Yale, moreover, he was attracted to the biblical theology of Frank C. Porter, whose lectures took him further down the liberal path that German scholars like Albrecht Ritschl and Adolf von Harnack had blazed prior to World War I. In working on his doctoral dissertation, titled "Ernst Troeltsch's Philosophy of Religion," he learned to see more fully the relative features of all Christian truths and to examine the historical and cultural context in which they were developed or interpreted. Finally, as president of Elmhurst College, he argued that if students were to address contemporary social problems on the basis of their religious faith, they needed to be exposed to the results of modern historical and scientific research rather than shielded from them.

The writings that follow illustrate Niebuhr's growing commitment to identifying the social applications of the Christian gospel to the mainstream of the American culture that his Evangelical Synod had entered more fully during the Roaring Twenties. They also demonstrate his firm conviction that turning back the clock to either the culture or the approach to theology of yesteryear would only inhibit the church's ability to engage the world around it.

---

11. H. Richard Niebuhr, *The Purpose of the Church and Its Ministry: Reflections on the Aims of Theological Education* (New York: Harper & Brothers, 1956), 43–44.
12. Gustav Niebuhr, "Modern Methods and Their Application to the Old Gospel Truth," *The Messenger of Peace* 12 (January 15, 1913): 1.

A Sociological Interpretation of Eden

When he wrote this article, Niebuhr was seeking to introduce his students at Eden Seminary to the same sociological perspective he was developing in the graduate courses he was taking at Washington University in St. Louis. In retrospect, the article appears foundational for much of his subsequent wrestling with the paradox of church and world. The viewpoint he urged the students and faculty at his school to assume for the building of a more "universal community" was world-centered rather than church-centered. He already emphasized at this early point in his career that God intended this important feature of his kingdom to be realized not only within the seminary family or through the work of the larger church but by joining forces with everyone in the wider world who had similar aspirations.

Source: *The Keryx* 12, no. 2 (February 1922): 8–11.

Eden Seminary is not an institution in the ordinary sense of that word, it is a community. The communal character of Eden life is its most distinctive aspect when the school is compared with other seminaries. And it is the hope of Eden that this characteristic will not only be maintained but also developed: for there is no education that can take the place of developing within a community. Whenever education is not connected with community living it is mere instruction and not education at all. As the family is a better educator than the public school, so the religious community is superior to the institution which teaches religion. In the community instruction and life are intimately connected; it develops personality and does not merely impart knowledge. To maintain the community character of Eden life and to foster its development is therefore a chief concern of its friends.

Communism as a term is associated today with the idea of common ownership of property; but the communism of Eden is not primarily economic. It is true that the community has its physical basis. The common home, the common meal, the common control over the physical environment play an important role in fostering the social spirit. Communism has been extended at times to other property. Soap, towels, rain coats and umbrellas, light bulbs, etc., have been frequently nationalized. But this economic communism is not an essential part of the social life at Eden. It tends perhaps more in the direction of disintegration than of integration—Eden's experience thus partly confirming that of Russia.

The Eden community is of course a political body. The Brotherhood represents democracy and exercises self-government. But more important is the fact that Eden men are members of a social community. They are ruled by the customs—conscious and unconscious—of their society. Is not the custom of disrobing partially in one's study before retiring to bed a folkway more binding than any state law? They speak their own peculiar language. The joke columns of *The Keryx* abound in examples. Customs and language change. Imitation, suggestion, the work of some great organizing genius, frequently help the community to make new adaptations to new situations. All the laws of the social process are illustrated in miniature in the changes as well as in the traditional continuity of Eden society.

What is of greatest importance however is that Eden is the name of a religious community. In the externals the social character of Eden religious life manifests itself in the attendance on common worship, common participation in leadership of religious meetings, in communion in the celebration of the sacrament. Common spiritual ideals and moral value-judgments, as well as co-operation in the realm of spiritual life, are not so easily analyzed nor pointed out.

Yet their existence is evident to the participant in the community religious life.

The religious community is united by its common memory. The students of Eden have not only the same social background on the whole, but they have been nurtured in a single spiritual tradition. It is also a community of common hope. Not only the expectation of all members to enter into the same life work, but, what is infinitely more important—their participation in the great hope of all Christians for the Kingdom, make these separate selves one body. The presence of this hope in a greater or small degree determines to a large extent the character of the community. The greater and more general the hope, the more closely is the group united: the weaker it is, the weaker are the bonds which hold the selves together. There are instances in the history of Eden which illustrate this truth.

There are many points perhaps in which the Eden community resembles religious communities of the middle ages. There is however one great difference. Our present society is not held together by authority, but can find its basis only in common memory and common purpose, in shared ideals, and in a united faith.

Here then is a characteristic of Eden life which is of tremendous value and which needs to be maintained and developed. For any community is subject to strains and to friction from within which need to be guarded against. The success of the brotherhood in the past in overcoming such strains is something of a guarantee for the future. The longer a society maintains itself the greater is the chance of survival. But a community, if it is to be successful—if it is to continue in being, must not only guard against internal frictions but it must grow. In every real society there is a tendency to become a universal society. The Eden community will become ever more vital only as it extends its relations. As a Christian community, of course, the tendency to extend its communion is always a present factor. But the universal community is not only to be apprehended in the inner life: the mystic's communion with God must have as its counterpart the desire to realize universal communion with mankind.

How may the Eden community extend its relations and thus realize itself within the universal community, or in the kingdom of God? Participation in the missionary enterprise is the first and most obvious way. Such co-operation becomes of greatest value to the community of course when the whole body co-operates as a unit, not in separate parts. The church which interests itself in the missionary movement as a church receives a much greater benefit for itself than when its individual members share in the movement as individuals. Unity of the group is fostered by the common interest and common purpose. A second extension of the Eden community may be sought in its relation to the church. An active sharing in the life of the Evangelical church by the society as such will benefit both church and the society. The Evangelical Forward Movement offers a splendid opportunity for such an extension of the local group, thru the extension of its interest. Again the community of Eden will maintain and develop itself thru [sic] participation in the ideals and in the enterprises of the church as a whole—of the American church and of the church universal. A common interest, a common sympathy with the hopes and aims of other Christians in other folds is the only possible basis for the realization of our denominational purpose of church unity. When the Eden community participates in this fashion in the spiritual life of American and of world Christianity, our church will be making a long step in the direction of real church unity. Interest in the immediate neighborhood, in the city, in the nation, in the international world, will foster the development of the Eden community and thus the development of its members. Sympathy with all of the aspirations of men toward God and His kingdom—whether those aspirations be expressed in the language of religion or of economics, whether in the language of the Catholic or of the Protestant, of the American or the German—sympathy of such a character is the basis of a fruitful communal life. Our own communities become of greater value to us as the interest of that community increase; they develop our personalities the better, the less self-centered they are.

Eden is on the way to realize its community life in such extension of interests and participation in the purposes and ideals of other communities. Its future will be determined by the progress made in this direction. If the community becomes self-centered it very quickly creates a tradition of narrowness and maintains that tradition as an individual maintains his habits. Community habits of wide interest and sympathy are as easily formed and as surely transmitted as are the good habits of any person.

The Eden community—to point out an important fact in conclusion—is not a local community. It numbers among the members of its body "the noble living and the noble dead" of its graduates. Contact between the brotherhood and the distant members increases and develops the community spirit of the local group and extends its interest. *The Keryx* as the organ of that contact plays an important role in the social life of the whole community. It is the main nerve of the Eden body. Its continued prosperity is of real interest to all who are concerned about the extension of the Eden brotherhood ideal. In bringing to the attention of all graduates the interests, needs, hopes and purposes as well as the memory of the Eden society, it helps to maintain the integrity of the whole body. A corresponding activity on the part of the graduates in making the interests, needs and purposes of Eden their own will tend to enrich their life, by participation in the life of their social body, while it will tremendously further the development of that body.

The Alliance Between Labor and Religion

For Niebuhr, Christianity and the labor movement in America were not enemies. On the contrary, they were natural allies in the struggle for social improvements. He stated this again in another article published in the same journal in 1929 entitled, "Christianity and the Industrial Classes." Both articles, by pointing to the historical connections between Christianity and the working classes and highlighting the accommodation of the church to capitalist ownership, underscore Niebuhr's strong commitment to getting his immigrant denomination to engage the world around it more fully. This article has been chosen not only because it is the earlier of the two but also because of its passionate appropriation of Social-Gospel rhetoric and the attention it gives to the religious points of connection between the world of labor and the church. Like the later article, it also helps account for the more comprehensive sociological analysis Niebuhr devoted in The Social Sources of Denominationalism *to "disinherited" religious groups.*

Source: *Theological Magazine of the Evangelical Synod of North America* 49 (May 1921): 197–203.

Since the days of Christ there have been frequent connections between Christian history and that other movement, whose origin lies in the inequalities of social life. We may call it the labor movement, if by that term we imply no restriction to those efforts only which seek to affect the situation of men as workers. Labor movements are not today, nor have they ever been, purely economic in origin or purpose. Socialism, anarchism, and syndicalism, trade unionism for that matter, as well as the peasant wars, the French Revolution and the Utopianism of the Nineteenth [sic] century are to be traced to deeper fountains within the human heart and to be followed to vaster ends than can be described in economic terms.

There is much that is akin to religion in them. It must be so, tho our only evidence were the historic connection.

The religious renaissance of Israelite prophecy was in the closest connection with the social movement that is reflected in the revolutions of the period both against despots and against the foreign faiths imported to bolster up their despotism. The time of Jesus was a time of social ferment and few but the poor in the land were open to the voice of the Carpenter of Nazareth. Paul's message was sown in the hearts of the workers, the poor and the ignoble, who had begun to stir restlessly under the oppression of a false Pax Romana. Luther's effort to dissociate the reformation from the peasants' uprising did not avail to cover up the close connection between the two movements nor the Reformer's debt to the social conscience, while it has made evident the evil resulting to church and peasant-worker alike from the divorce of their related enterprises. Nor do we [sic] lack lesser parallels: Huss and the Taborites, Wycliff and Wat Tyler, Hans Boehm, the reformer-revolutionist, Wesleyanism and the English social evolution of the eighteenth century, the religious movement in the United States, of which Charles G. Finney was the main representative, and the labor movement which found its leader in Robert Owen. These are but a few of the multitudinous connections between labor and religious history which present themselves. The evidence becomes too formidable to permit any ascription of the connections to the category of accident.

It is apparent that in almost every one of the religious movements mentioned there was a deep social enthusiasm for the rights of the workers; and that the social revolutions were impregnated with some sentiment of enthusiastic religion blended with confused dreams of the establishment of the kingdom of God on earth. The contemporary movements were kin to each other and partook of each other's natures. In our own day we are well enough aware what vitality and energy has come to some sections of the Christian church thru recognition of the social meaning of the faith. What is less patent to most of us is that the progress of the labor movement today is inspired by a religious sentiment, that it is an ally of religion by reason of origin within the same stirrings of the human heart and because of the similarity of its aim to that of Christianity. While it may be evident that in the past labor movements have frequently been of such a character as is claimed for them, it is more difficult to recognize these characteristics in a contemporary movement, whose deeper meanings are obscured by the limitations of some of its leaders, by the passions of the movement and by popular prejudices.

That the present phase of the labor movement bears an *implicit religious character* is a conclusion based upon its inspiring hope for a better world and its faith in the ideal, upon its bitter discontent with the sins of the present order, its insistence on the worth of personality, its sense for realities, and its underlying conviction of the solidarity of men. That these characteristics are often inarticulate in the expression of labor thru organization and organized movements is plain; that they are present beneath the surface and are underlying motives of action becomes equally evident upon closer scrutiny of the psychology of labor. As generalizations they are perhaps only half-true of a movement so complex as the labor movement, as they would be only half-true of the complex religion of the church. But the truth that is in them is sufficient justification for their emphasis.

The basis of any Christian attitude toward life is found in the Baptist's and Jesus' early message: "Repent for the Kingdom of the heavens is at hand." If we think of repentance as a state of regret for personal sins it is true that we shall look in vain for such an attitude on the part of the labor movement. But there is *repentance* in that state of bitter *discontent with* the *present order* and in that sense of need for succor, which characterizes its every expression; and such repentance is also religious. However diverse may be elements which make up the complex state which is the fore-runner of the religious experience, this element of discontent, this sense of need, this realization of the sin of society is one of great importance. It is basic in the religious experience of Moses; its overtones are clearly distinguishable in the prophetic call; such social repentance paved the way for the Reformation. Dissatisfaction with and distress over the injustice and immorality of the world is a primary element in the religion of labor.

The counterpart of repentance is the *outreaching* of the human heart *after the better world*. Where repentance is purely personal that desire remains also purely personal and the penitent craves only to know that he has made his peace with God. Where the social conscience is involved the hope of the distressed is for a better social order, for a kingdom of God and the salvation of humanity as a whole. Insofar as the labor movement shares this type of hope it is surely religious. Of course that hope may be very materialistic in form, but there is frequently less materialism and more ethical idealism in the socialist's and anarchist's and laborer's desire than in the crass dreams of heaven, which still play so large a part in the recognized religious life of our own day. The distinction is not to be made between the hope of the social movement and the hope of organized Christianity, but between desires of a materialistic and of an ethical order. The pronunciamentos of labor parties of every shade of radicalism and conservatism, the evident idealism of many of their leaders, the longings which fill the breasts of the poor in their land, coming to expression in simple and unobtrusive forms, give evidence of the power of the hope for a better world, which makes labor movements so akin to religion.

The *idealism* of *labor* reflects itself in still other forms than this. The gullibility of the rank and file, so frequently exploited by their false prophets, is not as much an indication of ignorance as it is of faith in the moral quality of others. It is true that labor movements have more frequently been characterized by hatred than by love. At least hatred has been a more apparent characteristic. But the hatred of the labor movement is not dominantly of a personal kind. It is hatred against those systems and typical persons that have been made representatives, by slogan and suggestion, of all the injustice of the present world. As such it can often be compared to the holy wrath of religion. Such hatred as this, harmful tho it be to the hater, is nevertheless a counterpart of idealism. The idealism of the labor movement is evident, as well in the support which it has lent to the idealistic reformers. Internationalism is nowhere so powerful as in the labor movement. Labor more than any other agency perhaps was responsible for the universal school system in the United States; its part in the overthrow of slavery seems to be far greater than historians as a rule assign to it; imprisonment for debt was abolished largely thru the efforts of labor; and in more recent times it was this group which responded most whole-heartedly to the idealism of such movements as the extension of suffrage to women, pacifism, disarmament, free speech, democratization of education and the protection of womanhood and childhood in industry.

In all of this idealism of the worker there is one outstanding characteristic which the labor movement shares with Christianity: *respect for individuality.* We are wont to boast that the church established the sanctity of all personality, that it gave to the child, to the woman, to the stranger within the gates, to the poor, to the outcast an equal standing before God, and consequently established their position in the world on the basis of equality. We are liable to forget that the labor movement has been in our own time equally responsible with, if not more responsible than, the church for those reforms. It is perhaps because of this fact more than any other that we have a right to speak of the religion of labor. Here it stands on common ground with Christianity. As the "Old Testament stakes its idea of God on the possibility of making the commonest Israelite a native within the things of eternity" and the New Testament on the possibility of regenerating the meanest of all men thru the spirit of Christ, so the labor movement is staking everything upon the possibility of carrying the principle of individuality into every department of society.

In its *appreciation of the solidarity of men* the faith of labor is no less akin to ours than in its sponsorship of the principle of personality. The solidarity of Christ with men made the Christian religion; the solidarity of believers in him continued it; faith in that solidarity and loyalty to its embodiment in Christ is the Christian religion. Perhaps the labor movement does not share that loyalty to Christ, but it is animated by a loyalty to humanity—it has the feeling of belonging together with others—it has a capacity for sacrifice in the interest of the body which gave it a definitely religious if not yet a Christian character. For is not the foundation of religion to be sought just in this capacity of man to identify himself with another and with humanity, to lose his life within the larger life? Where this spirit of loyalty and solidarity is lacking religion cannot enter in; where it has established itself there religion has been born.

The religious spirit of the labor movement, finally, shows itself in the *sense* for *realities* and *scorn* of *hypocrisy*. Christ penetrating the hypocrisy and conventionalism of Pharisaism to the heart of the moral relationships in His Sermon on the Mount is the typical example. This penetration is characteristic of labor. "To balance the hardship of a laborer's life, there are real compensations. There is at least a suggestion of Antaeus's contact with Mother Earth. A thousand conventions, harmless in themselves, but distorting to the mental vision when unconsciously regarded as vital, drop away. A thousand preoccupations that worry the soul of the well-to-do are as meaningless to the workingman as heraldic terms to the Hottentot." (From "The Diary of the Laborer".) It is easy to see why that should be so. Its effect is also apparent. The conventions that hide realities are the bane of all social and of organized religious life. The laborers lack of them may go far to explain why it has been just he who responded most quickly to the message of the true prophets of religion.

So akin by nature, so closely connected in history, Christianity and the labor movement might have been allies and seed-plots for each other's truth. That this has not been the case is the tragedy of both labor and the church. For the connection has rather been the occasion for frequent misunderstandings and for many feuds. So Luther disowned the peasants, radical Puritanism early lost its faith in the French Revolution, socialism and the Church discovered in each other bitter animosities. The church has lost not only the social enthusiasm and the energy of the labor class movement, but has failed also to appropriate for itself the spiritual qualities which labor could give to it; on the other hand it received from its connection with the leisure class qualities which stand often enough in direct contrast with spiritual realities: worldliness and satisfaction with the things that are; customs, habits of thought, conventions of every kind, that obscure the real things in life; a practical belief in the class-division of mankind into upper and lower groups and a spirit of narrow nationalism and racial prejudice.

The dividing force has not been only the worldliness of the church in these respects. Often enough it has seemed that the Church came to a real appreciation of the spirit of labor and made common cause with it for a while, just as we are seeking to do in our own time. But the division always came and we need to learn a lesson from history if we would adjust relations so as to prevent a similar disjunction of the two movements which are just beginning to arrive at a mutual understanding of each other.

The *dividing element* has been *labor's method of gaining its ends by force* and the *Church's interest* in the *preservation of law and order*. Certainly that seems to have been the cause of the momentous and irreparable break between Luther and the peasants, as it was one of those divisions mentioned. There are two considerations which need to be taken into account for a correct appreciation of the situation. The first is that the Church's opposition to force, justified as it surely is by the ethics of Christ, has not as a rule sought its basis there but rather has been founded upon interest of a far different nature. Interest in its own salvation when the force used by labor called forth the use of force by labor's enemy, interest in the material possessions of the Church and in the mere stability of a worldly society, wherein the church had made itself at home, seem to have dictated the opposition. It is one thing to preach the bearing of the cross which the injustice of society lays upon the man who fights that injustice. It is one thing to preach forgiveness as meaning condoning of the sin of the social order and resignation to its unalterable power, it is quite another thing to preach forgiveness to the enemy against whose sin relentless warfare is to continue that he may be saved along with his victims. Has not the Church's preaching been too often the former kind? It has not preached warfare against sin without hate of the sinner, but rather peace and law and order and condoning of sin that the sinner and his system might not be harmed. Not until the church is ready to fight the same battle that labor is fighting, but by the better method of aggressive suffering, will it be in a position to declare against labor's method in the fight. Because the Church has rejected the war together with the methods of labor's warfare, because it has sought to preserve false peace rather than to establish real peace, because it has had greater interest in law and order than in righteousness, it has alienated labor again and again and will continue to do so until it follows the suffering Christ.

The second consideration which presents itself when we survey the history of the church's connection with labor is this—that the *Church has not dared to stand alone*. Whenever it rejected labor because of labor's method of warfare, it also made common cause with labor's enemies. Thus Luther joined the princes and the nobles. At once the inconsistency of the position becomes apparent. The Church countenances those methods on the part of capital which it decried when labor used them, and because of which it forsook labor—war, force and bloodshed. Such an inconsistency is a necessary result of a confusion between the actual and selfish interest in the preservation of law and order and the ostensible, confessed interest in the methods of non-resistance and suffering to gain a just end. If the church is in reality interested in the establishment of justice, and in the establishment of that justice by methods of spiritual warfare, it could never, tho forsaking labor, battle against labor. Is there not always a third choice? Is not the church strong enough in the strength of Christ to stand alone? Because labor's method is not our method, our cause is not one whit the more akin to the cause of capital, of narrow nationalism or aristocracy. The kingdom of God may suffer violence, and the violent may seek to take it by force, but it remains the kingdom of God, and their violence is no disparagement of it and never can be a reason for rejecting that kingdom, tho only for a time being, in favor of a kingdom of this world.

The Church of Jesus Christ may soon need to make a decision weightier in import even than that which was forced upon Luther. Now it feels its kinship with the poor in the land and pronounces them blessed. Whether it will deny that kinship later and engage again in war against the movement with which it shares so much that is real in a world of shams—or whether it will strive, while there is yet time, to lead the way to the goal by way of the cross—or whether, not succeeding in that, it will forfeit its rights to all consideration as an agency of righteousness and as a carrier of the prophetic spirit, by making common cause with unrighteousness, will soon be determined. The lessons of history and the life of the Master are our only guides. But they are sufficient, if we will but heed.

THE PARADOX OF CHURCH AND WORLD

Christianity and the Social Problem

The Evangelical Synod of North America had one foot each in the Lutheran and Calvinist traditions of the sixteenth-century Reformation. Niebuhr tended to favor the latter because he believed it nurtured the greater sense of social responsibility he was encouraging his denomination to assume. He also thought that the "higher righteousness" of the Social Gospel effectively addressed the pressing needs of a society dehumanized by industrialization and tottering on the brink of moral collapse. This article is both sweeping in its analysis of America's social ills during the 1920s and specific in terms of the remedies that Niebuhr calls on the church of his forebears to apply not only through its proclamation of the gospel but also through its advocacy of reform measures. "The church needs not so much to preach Christ as to be Christ," the anonymous quotation with which he ends the article, is one that might just as readily be applied to twenty-first century, post-church American Christianity.

Source: *Theological Magazine of the Evangelical Synod of North America* 50 (July 1922): 278–91.

I

The social gospel is no new gospel. It is the *Sermon on the Mount* and the *message* about the *Kingdom of God*. It is the parable of the Good Samaritan and of Dives and Lazarus. It is the prophecy of the Old Testament and the good news of the New Covenant. It is Paul's description of the universal church and John's vision of the end. The social gospel is not new, but the viewpoint from which that gospel and the whole Scriptures are surveyed is a new one. The viewpoint of Protestant thought, especially of Lutheran thought, has been individualistic. It has said: Man's chief concern should be the salvation of his soul. The social gospel reiterates: Seek ye *first* the kingdom of God and all other things shall be added unto you. Individualistic thought has said: Original sin has been passed down from father to son. The social interpretation does not deny this, but it emphasizes another point of view: The sin from which men must be redeemed is not so much passed down from one individual to another, as it is ingrained in social institutions, and perpetuated in false social standards. The character of man is inevitably born out of this environment. The older view said: Love God and so you will love men. The new: He that loveth not his brother whom he hath seen, how can he love God whom he hath not seen? But the comparison need go no farther. The emphasis is clear. The social gospel is the gospel which proclaims that between man and his society there is the closest possible relation; that Christ sought to save individuals for the sake of the Kingdom; that He proclaimed the Kingdom for the sake of individuals; that none of us liveth to himself and none dieth to himself; that members of the human family must by the law of life suffer, sin and be saved together; that we are members of one another and that just this relationship between men is the point where the saving work of Christ begins and ends.

We can best summarize the content of the social gospel in three phases: the *value of the individual*, the *kingdom of God*, the *principle of service*. Under the first head these doctrines of the New Testament are subsumed.

1. The absolute value of human personality as brought out in teaching after teaching of Jesus and by his whole life of service to those whom the world esteemed without great worth: lepers, publicans, Samaritans, women, children, etc.

2. The comparative value of personality. Human lives are more valuable than human institutions. The whole teaching is brought

home to us in one phrase: Man was not made for the Sabbath, but the Sabbath was made for man.

Yet the value of human lives can be realized, according to the gospel, only in the losing of the individual life within the kingdom of God. Seek ye first the kingdom of God. Whether Jesus conceived that the Kingdom was to be established here or beyond is a question beside the point. It was to be realized as a Kingdom, as a social entity. The righteousness of the gospel is the righteousness of community conduct; to be lived out wherever men are in society, and have a mutual interdependence and mutual obligations. Finally the guiding principle—the law of the individual and of the Kingdom, the standard by which human conduct is to be measured and the value of human institutions determined—is the law of service, as it is presented upon every page of the teaching and embodied in the whole life of Christ.

II

From this vantage point of the gospel the Christian looks out upon the conditions of contemporaneous civilization. The conflicts between nations, the drawing apart of the social classes, unemployment, the conflict between laborer and employer, the rising of the crime wave in all countries, the growing prevalence of divorce, illegitimacy, and desertion, the falling of the birth rate, the recrudescence of racial conflict in America, the post-haste legislation against every manner of evil, the suppression of free speech and free assembly upon the slightest provocation—all these are symptoms to him of an underlying evil. Constructive efforts are being made too; there is an ever growing interest in all kinds of social service; we hear of various attempts at the formation of community groups, of radical pronunciamentos against the present order; earnest efforts to apply the doctrines of Christ to the conditions of social life. These also the

Christian can test by the standard of Christ's statement of the social law.

But it is not enough to test and to condemn. The ascetic, the world-fleer may do that; not the follower of that Master who sent his disciples as sheep into the midst of wolves. Nor is it sufficient to content ourselves with hope of the heavens that open to the faithful, if that include a shirking of our responsibility toward the coming generations and toward the present, or any neglect of the prayer: Thy will be done on earth as it is in heaven. The world of business and labor and government needs not only criticism, but constructive criticism; the church's demands for justice must deal with realities and not with abstractions; they need to be based upon sympathetic insight into the situations of the day, on a whole-hearted desire to identify itself with the world of sin and help it to work out its redemption, as Christ identified himself with the sinner and led him to the realization of a fairer life. The primary condition for Christendom and the church to fulfill if they would assist in the construction of a more Christian social order will be the abandonment of an attitude of self-righteousness, whole-hearted recognition of their share in the sin of the world and their express recognition for the evils of that social life, of which they ought to have been the conscience. Measured by the standard of service, the church will find itself sadly lacking as a social institution; realizing the vital truth of the supremacy of human individuality and of the sole desirability of the kingdom of God we will not fail to accuse ourselves of having set our own interests as a churchly institution before these.

Having made this confession so good for the soul and being ready to identify itself with the sin-stricken social order, the church may turn its attention to those specific ills of the world of today which call for the diagnosis and the remedy of the gospel. These evils we may consider under two heads: insofar as they violate the principle of the kingdom of God, they show themselves in rampant individualism; insofar as they are denials of the supreme value of the individual, they appear as the suppression of personality.

III

Let us reiterate the principle of the kingdom: that individual life finds its purpose and its realization in the identification of its interests with the interests of the kingdom of God. The end of life is social. This is not an esoteric truth. It is as fundamental law of life. Individualism leads always and everywhere to destruction. Consecration of self to the cause of the social group leads to a self-realization, tho complete self-realization be impossible until the social group include the whole of man's social environment, God and mankind.

Let us measure the conditions of our own time by this law of the losing and the finding of life. We note on all sides symptoms of a rampant individualism which finds its end in itself rather than within the social group. Symptoms of especial significance are those relating to the family. The increasing prevalence of *divorce* is a phenomenon adequately noted by all agencies of church and state alike. That the essential causes of this factor are to be sought not in the economic but in the psychological and ethical realms seems evident. Not because the age of marriage is so much longer postponed today than was the case in natural civilizations, nor because poverty is the great disrupter of the family—important as these causes are—but because the social standard of individualism countenances divorce, has this evil become so ominous an appearance. The rights of the individual or his claims are placed higher than his duties and the result upon the family is evident. This same result of excessive individualism is of course also to be noted in the world of industry. There the law long prevailed and largely still prevails: "That they shall take who have the power and they shall keep who can." The result has been the *exploitation* of the worker by the employer in matters of wages, hours, and lack of provision for care in case of accident, etc. There are signs of the passing of the era of excessive individualism in industry, but we are still dealing with the results of that era in the grievances of labor against capital and in the adoption on the part of labor of a similar attitude in many cases. Group exploitation has taken the place of individualism: the corporation has supplanted the individual employer, and the union the individual laborer. The ethics of the group however remain frequently, almost always the ethics of individualism, for the group is never the whole group of those interested, but an individualistic group, whose mores are those of the fight and of the rule by power rather than by co-operation.

There are other symptoms of excessive individualism in the increase of crimes both against life and against property, a phenomenon which Europe shares with America, tho in a smaller degree. The general lack of respect for law and for authority is of a similar nature.

There seems to have been, or there exists in the world now, a *general breakdown of morals*, of the moral sanctions whereby society kept the individual within bounds and sought in a practical, tho often far from righteous and ideal way, to express and guide itself according to the law whose universal validity Jesus discovered for mankind—that the end of the individual lies in the social group.

We know the reasons for this breakdown in part at least: 1) The *abuse of authority* and the suppression of the individual under monarchies and hierarchies, economic tyrannies and political oppressions, which brought about the reactions of the Reformation and the French Revolution and ended in the one-sided development of the principle of individual liberty. It has often been said that this reaction reached its climax in the French Revolution. It seems exceedingly doubtful to competent historians and sociologists, in view of the individualism of our own day, whether the crest of the reaction has as yet been reached. "Our fathers rightly thought that the emancipation of the human spirit was one of the noblest causes to which men could devote themselves. They even thought that human history might be interpreted as such a progressive emancipation. They could scarcely have been expected to foresee that in the name of such 'emancipation' individuals would demand to be released from a well-ordered and stable family life, that women would demand to be emancipated even from the natural burdens of motherhood, and that some men would demand to be freed from the restraints of any moral code whatsoever. While, therefore, historically the individualistic movement has conferred some of the greatest benefits upon Western civilization, and in many countries has still much beneficent work to do, yet it must be judged at the same time as perhaps the greatest menace of the present to social order, and so to civilization" (Ellwood: *The Social Problem*, p. 77).

2) The second factor contributing to modern individualism was the discovery of the steam engine and the *introduction* of the *machine*. Thereby excessive power was placed into the hands of individuals who were wealthy enough to be the owners of machines. Power is always temptation to exploitation, in industry as in politics. Thru the introduction of the machine the individual was separated from the family, the former unit of production, and placed into a factory. The individual became the economic unit of production. Both the employer and the employee thus became more conscious of their individuality and of the separateness of their life thru the introduction of the machine. A further result of the industrial revolution was the enormous increase of wealth, the establishment of standards of luxury and the emancipation of a large class of humanity from the fear of want. "The enormous wealth of modern times has stimulated luxury and self-indulgence almost beyond belief in some classes of

society." The standards of selfishness there established have been imitated in greater or less degree by all classes of the population. Finally the industrial revolution thru the establishment of classes in the population has worked for the creation of class consciousness, an individualistic principle, tho it be the consciousness of a group. Class consciousness, let us point out here, is to be found to a much higher degree among the so-called upper classes, than among those most often accused of it—the laborers.

3) Another set of factors which have been especially potent in American life and are important causes for the larger individualism of American civilization, are to be sought in the fact of *immigration*. Thru immigration the most various groups with widely varying standards of conduct and morals have been brought into the closest juxtaposition. Whenever varying civilizations mingle we can look for a mutual breakdown of the morals which guided the conduct of each group so long as it was separate. Like-mindedness, which is especially important for social peace and solidarity is especially absent in American society as a whole. It is possible and it is to be hoped that this intermingling of the most various civilizations and the conflict of divergent social ideals and customs will finally result in a higher type of society, combining what is best in each of the component groups. For the present it has resulted in a breakdown of the morals of each group and a consequent dependence on the individual upon himself for his standards of conduct.

We are facing therefore a situation which is not to be ascribed to human selfishness and therewith dropped. *The conditions of our times are such that human selfishness is given an especial opportunity to assert itself. The fault does not lie only within human nature—it lies within the social structure to which this human nature must make its adaptation.*

Such a breaking up of morals, such excessive individualism, may, it is true, eventually lead to the adoption of a higher morality than that found in all of the books of the law. But let us remember the parable of Christ: of the one demon driven out, the swept and garnished house and the entrance of the seven demons. There is only one thing that ought to supplant the righteousness of the Scribes and Pharisees, and that is the higher righteousness of the kingdom of God.

What then is the specific social *mission* and the goal of the *churches* of Jesus Christ, representatives of the Kingdom Gospel, under these circumstances? In the first place, certainly, the conditions present to the church a great opportunity and an immediate demand to preach that higher righteousness, the righteousness of love, of service and of fellowship. Now if ever we ought to and we will proclaim: Ye have heard that it has been said of old time: An eye for an eye and a tooth for a tooth, but I say unto you that ye resist not evil. Ye have heard that it was said by them of old time: Thou shalt not kill; but I say to unto you: that whosoever is angry with his brother without cause shall be in danger of judgment. The message of our Lord in the *Sermon on the Mount* must be the message of the Christian church *now* as *never before.*

The church is in great temptation to refer the matter of law to the state. It urges upon the state the establishment of a uniform divorce law, abolition of child labor, protection of women in industry. Certainly the state should do these things. But the church has a larger task than that of urging state action. It has before it the task of creating a new set of morals directly in the hearts of the people. No law is of any value upon the statue books. No law can ever be enforced until the conscience of the people is behind it. The suggestion has been made that these should be placed in parallel columns the numerous requests of the Protestant church to the state to pass divorce and marriage laws on the one hand, and the sermons and S[unday] S[chool] instruction upon the same subject on the other hand. It would be found, one surmises, that as yet the churches have scarcely begun to use the power which they possess for preventing the evils that they urge the state to rectify by legislation. This then seems to be the immediate task of the church and of the church only: to educate, to admonish, to preach with all the power at its disposal that those only shall find their life who shall lose it, that the higher righteousness has concrete application to the problems of the day, that Christianity demands not less but more righteousness in every specific instance: the proclamation of the social gospel directly applied to the actual problems, not as new legalism might be preached, but as the new righteousness may be made specific, tho it be the righteousness of the spirit. The church deals still with individuals but must deal with them as *social* beings, with a social goal in life.

Laws are frequently effective tutors unto Christ. The prohibition law may become such, if the social consciousness, supported and educated by the church, insists on its enforcement as the fulfillment of a righteousness. The church may well support and should support laws against child labor, laws regulating marriage, for these laws may educate to the acceptance of the righteousness which they aim at, and they may prevent the exploitation of the weak by the strong. The Evangelical Synod is hardly in danger of erring upon the side of legalism. Perhaps some recognition of the educative power of laws and consequent support of them would be an effective contribution to the social life of our nation.

Finally the social gospel leads to the realization of the righteousness which it proclaims within a social group. The lack of homogeneity in American life is, as we have seen, a powerful factor in the promotion of excessive individualism. The creation of such a homogeneity is part of the task of restoring to our social life the value of a social ideal held in common. As Jesus *made* the twelve, according to Mark's expression—not only making them as individuals but making the group, the first Christian community—so the interest of the church lies in the development of the communities in which the higher righteousness shall come to group expression. Not only the church constitutes such a group. Certainly the neighborhood in which the smaller group of the church exists may expect the social ministry of the church and its assistance in the formation of an ever more Christian community, with one mind and one ideal. As Christ was interested in the lesser righteousness of the Pharisees, as well as in the righteousness of the Kingdom thus also the Christian churches may bring to their communities an active interest, and an earnest assistance in every enterprise that promises to create a common bond of fellowship and a common respect for the laws that govern, tho they be less than ideal.

IV

Thus far we have dealt with one aspect of the modern situation and applied one of the principles of the social gospel. There is another aspect, quite opposite to the first—and another principle, the other pole of the social gospel, to be considered. The principle is that of the *value* of a *human personality;* the violation of that principle in modern life, the suppression of personality and of personal values is the evil which it uncovers.

If on the one hand the gospel is certain upon the point that the end of individual life does not lie within itself, it is equally outspoken upon another point; that neither human institutions nor the kingdom of God, nor any social entity, may have their ends in themselves. The relationship of the King to the citizen of the Kingdom is that of service. The relationship of every human institution to its members or to individuals in general must be that of service if the institution or group is to realize itself. "The Sabbath was made for man and not man for the Sabbath." Here once more Jesus in His doctrine of the

Kingdom and in His embodiment in His life of the truth He also taught by word, reveals and discovers a universally valid principle, whose general truth we need not stop to illustrate from the history of societies.

The violation of that principle is found in modern times in the suppression of individuality—in the tendency of institutions and social entities to find their ends in themselves rather than in the individuals whom originally they were meant to serve.

The era of suppression, and of the dominance of social institutions over individual life, is contemporary with the era of excessive individualism. In part it is simply the suppression of individual by individual. Where excessive individuality prevails there also suppression of other individuality is the necessary result. For individualism with its corollary, competition, results in the *control of the weak by the strong* and the ethics of the jungle. Again excessive individualism has resulted in the denial of personal values thru its enthronement of the material values. Individualism has issued in a mania for the acquisition of wealth and the retirement of ethical human values in favor of economic values. The end of individual life, when it is no longer the welfare of society, is necessarily found by many in the acquisition of possessions and in the satisfaction of creature comforts. Thus by its fostering of materialism and of materialistic standards of morality, individualism has effectively suppressed true personality, which must find its expression in service and social ethics. In the third place individual interests have tended to become vested in certain institutions, —in the institution of private property for instance, or in the institutions of industrial life—and these have become suppressors and oppressors. As the Jew enthroned the Sabbath above man so we have witnessed the enthronement in Western civilization of the principle of property above the human beings whom property was meant to serve; the exaltation of industrial production above the interests of men for whom that production was to be made; the lifting of the government above the citizens, for the protection of whom the government was founded. Finally the era of individualism has made men conscious to an unusual degree of the separateness of their personalities, of the nature of their rights, of the inviolability of human individuality and has thus made them extremely sensitive to the violation of the sanctity of their personality. Thereby it has become possible for men to assert themselves much more violently, and to react much more quickly against any infringement of their personal values.

Let us make clear to ourselves the actuality of the suppression of individuality in modern life. Such a suppression is to be found in the first place in the growth of cities, the establishment of ever more rapid means of communication, the general tendency of the day to bring men into ever closer juxtaposition to each other. The public opinion of the moment, rather than group morals, is brought to bear upon the individual with extreme rapidity. Our minds and our instincts are adapted to a less completely socialized life and a reaction to a situation which is more or less unnatural is bound to make itself felt again and again.

But it is in the *institution* of *modern industry* that this suppression of individuality is to be especially noted, for here it is of prime significance. Under the conditions of modern industry economic values have come to take the place of human values as in medieval days ecclesiastical values tended to supersede personal worth. Industrial and economic conditions encourage the worker to find the value of his life in the pay envelope. They have developed a standard of success measured entirely by the dollars accumulated. Furthermore the modern industrial situation has become inimical to the realization of personal and ethical values, to the building of character as well as to the expression of freedom, thru the fact that they have *deprived* the *worker of economic freedom*. First there came the loss of land freedom. This is well illustrated in Germany. In 1816 came the edict which freed the German peasantry from feudal laws and deprived them at the same time of 1,650,000 hectares of land. Between 1816 and 1865 another 1,760,000 hectares passed out of their possession into the hands of the capitalists because of the inability of the peasant to compete with the "Grossgrundbesitzern." In America very much of the same thing is taking place. There are indications aplenty of the fact that the small farmer is losing possession to the capitalist landlord, and is becoming a renter and economically a dependent man. In the second place there is the loss of industrial freedom, the freedom to work. When, where and how the worker is to work is dictated now by the machine. The impersonal board sitting in a financial center such as Wall street [*sic*], determines what factories of a trust are to resume, or where they are to cease production, and controls of the laborer's freedom to work. Economic freedom is at least as important as political freedom. The denial of economic freedom is a much more serious infringement of the rights of personality than the denial of political freedom. Man's life as a citizen of his state touches his personal life much less acutely than does his existence as a worker, as an earner of bread for himself and his family. Again there is the suppression of personality thru the machine and the subdivision of labor. The power of man to create a thing, to express his self in the work of his hand—as the workman has no less a chance of doing in his making of shoes and hewing of wood, than the artist has in his sculpture or the preacher in his sermon—is a thing of infinite value to the individual and often to the world. "To respect it in one's self and others makes up nine tenths of the good life," says Bertrand Russell, and we can well agree. "In most human beings it is rather frail and easily destroyed or disturbed; parents and teachers are often hostile to it; and our economic system crushes out its last remnants in young men and women. The result is that human beings cease to be individual, or to retain the pride that is their native birthright: they become machine-made, tame, convenient for the bureaucrat and the drill sergeant, capable of being tabulated in statistics without anything being omitted. This is the fundamental evil resulting from lack of liberty; and it is the evil which is being continually intensified as population grows more dense and the machinery of organization becomes more efficient." And this loss of liberty due to the introduction of the machine is a factor in the life of the world today which none who would serve humanity can fail to recognize. "Today the machine in its character fixes the man's speed of work . . . limits his thoughts in the day, and in the end molds for his life the very processes of mind, and thus determines how he shall worship, vote and find his pleasure" is the statement of a most acute observer.

This control of the life of men by economic factors and standards and this exaltation of machine over the man have become embodied in institutions which are given a higher veneration by the people of today than they give to individual personality. Thus the *institution* of *private property* which certainly was made for man, has become the institution in which has become vested the right of capital to take and to keep the peasant's or small farmer's land. It protects not so much the rights of the free-holder as it protects the right of the large interests which have taken from him thru their economic power his economic independence. Industry has become a vast institution much more important than human life. Whether or not its workers suffer is not a question. It must produce at highest speed, or cease to produce and thus cause misery either thru over-work or thru unemployment according to the interests of the industry, not of the worker nor of the consumer.

Is there any doubt that such an organization of society is absolutely contrary to the principle of Jesus that man was not made for the Sabbath but the Sabbath was made for man? Are we not affirming by the very patent situations of our present day that man was made for the production and production was not made for man? The condition is intolerable and loaded with dynamite. The church is profoundly interested. Not so much because it would avert the final reaction of human personality against government of itself by the impersonal factors of the machine, of capital and of industrial organizations, but because this is a crying evil. The hire of the laborers crieth out to heaven. Not because of the inadequacy of wages, but because of the inadequacy of the wage in personality, in self-realization, in opportunity for self-expression, the inadequacy of the wage in liberty.

Again in the case of private property, the principle of Christianity that all things are God's and that men may only hold in trust must be directly asserted against the application of the laws of private property in our day. Is it not the church's duty at this time to assert in the clearest and most unequivocal terms that not only the ownership and administration of private property are to be regarded in the light of a trust but that the acquisition of property must be made to conform to the principle of service, if there is to be anything that is Christian in our present economic order.

It seems from the viewpoint of Christianity that the organization of industry is an institution of service rather than as an institution for selfish aggrandizement involves recognition primarily of the human factor, the enthronement of personal values above economic values. The demand for the recognition of the human factor in industry has taken the following forms as well as some others in the present day:

1) the *right of labor* to *organize*. The union has been the one means whereby the worker has been able to assert any kind of economic independence from capital.

2) The enthronement of personal values above economic values is sponsored in the second place by the movement which asks for the *recognition of the worker* to *share* in the *control of industry*. No less than this must finally come to pass, if there is to be economic and hence also political and religious liberty on the part of the worker. As at present constituted only the sacred rights of the owner of the capitalist are vested in industry. The sacred rights of the worker who is so much more dependent upon that industry need to be recognized in an ever larger degree.

3) In the third place the dominance of the machine over human life must be counteracted if human values are not to be destroyed by production values. The machine cannot be done away with. Sub-division of labor will hardly decrease—we may rather look for an increase. But this fact only makes so much more necessary the recognition of the human factor outside of industry. If man is to be more and more mechanized in industry, he must be given opportunity to an ever greater extent to find the realization of himself outside of industry. The church of Christ cannot but have sympathy with the demands for reduction of the labor day and for the steady increase of wages to the point where the service of the worker rather than the service of material things, of capital, is fully recognized. It is interested in this demand because of its interest in the family as well as because of its interest in the establishment of the rule of service in business.

The recognition of the human factor as the most important factor in the economic life of the world will involve a host of changes in a system which is founded upon the exact opposite of that principle, namely upon the principle of private profit and of the superiority of the economic factor. We may expect the full recognition of industry of its responsibility to provide for its workers at all times the consequent abrogation of unemployment; we may expect special provision for the protection of motherhood and womanhood in industry and other steps of a similar nature. The social gospel as applied to industry will be revolutionary finally in its outworkings.

How now may the church apply this social gospel to so un-Christian a situation? It is enough to say that if the gospel of Christ were not followed there would be no conflict between capital and labor. Cannot we say with equal right that if the gospel were followed there would be no sin? Let the application of the social gospel be in the first place *sympathetic*. The employer and the employe [sic] of today are the results largely of their environment. Individual capitalists are finally as little to blame as individual employes [sic] for excesses. The sin is ingrained in the whole situation, in the institutions and in the social standards. To convert individual capitalists or individual laborers to the gospel of the losing of life will not solve the situation. The church of Christ is interested in the establishment of a valid social standard and the conscious recognition of the supremacy of personality, not by individuals only but by the whole social group. To recognize the social character of the sin is to become sympathetic to those who have been caught in its toils, tho it will not mean condonement of sin.

In the next place the preaching of the church might be *definite*. There are specific problems to be met. The reorganization of industry will not take place except by evolution. Cannot the church seek to be definite in its application of the social gospel to the definite problems?

And finally may the preaching of the social gospel be *Christian*. May it preach the law of sacrifice to the employer and employe [sic], but sacrifice not for the sake of present peace. Sacrifice for the sake of the attainment of the kingdom of God. The burden of the sacrifice falls upon capital, which has the power under the present system. It is not sacrifice for the sake of others so much as sacrifice of those things possessed under unchristian conditions which needs to be thought of. And not sacrifice of money and wealth so much as the sacrifice of power and spurious personal rights.

But the most effective method at the disposal of the church to hasten the growth of a Christian social order is the method of *self-sacrifice* for its ideals and convictions. "The church needs not so much to preach Christ as to be Christ."

The Relativities of Religion

Although it was published in The Christian Century, *this article generally gets overlooked in standard H. Richard Niebuhr bibliographies. Its emphasis on "relativity" documents the influence of Ernst Troeltsch upon his thinking. It also stands out as an eloquent defense of this feature of liberal Protestant scholarship, which Niebuhr came to regard as one of its enduring contributions. For Niebuhr, the perspective of any contemporary Christian believer influenced the interpretation of any belief as much as the time and circumstance of the period in which it originated. Was he in fact making the relativity of everything into an absolute, as some of his later critics would contend? As Niebuhr put in his closing line "We may be confident that what we have seen darkly is really there, and that new points of view will not destroy but fulfil the promise of our best insights and highest aspirations."*

Source: *The Christian Century* 45 (November 29, 1928): 1456–58.

Every age is in a real sense the creator of its own past. Of course the past produced it. The faiths and facts, the institutions and laws, the economic life of yesterday have determined what today shall be. But the determination is not complete; the new day is also self-creative. As the individual selects for cultivation certain elements from his biological heritage—brain rather than brawn or brawn rather than brain, ear rather than eye or eye rather than ear—so also society chooses out of the massive heritage of the past's ideals and habits some to which it will particularly attend and so incorporate them into its own character. Such a selection, to be sure, is made half-unconsciously, under the pressure of needs and suggestions; but the choice is conscious for the other half, involving the judgment that this or that element is best and deserves attention.

Creative epochs in history are therefore always repristinations, yet the restoration is always creative. The Hebrew prophet inaugurates a new day by setting forth again the old ideals of nomadic life. The Augustan age is celebrated as a palingenesis. Zwingli and Luther restore primitive Christianity. The French revolution is nurtured on the ideals of an uncivilized age. We clamor for the restoration of the old freedom or of the medieval guild or of a vanished aristocracy. Every revolution is a return of the cycle, every reformation a retrieval. But the cycle does not repeat itself completely and not all of the past is retrieved. There is a creative element in selection; the analysis of the past and present is but the first step in a new synthesis. Prophetic ideals are not merely a rehabilitation of Mosaic virtues and Protestantism is not primitive Christianity. Reformations and revolutions create the past out of which they create themselves; and they do so by making a judicious selection from their heritage.

The Present Looks at the Past

Choice, however, is not the only means whereby the present remakes history. It sees the beliefs and ideals and customs of the past through the medium of its own atmosphere. It occupies a peculiar point of view; it inhabits a point-instant which has never before and will never come again. Hence, when it regards the things of yesteryear it notes high-lights which other ages did not see because they were not there; it finds proportions which could be revealed to no other standpoint. So the forms which old ideals assume may be in some respects quite strange to the days when those ideals were born.

Selection and creation of this sort is not only inevitable but also justifiable, or perhaps it is justifiable because it is inevitable. Only by such recreation of the past can the needs of the new day be met and only so can old ideals be made effective. The interpretation must of course be kept subject to the criticism of the past ideal itself.

The new point of view may not read into the old faith whatever is desired. But the antiquarian has no right to bind interpretation to the point of view of the ancient time. He has his role to play as the watchful guardian of essential principles in the old doctrine. Let him be content with that and not seek to dictate to the new time what must be its point of view. If he does so he deprives the past of all opportunity to exert effective force upon the present, and mummifies it in the grave-clothes of its contemporary point of view. Upon the other hand, the present interpreter has reason to beware of making the same error, that is, of regarding his relative discovery as a universal truth *quod semper, quod ubique, quod ab omnibus creditum est.*

Creative Visions of Jesus

Applied to the present situation in religion the right to interpret means that it is as justifiable as it is inevitable that our views of Jesus and of his gospel should be creative visions and not merely attempts to apprehend the point of view of the first century. They are inevitably and justifiably selective. Even the most earnest believer in the Bible "from cover to cover" indulges his preferences. He chooses from the book those statements and those facts which persuade him to believe it from Genesis to Revelation; he attends to these until they live in him.

So it is with the gospel and the kingdom of God. In that conception of Jesus many Christians of today have found that which, in Coleridge's phrase, finds them. They may turn the pages of the epistle to the Romans and read with great appreciation that the just shall live by faith, but the phrase does not speak to them as it spoke to Luther. Paul's despair and exaltation arouse answering echoes in the heart but not the mighty reverberations the people of the reformation knew. But when they turn to Matthew, Luke and Mark the voice that speaks to them there receives more than approval. It is the voice of longed-for leadership, which gives expressions to their vague desires, hopes and purposes; which inspires with a new dynamic because it gathers scattered energies into a unity of will.

The synoptic gospels are as much the keys to Christianity's meaning today as Romans and Galatians were for another era. Selection is present in both instances, and who can say that the one selection is better than the other? Even the point of view of eternity will be a different point of view than either that of the sixteenth or that of the twentieth century. It must provide for both, yet only by transcending each. The selection of the gospel of the kingdom is no random choice, which men may take or leave. It is rooted in the needs of the day. What men will find in Christ is determined not only by what he is but by what they require. Such is the richness of his life and death and teaching that he can be all things to all men, granting of the fullness of his grace that which is sufficient for each man's need.

Today's Salvation

Perhaps the main reason why interpretations of Christ and God differ so much is because the sense of sin is so various in various times and groups. The first question one must ask about every theologian before one can understand him is this, What does he mean by sin? Only then is it possible to understand his interpretation of Christ and God and salvation. For Augustine sin is concupiscence, for Luther it is guilt, for Calvin it is secularism, for Wesley frivolity and vice. But the conception of sin in the modern world, or, to speak more modestly, in American Christianity, is rather that of ethical failure. We know that we have missed and are continuing to miss the mark. And this missing of the mark is not just an individual matter; it is social failure. Or again, sin appears today more under the form of selfishness than of sensuality. To be sure, men continue to be aware of guilt and concupiscence, of secularism and vice, but the deep division of their souls appears less as the conflict of the flesh with the spirit and more as the warfare of their selfish with their social purposes.

The salvation that is required is salvation from the body of that death, a forgiveness that will bring the communion of man with man under the fatherhood of God. This is the need that determines the selection of the gospel of the kingdom. It is not quite the same as the need of first century Rome, not quite the same as the need of sixteenth century Germany, not quite the same as the need of eighteenth century England. It is, indeed, an aspect of the universal human need; it also is the need of sinful, mortal men. But these sinful, mortal men contend with new types of sin and with new forms of morality. And they sin more in the lump; they die more in the gross. They find in the gospel of the kingdom a gospel which speaks to their needs; have they not as much right to their selection as Augustine and Calvin and Luther and Wesley had to theirs?

Yet the gospel of the kingdom is not only a selection. It is also an interpretation. The ideal we discover in the words of Jesus is not the same ideal which James and John and Peter heard, even though they may have harkened to the same words. The city of God we see is not quite the same as these saw. The high lights [*sic*] are different. The point of view has changed the proportions. Every gospel we read in the New Testament we partially read into it. When we read of the infinite value of the human soul we think in terms of personality; the blow upon the right cheek and the left contains for us subtle connotations, memories of chivalric codes, and a score of social implications. The kingdom as we see it cannot be a photographic copy of the kingdom as Jesus portrayed it; at best it may be an impressionistic attempt at reproduction.

Relativity of Interpretation

Yet we have the right so to interpret if we remain close to fundamental principles and do not seek to exalt our point of view into a universal standpoint which all men everywhere and always must occupy with us. The New Testament scholar cannot tell us what the kingdom of God is like, merely by interpreting Jesus from a contemporary and Galilean point of view. Such an interpretation of the kingdom is just as limited, just as impermanent as ours. He has no right to bind men again in the fetters of a letter which killeth; but his may be the greater task of transmitting a spirit which will make alive the material conceptions which our needs and problems will supply. The modern Christian has no license, of course, to fashion his Utopia as he pleases and then to force on Jesus that construction. The interpretation still remains an interpretation of an ideal. It is creative in being recreative. It is a new synthesis which cannot be made save after analysis of other points of view.

If it is necessary and desirable then upon one hand to accept boldly our contemporary point of view and to make our interpretation with all confidence, it is equally necessary to beware of the exaltation of that twentieth century, and perhaps American, synthesis into a universal and obligatory dogma. How proudly we sit in judgment on puritan and Lutheran today, blaming them for not seeing in the gospel what we see. How cavalierly do some writers on the social gospel treat Saint Paul—because he did not live in the machine age, in democratic society. How easily we discern the relativities of the past but regard our own relative visions as final insights, which all men might have had.

To discern the relativity of our interpretation is not to rob our gospel of its power. The relative may have an absolute claim on us without having an absolute claim on all men everywhere. We not only may, but must take it to our heart as our categorical imperative, our highest and our best. And if we have been as true as we could be to the spirit of the author of our ideal and to the need of our own souls, we have a right to the faith that our point of view has not betrayed its object completely. We may be confident that what we have seen darkly is really there and that new points of view will not destroy but will fulfill the promise of our best insights and highest aspirations.

Fundamentalism

Niebuhr viewed the fundamentalism that had gained notoriety with the Scopes Trial of 1925 as an anachronism driven by a resistance to accommodating the Christian faith to modern science and the new realities of an industrialized and urban way of life. Hence, he erroneously believed the movement might be doomed to extinction. At the time he wrote this article, fundamentalists had chosen to remove themselves from the public eye, and as later historians have consistently shown, were in fact quietly growing and actually beginning to expand their network of churches, schools, and Bible institutes. Later in his career, Niebuhr also failed to draw any distinction between fundamentalism and the post-fundamentalist evangelicalism that burst on to the American scene with the advent of the popular evangelist Billy Graham. In any event, his conviction at this point was that fundamentalism was not a viable option for churches intent upon engaging the contemporary culture and addressing its social problems.

Source: *The Encyclopedia of the Social Sciences*, vol. 4, ed. E. R. A. Seligman (New York: Macmillan, 1931), 526–27.

FUNDAMENTALISM is the name of an aggressive conservative movement in the Protestant churches of the United States which flourished during the decade after the World War. It manifested itself chiefly in the Baptist, Disciple and Presbyterian churches but received considerable support from other ecclesiastical groups. It was characterized not only by its conservatism with regard to traditional popular Christian beliefs but also by its aggressive efforts to impose its creed upon the churches and upon the public and denominational schools of the country. Its conservative supernaturalism was expressed in the "five points of fundamentalism," which included the doctrines of the inerrancy of the Bible, the Virgin Birth of Jesus, the supernatural atonement, the physical resurrection of Jesus and the authenticity of the Gospel miracles. The first of these points was interpreted by fundamentalism to apply particularly to the Biblical account of the creation of man in opposition to the theory of evolution, which became the central question of the fundamentalist controversy.

The movement was directed against liberal elements within the churches and against the purely scientific or secular interests in American civilization. In the former sphere it attempted to exclude from the churches and particularly from the control of their educational institutions those who did not share the conservative faith. The effort was not generally successful, but in a number of denominational colleges the teachers were required to subscribe to the fundamentalist creed on pain of dismissal and in other instances new colleges in which the creed was made obligatory were founded. The effort to control the public schools in the interest of the conservative dogma was expressed in the attempt to induce state legislatures to pass laws prohibiting the teaching of evolution. This political phase of the fundamentalist movement was strongest in the southern and border states and made itself felt in the middle west but was weak or absent in the New England, middle Atlantic and far western states with the exception of California, where considerable controversy developed around the textbook question. The legislature of Tennessee enacted a bill in 1925, reaffirmed in 1931, which made it unlawful to teach in any tax supported school any theory "that denies the story of the Divine creation of man as taught in the Bible and to teach instead that man has descended from a lower order of animals." The constitutionality of the law was tested and upheld in the Scopes trial at Dayton, Tennessee, in 1925 and in a later decision in 1927 by the Supreme Court of the state. This trial formed the dramatic center of the fundamentalist controversy. A similar law was passed in Mississippi in 1926, while textbooks teaching evolution were barred in Oklahoma from 1923 to 1926. The Florida legislature adopted resolutions disapproving the teaching of evolution but failed to enact a law. In many other states, including Louisiana, South Carolina, Texas, Arkansas, Kentucky, Georgia, Alabama, Missouri, and West Virginia, attempts to pass restrictive legislation of this sort were unsuccessful, but it became evident through them that the strength of the fundamentalist movement was considerable. Its effect upon the schools was measurable not only in terms of laws passed but also in terms of social pressure, particularly in many isolated communities in these states. In some instances local or state boards of education were prevailed upon to exclude textbooks unsatisfactory to the conservative sentiment or to exert corresponding pressure upon the teachers.

While fundamentalism drew amount of sympathetic support from the conservative religious groups, such as Roman Catholic and Lutheran churches, and from conservative parties in other churches it often failed to enlist them in its aggressive efforts to influence legislation; and it remained distinguished from them by the manner in which it threw the weight of its interest upon the popular dogmas of Biblical inerrancy and miraculous supernaturalism while conservatism remained primarily interested in the doctrines of human sinfulness and divine atonement. Fundamentalism shared with conservatism distrust of human nature and reacted with it against the romantic and liberal dogma of human goodness and self-sufficiency, but in accordance with its non-theological and popular character it placed its emphasis on myth rather than doctrine.

In the social sources from which it drew its strength fundamentalism was closely related to the conflict between rural and urban cultures in America. Its popular leader was the agrarian W. J. Bryan; its rise coincided with the depression of agricultural values after the World War; it achieved little strength in the urban and industrial sections of the country but was active in many of the rural states. The opposing religious movement, modernism, was identified on the other hand with bourgeois culture, having its strength in the cities and in the churches supported by the urban middle classes. Furthermore, fundamentalism in its aggressive forms was most prevalent in those isolated communities in which the traditions of pioneer society had been most effectively preserved and which were least subject to the influence of modern science and industrial civilization. Its rejection of a dynamic conception of creative processes was due partly to the inadequate development of educational institutions for both clergy and laity in isolated and poor communities or religious groups, partly to the static character of the culture prevailing in these societies. The contrary movement was associated with an industrialized civilization in which the acceptance of change as a primary law of life was encouraged by the dynamic and changing character of the social process, especially in the economic sphere, as well as by the more effective contact with modern science through its schools. Again, the fundamentalist attitude reflected the distrust of reason and the emphasis upon emotion, the doubt of human ability to solve ultimate problems and the reliance on divine agency which are characteristic not only of much traditional Christianity but also of those groups which have received the least profit from a rationalized culture and of pioneer or isolated rural societies which remain most conscious of dependence for their livelihood on those processes of nature which are least subject to human control. The rationalism and self-reliance of the opposing groups, on the other hand, had been fostered not only by the science and education but also by industrialized culture with its rational and artificial methods of production and its immediate urban environment, all largely subject to human control.

The fundamentalist movement was related in some localities to the Ku Klux Klan and to similar types of intense racialism or sectionalism. With them it shared antagonism to changes in the mores which the war and its consequences, the rise to power of the previously submerged immigrant or racial groups and other social processes, brought forth. The political effectiveness of fundamentalism was due in part to this association and to the support which it gave to political leaders, who found in it a powerful symbolism representative of the antagonism of political and economic minorities against the eastern or northern urban industrial majority.

3

Worldly Impediments to Churchly Integrity

During his second tenure on the faculty at Eden Seminary and as the school's academic dean, H. Richard Niebuhr drafted his first book. When it was published in 1929, *The Social Sources of Denominationalism*[1] broke new ground in the sociology of religion. Niebuhr's work on the subject was an outgrowth of his doctoral study of Ernst Troeltsch at Yale. As the great Berlin professor had done in his work *The Social Teaching of the Christian Churches*, Niebuhr attributed denominational divisions on the American church scene not simply to differences in doctrine and practice but to the social, political, and economic factors that could affect the behavior of any religious group. In the context of European ecclesiastical establishments, Troeltsch had drawn a distinction between "churches" and "sects." The American setting was one of religious disestablishment, yet Niebuhr was able to use both categories effectively for the purpose of explaining the proliferation

---

1. Hereafter referred to as *Social Sources*.

of denominations. At the same time, *Social Sources* was a moral indictment of the church in America. Niebuhr provocatively entitled his opening chapter "The Ethical Failure of the Divided Church," and on the pages that followed he called denominationalism an "unacknowledged hypocrisy" and a "compromise" of the church with the world. "It represents the accommodation of Christianity to the caste system of human society,"[2] he wrote. "It draws the color line in the church of God; it fosters the misunderstandings, the self-exaltations, the hatred of jingoistic nationalism by continuing in the body of Christ the spurious differences of provincial loyalties; it seats the rich and poor apart at the table of the Lord, where the fortunate may enjoy the bounty they have provided while others feed upon the crusts their poverty affords." He recognized that any church, as it sought to carry out its work *in* the world, could easily become *of* the world.

Niebuhr's concern was apparently developed by the emergence of a more prosperous and consumer-oriented middle class during the 1920s. While he was urging his own Evangelical Synod to enter the mainstream of American culture more fully than it had prior to World War I, he also issued words of caution about such engagement. Some of these appeared in the *Evangelical Herald*, a magazine widely circulated among the membership. "As we leave the sectarianism of race behind," he wrote in 1924, "we need to be on our guard lest a worse sectarianism, that of economic class, overtake us."[3] Niebuhr feared that as the farmers and small businessmen who were well-represented in the Synod's congregations prospered, his denomination might become "just another middle class church."

---

2. H. Richard Niebuhr, *The Social Sources of Denominationalism* (New York: Henry Holt, 1929), 6.
3. H. Richard Niebuhr, "The Kingdom, Our Country and Our Church," *The Evangelical Herald* 24 (November 19, 1924): 760.

In *Social Sources*, Niebuhr heaped an abundance of criticism on the "churches of the middle class." His longstanding interest in sociology had made him well aware of Max Weber's thesis on Calvinism and the rise of modern capitalism. Like Weber, he believed that Calvinism, through its emphasis on a morality that enhanced the growth of trade and industry, had helped to make a vibrant middle class possible. But in his estimation, the middle class also modified John Calvin's teaching in order to meet its own desires. Bourgeois self-conscious individualism and an "activist attitude toward life" had conspired to make sin a matter of wrong deeds rather than a perverted state of the soul, to reduce righteousness to a personal code of conduct, and to view faith as more of a task to be accomplished than a freely given promise. As a result, the rising middle class came to view poverty as a moral failure and riches as a reward for a virtuous life, and its gospel of self-help became the key for unlocking the mystery of divine providence. This "God-helps-those-who-help-themselves" accommodation to the middle-class world, as Niebuhr saw it, not only helped to create separate denominations; it served to keep congregations from recognizing society as a legitimate sphere of ministry and to inhibit the ability of their pastors to arouse much sympathy for the causes of the working classes.[4]

There is a similar ambivalence in Niebuhr's writings during this period toward some of the theological directions in which liberal Christianity in America appeared to be heading. The terms *liberalism* and *modernism* are often used as synonyms. Indeed, both terms refer to those members of the Protestant family who believed that orthodox Christianity was too deeply embedded in a civilization that the world was outgrowing, and who for this reason were offering a more contemporary version of the faith that had been bequeathed

---

4. Niebuhr, *Social Sources*, 105.

to them. On the other hand, *scientific modernists*, became convinced that updating the old faith was a lost cause. Instead, they wanted to start over with the presuppositions of the natural and social sciences, subjecting traditional Christianity to a complete overhaul. According to Shailer Matthews, in his 1925 book *The Faith of Modernism*, all doctrinal statements about Jesus Christ as the revelation of God needed to be tested and applied in the same way that chemists and historians did with the objects of their studies. While Niebuhr did not disagree with the modernist emphasis on a more vigorous application of the scientific method to religious phenomena, he tended to feel that the *new religion* they were concocting was resulting in a dismissal of too many essential features of the Christian faith. It all added up, in his estimation, to another instance of accommodation on the part of the church to the world.

For this reason, Niebuhr welcomed all signs of a fresh emphasis on the transcendent reality of God. During his graduate school years at Yale, D. C. Macintosh had shown him how a theologian could both investigate scientifically the experiences of a religious subject and still retain faith in the reality of God as its object. At the Elmhurst Service Conference that Niebuhr had called in 1927, and with the members of his Evangelical Synod as the greater audience in his mind, he spoke of "planetary provincialism" and "cosmic faith," a distinction that would also appear in his later writings. The former was "provincial" because it made humankind "the measure of all things" and tended to result in "a narrow selfish way of thinking and looking at things." The latter was "cosmic" because it pointed to things greater than self, and as such provided the only real hope of grappling with the problems of the day and realizing human "brotherhood."[5]

---

5. H. Richard Niebuhr, "Planetary Provincialism and Cosmic Faith," quoted in "The Elmhurst Service Conference," *The Evangelical Herald* 26 (April 28, 1927): 344–45.

Among the crisis theologians who had become disillusioned with the faith that liberal Christianity had placed in the course of Western civilization, Niebuhr was drawn to Karl Barth. Niebuhr's commitment to keeping the church at work "in the world" always kept him from completely embracing Barth's theology. But in Barth, with his emphasis on a God who is "wholly other" from human experience, he found a companion to assist him in keeping the church's tendency to become "of the world" in check.

Given Niebuhr's efforts during the 1920s to push his immigrant church into finding new ways to make a difference in its American context, it may seem odd that he would simultaneously use as a positive example a moment in the church's history that employed a strategy of *withdrawal* from the world. In his estimation, this occurred during the Middle Ages, when monks and friars, in order to call for reform of the church, retreated from the world around them. This monastic metaphor is one that Niebuhr would continue to employ in formulating his thoughts on church-world relationships. In his second book, *The Kingdom of God in America*, for instance, he saw a similar dynamic at work in the life of various New-World Protestant orders, such as "Methodist preachers, with their saddlebags and books of discipline," who chose to focus their attention directly on a sovereign and living God rather than secondhand sources.[6]

In *Social Sources*, moreover, when Niebuhr followed Troeltsch in evaluating "churches" and "sects," it was the world-fleeing sects that he seemed to view more favorably. To him, the accommodation of church groups to the cultures of empires and nation-states began with the conversion of the Roman Emperor Constantine in the fourth century. "From that time onward," he stressed, "the doctrine of Christianity came decreasingly to be the presentation of the teachings

---

6. H. Richard Niebuhr, *The Kingdom of God in America* (New York: Harper & Row, 1937), 75.

of Jesus and increasingly the religious formulation of prevailing ideals." By contrast, sects retained the early Christian ideal of a "kingdom of God opposed to the kingdom of the world." This difference, he argued, appeared in their institutional structures, their forms of worship, and their ethics. Sects could and did oppose wars between nation-states, whereas churches felt compelled to endorse the conflicts and accept their catastrophes. According to Niebuhr, sects formed the only real counterforce to churches, which were so culturally compromised that they were not prone to seek social reforms. More often than not, they remained bulwarks of "political conservatism."[7]

Was Richard Niebuhr at this time endorsing a separatist approach to culture on the part of the church, only to abandon it at a later time in *Christ and Culture*? The writings that follow will demonstrate that what he was seeking to assert already in the 1920s was the paradoxical nature of the church-world relationship. His hope was that the church, by stepping away from worldly entanglements, might regain its primary allegiance to its Lord, and thus begin to do a better job of becoming a church *for the world*.

---

7. Niebuhr, *Social Sources*, 106–34.

Back to Benedict?

The following article illustrates the intensity with which Niebuhr, already in 1925, was wrestling with some of the moral and the intellectual features of the paradox of church and world. In order to influence the world, a church such as his own Evangelical Synod could not remain an isolated, immigrant denomination, but needed to attune its version of the Christian experience to twentieth century America. But at the same time, Niebuhr knew that this culture, which was rapidly becoming more materialistic, could so condition the church's life that its members might cease to respond to the transcendent dimension of the gospel it was endeavoring to preach. The monastic movement in the church's history, as he saw it, promised a potential way out of this dilemma.

Source: *The Christian Century* 42 (July 2, 1925): 860–61.

Christianity has made a startling discovery in recent years. It has suddenly become aware of the steepness of the ideal of Jesus and of the intransigent character of his ethics. At the same time it has been painfully disillusioned of its dream of the automatic progress of the world toward the kingdom of God. The old antithesis, long conveniently forgotten, is again with us: the world, the flesh and the devil over against a transcendent God, the state against the church, mammon against Christ. With this disillusionment and the realization of the utter steepness of the demand of Jesus there has come upon Christians in general and upon many proponents of the social gospel in particular a new resurgence of the old pessimism so far as the present world is concerned.

Human sin appears once more as a bitter and murderous reality; the hope of the kingdom of God on earth is obscured by the clearer and more certain prophecy of the doom which must overtake this pitiful planet and the race which has "for a moment disturbed its solitude." The astronomer is our Isaiah, the psychologist our Amos, who tells us, "The day of the Lord will be darkness and not light." Perhaps it is the mood of the "tired radical" which is descending upon the evangelists of the social gospel; perhaps it is the pessimism and the optimism of Jesus turning his face toward Jerusalem. But they are not going to Jerusalem and to Calvary; most Christians will seek a less painful martyrdom and will vainly hope to conquer the citadel of evil by a less heroic attack. Now as once before the way out may be the way of the monk, for though monasticism be no final road to the city of God, yet it may lead us nearer to the hope of the ages.

Why Monasticism?

The old monasticism arose under conditions which have many a parallel in our own day. Pessimism regarding this present world and the evident necessity of compromising the Christian idea as soon as the church allied itself with the interests of the empire, the psychological necessity for replacing the "ardors and endurance" of a century of persecution by new and no less taxing demands upon the self, the desire for solitude and for simplicity in the overly complex civilization of later Rome, the need of leisure for the pursuit of knowledge in a time when circumstances were unfavorable to the pursuit of knowledge, the necessity for saving one's soul—not necessarily to eternal life, but for the purposes of self-respect—these were among the conditions, external and internal, which furnished fruitful soil for the growth of the old monasticism. No doubt the external conditions of the modern world are different from those which prevailed between 300 and 600 A.D. Yet they are curiously like the latter in their effect upon the psychical life. Pessimism, the conscience-stricken consciousness of compromise, the need for hardness and for martyrdom in a comparatively soft time, the desire for simplification—these are all with us now as then and as they have not been with us during the years between.

Meanwhile the Protestant protest against the cloister and the nunnery has lost its force. That protest was based not only on the corruption which had invaded monastic life but just as much on democratic repugnance for a spiritual aristocracy, and on the Protestant's diplomatic alliance with the nationalism whose hardiest foe was the Black International of the monasteries. Furthermore, the Protestant conception of Christian ethics as a this-worldly ethics and of the "several callings" of earthly life as the sphere of Christian vocation operated against monasticism with its other-worldliness and its exaltation of the special vocation of Christians. Now Protestantism has grown sick of its bargain with nationalism while the divorce between Christian ethics and the ethics of business and industry is so complete that the application of Christian principles in commercial life is one of those rarities which are worthy of the wide publicity and universal commendation reserved for the unique. It has been possible to keep up the myth of Christian vocation of our "earthly callings" only by eliminating the essentially Christian content of the concept of vocation, as, for instance, in the contemporary use of the idea of service.

Return to Monastic Life

It is worthwhile raising the question, therefore, whether Protestantism can and ought to continue to reject the monastic ideal out of hand. The situation of Christianity in the modern world seems to require and to be conducive to a modern revivification and adaptation of the Benedictine order of life—a new monasticism.

A complex era demands simplicity; a luxurious and self-indulgent age requires hardness and martyrdom; and a materialistic time is moving toward mysticism. Perhaps simplicity, hardness and mysticism seem attainable in other ways than by monasticism, but the golden mean is never practicable. Progress comes only by the over-emphasis of antithesis. The pendulum has swung about as far as it may toward this-worldliness; its return will not stop at any dead center; nor is it desirable that it should. The old monastic virtues need to be over-emphasized if they are to make a sufficient impression upon a time which has almost completely forgotten them.

The first of these virtues is the virtue of an undivided interest in the spiritual world, conceived as standing in opposition to the present world. As a reaction against the implicit materialistic monism of our time, which has made its presence evident in many a soup-kitchen caricature of the social gospel of the kingdom, a trend toward the monastic ideal is perhaps inevitable. All efforts to define the world monistically have only succeeded in reducing the spiritual to the level of the material; and all this-worldliness, despite its high claim of bringing the other world into the present sphere, has only succeeded in banishing the spiritual realm from human thought. Dualism is perhaps not so discredited a philosophical doctrine as the fashion in thought would have us believe; at all events a practical dualism is emerging out of the critical antithesis modern men experience between the ideal and the real.

New Interest in Mysticism

If the basis of spirituality is dualism, its realism of practice is mysticism and the modern world is assuming an interest in mysticism. The great mystics, and the mild mystics too, flourished there where it was possible to engage in "spiritual exercise," in "fasting and in prayer," and without "fasting and prayer" there is no mysticism—which is as much as to say that without intensive attention to the realm of the spirit no knowledge of the spiritual world is possible. Without something of the ascetic rule, extreme or gentle, we shall be hard put to it to discover in our modern life with its blatant advertising of material values any element of the brooding spirit.

What then of the sterner demands of the ascetic life, what of obedience, poverty, and chastity? May not these also have their place in the twentieth century? One wonders whether the historian of the future will agree with the orthodox Protestants who ascribe to the monastic ideal of chastity an evil influence on family life. It is true that the morality of the dark and middle ages was sorry enough in sexual matters, but many other considerations besides the influence of monasticism must be weighed in accounting for the low estate of the mores. May not, for that matter, the sorry state of American family life be ascribed with equal right to Protestant ethics?

It is not the celibacy of the continent but the celibacy of the unrestrained with their new morality, so called, which needs to be feared today and the monastic ethics in sex matters deserves a new emphasis. The voluntary and harshly self-restrained celibacy of the early Benedictine would be not only an effective protest against all looseness but an example worth the imitation of those whose celibacy is not founded on resolution but on social conditions. The celibacy of the dark ages was not, for that matter, entirely voluntary. In part it was due, it may be assumed, to the pessimism which asked whether it were right to bring children into an evil world, in part undoubtedly it had its cause in economic conditions. The practical abstention from marriage or from conception in our time may be similarly motivated but the ideal celibacy of monasticism is a better answer to the problem.

Involvement in Social Wrongs

In a time when a man cannot own a square foot of property or accept a salary without coming dangerously near to compromise with the whole evil and selfish system which issues in class and race exploitation and murder, the monastic ideal of poverty is not an unreasonable answer to the moral problem of property. Furthermore, it has become evident to men that there is no freedom available for them unless there be economic freedom. The economic freedom of the wealthy is attainable by few and it implies a bondage as fearful though not as feared as the slavery of the poor. There is another kind of economic freedom. He who had not where to lay his head was freest of all. The monk who was willing to be robbed of his sole property—the breviary—and of his life, because he knew the first by heart and would gain the bliss of heaven through the loss of the latter, is more envied than the economically "free" man who trembles at each fluctuation of the market and at each new headline about Russian communism.

The over-indulgence, not the under-satisfaction, of the instincts of acquisition makes man poor. To be sure, organized monasticism in the past compromised eventually with all sanctified and vested selfishness and would probably do so again in the future, but it remained free for centuries before it fell and, rejuvenated, might succeed better in the future. At all events its compromise could be no worse than that of Protestant ethics.

Finally, there is the ideal of obedience. It is scarcely necessary to point out the antagonism between the modern ideal of liberty, in political life, art, education and where not, and the ancient ideal of *obedientia*. Yet what educator and what parent, what scientist, what lover of beauty and of truth is not ready to declaim upon the necessity of restraint in our time? It is not obedience to superior force that is wanted but the hard and unyielding honesty of those who understand the command of their own categorical imperative in the pursuit of beauty, truth and goodness. The iron self-discipline of monasticism cannot be without defenders in these days of luxury and self-indulgence.

Monasticism, the ascetic ideal, is even now in the air. The youth movements with their demand for simplicity and the growing monasticism of the Anglican high church may be straws in the wind. Were Christianity to adopt the ideal seriously once more it would mean that it would abandon the policy of boring from within. Separating itself from the world it might recover its integrity for a while until confronted with another Calvary it either suffered crucifixion or made its uneasy compromise with pharisee and sadducee. There is nothing unsocial about this attitude. It is not for the love of self the monk retires from the world but for the love of his brethren who may be saved by no other means.

What Holds Churches Together?

"A man is not a Baptist because he believes in adult baptism by immersion," Niebuhr observes in this article, "but he believes in adult baptism by immersion because he is a Baptist." His study of Ernst Troeltsch had sharpened his awareness of the social behavior that tended to separate denominations from each other. By accommodating itself to the world in this way, Niebuhr believed, the church had become its own worst enemy. The problem was clearly one of churchly integrity; in his estimation the real issue involved choosing "between the gospel and the world." This same prophetic indictment of institutional Christianity in America is still being issued in the twenty-first century, especially by those who have chosen to remain outside the churches.

Source: *The Christian Century* 43 (March 18, 1926): 346–48.

Most programs for the unification of Christendom are afflicted with the intellectualist fallacy. Both in their diagnosis of the disease and in the recommendation of a remedy they fall into the error of thinking in creedal terms of denominations as well as of the faith as a whole. They regard the churches, sects and groups as associations gathered around formulations of belief and as possessing their distinctive characteristics in their confessions of faith. Until very recently the only study of denominational characteristics and differences carried on in theological schools was the study of "symbolics," which taught the student that a man was a Presbyterian because he subscribed to the Westminster confession, or a Lutheran because he believed the content of the Augsburg confession or a Roman Catholic because he assented to the decrees of the council of Trent. This method of defining the character of the denominations is as fallacious as would be the attempt to define the present character of the American political parties on the basis of their platforms or of the manifestoes issued by their early leaders.

Man Not Primarily Intellectual

The error is based upon an incorrect apprehension of human nature—the idea that it is primarily intellectual—and upon an incorrect view of the social groups, the churches. These are regarded as free associations of individuals who have contracted to work and worship together because they believe the same things. It leaves out of account the fact that the churches are true social groups, subject to the various influences which play on every society within the larger complex of a culture and that as societies they are not contractual relationships but growing organisms in which a variegated social heritage plays at least as important a part as does the creed of individual members. In its beginnings a church may have stood for certain principles of belief and practice because the individuals who composed it held those principles; now the individuals believe because the church does. A man is not a Baptist because he believes in adult baptism by immersion but he believes in adult baptism by immersion because he is a Baptist.

When the social character of the denominations becomes apparent to us we realize that the theological approach is quite insufficient to do justice to denominational characteristics and that a sociology of the denominations is needed to do that. The sociological approach calls our attention to the fact that theological differences are often the result of more fundamental differences in sociological structure and to the further fact that the character of the churches is due at least as much to non-religious, social influences as to creedal background.

THE PARADOX OF CHURCH AND WORLD

Three Types of Christianity

In his great work on *The Social Doctrines of the Christian Churches and Groups* the German historian and theologian, Troeltsch, defines three types of Christianity, distinguished primarily by their varying sociological structure and only as a result by theological differences. The three types are church, sect and mysticism. The first represents the dominantly social type of Christianity; the last is so completely individualistic that it rarely brings forth real groups or associations. The sect occupies an intermediate position.

An interesting point in Troeltsch's differentiation of the character of church and sect is his tracing of doctrinal differences back to an original difference in sociological structure. The Christ-dogma, for instance, which itself grew out of the social need of the first community, receives a very different interpretation according to its development in church or sect or mysticism. The Christ of the church is the Savior who accomplished salvation and justification once and for all through his work and who grants the results of this work to the individual by means of his continuous miraculous activity in the word, the work and the sacraments of the church. The Christ of the sect is the Lord, the pattern and lawgiver, who possesses divine dignity and authority, who leads his community through shame and misery to a salvation which has not yet been really accomplished but which will be completed at the time of his return. The Christ of mysticism is an inner spiritual principle, present in every manifestation of religious feeling. What is true of the Christ dogma is true of other doctrines. The fundamental difference of sociological character expresses itself in corresponding differences of creed.

Social Factors Behind Churches

When the problem of denominationalism is approached from this point of view it becomes apparent that differences in creed and polity form a more serious barrier to Christianity than is generally recognized. In our non-theological time creedal differences seem unimportant to many and unity appears to be an attainable goal. But back of creedal expressions lie more stubborn sociological structures which will not yield so readily to efforts at harmonization.

The sociological study of denominationalism does not confine itself to the examination of the fundamental social structures which lie back of creed and polity. It seeks also to understand to what extent social factors in the complex culture wherein Christian denominations exist have influenced the rise and development of the groups.

It need not be denied that intellectual considerations play a larger role in the social as well as in the individual life than it is the present fashion to concede. Yet it is evident also to the observer, that the division and subdivision of Christianity and the tenacity with which the resultant groups cling to their separate identities are due to other than intellectual causes. The creeds, it seems, are often rationalizations of organizations and established customs whose origin was due to less noble but more effective motives than the average denominational theology furnishes. Among these moving forces, responsible for much of our denominationalism, racial and economic factors play an important part. In some cases they are responsible for the rise of new groups; in almost all cases they must be held accountable for the preservation of group identities. The churches and the sects are racial and economic groups to at least the same extent that they are religious groups.

It is not a strange coincidence that America, the land of many races, should also be the land of many churches. Our religious life is but a reflection of our political character. The anarchy of American church life is the direct result, to a large extent, of the anarchy prevailing in European international life. We gather the representatives of a score of countries in a single city and then apologize to the visiting European because twenty church associations have grown up where there should be but one. Yet Europe, not America, is the mother of these children. A brief survey of the list of more than two hundred American denominations indicates that a very large proportion are national churches brought over by immigrants, along with other native customs and institutions. These churches frequently serve to conserve other racial customs and characteristics, particularly language. Such, furthermore, is the strength of religious conservatism that they usually outlast all the rest of the social heritage of the immigrant group and continue as the only remnant saved from the process of "Americanization." Even churches which have, apparently, been completely naturalized retain marks of this racial origin; often they remain strongly racial in character, though the fact is not recognized by their adherents.

Racial Origin of Churches

The names of many denominations indicate their racial character and origin. In the list of American denominations one finds an Armenian church, a Russian Orthodox church, Norwegian, Danish, Swedish, Icelandic, German and Slovak Lutheran groups, a Polish national church, the Welsh Calvinistic Methodist church, the Hungarian Reformed church and others. It is evident that the strong Lutheran bodies are German; the Reformed churches still carry their German or Dutch heritage with them; the Protestant Episcopal church is better designated by the term Anglican and Presbyterianism remains beloved of the Scotch. The denominational affiliations of persons whose names begin with Mack or O' or Sch can be guessed with considerable accuracy.

National differences usually operate indirectly, through differences in polity, in type of worship and so also of doctrine. National character may be more the result of cultural environment than of heredity but it is nevertheless a stubborn and unpliable factor. Its influence upon the polity and cult and doctrine of the churches may be noted in the connection of Roman Catholicism with the southern races of Europe, of Protestantism with the northern, and of orthodoxy with the eastern. Each group of nationalities has carried into its religious cult its characteristic temperament which finds expression also in its political and general cultural life. The social heritage of customs and mores has also entered into the religion of each nation and the result has been a different type of cult and doctrine in each case. Rome brought into the faith of Paul not only the legal mode of thought and the organization of the empire but also the disguised polytheism of the masses it won for the new faith. The individualism and democratic organization of Teuton tribes lies back of much protestant theology and polity. A clear recognition of this fact would have saved the fathers much laborious searching for proof-texts.

Next to nationalism and racial character the economic factor has probably been more important among social motives in the process of Christian disintegration. While on the one hand the history of Christianity promptly denied the fact that in Christ there is neither Jew nor Greek, it went on to demonstrate on the other hand that the distinctions between bond and free could also be maintained within the form of Christianity. There seems to be much truth in Max Weber's thesis that the economic character of a civilization depends largely upon its religious character, but the relation is one of interaction. Economic forms and classes have influenced the formation of Christian groups and of Christian thought to a pronounced degree.

Economic Motives

Back of the strife between Lutherans and Anabaptists, which was fought with the weapons of theology, there were unconscious but potent economic factors. Back of the rise of Methodism there was not only the evangelistic fervor of Wesley but also the economic cleavage between classes in Anglicanism. Back of the present day movements toward popular forms of Christianity, as in the Pentecostal groups, lies the economic class division of Christians.

The classes of the poor and the uncultured have always been the cradles of religions and of churches. Only among them, apparently, is religion to be found in its naive and native force. What was true in Palestine and Corinth remained true in Germany and England. In the course of time—partly it may be because of the influence of religion in cultivating habits of thrift and industry—the classes which brought forth new forms of faith in the days of their poverty rose in the economic and cultural scale. New classes of new people or new classes of the poor came in to take their places and these did not find themselves welcomed or at home in the churches which were once the meeting places of the lowly but had become the ecclesiastical establishments of the well-to-do and the educated. A new seed-plot had been made ready for the cultivation of a new church, which would meet the demand of the untutored for a form of religion offering the sort of cult and opportunity for emotional rather than intellectual expression which alone is adequate for the unschooled. The process can be followed frequently in the history of the religious organizations of a single locality. [James M.] Williams' study of *An*

American Town furnishes many interesting sidelights on one such process.

It would be rash to attempt to classify the denominations of America by means of an economic scale, yet such a classification suggests itself and, on the whole, it would probably represent the actual facts of divergence between denominations as accurately as a theological classification represents them.

One economic distinction is of especial importance. The religious forms of a group are influenced not only by its economic status but also by the general type of occupation of its members. The present cleavage in the denominations between fundamentalists and modernists is apparently due just as much to the transition from an agricultural to an industrial civilization as to the influence of science and philosophy upon religious thought. The liberal's emphasis on ethics is surely in part a product of modern city and industrial life with all the interdependence of human beings this civilization brings with it. The fundamentalist's emphasis on the direct activity of God is not without connection with the agriculturalist's dependence on the forces of nature.

There are many other factors in the culture complex which influence the organization of religious groups and the formulation of doctrines of belief. The standard of education which prevails in a certain class comes to expression in its church. The connection of political forms with religious thought and organization has often been noted. These various influences can cut across each other and combine in various ways to form the distinctive characteristics of each denomination. Religious thought or experience itself plays its important part, of course, but it does not always nor probably very frequently take the leading role. On the whole it seems that the other factors—economic, racial and cultural—are more potent than theological or religious influences in continuing the anarchic condition of church organization.

The problem of Christian unity is not primarily theological in nature; the issue is not that of adjusting conflicting polities. The problem is the problem of Christianity; the issue is that between the gospel and the world. The churches seeking to preach a gospel which recognized no differences of race or economic status, have reproduced within themselves those same cleavages which they purport to overcome and they continue to support through their own organization the caste system which their pulpits attack. Are not the churches the church's worst enemy?

Theology and Psychology: A Sterile Union

Neither Niebuhr's affirmation of the efforts made by Protestant liberalism to update traditional Christian theology nor intermittent opposition from conservatives within his own Evangelical Synod threw him into the camp of the "scientific modernists." He could not agree with Harry Elmer Barnes that "intelligent and educated theologians must surrender their age-long pretension to special if not unique competence in clearing up the problem of the nature of God and his laws."[8] When understood in this way, the psychology of religion for Niebuhr became evidence of the church selling out to the world. While this field of scientific study might better explain certain forms of religious behavior or even help diagnose what was ailing Christianity, its tendency to make theology subservient to its subjective assumptions could easily terminate the life of the patient.

Source: *The Christian Century* 44 (January 13, 1927): 47–48.

The union of psychology and theology is more than a hundred years old despite the fact that it is sometimes referred to as a recent and brilliant match. The courtship began when Berkeley, Hume and Kant succeeded in transferring the point of view in philosophy so that henceforth the subject displaced the object in the center of attention, and psychology with epistemology were called upon to lead the way into every philosophical discussion. The marriage was consummated when this new method was introduced into theology by Schleiermacher, who defined religious doctrine in terms of social consciousness and of individual experience. Since his day many theologians have been prone to regard psychology as the only fit consort of the erstwhile "queen of the sciences." But the union has been sterile.

---

8. Harry Elmer Barnes, *The Twilight of Christianity* (New York: Vanguard, 1929), 437.

England and America were slower to accept the new alliance than Germany, where Strauss, F. C. Baur, and Feuerbach became its champions or—to return to the earlier figure—where their systems of thought were revealed to be the offspring of the new union. It is true that Hegelian philosophy rather than Kant's critical rationalism or Schleiermacher's psychology furnished these theologians with their approach, but the net result remained the same, for the point of view was subjective and theology directed its attention to the idea rather than to the object. In France positivism led to similar results, issuing at last in the social subjectivism of Durkheim and Levy-Bruhl.

Influence of William James

In America, and eventually also in England, the revolution was introduced by William James and his followers as well as predecessors in the psychology of religion. They made the psychological approach the orthodox introduction to theology while in Germany the theory of knowledge was regarded as the necessary prerequisite of all thought upon the nature of religion and of God. The net result was about the same in both cases. American psychology of religion led to a psychological theory of religious knowledge, pragmatism, and German epistemology, starting with the subject, failed as a rule to discover the categorical element in religious experience and ended by consigning the whole of that experience to the tender mercies of psychological analysis.

There are many who believe that theology, and with it religion, is being well served by this partnership with psychology. Sufficient work has been done in the psychology of religion during the last century, and especially during the last quarter of that period, to enable the student to estimate the worth of the combination and to evaluate the profits which it has brought to theology.

Psychology, it may seem, has derived some advantages from its exploitation of the religious consciousness and its analysis of religious behavior. It has found an additional field wherein it may apply its hypothesis about the unconscious, suggestion, sublimation, transfer, the sentiments, and the like. Social psychology has been interested in the religious representations and behavior of groups, and has profited not a little by its study of religion. Genetic psychology has yielded to the attraction of the night "in which all cats are black" and all theories seem bright—the night of primitive religion—where it has demonstrated how nicely its hypotheses fit into a situation which has been constructed to fit the hypotheses.

Effect of Psychology on Religion

What benefit, upon the other hand, has theology received from its alliance with psychology? The net result of psychologizing about religion has been the apparent subjectivization of religion. Psychology has substituted religious experience for revelation, auto-suggestion for communion with God in prayer and mysticism, sublimation of the instincts for devotion, reflexes for the soul, and group consciousness or the ideal wish-fulfillment for God. It is true that it does not often profess to do these things and, in the opinion of the philosophically minded, may indeed do none of them, but this is the result which it has achieved in the minds of many psychologists, of some theologians, and a great many of those whose acquaintance with psychology, theology, and philosophy is only casual. Even where the result is not consciously accepted it frequently exercises an unconscious influence, so that God, prayer and revelation are left out of account as realities though their reality is not denied.

It was the claim of the psychology of religion when it began its work that it would greatly further the cause of religious education and that, by demonstrating the laws of religious life, it would make the development of that life by pastors and teachers a matter of scientific control. It has failed to justify that claim. What improvement has been made in the work of religious education in recent years has been sponsored by the psychology of education rather than by the psychology of religion. It is true that certain refinements in the use of the appurtenances of worship and in the methods of arousing religious emotions may be traced to the study of psychology, but the refinement of method does not compensate for the great diminution of the sense of the reality of the Object of worship, which is also due to psychology. Many modern discussions of prayer and of the conduct of worship are tragic confessions of that loss. They appear as sterile and pitiful efforts to hold fast to a fiction which must be maintained as long as possible ere sad disillusionment robs the race of the values it affords—hectic efforts to develop a method of suggestion and auto-suggestion to take the place of communion.

What Theology Has Sacrificed

Apart from the gain of some interesting side-lights on special problems, such as sin and conversion, theology has derived only two considerable benefits from its association with psychology. Religion has been revealed to be an inalienable part of the psychic life, and the critical faculty of theology has been strengthened. The first of these results, however, is by no means an undisputed finding of the psychologists. A few of them, notably James, have maintained that this is the case, but a larger number, explicitly or implicitly, have defended the opposite conclusion, seeking to show that religion is an epi-phenomenon—a fiction, indeed, explicable but quite unnecessary. So far as the second contribution of psychology is concerned, the gain for theology may be only specious. For while psychological theology has been taught the characteristics of the purely psychological and thus learned to isolate it, it has lost its sense for the rational and the real. Hence the net result is that the whole realm of religious experience is often consigned to psychology. The extreme pragmatic tendency, as distinguished from the discriminating pragmatism of William James, makes room for every sort of irrationalism which is psychologically palatable and edifying and makes psychology the final arbiter of truth. Theology has, therefore, become less, rather than more, scientific under the tutelage of psychology. It has sacrificed even the modicum of precision it possessed to gain a method characterized by formlessness and uncertainty of its object.

If it were evident in any way that psychology of religion led men nearer to the truth, then the result for religion would indeed need to be regarded as a bitter but necessary disillusionment. But too much of modern psychology rests its structure of theory upon the basis of value-judgments, rather than upon adequate evidence of soundly established facts, to make its results of important value for theology. Distinguished and qualified scientists are at work in the field and when their work has led to some assured results, which have bearing upon religious life, it will be necessary for theology to assimilate these. So far, however, the assured results of psychological research lie in the field which has no important bearing upon religious life, and it has been the hasty generalization, the tentative hypothesis, which has been exploited too much in the psychology of religion. So far as psychology is a science, it has little to say about religion. When it deals with the subject it abandons scientific procedure all too often.

Schleiermacher's Blind Alley

Has Schleiermacher led theology into a blind alley comparable to the blind alley into which the early physicists might have led the natural sciences had they begun their work by observing and analyzing man's consciousness of physical objects, his sentiments about them, his reaction toward them? These left the question as to the "how" of man's knowledge of nature to philosophy and concerned themselves with the "what," working out a method oriented toward the object and not toward the subject. Sophisticated subjective idealists may seek to reduce the world science has revealed to an idea-world, but the net result of their labor remains the sterile recognition that "idea" is the philosophical name for "thing." The empirical approach has been fruitful not only for science but also for philosophy; the theory of knowledge which builds on the basis of the scientific method, and the metaphysics which is constructed with the materials furnished by an objective science, are incomparably superior in precision to all introverted philosophies.

If theology would resolutely turn its back on all psychologism, if it would devote itself with the wholeheartedness which characterizes the natural sciences to the observation and intense study of its object as it is revealed in history and in the ethical and spiritual life, then it might eventually be found worthy of the name of science and its results might become as valuable for the religious life as the results of the natural sciences are for physical existence. Such a theology, as it has been set forth by Professor D. C. Macintosh, is truly an empirical science and not an empiricist philosophy in which object and subject are dissolved in psychological experience. A critical theory of religious knowledge is, of course, eventually indispensable, but this theory must be as independent of psychology as is any epistemology, which takes psychological facts into consideration but grants them no special position of pre-eminence over the facts of other sciences and disciplines. Empirical theology of this type is no longer the obsequious servitor of psychology but returns to its true vocation as the handmaid of religion.

From the Religion of Humanity to the Religion of God

This article illustrates Niebuhr's competence as an intellectual historian, his ability to hopscotch his way across several fields within this discipline, and his knack for finding a synthesis amid a host of divergent comments about a given subject. It also shows that he clearly recognized the close of World War I as a turning point in much of Western thinking. In reaction to the church's efforts during the previous century to accommodate itself to the "anthropocentric" turn that theology had taken during the Enlightenment, a fresh emphasis was being placed once again on God's objective reality and on religious knowledge based on God's self-revelation. Particularly noteworthy is Niebuhr's discussion of the work of his American mentor, D. C. Macintosh, in comparison to Europe's leading exponent of the new crisis theology, Karl Barth. Niebuhr, it seems, was positioning himself theologically in order to keep church and world in their proper tension.

Source: *Theological Magazine of the Evangelical Synod of North America* 57 (November 1929): 401–9.

"We advance inevitably from a religion of humanity to a religion of God," the words are not quoted from a theologian but from a psychologist, William Brown of Oxford. They may be taken as the motto not only of the experience of many a devout man but also of a tendency in modern thought as a whole. There is good reason for the belief that a new age of faith is at hand; or if that is too optimistic a conclusion, it is yet evident that fewer theoretical difficulties will be placed in the path of faith in the future than has been the case since the beginning of the nineteenth century.

In support of this thesis two main tendencies in modern thinking may be described: the tendency in theology and philosophy of religion and the tendency in natural science. There are, of course, other movements in the modern world which make it more susceptible to religious influences than it once was. Among these the primary place is occupied by man's disillusionment with himself. It may be this is the most fundamental of all characteristics of the contemporary intellectual climate. For pride and human self-sufficiency are the arch-enemies of faith and when these go both the possibility and the need of faith may enter the soul once more. The pride of the nineteenth and early twentieth century in the achievements of men, the sophomoric vainglory of popularized science, the arrogance of democracy have all been chastened not only by the tremendous experiences of the world war but by the sober second thought which reveals limitations unattended to by civilization in the period of its expansion, and insufficiencies unacknowledged by an adolescent culture in its years of discovery.

In science, political and cultural life a new humility has manifested itself which cannot but ultimately affect the popular temper and be conducive to the reassertion of religious faith. For the present, it is true, the pride in human achievement, which leaves no room for religion, and the contentment with a present world of material comforts, which does not allow the restlessness of the soul for God to come to expression, still prevail among large masses. The temper of the popular mind is frequently determined by the temper of the scientific mind in the previous generations; leading ideas require a long time to work down into the social consciousness; the practical results of the scientific labor of one generation do not become apparent until much later, for applied science necessarily lags years behind theory, while it is this applied science which influences the popular psychology most effectively. The effectiveness of the new tendencies in theology and philosophy of religion upon the one hand and in natural science and philosophy upon the other hand may not become apparent for many years, yet their appearance is significant for the future.

I

The advance from a religion of humanity to a religion of God is strikingly manifested in the changes which have taken place in theology during the last ten years. The culture of the nineteenth century was in almost every respect anthropocentric. Its interest in man as the measure of all things came to expression in the great democratic movements which, starting with the American and French Revolutions, culminated in the Russian Revolution and which, in the interval of more than a hundred years, democratized almost all the nations of the earth. This same interest in man, in his emotions, in the subjective aspects of his experiences was revealed in literature, where the romantic tradition replaced the classic. From [*The Sorrows of Young*] *Werther* on the literature of the nineteenth century was under the influence of this anthropocentric point of view. The psychological novel, as illustrated in English literature by Henry James, by Hardy and even Conrad, ego-centric poetry as exemplified by Browning, Francis Thompson and Tennyson's "In Memoriam," has been followed in our own time by the psychological biography. The extreme form of the arts, from music to sculpture, betrayed the same concentration upon the emotions and impressions and expressions of the self. Objective standards everywhere were replaced by subjective standards.

This spirit of nineteenth century civilization was partly expressed in, partly derived from its philosophy. The philosophy of the period was anthropocentric with a vengeance. The dominant school was the idealistic school which found its starting point or the fulcrum from which it sought to move the world in the dictum of Descartes, "I think, therefore I am." Berkeley, Hume and Kant with all their followers in England and Germany could not emancipate themselves from this point of view. Experience was regarded everywhere as the key to knowledge and the decisive thing about experience was that it was the experience of a subject. With Hegel and Hegelianism this point of view became the source of a great *Weltanschauung* in which the whole world was regarded from the interior point of view and human experience of self-consciousness was made the pattern of the universe.

Theology under the influence of the general *Zeitgeist* and, especially, under the guidance of philosophy followed the dominant tendency. Romanticism and idealistic philosophy met in Schleiermacher who defined the essence of religion in the highly subjective terms of feeling and the content of theology in the psychological terms of Christian consciousness. To quarrel with historical tendencies and to criticize Schleiermacher for what was in his day a most necessary and highly fruitful discovery is as unnecessary as it is unjustified. Certainly Schleiermacher's contribution remains of supreme importance. But, like all theological insights it was influenced by the temper of the times and it was one-sided. The human aspect of religion, as the only one available for analysis, alone came to expression and from this time onward to our own day theology remained under the influence of an anthropocentric point of view. The heresies of a period are as enlightening for the understanding of its character as are its orthodoxies, for usually heresies are simply the completely rationalized, extreme developments of some item of orthodox belief. The heresies of the nineteenth century, if one may use that phrase, came to light in Strauss and Feuerbach. In the latter especially the anthropocentric tendencies of the nineteenth century were illustrated in their extreme form. For Feuerbach the only possible view of religion was the psychological view. Theology is anthropology, the gods are wish-beings; but one factor is present in religion—the human; human experience, human wishes, human feelings these are the factors which make up faith.

A more adequate but still anthropocentric point of view was expressed in the pragmatic theology of the late nineteenth and the early twentieth century and in those forms of the social gospel which are most akin to pragmatism. The question which was raised in these schools was the question as to the human value of religion. Religion was defended because it is serviceable to the mundane life of man. Even American Lutheranism succumbed to this tendency when it advertised itself in the days of the "Great Red Scare" as an antidote to Bolshevism and, by implications, a safe-guarder of property. In some highly provincial forms of the social gospel Christianity in particular and religion in general are regarded as exclusively ethical, exclusively mundane, exclusively human endeavors. Again, as in the case of Schleiermacher, there is an obvious truth in the claim that faith has a social task as well as some social origins but the one-sided emphasis indicates the pre-occupation of the period with man and his mundane values. The most important of the contemporary manifestations of this nineteenth century and anthropocentric point of view are to be found in the field of psychology and sociology of religion, where the sociological rather than the ethical and psychological rather than the empirical interests of modern times meet. Such a work as [Edward Scribner] Ames' recent *Religion* falls completely within the category of anthropocentric theology. Following his masters, Durkheim and Levy-Bruhl, Ames regards religion as the purely human enterprises of pursuing purely human values and believes that its nature can be explained completely without reference to any objective Deity solely by reference to psychology, sociology and ethics.

This anthropocentric theology which remains symptomatic of the past century though it continues to manifest itself so late as 1929, has its undoubted values, historically and intrinsically. Historically its value lies in the rediscovery of the inner life in religion and of the social task of faith. It was a most desirable and necessary revolt against the intellectualism of Deism and Orthodoxy which both found the essence of faith in the acceptance of intellectually formulated beliefs. Intrinsically the value of the anthropocentric tendency lies in its reassertion of the ethical factors in religion, in its emphasis upon practical activity, in its cultivation of an inner piety of feeling, and in its development of an adequate critical apparatus by means of which men are better able to examine and to criticize both their own ethical and religious life and the ethical and doctrinal mixture of philosophy and religion, of social and Christian ethics which prevails in all institutional and historical forms of faith. But the deficiencies and evils of an anthropocentric theology have also become apparent. In its extreme forms it robbed men of the consciousness of God, substituted auto suggestion for prayer, pursuit of values for devotion to God and self-help for salvation.

II

Hence the reaction against the subjective point of view which has set in in theology is to be warmly welcomed by all for whom religion means not only the seeking after God but His self-revelation also, not only pursuit of values but also obedience to the Divine Will, not only striving but also trust and assurance, not only the energizing of the will but also its salvation, not only the Kingdom of God in its social aspects but also immortality and redemption. This reaction has undoubtedly set in. Perhaps the year 1918 may be taken as the year of the turning point in theology, when from a religion of humanity it moved inevitably again toward the religion of God.

WORLDLY IMPEDIMENTS TO CHURCHLY INTEGRITY

The closing years of the world-war were marked by the publication in Germany of [Rudolf] Otto's *Das Heilige* and Barth's *Roemerbrief*, in America of Macintosh's *Theology as an Empirical Science*, in England of [Burnett H.] Streeter's and his associates' studies. All the movements which have been influenced by these publications or their authors have one element in common—the re-emphasis upon God as the fundamental factor in faith and of the revelation or knowledge of God as the essential element in religion. This is not the place to examine the very wide differences between the positions occupied by the various men mentioned. Some of these are due to differences of background and terminology. One reason why German and Anglo-Saxon theology seem to vary so greatly is that they build upon entirely different philosophical foundations. The term "empiricism," for instance, has an entirely different connotation in German thinking than it has in Anglo-Saxon philosophy. It makes a great deal of difference whether nations have thought for a century in terms of Kant or in the terms of Locke. They may be much nearer to each other in essentials than they believe but their kinship is hidden because they speak different languages even when they employ the so called precise terms of philosophy or theology. Despite specious and real distinctions, however, there is the common note in the new theology—the insistence upon the fact that in religion the primary element is God, not man and that in faith there is actual commerce with the Father. For the new German theology this position demands this rejection of empiricism; for American and, in part, for English theology it requires reinterpretation of experience from a realistic point of view. In the nineteenth century experience, including religious experience, was examined from the point of view of the subject. The psychological and perhaps logical aspects were analyzed but toward the thing-in-itself, that which was experienced, a negative agnostic attitude seemed alone possible. Today realism is in the saddle as much as subjectivism was. The temper of the times demands realism in literature and art as well as in science, and theology is profiting by this general reversal. Empirical realism of this sort may, it is true, be so cautious as to make very little advance on the idealistic or psychological empiricism of a previous generation. Such a cautious and inadequate realism is presented in the works of [Henry Nelson] Wieman, who maintains the independent reality of God but proceeds then to define God in terms which allow for the interpretation of almost any kind of dependence upon the world as religious. In Macintosh realistic empiricism is much more adequate and more realistic. It is the contention of Macintosh's theology that men know God as they know any other reality, for instance the reality of other persons. Within the complex of sensations which the subject experiences when he sees another person he directly intuits, knows, the reality of that other. So within the experience of salvation, man intuits God. Religious experience is primarily an experience of God, though it is also the experience possessed by a subject. Such experience is at once revelation and discovery. From the purely human point of view it is discovery, but the man who experiences God in the answer to prayer experiences him as active, self-revealing will. Because men may know God directly, as the dependable factor on which they can count for salvation when they make the right adjustment to him—that is the adjustment which Christ has made possible—therefore it is possible for theology to become an empirical science which will describe the Object which appears in the experience of the stars. There is a tremendous difference, of course, between the inactive object of astronomical experience and the living God of religious experience but this is common to both types—that in them an object independent of all human wishes, of all purely psychological elements comes to appearance. By making religious experience at its best rather than religious experience in its least developed forms the source of knowledge about God Macintosh is able to go far beyond Wieman in his theological theory. The God who seeks men and who responds to them when they come to Him in the spirit of Christ is not only a dependable factor, but an evidently personal God of love. Macintosh's theory, by the way, must be judged primarily by reference to the book named above rather than by reference to the apologetic work on *The Reasonableness of Christianity*.

In German theology the theocentric tendency is most pronounced. It is so pronounced in fact that it is almost possible to speak of a theo-centric predicament in the Barthian theology comparable to the ego-centric predicament of romantic theology. For while the anthropocentric theology of the nineteenth century began with man and then discovered that it was very difficult to find a way from man to God, so the theo-centric theology of Barth and his followers begins with God and finds it hard to discover a way from God to man. Eventually it is forced to rely more on the Logos doctrine than on the Jesus Christ of the New Testament and on metaphysics rather than on the history of salvation. The predicament in which each type of theology is placed illustrates simply the chasm which exists between life and intellect and the danger to which thinking leads when it sets up one absolute principle and seeks consistently to follow out its implications to their rational consequences. The mystery and the power of Christianity seem always to have resided in the tension between dual principles and in the movement of life back and forth between these poles rather than in the consistent application of a single idea. This tension, irrational but fruitful, is illustrated in the Trinitarian and Chalcedonian formulae, in the emphasis upon God's unity and God's diversity, on Christ's humanity and deity, in the further hiatus between divine justice and divine mercy. The Barthian emphasis upon the majesty of God, on his over-poweringness and sole reality, on Christ the Logos rather than on the Jesus of history, betray the movement into a difficult position in which many of the values of the Christian faith are imperilled. But with all these difficulties and dangers—and what great theology is without its perils?—there is in this new German movement the great, hopeful, realistic note of emphasis upon the absolute objectivity and reality of God.

This is the tendency which characterizes the new theology, whether in Germany, America or England. And as theology is always responsive to the temper of its times so this theology is significant of a new temper in religion—of a new emphasis which is yet the old emphasis, namely that faith is life in God and not within the confines of human consciousness. Whether or not this theology will become as one-sided in its emphasis as nineteenth century thought was remains to be seen. For the present that danger exists, but no new movement, it seems, can make its contribution to the truth without over-emphasizing and so distorting the truth. There is need today as always of quiet and well-balanced minds which will refuse to fall into the apparently courageous but over-zealous, and dangerous attitudes of an "either-or" theology or philosophy and which will endeavor to continue the less spectacular but truer task of finding the meaning which resides in the antinomies of the religious life and of doctrine.

III

The movement from a religion of humanity to a religion of God is not confined to theology. In secular philosophy a similar tendency is manifesting itself. In part this tendency is due to that greater appreciation of the reality of religion which has made itself manifest in scientific circles since the days when [William] James' *Varieties of Religious Experience* was first published; in part the tendency is due to the unsatisfactory nature of the conclusions to which an irreligious philosophy was forced; in part it derives from the new developments within science itself.

Biology, to take up one example, has gone a long way from the position occupied by [Ernst] Haeckel. In [Hans] Driesch, J. A. Thompson, [Stanley] Coulter and many others, in the philosophies of [Henri] Bergson, [Leonard Trelawny] Hobhouse, [Friedrich] Schiller and James the mechanistic hypotheses of an earlier day have disappeared and the *Weltanschauung* which builds upon the basis of the concept of evolution either shows its need of or provides a definite place for a theistic interpretation of the program of life.

In the new physics, however, which more than anything else is overthrowing the mechanistic, godless world-views of an earlier day, which is restoring humility to the list of scientific virtues and which is showing forth again the reasonableness or necessity for belief in God, from a purely intellectual point of view. The extent to which modern physics has overcome its mechanistic antecedents and tends in its philosophic movements to extend a welcome to the religious interpretation of the universe is indicated especially in the recent Gifford lectures of the great English astronomer, A. S. Eddington. The final conclusions of his examination of the new physics are worth quoting:

(1) The symbolic nature of the entities of physics is generally recognized; and the scheme of physics is now formulated in such a way as to make it almost self-evident that it is a partial aspect of something wider.

(2) Strict causality is abandoned in the material world. Our ideas of the controlling laws are in process of reconstruction and it is not possible to predict what kind of form they will ultimately take; but all indications are that strict causality has dropped out permanently. This relieves the former necessity of supposing that mind is subject

to deterministic law or alternatively that it can suspend deterministic law in the material world.

(3) Recognizing that the physical world is entirely abstract and without "actuality" apart from its linkage to consciousness, we restore consciousness to the fundamental position instead of representing it as an inessential complication occasionally found in the midst of inorganic nature at a large stage in evolutionary history.

(4) The sanction for correlating a "real" physical world to certain feelings of which we are conscious does not seem to differ in any essential respect from the sanction for correlating a spiritual domain to another side of our personality. (*Nature of the Physical World*, p. 331–32).

It is at the latter point that this new tendency in science differs from the rationalism of the eighteenth century in its efforts to prove the existence of God by means of man's experience of nature. The tendency which Eddington represents and which many scientists share with him is simply that of recognizing the limitations of their science and of acknowledging the validity of religious perceptions.

Yet secular philosophy [*sic*] today indicates its interest in the theistic world-view by reviving natural theology as well as by showing the inadequacy of mechanism and the validity of religious experience. In so eminent a scientist and philosopher as [Alfred North] Whitehead as well as in [Samuel] Alexander the return to the concept of God as a necessary philosophical concept becomes pronounced. It can be objected that such natural theologies do not give us God, but at best some pale and abstract principle, like Whitehead's "principle of concretion" or Alexander's "principle of emergence," which is far removed from the God and Father of religion and theology. The objection is doubtless justified if anyone seeks to substitute the scientific principle for the religious object but if the scientific principle is regarded as the discovery of one aspect of

Deity, an aspect available to philosophy without recourse to religion, then these approaches to theistic philosophy can only be welcomed as verifications from another realm of experience of that which is most manifestly and fully revealed in faith.

These are some of the signs of the times. They indicate that the brief period of modern culture's adolescence is over. Pride in human achievement and reliance upon human power alone, the idolatry of science and romantic pre-occupation with the self and its feelings are giving way to a chastened yet illuminated mood. "We advance inevitably from a religion of humanity to a religion of God."

4

First Prescriptions for Church Revitalization

While history does not repeat itself, there are some striking similarities between the early years of the twenty-first century and the 1920s with respect to the condition of religion in America. "Religious Depression" is the term church historian Robert T. Handy used to describe the climate of indifference and hostility toward religious institutions in particular that became increasingly apparent following the close of World War I.[1] Mainline Protestant church and Sunday School attendance were on the decline, and despite the new prosperity much of the country was experiencing, missionary funds and fervor were also trending downward. Internal battles weakened the once-powerful Northern Baptists and the Presbyterians, as liberal and conservative leaders jockeyed with each other for control of their denominations. The new business frenzy that Republican presidents like Calvin Coolidge trumpeted as the *business* of the nation became a freshly-paved road to social salvation for many of the church-

---

1. Robert T. Handy, "The American Religious Depression, 1925–1935," Facet Books, Historical Series Vol. 9, edited by Richard C. Wolf (Philadelphia: Fortress Press, 1968).

going faithful. Prosperity evangelist Russell H. Conwell, who had already preached his "Acres of Diamonds" some six thousand times, died in 1925. But into his shoes stepped advertising executive Bruce Barton whose best-seller, *The Man Nobody Knows*, lauded Jesus for his entrepreneurial skills and leadership. As a result, the Social Gospel, a movement that prior to the war had robustly championed the cause of society's *have-nots*, not only failed to gain any new traction, but only succeeded in adding to its woes when some of its leaders chose to embrace the alternative political strategies of socialism and Marxism. Protestant churches in America during this same period, as Sydney Ahlstrom has assessed it, did not lose their "historic hegemony," but "were made sharply aware that their ancient sway over the nation's moral life was threatened." Their last great victory turned debacle of prohibition, moreover, in reality served as "evidence and cause of the churches' loss of authority in a culture where urban values became primary."[2]

The ecumenical movement, on the other hand, did provide some hope for religious renewal. The Federal Council of Churches was gaining additional members during the 1920s and becoming more global in its vision of cooperation. Six hundred delegates from 37 countries in 1925 also came to the Stockholm conference, where the spadework was done for the ecumenical Life and Work movement, which advocated joint efforts to address the world's problems. Two years later, another such conference in Lausanne, Switzerland, put the wheels in motion for a Faith and Order movement toward Christian unity. These developments quickened the *union* church instincts of H. Richard Niebuhr's Evangelical Synod. His work on *The Social Sources of Denominationalism* made him realistic, if not pessimistic, about possible institutional mergers for the sake of Christian unity.

---

2. Sydney E. Ahlstrom, *A Religious History of the American People* (New Haven, CT: Yale University Press, 1972), 915.

FIRST PRESCRIPTIONS FOR CHURCH REVITALIZATION

As Niebuhr saw it, the best hope of "overcoming some of the evils of the prevalent anarchy" lay with those churches with a high degree of social affinity. After all, some of his Synod's "Lutheran" cousins, who were primarily German and Scandinavian in origin, had recently succeeded in merging their separate denominations. So why not the "non-Lutheran German groups?"[3]

This may have been the reason, Niebuhr consented to chair the Evangelical Synod's Committee on Relations with Other Churches, and as such took the lead in its negotiations with the Reformed Church in the United States and the United Brethren in Christ. The joint meetings resulted in consensus on a *Plan of Union* that included seven key planks, the last of which revealed Niebuhr's influence because it recognized the "present" and the "social" dimensions of the kingdom of God. The proposal of a "United Church in America," in his estimation, was "an effective step toward the achievement of the ideal for which our Evangelical Synod has always stood."[4] But his high hopes were soon dashed when the United Brethren found it difficult to give up their episcopal form of church polity and withdrew from the negotiations. The disappointment was one that may well have contributed to his more general observation that "churches are social organisms and like all other groups are keenly interested in self-preservation."[5]

In any case, Niebuhr chose in 1930 to resign from his denomination's church-relations committee. While he supported the "organic union" of the Evangelical and Reformed Church in 1934, as well as the eventual merger with the Congregational Christian Churches in 1957 as the United Church of Christ, never again did

---

3. H. Richard Niebuhr, "Churches That Might Unite," *The Christian Century* 46 (February 21, 1929): 260.
4. H. Richard Niebuhr, "A Summary of the Plan of Union," *The Evangelical Herald* 28 (March 21, 1929): 230–31.
5. Niebuhr, "Churches That Might Unite," 260.

he see this kind of church-centered ecumenism as a prescription for church revitalization in America's culture. While he agreed that the church could not effectively preach "brotherhood" until it practiced that doctrine itself, he also found himself asking, "[H]ow can it practice that doctrine until brotherhood between classes, nation and races has been established?"[6] A kingdom-centered ecumenism that focused its attention on healing of a broken and divided world, he said already as this point in his career, was the far more effective approach for the church to take. In his concluding chapter of *Social Sources*, he in fact called upon the churches to search for, and to make it the guiding star for all of their activities, a *"summum bonum,"* a principle capable of bringing together the whole human family because it mirrored the "eternal harmony of love."[7]

As the decade of the 1920s drew to a close, Niebuhr's search for a prescription for church revitalization also led him to sift through the various strands of Protestant thinking in the areas of theology and ethics. He did not waver in his positive assessments of liberalism's insights into the relationship between religion and culture in both biblical and modern contexts, and he continued to value the emphasis it had placed on the social dimension of the church's work. But he felt that what liberal Protestants had ignored was the social character of sin as well as the corrupt side of every human being. Because of their proclivity for utopian thinking, moreover, many of them failed to put current realities under the microscope of religion. When weighed in the balance of post-war disillusionment, therefore, the faith that liberalism had placed in humanity and in the inevitable progress of western civilization was found to be wanting. In Niebuhr's view, neither fundamentalist nor similarly conservative Protestant groups

---

6. Ibid., 261.
7. H. Richard Niebuhr, *The Social Sources of Denominationalism* (New York: Henry Holt, 1929), 265.

were offering a viable alternative. What claimed their attention was the individual rather than society, and in the face of many changes in the world around them, they not only sought refuge in the past, but continued to fight old battles over doctrinal and ethical issues, thus rendering themselves incapable of addressing more recent intellectual developments and the new moral problems that the industrialization of the Western world had created. In the revolt on the European scene of against liberalism, Niebuhr found a more realistic assessment of human nature and a return to a transcendent point of view, one that re-emphasized human dependence on God's grace for salvation. But at the same time, he insisted that any new theology must not divorce religion from social ethics or restrict the sphere of salvation to the individual human being.

The selections that follow demonstrate the dialectical pattern that Niebuhr's reflections on church-world paradox were beginning to assume already in these early years in the Evangelical Synod. Called to be *in* the world and to attune its message to contemporary intellectual and moral challenges, the church inevitably accommodated itself to features of particular cultures that in this process served to compromise the universal gospel it sought to proclaim. Lest it become *of* the world, therefore, the church needed to experience antithetical movements of retreat from the world for the purpose of renewing its primary allegiance to its Lord. To Niebuhr, such *withdrawal* required that the church take a hard look at itself and follow the often-painful path of repentance. But this step was only a temporary one, to be followed always for the sake of more robust efforts on the part of the church under the cross of Christ to engage the world.

Of particular note is the article of 1929 that Niebuhr entitled "The Church in the Modern World." Here he metaphorically described the same church-world dynamic as being like "the rhythm of the waves that wash upon the beach."[8] When he applied it to the field of ethics, the course he plotted involved a separation of religion from any value system that identified God with human goodness not in order to make ethics more metaphysically palatable or to let religion become a strictly *private matter*, but so that ethicists might rediscover the transcendent basis of moral obligations and that religious leaders might become more prophetic in the combatting of social ills. For the struggling Social Gospel movement, it meant abandoning not the world it was seeking to save, but the liberal theology with which it had aligned itself, with the intention of finding the theological convictions necessary for the breathing of new life into its efforts. For Niebuhr's Evangelical Synod, moreover, it implied entering the mainstream of American culture in order to more vigorously address its social problems, but without surrendering its gospel-centered theological heritage or succumbing to the temptation to become "just another middle class church."

---

8. H. Richard Niebuhr, "The Church in the Modern World," *The Keryx* 20, no. 3 (May 1929): 18.

FIRST PRESCRIPTIONS FOR CHURCH REVITALIZATION

The Church in the Modern World

In this article, which appeared in the student publication of Eden Seminary, Niebuhr used the term paradox to define the relationship between church and world. This relationship, as he saw it, involved the church in an ongoing rhythm of accommodation to the world and withdrawal from the world. The problems that these two movements inevitably created were not resolvable, thus making it all the more necessary to maintain the dynamic tension between them. He also made it clear that withdrawal of the church from the world was not a prescription for revitalization. While it might be necessary at times, it was always to be viewed as a temporary and unselfish measure designed to permit Christians theologically and morally to renew their ability to serve the world and thereby to make a fresh effort to transform it.

Source: *The Keryx* 20, no. 3 (May 1929): 9–10, 29.

The problem of the church in the modern world is only the contemporary aspect of the age-old question of the relationship of church and world. It is the problem of accommodation or transcendence, or, better, of accommodation and transcendence. In every period of Christian history the problem has been difficult, not only as a subject of academic discussion but also as a complex practical question. How far could the church dare to go in trying to be all things to all men in the days of Hellenistic civilization? How far did it need to go in endeavoring to keep itself unspotted from the world? Church fathers, medieval popes, Protestant reformers, eighteenth century rationalists and revivalists faced the problem in the same way in which the modern Christian must face it. Of course the contemporary world offers particular difficulties and challenges to the church; science, industrialism, international relations, the growth of cities, rapid communication—these aspects of present-day culture

THE PARADOX OF CHURCH AND WORLD

demand recognition in all their novelty and in all their complexity. Yet in principle the question of accommodation and transcendence is neither new or old; it is chronic.

I

It is necessary that the church adapt itself to the surrounding culture if it would be effective. It must seek to become all things to all men that, haply, it may win some. What ecclesiastical tragedies have not been enacted because some preacher, some congregation, or some denomination has only offered an unyielding front to the changing civilization round about. They have persisted in the methods developed in some old environment long after that environment has passed away. They have sought to speak the languages of agricultural civilizations among people removed by generations from the soil; they have employed the methods of the frontier long after the frontier and its pioneers had been forgotten and when a stable, agricultural or urban society had replaced the old border. They have continued to use the thought-forms of ancient monarchic or feudal cultures as empty symbols among peoples who were devoid of any intelligent appreciations of the remaining of those forms. In their use of language, church methods, symbols, in battling with the ethical problems of some hoary past, in fighting doctrinal controversies of a by-gone era they have failed to accommodate themselves to the changing and complex world; and so they have fallen into complete ineffectiveness. There are a score or more of denominations in the United States, mere survivals of once flourishing churches, which continue to live in the environment of Europe or of early nineteenth century America and which have sacrificed all usefulness in the contemporary world because they have failed to accommodate themselves to it. There are churches which insist that every new constitution must contain a paragraph denouncing not race discrimination, but slavery; they continue to live in the eighteen-forties. There are churches which resist the use of hymns, of organs, of Sunday school literature, churches which antagonize foreign missions—because these things were unknown in their ancient past. They prefer to break rather than to bend. And they are breaking.

II

The problem of accommodation is not only one of method. It is also a problem of doctrine. Language changes from generation to generation. The words which conveyed one meaning to a people living in an agricultural, or in a monarchic, or in a provincial society have another connotation to the men who dwell in different surroundings. Theology can never be absolute because an absolute content can be transmitted into a changing vocabulary and in fluent thought-forms only by means of constant reinterpretation. Even the simple language of the Apostle's Creed has a different meaning for men today than it had for the Christians of the fourth century. Moreover, new experiences of nature, new interpretations of the physical cosmos, new observations of human nature and new explanations of social relationships which become established in the conscious and unconscious mind of contemporary men demand that the church adapt its teaching to the mental environment if it would continue its old testimony in all its vigor.

Accommodation is necessary also in the moral realm. New moral problems arise as industrialism takes the place of slavery and as the corruptions of democracy supplant the vices of monarchy; new ideals emerge, or old ideals rise in new forms, as the primitive social organization blends into the complex, cosmopolitan society of a shrunken planet. Old sins remain but they arise amid new temptations; the old instincts assert themselves but they acquire more deadly force as they are expressed in machines and communicated through the close-knit social fabric.

III

Yet the necessity for adaptation on the part of the church is not only due to changing character of the environment. To be *in* the world means always to be somewhat *of* the world. It means that the social organization, like the individual, must become subject to physical and social laws, and that it can be effective only by observing its limitations. As soon as a principle is organized it is compromised. Freedom has the blessed sound of a pure ideal so long as it does not need to be written into a constitution. Christian brotherhood is a reality so long as it does not need to adopt bylaws. The position of the church as an organized society within organized civilization brings with it the inevitable accommodation of the church to the political, economic, and cultural structures of the environment. Indeed, the church may be regarded as a sociological structure subject to all the social laws to which any other social entities are subject. It is conditioned through and through by the surrounding culture with its language, its economic methods, its racial character, its fundamental intellectual attitudes. Hence it becomes a class church which must use revivalism or liturgism in order to reach its charges but which becomes influenced in doctrine and its whole conception of the Christian life by the method it must espouse. Or it becomes a national church which must use the language of its nation, but is separated by language and national genius from other branches of the church universal. Or it becomes a racial church which becomes all things to some men only by sacrificing the ambition of becoming all things to all men. This is the central element in the problem of the church and the world.

Accommodation is necessary, but accommodation leads again and again to a radical denial of the universalism or of the righteousness of the gospel. Accommodation has brought in its train the church's sanction of slavery, of war, of race discrimination, of nationalism, of class inequality, of unchristian treatment of criminals and of a score of other evils. It has made the church condone a thousand other social sins which it either lacked the will or the courage to attack. Its constant temptation has been toward compromise lest it lose its position of cultural leadership.

IV

It is evident that transcendence over the world is demanded of the church even more than accommodation. The demand is that it keep itself unspotted from the world, that it represent not so much the ideal of becoming all things to all men as the ideal of a holy and righteous community within an evil world. This demand is more imperative for today than it has been for many centuries, for the world is growing constantly more frankly pagan. In family relations, in international relations, in business, the pretensions of maintaining Christian principles are being consciously abandoned in many an instance. How can the church make itself effective in proclaiming the gospel unless it openly cuts itself adrift from all involvement with the powers of this world which are so openly antagonistic to the ideals which the church must hold dear? The problem is an individual just as much as an ecclesiastical problem. Some souls animated by an intransient motive for consistency find it necessary to sever all ties that bind them to the world and to adopt a new form of monasticism. They take the vow of poverty that they may transcend the economic life of the world, the vow of pacifism that they may cut themselves loose from the sins and compromises of nationalism, the vow of celibacy that they may not be tempted to substitute loyalty to kin for loyalty to humanity. And yet their transcendence remains incomplete; for they cannot entirely divorce themselves from their civilization without divorcing themselves from the very humanity which they love and which they wish to serve. In the case of churches such efforts at transcendence are exemplified by the establishment of monastic orders and of the sects which prefer holiness to universalism. The Quakers remain to this day an outstanding example of an ecclesiastical effort to transcend the world. And the history of this group, like the history of monastic orders, is a typical example of the fate of most or all efforts of the sort. Transcendence leads again to accommodation. The holy community becomes wealthy and self-sufficient, as the holy individual tends to become Pharisaic.

V

Ultimately the problem of church and world involves us in a paradox; unless the church accommodates itself to the world it becomes sterile inwardly and outwardly; unless it transcends the world it becomes indistinguishable from the world and loses its effectiveness no less surely. Like all other paradoxes the paradox of church and world merely states, it does not solve, the problem. It is descriptive of a process whose rationality has not been discovered; it is scarcely the definition of an absolute, metaphysical fact. The process of the world in the church must be a constant rhythm of identification and withdrawal. The two poles of the rhythm are defined by the nationalist church and by the world-fleeing sect. It seems that in history ever new sectarian movements are necessary in order that the church may transcend the world to bethink itself again of its own peculiar character and of the imperative nature of the ethical demands made upon it. But in the same history movements of approach are no less necessary that the church may not lose its powers of driving into the chaotic material of civilization with its organizing gospel of love. The rhythm of approach and withdrawal need not be like the swinging pendulum, mere repetition without progress; it may be more like the rhythm of the waves that wash upon the beach; each succeeding wave advances a little farther than its predecessor, and after each withdrawal the church may enter a little farther into the world with its cleansing gospel before that gospel becomes sullied by contact with the earth.

Perhaps a period of withdrawal is now upon us. The easy identifications of church and world, of kingdom of God and civilization of natural and Christian ethics which have prevailed for the past generation are even now issuing in a strong reaction, which is most necessary if the Christian community is to realize the uniqueness and the imperativeness of the demand laid upon it. But such withdrawal will be ineffective if it does not lead in turn to a new reaction of identification.

Ways to Unity

This selection is the last chapter of Niebuhr's first book. It deserves to be classified as one of the great passages of Christian discourse of all times and places. Nearly Lincolnesque at some points, the sheer literary strength of it is amazing for a thirty-five year old scholar. The chapter reveals both the depth of his dismay over the failure of Christian denominations in America to live up to their own ideals and the reservations he had about the ability of Karl Barth's crisis theology to serve as an alternative to liberal theology's cultural compromises. It communicates his passion for an ecumenism that included not only his Evangelical Synod and the rest of Christendom, but all of Western civilization. In his estimation, only an ecumenism aimed at the reunion of all members of the human family would truly further the cause of church revitalization.

Source: *The Social Sources of Denominationalism* (New York: Henry Holt, 1929), 264–84.

I

The history of schism has been a history of Christianity's defeat. The church which began its career with the promise of peace and brotherhood for a distracted world has accepted the divisions of the society it had hoped to transform and has championed the conflicts it had thought to transcend. It began its mission with the heroic proclamation of a new humanity "where there cannot be Greek and Jew, circumcision and uncircumcision, barbarian, Scythian, bondman, freeman," but where "Christ is all and in all." It has lost the radiant hopes and high desires of its vision-attended youth and, having accepted the cynical distinctions of the old humanity, it has maintained and reinforced these by its denominational structure, often giving the sanction of the spirit to the warfare of the flesh.

FIRST PRESCRIPTIONS FOR CHURCH REVITALIZATION

From its position of leadership in the task of integrating humanity it has fallen to the position of follower in a social process guided by economic and political forces. In its denominational aspect, at least, it has become part and parcel of the world, one social institution alongside of many others, a phase of the total civilization more frequently conditioned by other cultural tendencies than conditioning them. The old vision of the time when the kingdom of this world should be transformed into a kingdom of our Lord and of his Christ has faded into the light of a common day in which the brute facts of an unchanging human nature, of the invincible fortifications of economic and political society, of racial pride, economic self-interest and *Realpolitik* appear in their grim reality. The denominationalism which has been built on these foundations is the church's confession of defeat and the symbol of its surrender.

At the same time the victorious forces of divisiveness stand self-condemned in the moment of their triumph. Modern civilization, aghast at the results of a conflict between societies which had acknowledged no higher ideal than the pride of an ignorant nationalism, looks forward fearfully and almost helplessly to a yet mightier conflagration of hates and passions it has nurtured. Remembering the holocaust which ethical stupidity ignited and science fed with fuel, it fears to face its foreboding of a yet more fateful application of the destructive knowledge which its warriors are feverishly seeking. It envisions the prospect of its death at its own hands. It contemplates the not impossible decline of its intellectual, religious, artistic, and economic activity into the unconscious, vegetative functioning of a race of fellaheen. It recalls and foresees the murder of its millions of young men, the destruction of its treasures, the enslavement of debt-ridden populations. And it knows that the way of divisive egotism is the way of doom. It regards the injustices of a class-organized, economic social order, which apportions its rewards neither according to merit nor to need, but according to the power of the strong to take the spoils; it looks upon the maddening rush of an acquisitive society intent upon the gain of possessions and yet more possessions, irrespective of their cost in spiritual and moral values; it begins to tremble before the mastery of the machine it has invented. It sees the growing fears, suspicions and hatreds of races long exploited by the nations of the West. And in its saner moments it becomes aware that it can save neither its self-esteem nor its existence nor yet the finer values its thinkers, prophets, artists and its toiling masses have wrought out, unless it is made captive to some compelling and integrating ideal which will restore to it a sense of the whole and will equip it with an ethics commensurate with the scope of its interests and of its world-embracing organization. The problem of the world is the problem of a synthesis of culture—of the building up of an organic whole in which the various interests and the separate nations and classes will be integrated into a harmonious, interacting society, serving one common end in diverse manners. Such a synthesis of culture can be built only upon a common world-view and a common ethics. Without these no civilization has flourished or left a contribution for the future. And every civilization which has possessed itself by possessing such a synthesis has received it from its religion.

For the simple and small world of Greece the religious ideal of the city-state sufficed. In it governor, warrior, artists, and artisan found their common *summum bonum*, transfigured by faith into a divine Athene and established upon the will of the gods. The medieval world was fashioned out of the remnants of empire and the raw materials of barbarism by the Catholic philosophy and ethics of the divine government. In these, the knowledge and the interests and the social life of the period were integrated, practically as well as theoretically, into a graded system, an organic whole. Compared with these ethical syntheses of its cultural forebears the modern world is atomic, confused, divided. It is at conflict with itself, for it knows of no supreme value to which it can subordinate the selfish desires of its groups and individuals and by means of which it can integrate its interests. The values to which it gives the greatest abandon are values which inherently lead to strife and conflict. They are political and economic goods which cannot be shared without diminution and which arouse cupidity and strife rather than lead to co-operation and peace. Civilization, which has always in the past depended upon its religious faith for the discovery and assertion of its values, cannot produce out of itself the devotion to a common spiritual end which will unite rather than divide it. It pins its hopes on education and science but discovers that, while these are effective in propagating ideals previously accepted and in devising means for the attainment of acknowledged values, they are ineffective as methods for the revelation of ends or for securing for the supreme value the devout loyalty of the people. The synthesis of culture, the discovery of the *summum bonum*, and the growth of devotion to this divine value, wait now as always upon a faith that can arise only out of man's commerce with the ultimate realities of the cosmos. Civilization today must look to religion for the authoritative word which will enlist its forces in the co-operative, organic endeavor to achieve the highest good. But the dilemma of the Western world lies in the fact that while it depends upon religion for the creation of a common mind and the birth of a common loyalty, the only religion available seems incapable of establishing, even within its own structure, the desired harmony.

Hence there is abroad the cry for a new religion; homesick souls delude themselves with the belief that some Eastern temple, redolent with the incense of quiet centuries, will offer a refuge from the distractions of a divided world. But new religions do not rise at the call of need; if they do appear they come in organic, evolutionary continuity with the religions of the past which they absorb and reaffirm. And it is vain to look for salvation to an Eastern faith, whose thought-forms are strange, whose spirit is foreign, whose ideals and ideas are in radical opposition to the philosophy and the interests of the modern world. Amateurs of the foreign, sentimentalists and romanticists who have no regard for the facts of their own cultural heredity and are unaware of the massive power of customs, institutions, and the established tendencies of social history, may beguile themselves with the dream of grafting upon the progressive, activist, democratic, individualistic history of the West the quietistic, impersonal, metaphysical religion of the East with its ethics of a sad compassion. The realist observer of social life, while acknowledging the aesthetic beauty of an Oriental creed, knows that the day is too far spent, the working day of the West too far advanced, for the realization of such a new dawn of Eastern light. He realizes that however great may be the distance between the creed and practice of Christendom, yet this civilization in its whole structure, from fundamental, unconscious ideas about personality and progress to the character of its economic and political life, has been conditioned by its religion. It can no more deny this fundamental factor in its cultural heredity than it can gainsay its biological sources. It is the product of its faith and by its faith it stands or falls.

II

Can that faith save the Western world? It is evident that it cannot do so in its present ecclesiastical forms, subject as these are to the very same influences which have brought civilization to its plight. Christianity as represented by denominations, which in turn are representative of the divided culture and its divisive interests, is no more able to stem the tide of disintegration in the world that it is able to set bounds to the process of disintegration within itself. Following

FIRST PRESCRIPTIONS FOR CHURCH REVITALIZATION

the leadership of nationalism and capitalism, it cannot but continue the process of schism which has marked its entire past history.

It is true that under the influence of social forces which are arising out of the modern world, with the extension of communication, the passing of provincialisms, the rise of once suppressed economic groups to financial respectability and the acceptance on the part of a vast majority of such a population as the American of a standard common culture, old lines of cleavage are being erased and the possibilities of church union on the basis of a common social background are being established. The transition from cultural heterogeneity to cultural homogeneity on the part of the American people is reflected in the tendency of the various churches to accept a common attitude toward doctrine, a common piety, and a common type of worship. The social causes which divided the denominations of the immigrants and of the sections have long ceased to be operative in many churches which continue to maintain their separate existence merely because of the pure inertia of long hallowed custom and denominational pride. But the existence of the social presuppositions of church union is no guarantee of its achievement. Some active motive sufficient to overcome denominational self-consciousness and inertia is required for the actual union of churches. Such a motive may be supplied in some instances by the necessity of competition, whether with larger Protestant groups or with Catholicism. Yet union achieved on this basis as the outcome of the counsel of expediency, is of no significance as a moral factor in the ethical integration of civilization. The efficiency of churches as educational and self-propagating societies may be improved by mergers of this character; their ethical effectiveness is scarcely touched.

Sole reliance on social factors, moreover, cannot lead Christianity very far in achieving even an external union. The social process is as likely to bring about new schisms, or the accentuation of existing divisions, as it is to produce new alliances. The impact of nationalism and nationalist culture upon the churches may lead to the unification of denominations within the states but the same process may be responsible for the emphasis of differences between such national churches and for the dangerous division of organized Christianity along political lines. A movement toward nationalist churches is, in fact, evident everywhere in Christendom. Though state churches are passing, the integration of provincial, sectional, and class denominations into great popular organizations is in process in Europe and America, as also in the development of independent Indian, Chinese, and other Eastern churches.[9] Such churches, though separate from the state, are always in danger of representing the political and cultural interests of their nations more truly than a common, international Christianity. Desirable as is the organization of an American Protestant Church from an ecclesiastical point of view, desirable also as is the growth of an indigenous Christianity in missionary lands, yet the development of these denominations may lead to an even greater subordination of Christian ethics to nationalist ethics than now prevails and to the opening up of more serious rifts in Christianity than now exist. The growth of such churches can be of ethical significance only if the social forces operative in their development can be brought under the control of the Christian ideal.

The continued division of the classes, which has been reflected in the rise of socialism as a religion—in Russia most of all but also in other European countries—will scarcely fail to issue in new schism or in the increase of antagonism between this new faith of the poor and the religion of the upper classes, if social forces alone are allowed to determine the processes of Christian history. It may be,

---

9. Niebuhr note: [Cf. Keller and Stewart, *Protestant Europe;* Rowland, *Native Churches in Foreign Fields.*]

indeed, that the continued prosperity of some nations, especially the United States, will tend to diminish the lines of division between the classes and so prevent the economic schism of religion. But it is no less probable that the coming of economic maturity and senescence with the exhaustion of raw materials, the increase of population and the growing power of a capitalist aristocracy will lead in the New World, as elsewhere, to the rise of antagonistic classes, which will assert their hostility in religious as well as in other forms. At all events the independent operation of economic and political forces no more guarantees the religious integrity of national life than it guarantees its economic and political unity. Far less does it provide for the international integration of Christianity and of humanity; in this sphere these factors alone are more likely to produce schism and new misunderstandings.

A wise leadership will avail itself of the social forces which make for union and will encourage the development of truly indigenous churches in missionary lands. It will not seek the impossible ideal of a church divorced from all of the cultural conditions of its environment. Least of all will it attempt to impress upon the Christianity of the Orient the purely European and American elements in the Western adaptations of the faith. But it will endeavor to find the line of distinction between the acceptance of merely cultural elements and the adoption or preservation of non-Christian social ethics—such as supreme devotion to the local state or to the interests and thought-forms of a social class. For helpful as the acceptance of a national language and of local forms of ritual or government may be in providing for the extension and inner assimilation of Christianity, just so perilous is the adoption of the ethics of a local nationalism, sectionalism, or racialism.

The determination of this line of division is ever one of the most difficult duties of the church. But it is not an impossible task. The individual Christian is confronted with the problem not only in the cries of nationalism, when he must determine the limits of his loyalty, but also in every adjustment which he is required to make to the economic and cultural society of which he is a part. Though he finds the decision difficult and always less than wholly Christian, he does not find it impossible. It would be far easier for him were he guided and supported in his decisions by a church which had made the attempt as a society to discover the principles which should determine the choices of individuals as well as of groups. And in many respects it is less difficult for the church to draw the line between a reasonable adjustment to social conditions and an un-Christian compromise than it is for the individual to do so. Group action in such matters is always more stable than individual action can be. Once the decision has been reached it is more likely to stand than it is in the case of the individual. In reaching its decision, also, the group finds larger support in tradition than does the individual, while the sense of group solidarity and power is no small aid in fostering the courage which is necessary for such a step. The difficulty of the task of finding the *via media* between adjustment to culture and compromise with prevailing social ethics cannot be an excuse for refusing to attempt it.

The problem itself points to the need of some other type of Christianity than the religion which merely adjusts itself to the social conditions whether these make for union or for schism. The church which seeks universality by means of such adjustment sacrifices its claim to universality. It becomes an organization intent upon the promotion of its own interests, without a sense of its responsibility to the world as a social whole. And it loses its integrity in the very process of seeking universality, because its adjustments are made to a world which, far from being a universe, is divided in many ways. A universalism which is sought by adaptation only defeats itself.

Denominational Christianity, that is a Christianity which surrenders its leadership to the social forces of national and economic life, offers no hope to the divided world. Lacking an integrating ethics, lacking a universal appeal, it continues to follow the fortunes of the world, gaining petty victories in a war it has long lost. From it the world can expect none of the prophetic guidance it requires in its search for synthesis.

III

There is another type of Christianity which is quite as ineffective though perhaps not as destructive in its contacts with civilization as is denominational Christianity. The other-worldly faith which regards the message of the gospel as applying to the individual's relation to a transcendental sphere alone and condemns every aspect of the present world, including culture, religious striving, and every attempt at amelioration of social evils as the expression of a depraved and lost will, has been resurrected today by the crisis theology of Germany and is receiving no small attention throughout Christendom. It has become a refuge for disillusioned followers of the social gospel, who have noted how much of evil may lurk in every attempted reformation, how stubborn are the instincts of individual and collective humanity, how much of hypocrisy is associated with every effort to realize the ethics of the gospel. Once more the old doctrine of the Reformation is emphasized: man and all his works are evil; there is none good save God. The only hope of men lies in the miracle of divine mercy and the only promise of the kingdom of God that men can cherish is the promise of a radical, cosmic revolution which will substitute for the present world with its natural laws as well as its social evils a new heaven and a new earth entirely different from the cosmos as it now exists. Every human effort, whether it be that of religion or of ethics, is not only futile but damnable.

Valuable as the other-worldly, transcendental version of Christian theology is, necessary as it appears as the complement of a frequently provincial social gospel, important as every individual finds its conclusions in his religious life, yet it appears simply irrelevant so far as the social task of Christianity is concerned. It is true that the eternal fate of every individual is hopeless save that divine mercy purge his compromises, forgive his sins, fulfil his thwarted desires after goodness, and redeem him from the destruction that lurks within. It is true that the ultimate, cosmic significance of the kingdom of God must far transcend all mundane versions of the ideal for which men labor. Yet is there no relationship between these ideals and the cosmic fact? Is there no continuity between the divine mercy and those angels of man's better nature which struggle with the demons of the jungle in his individual and corporate life? Whatever be the final outcome for the individual or for society—and this the religious man cannot but leave in the hands of God—the duty of dealing with the present world in the light of our highest ideals and best insights remains inescapable. And the situations in the "here and now" do not yield to the simple device of condemning, as equally sinful, the reformation and the evil to be reformed, the search for unity and the divisions to be overcome. Between the white and black of absolute good and absolute evil there are infinite numbers of shades of gray and between any two of these shades there may be vast and important distinctions. The church cannot escape responsibility for the present order of civilization by referring men to some transcendental sphere where all their efforts are revealed as equally marked with guilt and imperfection. There remain in addition to the realms of perfection and sin various degrees of imperfection, of justice and injustice. To say, as the crisis theology says, that religion as a human enterprise stands self-condemned by its mundane and human character is to ignore the obligation which lies upon religion, just as a human enterprise, to substitute the better for the good or the less bad for the bad and to penetrate the stuff of existence, so far as possible, with so much of saving knowledge and so much of redeeming effort as are available. To anticipate attainment too easily has ever been a weakness of religion; to anticipate the attainment of peace with God by reliance upon His mercy rather than on human effort is an inescapable necessity; but to anticipate the attainment of His righteous rule by reliance on eschatological miracle and meanwhile to condemn all efforts to work out human salvation by the best endeavor of which men are capable, is to reduce religion to an ethical anodyne.

If denominational Christianity is surrender to the world, this sort of theological Christianity is escape from the world. Neither variety offers any hope for the church or for mundane humanity. Is there not available some form of the Christian faith which possesses both the compelling ideal that can bring inner unity to the world and courage to undertake the penetration of human society with that ideal despite the difficulties and confusions which tempt to surrender or to flight?

IV

The Christianity of the gospels doubtless contains the required ideal. Its purpose is not the foundation of an ecclesiastical institution or the proclamation of a metaphysical creed, though it seeks the formation of a divine society and presupposes the metaphysics of a Christlike God. Its purpose is the revelation to men of their potential childhood to the Father and their possible brotherhood with each other. That revelation is made not in terms of dogma but of life, above all in the life of Christ. His sonship and his brotherhood, as delineated in the gospel, are not the example which men are asked to follow if they will, but rather the demonstration of that character of ultimate reality which they can ignore only at the cost of their souls. The *summum bonum* which this faith sets before men is nothing less than the eternal harmony of love, in which each individual can realize the full potentiality of an eternal life in self-sacrificing devotion to the Beloved Community of the Father and all the brethren.

The appeal of that ideal to the world is unmistakable. Adumbrated by social and ethical science, gropingly anticipated even by economics, illustrated in the life of the family at its best, allegorized in the nobler aspects of patriotism, fumblingly essayed in the endless political experiments, seen in the dark glass of reason by philosophers and prophets, it is the unknown good which men have ignorantly worshipped and long sought after that haply they might find it. The Christian ideal wakes an answering response in many a human heart. It is able to command a loyalty far deeper and more extensive than that which the church in its mundane aspects can claim. Leaders of Oriental nationalism and Western socialism, remote though they may be from the church and its dogma, are often not far from this ideal of the kingdom of heaven. Among the masses of men betrayed into useless toil and murderous warfare by the ethics of the world, the yearning for a fairer social order is frequently readier to accept the guidance of this faith than the cynical counsel of self-interest and class warfare. Throughout mankind there is a vast fund of latent energy and devotion which awaits release and guidance by such an ideal as that of the Gospels. In this ideal of the highest good, in this world-view of the kingdom of love and in this conception of the ethical life of men, if anywhere, there is the available material for the creative synthesis of human culture and for the organic integration of mankind into a functional whole.

For the proclamation of this Christianity of Christ and the Gospels a church is needed which has transcended the divisions of the world and has adjusted itself not to the local interests and needs of classes, races, or nations but to the common interests of mankind and to the constitution of the unrealized kingdom of God. No denominational Christianity, no matter how broad its scope, suffices for the task. The church which can proclaim this gospel must be one in which no national allegiance will be suffered to infringe upon the unity of an international fellowship. In it the vow of love of enemy and neighbor and the practice of non-resistance will need to take their place beside the confession of faith and the rites. For without complete abstention from nationalist ethics the universal fellowship of this church would inevitably fall apart into nationalist groups at the threat of war or under the influence of jingoistic propaganda. In such a church distinctions between rich and poor will be abrogated by the kind of communism of love which prevailed in the early Jerusalem community. This communism differs as radically from the dictatorship of the proletariat as it does from the dictatorship of capitalism. The principle of harmony and love upon which it alone can be established requires that each contribute to the community according to his ability and receive from it according to his need, not according to some predetermined principles of quantitative equality or of privilege. Furthermore, this church of love will need to bridge the chasm between the races, not only by practising complete fellowship within the house of God but by extending that practice into all the relationships of life. It will need to mediate the differences of culture by supplying equality of opportunity to tutored and untutored alike and by giving each their share in the common task and in the common love.

Only such a church can transcend the divisions of men and by transcending heal them; only such a church can substitute for the self-interest and the machinery of denominationalism the dominant desire for the kingdom and its righteousness and the free activity of familiar fellowship. It requires from its members the sacrifice of privilege and pride and bids each count the other better than himself. It can plant within the nations a fellowship of reconciliation which will resist the animosities nurtured by strife for political and economic values—a fellowship which, doubtless, may often be required to carry crosses of shame and pain when the passions of men have been aroused for conflict.

To describe such a church, it will be objected, is only to describe another sect, which will be added to the denominations and increase the confusion. But the church of fellowship in love need never be a sect. Rather it has always existed as a church within the churches. It is no mere vision born of desire. It is a fellowship with a long history and a record of many victories. It flourished in the primitive church of Jerusalem, where all were one in Christ. It came to appearance in the brotherhood of the early friars under Francis' leadership. It has functioned in every movement of mercy and reconciliation. The sects which it has founded have failed to hold fast to the ideal and have become partisan champions of a provincialized gospel. They have succumbed to the interests which corporate societies must take in their own welfare and existence. They have sought to transmit the heritage of the spirit through inelastic rules and creeds which often have come to belie their original meaning. But though its sects have failed, the fellowship has continued. Again and again it has been the creative center of movements of the spirit which have penetrated the world. The band of disciples, the communities of Jerusalem and Antioch, did not fail when the sect of Jewish Christianity perished. The fellowship of love which had been nurtured among them impressed its ideals upon the ancient world. It did not change the whole world into conformity with its own pattern, to be sure, but it gave its savor, through the mediation of Paul, to the institutions of society so that family life, the relations of masters and slaves, and of the races were at least partially redeemed. The little brothers of the poor brought their influence to bear upon the medieval world in like manner. The Franciscan order was a failure, but the Franciscan movement which spread out from Portiuncula to the whole Catholic world was one of the great victorious marches of history. It penetrated palace and hovel, reviving practical piety and inscribing the grace of charity on hearts brutalized by centuries of war and oppression. The influence of George Fox and his Friends is not commensurable with the success of the Society in gaining members. The savor of friendship has penetrated from that source into regions untouched by the sect. Slavery has had to give way before it; the relations of employers and employees have been affected by it; the conscience of men at war has again and again been pricked by its example. There have been countless other, less dramatic appearances of the fellowship of love, but for the most part it does its work quietly, in hospitals under the tropical sun or in the icy north, in prisons where lovers of peace atone for the hatreds of war, in industrial establishments where owners and workers have learned to share their problems and their profits, in all the incidental and countless human contacts of men divided by color, tradition or estate.

The increase of that fellowship today is the hope of Christendom and of the world. It is the church which can save the churches from the ruin of their secularism and consequent division. It challenges the world to recall its better nature and to find unity and peace in the knowledge of the divine love upon which all stable and just social life must be built.

The road to unity which love requires denominations, nations, classes, and races to take is no easy way. There is no short cut even to the union of the churches. The way to the organic, active peace of brotherhood leads through the hearts of peacemakers who will knit together, with patience and self-sacrifice, the shorn and tangled fibers of human aspirations, faiths, and hopes, who will transcend the fears and dangers of an adventure of trust. The road to unity is the road of repentance. It demands a resolute turning away from all those loyalties to the lesser values of the self, the denomination, and the nation, which deny the inclusiveness of divine love. It requires that Christians learn to look upon their separate establishments and exclusive creeds with contrition rather than with pride. The road to unity is the road of sacrifice which asks of churches as of individuals that they lose their lives in order that they may find the fulfilment of their better selves. But it is also the road to the eternal values of a Kingdom of God that is among us.

Religion and Ethics

Niebuhr distinguished himself as a teacher of ethics in his time at Eden Seminary preparing students for pastoral ministry in the Evangelical Synod. In this area, we see unmistakable traces of the church-world paradox with which he was wrestling. To him, the failure of modern efforts to develop either an effective ethical system without faith in God (humanism) or an effective faith in God apart from ethics (crisis theology) showed that the two were inseparable. Yet they were not identical; each needed to reaffirm a cosmic basis for evaluating human behavior for different reasons. Niebuhr believed such renewal was bound to produce in religious leaders convictions capable of working real changes in society as well as in its individual members.

Source: *The World Tomorrow* 13 (November 1930): 443–46.

I

A characteristic feature of modern culture is the divorce between religion and ethics. The effort to differentiate the two is expressed, first of all, in the psychology of religion which emphasizes the element in faith that it does not share with ethics, art, or science. It does this by tracing the historical source of religious experience to the sense of awe felt in the presence of *mana* and by defining the object of worship as the Holy—that indefinable, majestic reality before which man experiences tremor and the feeling of unworthiness rather than any sense of kinship. Contemporary interest in mysticism—in which God is not so much an ethical will to be obeyed as a pure Being with whom union is sought—and in the development of worship—which, in opposition to service, is again regarded by many as the proper function of the church—also leads to the distinction between religion and ethics.

Even more significant than these religious and theological movements are the ethical tendencies which seek the same divorce of morals and faith but for antithetical reasons. In the theory of ethics tendencies of this sort are very old, going back to the moral philosophy of the Greeks, experiencing a great revival in the Illumination and with Kant, and moving forward with increasing vigor to our own times. Whether the ethical principle is sought in the realm of ideas or values, or in autonomous conscience, or in the desire for pleasure and the fear of pain, or in an instinctive sympathy, in a sense of obligation for social welfare, or in the value of self-realization—in every instance the effort is made to found morality upon a factor available to all men, irrespective of their religious or metaphysical beliefs.

This movement toward an ethics independent of faith has achieved a previously unknown significance in our day because of the popular increase of irreligion and the necessity for discovering a basis of worthy conduct for men whose faith in the moral authority of religion has been dissolved by the processes of modern civilization. The result is the humanistic movement which seeks not only to establish ethics in independence of religion but also to substitute moral ideals for faith and to win for the former the enthusiasms and devotions historically associated with the latter. Continental socialism, especially communism, shares two things with humanism: a desire to found a social ethic upon non-religious bases, and an animosity toward the metaphysics of faith as well as toward the moral codes connected with the dominant historic forms of Christianity.

The divorce of ethics from religion is, however, far more thorough and extensive than these limited social philosophies indicate. Theory, here as elsewhere, is the reflection of or answer to a social situation. The emancipation of business, state-craft, science, education, art and—most recently—the family from religious control has led to an effort to seek guidance from principles resident in "nature" or "reason." As with the institution, so with the individual. The emancipation of the latter from religious and social control, beginning with the Reformation and reaching its highest development with the atomization of life in industrial civilization, the division and conflict of interests which arise out of an individual's participation in unharmonized and conflicting social institutions—these have left him with a variety of codes of conduct, uncoordinated among themselves and uncoordinated with any religious faith. The latter, indeed, has become a purely private matter—an attitude toward the universe rather than a source of moral revelation and inspiration.

II

While the movement toward the separation of ethics from religion is of long standing, it is as yet impossible to speak with any assurance of its results. Up to the present time neither theoretical nor social and cultural ethics have been able to produce out of their own resources moral codes of recognized validity. They have achieved no such general recognition as is required for any really effective ethical standard. The types of ethical authority urged by the various theorists or accepted by the different groups are of so many sorts and so often conflicting that it is impossible to obtain a consensus. Individuals here and there, it is true, have found the basis for a worthy if not always a hopeful life in principles or considerations that have nothing to do with religion. But so far as the winning of a general set of principles is concerned, upon which men can build the structure of their social life—principles similar to the foundations of science—ethics without religion has made little progress. Russian communism alone has been able to produce an effective social ethics, and it has succeeded only by means of the double device of building its morals upon the metaphysical, semi-religious assumptions of Marxism and of enforcing them through the all-powerful authority of the state. For the rest, the effort to establish ethics without religion has left us with a moral anarchy in which each social institution is a law unto itself, where there is no good beyond that of the state, where business is business and art is carried on for art's sake, and where the last word to the individual is "Let your conscience be your guide."

On the other hand, the failure of the ethical movement to found a morality independent of religion is evident from the large extent to which it has unconsciously borrowed from the Jewish and Christian ethics, while consciously rejecting the metaphysics originally connected with these systems. This is true of theoretical as well as of popular ethical movements. It has often been pointed out that in his effort to develop a purely rational ethics Kant was not a little influenced by his pietistic education, and that the actual ethical principles which he sought to derive from his rationalism were definitely Christian in content. Later utilitarian ethics is likewise indebted to Christianity for its social ideals, while modern humanism seems to regard as "self-evident truths of reason" moral ideals and principles which have their historic roots in the prophecy of the Old Testament and in the gospel of the New. Nor is it an accident that many of the leaders of socialism have been Jews who, though they rejected the faith of their fathers, could not forget the cry for justice in the pages of Amos and Isaiah and Micah. The line of descent to other socialist programs leads from the Jerusalem community through early and medieval sects, Anabaptists and Quakers, to the nineteenth century. Socialism is definitely a western movement which has entered Oriental nations only after Christian missions prepared the ground for it.

What is true of social ethics is true also of those moral principles which govern the individual life in its less complex relations. Modern morality is characterized by the continuance of a considerable number of principles and habits which were derived from Christianity or Judaism but are now maintained apart from faith.

So it remains true that ethics without religion has thus far failed to produce or to make effective an independent morality. Religion without ethics must record an equal failure. Mysticism, like pure ethics, has been able to achieve some valid insights of its own, but when it has sought to communicate itself or to become a social and historical religion, it has found it necessary to re-introduce ethics into its faith; otherwise it has remained, again like ethics without religion, a purely private matter without authority save for the individual who achieved the mystical experience. A theology of pure transcendence eventually becomes a theology without content; it stops where it begins—with the assertion of divine transcendence. But if it seeks to make religion effective in the individual or the social life, it will inevitably associate itself with ethics.

III

Yet the justice of the two revolts—of ethics against religion and of religion against ethics—must be conceded. Because Christianity in its historic forms often associated itself with systems of metaphysical belief which became increasingly difficult for men living in the modern world to hold honestly, ethics was impelled to seek more certain foundations for its principles. That it involved itself in uncertainties at least as great as those from which it escaped is true; yet the effort remained necessary under the conditions. In the second place, the revolt of ethics against religion was inevitable because religion—Christianity in particular—had often become untrue to many of its own original, moral principles and had adopted an ethics inconsistent with its faith. So there appeared the remarkable phenomena of a Christian ethics which had adopted a non-Christian ethics. The third reason for the revolt of ethics against identification with religion lay in the demands made upon ethics by modern industrialism. The increasing complexities of the latter offered an opportunity for new ethical development and demanded the extension and refinement of inherited moral ideals. But theological and ecclesiastical conservatism prevented organized Christianity from making the adjustments required and meeting the opportunities offered. That failure called for an independent system of ethics.

The justice of the revolt of theology against ethics is less obvious, but the movement is not without legitimate foundation. The tendency to identify Christianity with western civilization, to define the religious object as well as religious endeavor in purely social terms, invited a reaction. It was inevitable that nineteenth century "religion within the limits of humanity" should issue in the extreme antithesis of a twentieth century "religion within the limits of deity."

IV

When these religious and ethical movements of our time are considered not merely as contemporary phenomena but in the light both of history and of the intrinsic relation between faith and morality, their meaning and the desirable though not necessary result of their interaction are disclosed.

Religion and ethics seem to be related somewhat as are the two natures of Christ according to the ancient formula: they are inseparable and indivisible, but are not to be confused or identified with each other. They have been inseparable in history insofar as all decisive religious advances have been made in close connection with new social experience and resultant ethical insight, and insofar as all great ethical systems—not those of theory but those of practical conduct—have been the product of religious movements. Moses and the prophets, Jesus and Paul, Gotama and Vardhamana, Zoroaster and Mohammed were not only the founders of great religious movements but the sources of great ethical systems. In theory also the relationship has been close. From Plato to Kant and Sidgwick and Hobhouse, ethical theory has revealed its need for a religious interpretation of the universe if it was to carry its thought to a worthy conclusion, while theology has been more rather than less dependent upon ethics for its definition of the essential constitution of the universe. Modern attempts to define goodness as value without metaphysical basis of any sort, or to define God as reality without any definition of his ethical character, end with unsatisfactory and ultimately intolerable constructions—houses without roofs. They leave one with only the choice between a complete relativism and a complete dogmatism, and so sap meaning and motive from both ethics and religion.

On the other hand, the identification of religion and ethics leads to a no less unsatisfactory and irrational result. Such identification, when made under the auspices of religion, either confounds ethical principle with the moral rules strictly relative to a certain historical and social situation and absolutizes a system of moral dogma, or it confines the definition of ethical truth to eternal principles from which no effective guidance for the moral life may be gained, so that individuals and especially social institutions are left without ethical control. Puritanism has tended toward the first of these fallacies, Lutheranism toward the second. If the identification is made under the auspices of ethics, however, religion is robbed of vitality, either because God is identified with social goodness as defined from the relative point of view of a particular epoch and social institution so that the transcendent and disinterested point of view of faith is lost, or he is defined in terms of ethical demand only, without that element of love which is beyond good and evil, yet gives both good and evil their tragic, redemptive meaning. If it would maintain its valid and vital element, religion must bethink itself not only of the goodness of God but also of those elements of divinity which constitute its "plus"—its beyond-good-and-evil, its transcendence and forgiveness. If ethics would develop its intention to the full, it must discover not only its eternal authority in a cosmic constitution, but also its responsibility to temporal problems and cultural values; it must seek not only the definition of the absolutely good and the absolutely bad, but it must remember its obligation to realize the better and to prevent the worse. The field of ethics is time, but the conditions of its effectiveness in time is its co-conscious awareness of eternity. The field of religion is eternity, but the condition of its realization of eternity is a co-consciousness of time. The peril of ethics alone is relativity, and the peril of isolated religion is the dogmatism of an absolute, irrelevant to time. The salvation of ethics is religion, and the salvation of religion is ethics.

Hence the relation of ethics and religion appears to be conceivable not so much after the analogy of the organism as after the pattern of social structure. It is a relation of support within a system of strains and tensions. At present the strains and tensions are more evident than the support. The development of rebellious tendencies within each sphere has been necessary not only for the sake of particular interests but also for the sake of the eventual support which they can give each other. Yet unless it leads to a new cooperation, rebellion will become its own nemesis. Whether a system of mutual support will again be realized, no one can prophesy; but it seems evident that, if it is to be realized, it must be worked out first of all in the field of practice—in the winning of ethical awareness of the cosmic basis of moral obligations—and in the gaining of religious convictions which will make a difference in the social and ethical life.

The Social Gospel and Liberal Theology

The article that follows is the last that Niebuhr wrote while he was still on the faculty at Eden Seminary. Unlike others who had become enamored with Karl Barth's crisis theology, Niebuhr was never ready to jettison the struggling Social Gospel. To be an effective force for change in America, the movement needed to become "as honest and as radical in its criticism of the social order of human sin as that order itself and the ethics of Jesus require." Revitalization meant finding a new theology that would replace the utopian faith in humanity and in the progress of civilization with which the Social Gospel had chosen to clothe itself. This prescription was one that Niebuhr would continue to advocate throughout the 1930s.

Source: *The Keryx* 22, no. 8 (May 1931): 12–13, 18.

Probably the outstanding theological development of recent years is the passing of the liberal theology. With the coming of the great disillusionment upon western civilization two of the foundation stones of that theology—its faith in man and in progress—have been undermined and the structure reared upon them shows signs of rapid disintegration. It may be only a question of a few years until liberalism will be as dead as fundamentalism is, which is to say that while it will continue to represent the orthodoxy of some sections of Christianity it will have lost vitality and meaningfulness, remaining often an inherited but unpossessed tradition. The drift of contemporary religious thinking is moving slowly but surely from the optimism of liberalism to pessimism, from humanism to theism, from immanence to transcendence, from subjectivism to objectivism. Liberalism in theology accompanies liberalism in political and economic thought and idealism in philosophy into a common decline. This fact does not mean that men, especially theologians, will ever be able to think and to live as though the liberal theology had never been; it is historic—an inescapable part of the past on which the future must build. Some of the results of the great liberal theology of the nineteenth century have become part of the theological capital of the future and will scarcely be abandoned. This appears to be true of the results of its critical research into the Biblical documents, of its painstaking labors in history, of its analysis of religious psychology, of its studies in the relation of religion and culture. These results may not seem as important to a new theology as they did to the old but though they become of secondary significance they will not thereby be denied.

A question which arises in view of this passing of liberalism is whether the "social gospel" will pass along with it. For the relations of social idealism with liberalism seem to have been very close. Many of the exponents of the "social gospel" were also liberal theologians, which may mean much or nothing. The doctrine of progress which identified the Kingdom of God with that perfect state toward which mankind was moving by sheer virtue of its inherent intelligence and nobility, was often uncritically accepted by the "social gospel." Both liberalism and Christian socialism frequently evaded the deeply religious question of the significance of the present moment and of the present generation and their relation to the eternal God, while they found the ultimate meaning of life in some state of perfection that was to be achieved in time. Both also inclined to forget the fact of sin or to reduce its significance. Despite these and other relations which might be pointed out it is not true that Christian socialism is the ethical consequence of liberal theology or that the two are inherently related. The relations between theology and ethics are never unilateral so that an ethical system can be treated as the direct result of a theological system. They do influence each other profoundly, but ethics influences theology as often as theology influences ethics and their combinations are sometimes more psychological and sociological in character than logical. A very important reason for the association of liberalism and Christian socialism in the past was the fact that the alternative to liberalism, fundamentalism so-called, was upon the whole inimical to the social gospel and represented that acceptance of a sinful world which allowed the radical protest of Christianity against sin in its corporate forms to sink into silence, preaching a repentance which failed to direct the attention of piety to an extremely powerful and vicious realm of human sin and satanic influence. A further reason for the association lay in the ethical emphasis of liberal theology; here was a theology which was apparently interested in social justice and which, though it spoke softly about present evils, did set forth the Christian hope in ethical terms. Under these circumstances the affiliation of "social gospel" and liberalism was at least explicable.

But the union has not been a happy one. During recent years Christian socialists have become increasingly restive in the affiliation. The liberal theology seemed totally inadequate to account for the toughness, the resistant power, the tremendous inertia of sin in its social character and those who felt this force and its penetration of all life, including their own, realized that the doctrine of original sin, however obscured by myth and allegory, had a meaning which liberalism could not grasp. The liberal theology, moreover, was associated in practice with the religion of rather comfortable middle classes whose preachers seemed much more interested in interpreting religion in inoffensive than in challenging terms and often devoted their whole attention to the task of making Christianity intellectually conformable to current world-views rather than to present the devastating judgment which that faith passed on our ethical worldliness. The students of "the social gospel" knew that whatever liberalism might say about the intellectual comfortableness of

Christianity, ethically it was hard, insuperably hard, a bed of thorns not roses. And they began to suspect that all of this pre-occupation with the intellectual interpretation of the faith represented an unconscious but very real evasion of its judgments upon man. Moreover the doctrine of progress and the Utopianism associated with the liberal theology failed to carry that note of imperativeness which the "social gospel" found in Christianity and in the actual needs of men condemned to death by nationalistic wars and to impoverishment of body, mind and spirit by the heedless processes of industrialism. The believer in the ethical mission of Christianity and in the infinite value of human souls in the sight of God could not finally reconcile himself to a program which regarded all present individuals from the viewpoint of a distant future as instruments of social progress rather than as ends. The crucial importance of the present moment, of this generation, seemed to him to be quite inadequately recognized in the liberal theology. These and other considerations showed that there was a hiatus between the liberal theology and the "social gospel" which was not accidental but went very deep.

It is not an accident that the revolt against liberalism in theology should have been led in Germany by men who in their earlier years had identified themselves with the Christian socialist movement, that the influence of such a leader as Hermann Kutter should have been great upon some of them, that of Ernst Troeltsch upon others, or that to this day some of the leaders of the new theology preserve a social radicalism of pronounced type despite the logical difficulties which they encounter in associating their ethics with their theology. It cannot be said that the revolt against liberalism in theology is a product of the social ethical movement, for it was the religious inadequacy of liberalism rather than its ethical inadequacy which was decisive in the beginning of the revolt, but the new movement was at least partially re-enforced by considerations which were due to the social ethical inquiry and interest. Whether or not the religious revolt will extend to America, it does appear necessary that in this country the "social gospel" movement dissociate itself as completely as possible from liberalism, not for the sake of turning to an equally impossible alternative, that of fundamentalism, but for the sake of maintaining its integrity as a movement which dares not compromise the absoluteness of the ethical demand it hears from Jesus by accommodating that demand to the innocuous optimism of liberalism and to the latter's penchant for investing the compromise arrangements of human self-interest with the sanction of divinity. The release from liberalism is necessary to the "social gospel" in order that it may be as honest and as radical in its criticism of the social order of human sin as that order itself and the ethics of Jesus require. Without the preaching of repentance the "social gospel" like the "individual gospel" has lost its salt and liberalism has failed the social gospel by reducing that element of the gospel to a minor note.

If the "social gospel" can no longer ally itself with liberalism, with what theology shall it associate itself? Perhaps the question is erroneously put, and should rather be phrased, what sort of a theology do the ethical convictions which are summarized under the term "social gospel" require? But to work out the implications of the social gospel for theology is not to frame a theology. There can be no such things as a theology for the social gospel if by that we mean a theology based exclusively on the social ethics of Christianity, for the ethical apprehension of man in society is not the only apprehension he suffers from the side of Eternity, nor is the condemnation to which he is subject only historical and social. The cry for justification can no more be identified with the cry for justice than the latter can be interpreted as wholly including the former. It was not only its ethical but also its religious failure which prepared the disintegration of liberalism. On the other hand the "social gospel" as the radical acceptance of the radical ethics of Jesus in their explicit and implicit references to man as a social being and to society as a sphere of sin and salvation must form an integral part of any theological system which grows out of the contemporary reading and interpretation of the Christian revelation. To leave it out is to leave out not only the vital social experience of the present but elements in the gospel which have been too often obscured. To build a theological system which omits the experience of social condemnation and the promise of social deliverance and the duty of social repentance in its premises while it seeks to add them somehow among the conclusions is to fail to relate theology vitally to one of the sources of religious life in the present. This appears to be one of the difficulties which the theology of crisis faces which despite its early relations to Christian socialism is drifting in some of its later expositions, especially in the case of [Friedrich] Gogarten, into an ethical conservatism which makes social evil and sin more an occasion for passive suffering than for radical repentance. On the other hand there are points of contact between the "social gospel" and the Barthian theology, perhaps especially in the eschatological connections of the latter and in its uncompromising doctrine of sin, which can only add energy and reality to the demands of Christian social ethics.

The passing of liberalism may, under the circumstances, be the salvation of the social gospel. But it needs more than ever as the new theology arises to insist upon the recognition of its validity and importance while disclaiming any exclusive right to determine the character of that theology. And it requires of its exponents that they think through its theological and ethical implications more intensively and radically than they have ever done before.

Niebuhr brothers in their student days, Richard third from right and Reinhold on far left.

Early 1920s photo of Eden faculty and students, Niebuhr in front row, second from left with Samuel D. Press in the middle.

Niebuhr as President of Elmhurst College.

New Eden Seminary, 1925.

Niebuhr as Eden's Academic Dean, top row, fourth from right.

PART II

The Crucible of the Great Depression

5

The Church in a World of Social Upheaval

The onset of the 1930s brought a period of significant change for H. Richard Niebuhr. Having completed seven commendable years of teaching, scholarship, and academic leadership at Eden Seminary, he began a nine-month sabbatical leave during the spring semester of 1930 that transported him and his family to Europe. Niebuhr's ambitious itinerary included research in the areas of religious philosophy and social ethics at leading universities in the British Isles and Germany, face-to-face conversations with the more prominent members of their religious faculties, and firsthand observations of church activities. A two-week tour of the Soviet Union was included as well. In addition, Yale University had recognized him as a scholar of special merit for his publication of *The Social Sources of Denominationalism* and awarded him a prestigious Sterling Fellowship. Early in 1931, Niebuhr was asked to join the faculty of its divinity school as an associate professor of Christian ethics. Although the prospect of terminating his important role in the Evangelical

Synod's program of higher education made the decision a difficult one, he accepted the appointment.

Like many an international traveler, Niebuhr found that his time in Europe altered some of his perceptions of his homeland as well as notions he had entertained about the countries he was visiting. His impressions were printed in eight articles that appeared in the weekly magazine of his church body, *The Evangelical Herald*. President Samuel D. Press of Eden Seminary also provided translations for subsequent issues of the *Herald's* counterpart in German, *Der Friedensbote*. Two other articles geared to a wider Protestant audience were published in *The Christian Century*. In one of these sabbatical articles, Niebuhr reported that Germans were using the term *Amerikanismus* in the same way that Americans used the term *Bolshevism*—to identify most anything they found undesirable, particularly the rationalization of the manufacturing process that large American corporations had first introduced. Once friendly German-American relations that had remained that way in World War I's immediate aftermath had changed for the worse. Germans were now recognizing that the war reparations imposed by the Treaty of Versailles were not just painfully compounding their country's poverty: as Britain and France used them to pay off their own war debts, American banks were in turn using the money to inflate their own nation's prosperity. In general, the German people seemed to Niebuhr to be weighted down with depression and feelings of despair. He also noted that one of their favorite words was *Schicksal*, which implied a sense of "resignation" to their postwar fate as a nation.[1] This helped furnish an explanation for the mounting appeal of fascism in Germany. To Niebuhr, Hitler offered the hope of

---

1. H. Richard Niebuhr, "German-American Relations," *The Evangelical Herald* 29 (September 4, 1930): 713, 715; "Some Observations on Religious Life in Germany," *The Evangelical Herald* 29 (August 28, 1930): 695–96.

release from the nation's "war guilt" and the promise of renewed self-respect and reform of moral and civic corruption. But his Nazi Party's blatant anti-Semitism, along with its ways of feeding Germany's appetite for chauvinism and militarism, clearly troubled him.[2] These concerns would be confirmed for him once Hitler came to power in 1933.

The state of religious life in Germany was just as eye-opening. Niebuhr often visited several different churches on a single weekend in order to assess the quality of the preaching, the proportion of young people in attendance, and attitudes toward social issues. When he attended the Lutheran celebrations of the four-hundredth anniversary of the Augsburg Confession on behalf of the Evangelical Synod, which recognized this document as a doctrinal standard, he felt that while this event seemed to signal a theological awakening in Germany, it also served to strengthen older disagreements between Protestants and Roman Catholics and to deepen more recent ones with socialists. It seemed to him that too many churches were still trying to live off past traditions. Alfred Dedo Mueller and Paul Tillich served as exceptions to this general observation. Niebuhr was particularly impressed by Mueller's efforts to promote reconciliation between the German labor movement and the church from which it had been alienated. Conversations with Tillich, moreover, helped alleviate some of his earlier concerns about crisis theology. Unlike Karl Barth, Tillich refused to exclude society from reconstructive efforts on the part of the church, and he seemed determined to keep every moment in time within the scope of God's self-revelation.[3] When Tillich's book *Die religiöse Lage der Gegenwart* was published

---

2. H. Richard Niebuhr, "Germany After the Election," *The Evangelical Herald* 29 (November 13, 1930): 911, 915.
3. H. Richard Niebuhr, "Some Observations on Religious Life in Germany," *The Evangelical Herald* 29 (July 10, 1930): 556–57; Ibid. (July 17, 1930), 575; Ibid. (August 21, 1930), 676–77.

as *The Religious Situation* in English in 1932, it was Niebuhr who provided the translation. Once Tillich left Nazi-controlled Germany the next year for America, moreover, he would continue to play a pivotal role in the development of Niebuhr's theological outlook on the church and the world.

On the basis of his firsthand observations in the Soviet Union, Niebuhr concluded that "a pessimistic view of the future of religion in Russia seems to be more justified than an optimistic one." During his two weeks there, he found churches and chapels on almost every corner of Moscow, and he visited as many as five Russian Orthodox worship services on a Saturday evening. Here he saw ample evidence of an old faith that was persisting as a source of comfort for the weary souls of every generation among the Russian masses. On the other hand, the obvious contrast between the drab poverty in which so many of them were now living and the luxurious artifacts of the church only appeared to lend credibility to Karl Marx's axiom that religion served as an "opiate" for such people. In addition, his visit to a monastery the Soviets had turned into an antireligious museum provided a graphic example of the link they were making between much of Russian Orthodox Christianity and the ignorance and superstition of the czarist past from which the Russian Revolution had achieved liberation. While Niebuhr acknowledged that a church's "baptism of fire" might prove to be a source of its "salvation," he was more convinced that "ethically and theologically the dominant faith of Russia continues to live in the Middle Ages."[4]

Niebuhr's assessment of the "Soviet experiment" was more positive. Americans for the most part tended to put communism in an entirely unfavorable light because of the threat it posed to capitalism, and for this reason many hoped that the Soviet version of it would be

---

4. H. Richard Niebuhr, "Some Observations on Russia," *The Evangelical Herald* 29 (October 9, 1930): 815–16.

doomed to failure. For Niebuhr, the visit to Russia seems to have produced a more balanced assessment of both economic systems. What impressed him the most was the commitment on the part of the Soviet government to the principle of equality. This commitment not only kept rental rates low enough for unskilled workers to live in housing comparable to that of more educated professionals but also appeared to energize the people, despite the gray monotony of their surroundings, as they went about their work of building a new nation.[5] In the years immediately following his European sabbatical, Niebuhr tended to stress points of convergence between Marxism and Christianity. Both, in his estimation, recognized that there were forces at work in history beyond human control, and both inspired a trust that something better would eventually emerge from the ashes of misery and discontent the present order had created. However, Niebuhr's optimism with respect to Russia would be tempered as the Stalinist purges came to light in the second half of the 1930s.

When he and his family returned to America, Niebuhr found their homeland sinking into the depths of the Great Depression. By the time President Herbert Hoover left office following the election of 1932, the national income had been cut in half and unemployment stood at fifteen million. Niebuhr's son Richard recalls witnessing some of the devastating effects of this economic contraction on frequent automobile trips his father made back to the Midwest from Yale's campus in New Haven, Connecticut: "Most conspicuous were the homeless men trudging along the roadside, asking for whatever food and milk we might spare from midday picnic meals we spread along the verge of the asphalt roads."[6] In this kind of crucible, political and religious views tend to gravitate to extremes. Christian

---

5. Ibid. (October 2, 1930), 795–96.
6. Richard R. Niebuhr, "Foreword," in William Stacy Johnson, ed., *H. Richard Niebuhr: Theology, History, Culture* (New Haven, CT: Yale University Press, 1996), viii.

Socialists, for whom Reinhold Niebuhr became a leading voice, renounced unbridled capitalist economics. A coalition of right-wing demagogues gained sympathy as well, led by Father Charles Coughlin, Gerald Winrod, and Gerald L. K. Smith. These men would use the medium of radio to feed their listeners a steady diet of anti-Semitism, anti-Communism, and criticism of New Deal programs. In addition, the repeal of Prohibition in 1933 seemed to signal a clear victory for America's urban civilization in its war against older mores, and in terms in church membership and financial support of the Protestant establishment, the "religious depression" that had been well underway since the mid-1920s only seemed to be continuing its downward spiral.[7]

Only three months after he joined the faculty at Yale Divinity School, Niebuhr gave an Alumni Lecture the he titled "Theology in a Time of Disillusionment." In it, he provided a sobering overview of the pessimism concerning the state of Western civilization that novelists, psychologists, and biographers were expressing in no uncertain terms. The devastating effects of the social upheavals he had witnessed with the onset of the Great Depressions in Europe as well as at home were clearly on his mind; they only appeared to strengthen the plea he had begun to utter already in the previous decade for the church to replace the "anthropocentric" viewpoint that had dominated liberal Protestant thinking for more than a half century with one that was more "theocentric" in character.[8] I have selected the articles that follow in order to demonstrate how these upheavals helped bring him to this point and shape his thinking as he continued to wrestle with the paradox of church and world.

---

7. See Sydney E. Ahlstrom, *A Religious History of the American People* (New Haven, CT: Yale University Press, 1972), 918–31.
8. H. Richard Niebuhr, "Theology in a Time of Disillusionment," in Johnson, ed., *H. Richard Niebuhr,* 102–16.

Some Observations on Religious Life in Germany

During his nine-month sabbatical in Europe, Niebuhr wrote four articles on the subject of German religious life. The last of them was selected because it contains a more wide-ranging set of observations. Niebuhr quickly discovered that the homeland of his forebears was mired politically and psychologically in the "war guilt" imposed by the Allies in the Treaty of Versailles. This problem, more than the depressed economic situation, seemed to cast a pall over the whole nation and to stir up old antagonisms between Protestants and Catholics. Hence he found the outlook expressed in German churches notably less optimistic than what he was accustomed to experiencing in America.

Source: *The Evangelical Herald* 29 (August 28, 1930): 695–96.

A characteristic feature of modern German culture is the sharpness of the antitheses which prevail in its various spheres of thought and activity. Whatever may have been the case in pre-war Germany, the national tendency today is toward sharp differentiation of opinions and toward the contrast rather than toward the harmonization of differences. In religion this tendency expresses itself not only in the conflict of theological opinions within Protestantism, but even more in the antagonism between Catholicism and Protestantism.

This antagonism is fundamentally political. Catholicism presents an almost united political front in the Centrum party of the Reichstag, and Protestants are very much aware of the fact that Catholics have played a decisive role in the politics of recent times. The Prime Ministers Fehrenbach, Kuno [Cuno], Wirth, and Bruening, and a large proportion of past and present Cabinet ministers were or are Catholics. From private and from semi-official sources one hears the complaint that the Catholic party is appropriating a disproportionately large number of civil service positions for the appointment of Catholics. An unusually large number of administrative positions in education, it is said, are filled by Catholic appointees. In all of this one sees a directed effort on the part of the Roman Church to secure a decisive position in Germany.

An interesting development is the appointment of professors to chairs of Catholic philosophy at universities. (*Katholische Weltanschauung*) When Troeltsch, professor of philosophy at Berlin, died in 1924 Catholic newspapers demanded that his chair be filled by a Catholic. So far the chair has not been filled but it was regarded as significant that a former Catholic, who still stands close to Catholicism was called, though he did not accept. At Breslau a chair for Catholic philosophy has been established and its incumbent also lectures at Berlin. At Frankfurt also a professor of Catholic philosophy has been appointed. In order to understand the significance of this one must remember that all German universities are state universities, and it is felt in Protestant circles that the establishment of Catholic chairs is a direct violation of the spirit of university education.

In addition to the political and educational conflict there is constant friction between the churches in their close associations in city and country. When Professor Seeberg delivered a radio address in commemoration of the four hundredth anniversary of the presentation of the Augsburg Confession Catholic newspapers outdid each other in pouring scorn upon him. There are constant conversions from Catholicism to Protestantism and vice versa, although the number of Catholics who become Protestants is considerably greater than the number of Protestants who turn to Catholicism.

All of this has its bearings upon the Lutheran renaissance in Germany. The return to the Protestant doctrine of the 16th century which marks contemporary German theology and preaching is in part a reaction against contemporary Catholicism, though it is also a reaction against socialism. The alliance of this reaction with social conservatism represents the weakness of Protestantism as the alliance of Catholicism with social reform movements represents the strength of the Roman faith. Catholic renaissance and Lutheran renaissance oppose each other with a sharpness of antithesis that has probably been rarely equalled since the days of Reformation and Counter-reformation.

At present politics occupy very much of the center of the stage in Germany. The dissolution of the Reichstag and the coming general elections, attempts to combine some of the many small parties into conservative and liberal groups, frictions within the parties leading to divisions and new political formations—these are not only the almost exclusive subject of newspaper reporting and comment but also a very general subject of conversation. Germany feels that it is moving toward a very important crisis and in many sections it is facing the crisis with little hope. In university lectures and in many sermons the note of hopelessness is strongly emphasized; it colors religious thought no less than political and economic discussion; probably it is even more pronounced in the former than in the latter two.

A favorite word here is *Schicksal*, which is used more in the sense of "fate" than of "destiny." It means resignation to the lot of post-war Germany, yet it often seems to imply something nearer to despair than resignation. Only rarely is it used in the sense of destiny, with an overtone of hopefulness and of encouragement to master fate.

One often wonders whether this attitude is based primarily on objective, economic and political conditions or on the psychological state of a nation which has had to make the tremendous readjustment which was required of the great pre-war Germany. The burden of taxation is exceedingly heavy, the number unemployed is great and increasing daily, the political leadership of the nation—as the

Reichstag dissolution indicates—is quite inadequate. To these must be added the moral problems which Germany feels no less keenly than do other nations—the problem of city youth and the decline of moral standards. And in addition there is the difficulty of adjustment to the new industrialism which has arisen out of the increased rationalization of manufacture. Germans seem to be far less reconciled to the machine than Americans are. Many of them rejoice in its possibilities, more of them seem to fear or to hate it. All of these problems increase the sense of crisis.

But there is another side to the picture. German unemployment does not seem to be as serious as that of England; it is probably no greater, proportionately, than that of America. Poverty is by no means pronounced; one is frequently told that people eat better now than they did before the war; a newspaper reports that the wool-growing industry is in difficulties because Germans use less of their own coarse but durable wool than they did in the past, requiring a finer imported wool; this applies not only to individuals but also to the army and railroads, which now specify the use of imported wool for uniforms. Such things may mean little. But they may mean that the weight which lies on Germany is more moral and psychological than economic and political. That does not make it less onerous, but more depressing. The sense of being oppressed, the knowledge that one must pay tribute—as they call it here, "reparations," as they say in former allied nations—for scores of years, that one is without military defense in a continent otherwise armed to the teeth—these are feelings, compounded of rebellion, resignation, fear which weigh more heavily upon the soul than do actual hunger or poverty.

The note of fate is a somber, heavy tone. It is the extreme opposite of the tone of Pollyanna optimism which one sometimes hears in American churches, but it may be no less dangerous in its final results.

Germany after the Election

Hitler's ascendancy as Chancellor of Germany was still several years away when Niebuhr wrote this article. Yet the election conducted in the fall of 1930 made it clear to him that Hitler and his fascist Brownshirts were a political force with which Germany and the rest of the world would need to reckon. In retrospect, Niebuhr appears to offer an evenhanded evaluation of the election; at the same time, he did not conceal his concerns about the politics of the Nazi Party. Once Hitler seized power he would come to recognize, along with Dietrich Bonhoeffer and those who joined his resistance movement within the Reichskirche, *how woefully unprepared the churches were for dealing with efforts to bring them into alignment (*Gleichschaltung*) with all of the policies Germany's self-proclaimed Führer was imposing upon the entire nation.*

Source: *The Evangelical Herald* 29 (November 13, 1930): 911, 915.

With the approach of winter the gloom which has been manifest in Germany all this year is growing ever thicker. The continuation and aggravation of the world economic crisis, which presses on this nation more heavily than on any other, the daily additions to the number of unemployed, the constant fear of a large number of workers that this week's or this month's pay envelope may be their last, the increase of taxes—already exceedingly high—for those still fortunate enough to have an income, the threat of large wage reductions in the great industries, the fear of political upheavals and a sense of impending catastrophe—these factors combined with the long and widely established belief that western civilization is dying and with all the agonies and burdens of the years since 1914, have bred a mood of despair which is not far removed from desperation. There are few light hearts in Germany today.

This situation explains, in part, the success of National Socialists and Communists at the recent elections and the growing popularity of all extreme views. Hope in the policy of democratic and national methods of improvement have [sic] been disappointed so often that the temptation to adopt radical measures, even if they have the slight chance to succeed, is very great. Hence the workers are increasingly attracted to Communism, the middle classes to Fascism.

These parties offer the alluring prospect of a complete break with the past, with the revolution of 1918, the treaty of Versailles, the Dawes and the Young-plans, the enrichment of war and inflation profiteers, the quarrels of parliamentary parties all intent upon promoting the interests of some economic group, the burden of war-guilt. And the German mood today is to say "Goodbye to all that." That does not mean that the nation sighs for the golden days of the Imperial period; Fascism does not appear to be reactionary in that sense; the primary motive is that of escape from the immediate past.

Viewed from this angle the increase of Fascism is not an entirely discouraging sign. If one disregards the negative elements in the movement and thinks of the positive appeal which it makes then one can see in it an expression of the German will to retrieve moral and national integrity; it is the assertion of a will to national reformation. Hitler's recent speeches—whatever may have been true of the pre-election appeals—are of a sort which would arouse enthusiastic response in any nation in the world. They are a challenge to sincere patriotism to put the interests of country above the interests of class and to break, therefore, with a political system which has made the class conflict—not only in the case of the socialists—the keynote of political life. Hence the attack of the national socialists is directed almost equally against capitalism and Marxism. In the second place the appeal of this party lies in its expression of the national self-respect, in its determined rejection of the German war-guilt theory, and in its assertion of the equality of Germany with the other great nations of the world. Intimately connected with this is, of course, the whole question of reparations. The romanticism of Fascism at this point lies in its failure to realize the inescapable fact that Germany lost the war; its justification lies in its stern refusal to carry any longer the hypocritical burden of sole war-guilt laid upon it by the treaty of Versailles. Apart from all argument pro and con, it must be evident that the vote for the Fascists contained much of this element of an assertion of self-respect. In the third place it is the will to effect an inner reformation which is expressed in the Hitler movement, the determination to do away with all the moral filth, the civic dishonesty and the cynical self-seeking, under which post-war Germany has suffered no less than have the conquering nations.

There are not only demagogs among the National Socialists, there are not a few idealists among them. And to leave the ideal motives out of account in evaluating their appeal to the German voter is wrong to both them and Germany. There are other factors, of course. These Fascists number many youthful romantics in their ranks—boys and girls, many students, who are animated by that ineradicable German romanticism which achieved its latest great expression in the German youth movement but which has not been absent from any period of German history. It is a beautiful spirit, but highly dangerous. Disillusioned romanticists are the world's worst reactionaries, and the romanticists of the Hitler movement may easily become the servants of reaction instead of the promoters of ideal purposes.

Idealism and romanticism are the keynotes of the party in many of its meetings and other expressions but other and sinister motives are combined with these and carry a threat to Germany and the world as much as the former carry promises of good. Most evident is the puerile anti-Semitism which has been dropped from public utterances since the election but which is an important part of the unchangeable program of the movement. Jews are made responsible for all the ills of Germany; reparations, immoral literature, Communism, the inflation and what not are ascribed to the machinations of this race. And half of the anti-capitalist program appears to be directed against them alone. At this point, as at many others, there seems to be a dubious hiatus between the public expressions of the leaders and the actual program of the party. This promises the exclusion of all Jews from public office, their disfranchisement and sometimes seems to threaten deportation. The converse of this measureless hate of the Jews is the old chauvinism, the old proud self-exaltation of isolated nationalism, and its associate—militarism. There can be no doubt of the fact that at this point German National Socialism speaks the same language, has the same hopes and struts about in the some [*sic*] overbearing fashion as does its hero, Mussolini.

Whether the appeal of the movement lies more in this latter, or more in the former group of idealistic factors only the future can reveal. At present it seems that the political crisis in Germany is the product of despair and of the will to conquer a nobler future. So far the victory of the Fascists remains a gesture. One trusts that there is reason as well as emotion in it.

Some Observations on Russia

In August of 1930, Niebuhr joined the Sherwood Eddy party, which included his brother Reinhold, for a two-week tour of the Soviet Union that took them primarily to Moscow and Leningrad. This article is the first of two that were published in the Evangelical Synod's popular magazine, and it reveals his positive impressions of the Soviet experiment. His evaluation of religion in Russia, which he initiates in this article, occupies the bulk of the second one. In Niebuhr's view, the more equitable society that the government and people seemed determined to construct in Russia stood in stark contrast to the class consciousness of the capitalist society with which he was more familiar as an American. He regarded the Soviet experiment as a possible model for the rest of the Western world to consider. Niebuhr soon changed his tune, however, once Stalin showed himself to be no different from Hitler in imposing his will upon an entire population.

Source: *The Evangelical Herald* 29 (October 2, 1930): 795–96.

General Impressions

The first impressions which Moscow, capital of revolutionary Russia, makes upon the visitor, are those of drabness and of intense activity. The gray monotony of the scene may be largely an inheritance from pre-revolutionary days, for Moscow was the deserted capital of the nation for two hundred years, while court and nobility transferred their building enterprise and gayety to St. Petersburg. Yet much of the drab appearance of this city of two and a half-million people is evidently the result of revolution. The crowds on the streets are crowds of proletarians, with scarcely a well-dressed man or woman among them. The somber poverty of their apparel is relieved now and then, only by the bright head-dress of a woman Communist, and by the red decorations on the khaki uniforms of the police. Half of the once prosperous shops now offer only dirty windows and empty show-cases to the view, while the others are occupied by government trusts or cooperative enterprises which are far too much absorbed in supplying the fundamental needs of the populace to give attention to the luxury of window display. The appearance of drab monotony is brightened by the swirling clouds of dust in every city street.

Moscow appears at first to be a city in decay. Unpainted buildings, crumbling stucco walls, broken tile floorings, empty stores, an obviously poor population frighten the visitor, who discerns traces of a past splendor, which the present seems little concerned to preserve.

Yet the second impression comes to relieve the first. For Moscow is a city of titanic enterprise and feverish activity. The faces of the people are neither happy nor unhappy—they are the determined faces of those who go to perform a task in which they believe. And everywhere one finds evidences of that will to achieve. Street after street is torn up, in order that the rough cobblestone pavements of centuries may be replaced by asphalt. A few hours' drive through the city discovers dozens of new building projects—government offices, workers' apartment houses, factories, workers' clubs. And here and there evidences of the new order emerge out of the chaos—completed streets and office buildings which in their western, industrial severity stand in marked contrast to the semi-oriental structures of the past. Such conversation as one can engage in by means of an interpreter or in German or English with those natives who command a foreign tongue, reveals that the construction of a new Moscow and of a new Russia is not alone the desire of the government but of the people in general. They know that they are making history, they know that millions of Western peoples want them to fail, so they build, not in despair, but with a buoyant optimism and a determination that is contagious. Despite the evidence of disorganization and of illimitable needs, despite the pioneer character of some of the construction which one sees, one cannot help but share much of the faith in the future which carries this nation along, through great privations, to be sure, and with great loss of what was good in the old order.

The dual impression which the merely external appearance of Moscow makes is paralleled by the dualism of one's reaction to the whole new civilization which Communism is building here after a pattern never used before. In its first stage, that it is in the present, it is a definitely proletarian civilization with all the vices and all the virtues of proletarianism. It is proletarian in its wide *equality*. Not even the history of revolutionary America, or of revolutionary France, reveals a comparable devotion to the doctrine of equality. There are differences of income, to be sure, between skilled and unskilled workers, between these and professional men—or cultural workers, as they are called here. But the difference is not always in favor of the latter (lawyers, for instance, are more poorly paid than artisans), and the degree of difference is infinitely less than in democratic countries. Moreover, the poorly paid worker enjoys advantages which are denied to his more fortunate comrade. The lower the income for instance, the lower is the rent—apart entirely from the quality of the dwellings. Equality reigns also in education, where the children of the poor enjoy better advantages today than the children of the old bourgeoisie. It prevails in the natural life, where every effort is made not only to open to the worker the stored artistic treasures of the past, in music, paintings and literature, but also to give him the ability to enjoy these things.

After equality it is the *energy* of the proletarianism which manifests itself in this civilization. It is the energy of the unsophisticated whose philosophy is simple, unqualified by reservations and doubts, undecked [sic] by too much reflection. It is an energy that grows out of physical vitality and that is released by the practical, tangible character of the ends a proletarian communism projects. This vital energy is displayed not only in the ardor with which enterprises of construction are launched and carried through, but also, it is true, in the brutality with which all obstacles which stand in the way are removed. It appears, furthermore, not only in the industrialization and communization of life, but also in its play.

The great Park of Culture and Rest in Moscow illustrates some of these points. Here communism has created a vast school and picnic ground in and where workers may come on each fifth day, after four days of labor, to attend a circus performance or a drama, to participate in the beautiful folk dances or to lie quietly in deck chairs on the river bank, to listen to concerts or to lectures on socialism, the abuse of vodka, venereal disease, or the five year plan. It is something of Coney Island, something of Central Park, something of a public library, something of a school. Here there is a model nursery where mothers may leave their children in the care of trained nurses and able kindergartners, while they go to enjoy a day of rest or pleasure. And withal the atmosphere of the park seems to be freer from immorality than any comparable institution in democratic countries.

Yet alongside of the energy, the wholesome fun, the air of equality, the interest in educational opportunities which prevail here, the disadvantages of proletarian civilization also come to light. They seem to be by no means comparable to the advantages; but the eye is struck by the homeliness and unkemptness of the scene and one is reminded that despite the professed interest in art, there is a noticeable lack of those refinements and of that love of harmony which distinguished older cultures. Perhaps the Russian eye would be as much offended by American bill boards, as the American eye is hurt by the crude red propaganda banner stretched across the beautiful white façade of the opera house, by the posters, cartoons and newspaper cuttings which hang on the walls of the art museum among oil paintings by the artists of the revolutionary period. So it is also in the park. The giant statues at the entrance, impressive in their bold simplicity, are flanked by advertisements of some government bonds or by propaganda posters proclaiming the five-year plan. And these impressions repeat themselves over and over, until one is tempted to make a generalization—which, like all generalizations about Russia, is probably untrue—this civilization contains a wealth of new and necessary justice, but little beauty, either old or new. Then one remembers a gorgeous opera production and is compelled to modify the generalization to the effect that while this new world may for the time being contain too little of the old beauty and less of the new, it does contain a wealth of new justice, energy and hope.

Religion in Russia

In the old days, before the revolution buried the old era and raised the new, Moscow was known as the Holy City of Russia. Today the world calls it the center of infidelity and of anti-religious propaganda. To the visitor it reveals its claims to both these titles. Over the roofs of the somber, gray houses, at the end of dreary vistas down dusty, cobblestoned streets, on the banks of the river, over the Chinese wall—everywhere rise the golden or brightly colored domes of the hundreds of churches which gave the city its repute for piety and supplied visual testimony to the claim that its sanctuaries numbered forty times forty. Some of these churches are only small chapels, but among them are great cathedrals, such as the church of Saint Savior's—a stately white pile with five great golden domes—and the famed St. Basil's with its oriental splendor, its uncanny beauty and its traditions of Ivan the Terrible's cruelty; among them are royal shrines, where the czars of an earlier period were baptized, crowned and buried, but also holy places where the poor forget their sorrows while they worshipped under the spell of the mysterious and mystic

Greek ritual. On almost every street another church—each with its legends, proud or humble, and each the symbol of a past devotion.

But one listens in vain for the sound of thousands of ringing bells which literature celebrates as the greatest charm of Moscow. Some of the towers, one notes, are empty, having yielded their bells to the cannon-makers or industrial foundries, but those which are not empty are equally silent. Beautiful Saint Savior's has been made a national museum, through which saunter reverent and irreverent alike to admire the beautiful ikons—those worshipping as they go, these sometimes deriding; yet once a week at least, the priests again take possession to conduct a service. One sees churches which have been converted into restaurants and worker's clubs, others with huge padlocks affixed to their doors, others made inaccessible by heaps of rubble which the laborers who are preparing the way for new pavement, have piled on the gates and on the stairs—and many others—whether closed or open—evidently crumbling into a sad decay, crumbling monuments to a piety that cannot preserve them. No one seems to know how many sanctuaries have been closed. One hears that sixty percent of the churches of Moscow are still open, and again that not more than four hundred are continuing their services. One guess is a good as another.

In Leningrad the situation is similar. Here one is unable to visit the great cathedral of St. Isaac, because, one is informed, preparations are underway to open it as a museum. A friend seeks out the Congregational Church previously maintained for English residents of the city and discovers that the building has been converted into the headquarters for an anti-religious society. A German Lutheran Church, however, is said to be still open. Village churches remain open, it is reported, so long as the majority of the population do not request their closing, but both the church and the priest are taxed so heavily (in some instances half of the priest's income is taken by the state as tax) that the pious wonder how long they will be able to maintain their worship. Churches, by the way, are taxed as trading organizations—because they sell candles to the worshippers.

Can German and American Christians Understand Each Other?

Personal interaction with some of the more prominent German theologians of the day was one of the chief aims of Niebuhr's sabbatical trip to Europe. He feared that the sharp criticism some of them had heaped upon the American Social Gospel as they chose to heed Karl Barth's summons to put God back at the center of religious thinking might make it impossible to conduct an intelligible dialogue. What was sorely needed, for him, was a theological framework that would facilitate the integration of the best features of postwar theological renewal in Germany and the longer-standing commitment of American Protestants to programs of social reform. Written for The Christian Century *while he was still in Europe, the following essay is an important one because it clearly demonstrates the immediate impact of Paul Tillich's "religious realism" upon Niebuhr's thinking. It not only offered the kind of mediating position for which he was searching but also served to help shape the more robust theological perspective he brought to bear on the church and the world throughout the 1930s and beyond.*

Source: *The Christian Century* 47 (July 23, 1930): 914–16.

I

It has been assumed at times that the theology of the country in which the "social gospel" has achieved its most intensive development can derive but little help from the Christianity of other nations. More especially have we felt in the United States that German theology with its strong metaphysical, often confessional, interest was moving in a direction opposite to the one taken by our own religious thought. This feeling was encouraged both by continental criticism of the American use of the term "Kingdom of God," at the Stockholm conference for instance, and by those reports on Barthian and post-

Barthian theology which reached us on the other side of the Atlantic. Yet it would be a sad thing if this were true, if it were a fact that in religion Germany and America were to take quite antithetical directions and these two of the few great leaders of Protestant thought were to drift farther apart and become increasingly unintelligible to each other in the very age when the Christian churches of the world most desire and most sorely need to develop an ecumenical consciousness.

There is another reason why such an estrangement would be tragic. In our present planetary age we have become exceedingly conscious of the dangers of provincialism and of the perils of relativity in ethics and theology. If anywhere a provincial relativism threatens American religion it is in its tendency toward a pure activism, degenerating at times into an exclusive and febrile passion for shortsighted reforms and into a Jesuitical acceptance of any means which will gain the desired end. Furthermore, this interest in measurable activity and in tangible results threatens to betray us into an anthropocentric, this-worldly, planetary provincialism which forgets that man may also be a citizen of heaven and that apart from his urge to identify himself with some transcendent meaning his being and even his ethical and social interests lose all ultimate significance. The danger of an American provincialism, which might at the same time be, in content, a planetary provincialism, becomes apparent in the expressions of the religious humanists, as the literary humanists well appreciate.

It would seem that American religious thought no less than German or English theology, can be saved from the danger of following a one-sided and ultimately self-defeating development only by engaging in that sort of active and objective debate with other types of thinking, which will enable it to find points of view outside of itself, from which it can criticize and correct its too partial emphases. Some German theologians and religious leaders are no less aware of their need for corrective influences from non-German sources. But if it were true, as has often seemed to be the case, that Germany and America had gone so far in opposite directions of theological development that they had become virtually unintelligible to each other, then no fruitful exchange of ideas, no necessary cross-criticism would be possible.

II

Another consideration must occupy the American thinker on religious and ethical themes as he surveys German theology. "The social gospel," he may be convinced, forms the heart of American Christianity. It represents no merely theological speculation, it is not the religion of mere assent to traditional confessions; it represents a conception of Christianity, which has grown out of the very life of American Christianity, out of its needs, out of its whole history, out of its struggle to understand its Bible in a new world and in the face of new-world problems. And yet, the social gospel which in Walter Rauschenbusch and Washington Gladden had its anchorage in an inclusive faith whose center was God in Jesus Christ and which in them was mated with a piety that did not ignore the peculiar needs of a man standing in solitariness before the final facts of life—this gospel has today often cut adrift from all God-centered religion. It seems at times to be a program of action only, lacking the support of the faith, of the complete philosophy or theology which can give meaning to the program and save it from the appearance of the fact of being a merely arbitrary personal choice.

The social gospel's need of a theology is apparent in the failure of ethics, in the revitalization of all moral choices which eventually reduces them to meaninglessness and which saps the fiber of our moral vigor. It is apparent in the disappointment of many a good worshiper who comes to church to find a mediator and discovers an accuser only; it is apparent, on the other hand, in the liturgical reaction which substitutes in the services of the church esthetic luxuries for the sharp voice of conscience and the sense of divine reality.

A similar problem, yet the complete antithesis of the American difficulty, faces German Christianity, which expresses a theology and a philosophy but no commensurate ethics, a faith but no effective social program. Hence the tremendous importance of such meetings as those of Lausanne and Stockholm. The deliverance from religious heresy as well as from patriotic provincialism seems to lie only in ever more active exchange of ideas between the Christian churches of the world.

III

It must not be assumed that a synthesis of partial tendencies is an easy task. It is not possible to unite German theology with American ethics, German theocentrism with American anthropocentrism, as one is wont to put together today various disparate chapters by various writers within the confines of two covers, calling the whole a book. The patterns of the American social gospel and of German theology do not fit into each other like adjacent sections of a picture puzzle. Each is claimed by many of its representatives to constitute an independent and self-sufficient whole.

In part, it is the old problem of religion and ethics which meets us here, each of these is represented by doughty champions whose war cries are "Either-or" and "Nothing but." They shout at us "theism *or* humanism"; "*either* fundamentalism *or* modernism"; "*either* religion *or* ethics"; "Christianity is *nothing but* justification by faith"; "the essence of religion is *nothing but* the consciousness of social values"; "man is *nothing but* an erect animal." And timid souls who had somehow believed that there is a rhyme as well as reason in the world and the conflicting values do not necessarily exclude each other forever, that somehow the disparate experiences and the apparently exclusive loyalties, which now require decisive choice, yet form part of one whole which will someday reveal its outlines—these minds are likely to become bewildered by the "either-orists" and the "nothing-butters," and by the stubborn patterns of the picture-puzzle pieces which refuse to fit into each other. And yet American and German Christianity, as little as religion and ethics, are not really independent. Neither forms a self-sufficient whole. Their ragged edges point out the need of complementation. What is required, we discover, is a third piece, one which will unite the two and in doing so change and reveal the meaning of the partial picture which appeared on either unintegrated block.

The search for this mediating element is the heart of the problem of theology. Christians may be practically convinced that the mediator, in this case also, is Jesus Christ. In him they find the living union of theocentric and anthropocentric faith, of religion and ethics. Yet in the interpretation of Jesus the conflict between opposite points of view breaks out afresh. And when one is convinced that it is in a common apprehension and evaluation of Jesus Christ and his gospel that unity must be found, not only as between American and German Christianity, but as between Greek and Roman and Protestant, as one is driven almost to despair by such statements as the following one, which is taken from a German Lutheran pastor's discussion of the meetings at Lausanne and Jerusalem. Writing about Lausanne he speaks of the "oft-repeated illusion that all the participants were one in Christ. They were not one in him and could not be. A Greek, who sees in the Nicene creed the expression of reality and a modernist who approaches this creed with the reservation of regarding it as historically conditioned, are not one in Christ. Love of truth commands us to say, 'Each has a different Christ.'" The situation of the churches therefore, he goes on to say, is a desperate one. One is inclined to agree with the last statement, for our situation is indeed desperate if we must continue to confuse our ideas and formulas with the reality we seek to express in them. Then Christ becomes Christology, God theology, and religion psychology.

The way out of the impasse appears to lie only in a realism which will apprehend in all their stubborn actuality the facts of history and the fact of God; which will neither substitute a romantic idea of natural man for the petty and ignoble creature whom our novelists have so often seen and described better than our theologians and which will not replace the God with whom the soul struggles, God the enemy and God the ultimate reality with some man-made deity, some projection of the wish or the social whole.

IV

The paths to a revitalized faith and to mutual understanding between the various groups of Christians are not different roads, but one and the same way; and an encouraging sign in contemporary development in theology—speaking now primarily of German and American Christianity—is the appearance in each country of a new leadership which is blazing the path of religious realism. Such realism is arising today in Germany in a variety of forms and is represented by a number of men of whom Paul Tillich and Alfred Dedo Mueller are outstanding representatives. What gives these theologians importance from the American as well as from the German point of view is their effort to combine religious realism with social idealism, or, to put it in another way, the sense of God's reality and willingness to let ideas retire behind independent reality in significance, with the passionate conviction that awareness of divine reality must exercise decisive influence on human activity in the social world.

One of the keynotes of this realism is emphasis on the apprehension of God in the present and the desire to understand history not by means of an impossible attempt to transplant ourselves into some remote past but by a resolute effort to wrest from contemporary experience its ultimate significance and revelational value. "Religious realism," says Tillich, "demands a revelation in which the Unconditioned Power, in whatever concreteness it may appear, invades my present." At this point two significant differences between American and German realism emerge; the latter is more historical in its point of view, more aware of the connection of the present with the past, and it is more objective, in so far as it gives little attention to the subject's adjustment to God and emphasizes the Divine Object's invasion of human life.

In realistic judgment of contemporary civilization and in the demand that religion be made effective in social life the religious realists move far away from the traditional Lutheran position which has been reaffirmed so often by post-war German theology. At the same time they do not venture to identify the work of social reconstruction with the building of the kingdom of God. Our reconstructive labors, they apprehend, are too strongly conditioned by contemporary evils, purposes, and tasks and too strongly infected with the vices that cling to all human effort to allow identification with the eternal and the divine. This very healthy distinction between the kingdom of God and social, political or economic measures detracts nothing from, but rather adds to, the radicalism with which gospel and contemporary civilization are placed in antithesis. It is not an accident that this ethical realism, especially in the case of Tillich, is closely associated with the religious socialism which is beginning to play an important role in contemporary German Christianity.

Religious realism may be a development which will arouse Protestant Christianity in central Europe to social effectiveness. It may also offer an opportunity for fruitful collaboration between German and American theology and it may greatly aid the social gospel to achieve that self-correction which will maintain it in harmony with a supporting faith and will eliminate from it those planetary provincialisms which often threaten to undo it. What the "theology of crisis" cannot do for America because its criticism of socialized faith is destructive and because its constructive ideas are entirely remote from our whole development, religious realism may accomplish because it unites a necessary criticism with an appreciation of the values involved.

It remains true that no theological movement can be transferred bodily from one religious environment to another without becoming something quite different—in attention, content and effect—in the process. But when appreciation of historical conditions is mated with desire for complete objectivity then the opportunity for mutual collaboration, mutual criticism and mutual understanding is present. American and German religious realism appear to offer this opportunity to each other.

The Irreligion of Communist and Capitalist

Firsthand observations of Russia seem to have motivated Niebuhr to draft this article for The Christian Century *before his sabbatical ended. The experience provided a measure of perspective on the tottering economy at home as well as the atheistic stereotype of the state communism he was witnessing abroad. Glimpses of the medieval trappings of Russian Orthodoxy helped him account for communist "irreligion." Its close connection with the sixteenth-century Protestant Reformation notwithstanding, modern capitalism to him was no less guilty of the same charge. In his view, the assumptions of both were equally "secular," and they both espoused values that were contrary to the Christian ethos. As the Great Depression deepened during the 1930s, Niebuhr would continue to develop his scathing critique of capitalist ideologies, and one suspects that he might deliver the same message to twenty-first century Americans inclined to fuse their Christian faith with free-market economics.*

Source: *The Christian Century* 47 (October 29, 1930): 1306–7.

Communist animosity to religion in general and to Christianity in particular has been regarded by the Christian churches and peoples of the world as one of the most revealing and condemnable elements in the communist movement. The association of Christianity and capitalism, on the other hand, has been looked upon by communism as one of the most characteristic and disreputable features of a class-governed world. If to the capitalist and Christian the campaign against religion is indicative of communist brutality, the alliance of faith and profit-seeking reveals capitalist and ecclesiastical hypocrisy to the Marxian.

Aside from the exaggerations of propaganda there is no small measure of truth in both judgments. It is a patent fact that since the French revolution, and especially since Marx and Engels, the attitude of the radical proletarian movement has been permanently anti-religious and that, where communism is in power, it seeks to eradicate Christianity along with other survivals of a pre-revolutionary civilization. No less obvious is the conservative and often reactionary part which the dominant Christian institutions have played in the history of western civilization since the days of Charlemagne; and it is notorious that today a majority of the Christian churches are enlisted on the side of social conservatism.

Fundamentally Similar Attitudes

Yet there is an important point which communists and capitalists as well as Christians overlook in their mutual recriminations. It is the fundamental similarity between the attitudes toward religion of both communist and capitalist civilizations, a similarity which is really due to the capitalist parentage of the bolshevist philosophy of life. From the point of view of a handicraft or agricultural economy, communism and capitalism are simply variants of the same economic scheme; from the point of view of ancient and medieval philosophy they are almost identical.

It is to be noted in the first place that communism undertakes the transformation of the religious attitudes of the people for precisely the same reasons that capitalism needed to wait for its development until a religious reformation had taken place in its civilization. Historians of economic life have pointed out that modern economy is unable to work with the "natural man." Natural man, or at least man as he has been conditioned by the ages of agricultural employment, is unfitted for modern industrial economy. His laziness, lack of punctuality and accuracy and his love of traditional processes unfit him for the tempo of an industrial civilization.

If capitalist economy was to succeed both the worker and the consumer, or rather men as both workers and consumers, needed to be remade. As workers they needed to be "educated" to develop greater wants so that they would continue to work even after their modest needs for food, clothing and shelter had been met; they needed to be weaned from their attachment to traditional methods of production so that they would be willing to learn and relearn new and more profitable methods of manufacture; they needed also to be torn out of the old, stately, unpunctual and easy-going rhythm of the seasons, the inexact, rule of thumb adjustments of agriculture, in order that they might be fitted into the nervous, clock-like, mechanical rhythm of industry into the accurate, precise adjustments of machine production.

Capitalism Remakes Men

It was equally necessary for the success of the new economy that men be reconditioned in their habits as consumers, so that their love for the old customary articles and the modesty of their desires might be replaced by interest in novelties and by a desire for the immense quantities and the new qualities introduced or produced by the new methods. Such a revolution in human nature, such a break with the habits and attitudes of centuries, was accomplished gratuitously for early capitalism by the Reformation and the Renaissance; for the later capitalism by revival and revolution. The part which religion played in accomplishing this revolution in human nature was probably more significant than its role in producing entrepreneurs, according to the well-known theory of Weber and Tawney. At all events, capitalism was the heir of the religious reformation in one respect as much as in the other.

Russia, however, enjoyed no religious transformation. Its Christianity, like its economy, remained medieval down to the 20th century. If its economic revolution—not so much as a communist as an industrial revolution, which it is—was to succeed, a reformation of the tradition-loving, easy-going agricultural laborers was required, just as had been the case in capitalism. Nothing but a religious reformation would suffice inasmuch as custom had been molded and guarded by faith, and habit was intertwined with the fundamental religious attitudes of life.

Communism as Revival

Since the reformation in this instance had not been carried under religious auspices it needed to be introduced under the only authority available, which was anti-religious. Yet as [Gerhart] Schulze-Gaevernitz, a German economist, puts it, "The battle of the soviet government against traditional religion is significant above all as a battle against the traditionalism of the peasantry. The world historic mission of the Russian revolution does not lie in the dictatorship of a minority nor in the communist experiment but in the replowing of the psychical soil." Regarded from this point of view communism and capitalism have, in their inceptions, the same interest in the breaking up of old religious attitudes, if not in the formation of new ones.

There is a second and more important similarity between communism and capitalism in their relation to religion. Both are fundamentally secular, this-worldly and irreligious in their outlook. In this communism is really the child of capitalism, which is the real parent of the secular spirit of modern life. The secularism of contemporary civilization lies in its hedonism, in its conception of the end of life as enjoyment, in its temporalism, that is to say its assumption that all enjoyment must be gained in this world, and in its humanism, its belief that the conditions of life and life itself are subject to human control. Its first proposition implies the denial of all transcendental values; its second the denial of immortality; its third the denial of God.

Secularism and the Child of Desire

This secularism of western civilization is sometimes traced to science because of the latter's predilection for the tangible and measurable phenomena of nature. But secularism is not so much an attitude of mind as of desire, and science has been far less effective in influencing human attitudes than industry has been. When modern men speak of science they usually mean applied science, invention rather than discovery, technique rather than ideas, Edison rather than Einstein.

Secularism is both prerequisite to and consequence of capitalist production; it is also the prerequisite of communism and whether as capitalist or as communist secularism it is the real enemy of religion in the modern world. It is a prerequisite of capitalist economy because this economy requires a dominant interest in the consumption of goods in its sphere of influence and a dominant interest in profit on the part of the promoters of its enterprise. Individuals engaged in the vast institution of modern economic life may follow other aims for themselves but the purpose of their economic activity remains profit. The basis of capitalism is the economic man.

Fostered by Capitalism

Secularism is the result of capitalism inasmuch as the economic enterprise has become the great educational institution which moulds the modern outlook upon life. Its influence is the more powerful because it changes attitudes not so much by what it preaches as by what it takes for granted. When all success is measured in terms of economic gain, when all the world is a show-window and an advertisement, when children are conditioned from their earliest years to want things, when the conscious, continuous effort of the most active elements in civilization is directed toward the increase of wants among men, then secularism is inevitable. Modern civilization is the most discontented of all cultures because it must depend for its vitality upon the increase of discontent. By exalting physical, temporal and individual values into the primary place capitalism results in the decline of faith and the exaltation of secular ethics, secular psychology and secular politics, all of which rest upon secular economics.

Communism's Secularism

Communism has done no more than to accept this secularism which capitalism has developed as it has accepted the machines and factories of the capitalist world. It professes openly what it has learned in secret, that the chief end of man is the enjoyment of physical satisfactions before death overtakes him and that men must look to themselves alone for the satisfaction of their needs. Communism is as naïve in assuming that the ideology of materialist philosophy explains its irreligion as capitalism is ignorant in failing to see its fundamental disagreement with the religion it sometimes professes to cherish.

There is a third point in which communism agrees with capitalism in the rejection of Christianity. The ethics of love is as foreign to the one as to the other and it is not too much to claim that the younger system of industrial civilization learned its cynicism, its reliance upon force and its doctrine of the class conflict from the example of the elder. In all these things communism boldly, brutally but honestly proclaims the principles which capitalism followed but did not profess. Hence the communist has the advantage of possessing a good conscience; his principles have been made to agree with his practice, while capitalist civilization remains a divided self, haunted by the sense of its hypocrisy.

Homeless Christianity

For Christianity the alliance with the capitalist civilization remains as fraught with danger as does the open warfare of the communist revolution. It is as homeless in the two spheres of the modern world as it was in the Roman empire which persecuted it and in the medieval feudalism which patronized it. If anything, it is more an alien in the modern world than it was in these cultures which at least retained some sense of transcendent goals, some contact with the spiritual environment, some modesty in their estimate of human sufficiency and some recollection of the ancient truth that discipline rather than satisfaction is the source of joy.

The time seems to be coming when Christianity will realize this homelessness to a poignant degree. Then it will break the ties which bind it to the optimistic secularism of capitalist civilization even as communism broke the ties which attached it to faith in the old utopian days. Then also the great temptation of faith will return—the temptation to find a resting place for its homelessness in some heaven of anticipated attainment where it can "let the rest of the world go by!"

Nationalism, Socialism and Christianity

The World Tomorrow was founded following World War I by the Fellowship of Reconciliation, a pacifist organization, and over the following decade and half it exhibited socialist political leanings. Niebuhr appears to have chosen to publish his response to Hitler's ascent to power in an issue of this magazine because he was convinced that German socialists and Christians had repeated the same mistake they had made prior to the outbreak of World War I. Both had underestimated the power of patriotism as a social force that was capable of rallying people of all persuasions. The economic reductionism that tended to control socialist thinking had only served to drive the German capitalists into the arms of the Nazi Party. The failure of German Christians to assert their independence and to leverage their influence among their fellow citizens on behalf of a wholesome set of national goals, moreover, had rendered them equally incapable of reversing the course on which Hitler was taking their country. The ensuing German church struggle would only serve to confirm Niebuhr's analysis. Were there lessons from the German scene of the 1930s that American Christians might apply to themselves in midst of their own world of social upheaval? Niebuhr believed that there were, and in this article he provided a foretaste of what he would go on to assert more forcefully and at greater length in The Church Against the World.

Source: *The World Tomorrow* 16 (August 1933): 469–70.

Among the major reasons for the frequent failures of Christian churches and socialist parties in their social conflicts is their oversimplified analysis of the strategic situation. The orthodox interpretations of life as a battle between religion and secularism, idealism and materialism, or the equally orthodox view of it as wholly determined by the class struggle both leave out of account the fact that there are social forces which are probably quite as important as religious or class loyalties and which may become allies or foes in the religious or class struggle. The effort to reduce the interpretation of the social process to economic terms is like the effort to define the organic process in terms of digestion only. The attempt of religious idealists to understand political and economic conflicts in terms of ideals is like the attempt to analyze the psychophysical organism in purely psychical terms. No one doubts the importance of diet and digestion nor the importance of right mental adjustments, but a medical art which takes only one or the other of these factors into consideration is likely to be not only fanatical but also highly dangerous to many a patient to whose condition this particular analysis does not apply. If no sane physician will ignore these factors, neither will he attach exclusive importance to them in his diagnosis and treatment.

In their attitude toward nationalism both socialists and Christians show the limitations of their understanding, and in their frequent defeats by capitalistic nationalism on the one hand and by secularistic nationalism on the other they demonstrate the evil effects of their bad theory. Orthodox socialism explains nationalism as a middle class movement in which that class hides its economic interests behind the cloak of patriotism. Idealistic Christians are likely to say nationalism is an idolatry in which the nation takes the place of a universal God. Both statements are probably right within limits. But in both of them there is not only analysis but also moralistic judgment and where this moralism begins analysis stops. There is a neglected factor here, something the socialist and the Christian cannot understand in the terms of their orthodox theory, hence they ascribe it to moral perversity, to hypocrisy, or to self-interest. When the socialist and the Christian face each other in opposition they simplify each other in the same way and ascribe what does not fit into the simple scheme to ethical perversity. The socialist becomes for the Christian an industrial worker who hides the interests of his particular group, in conflict with [the] middle class and agriculturalists, behind the ideals of a classless and international world, while the Christian appears to the socialist to be a capitalist who practices religious hypocrisy for the sake of retaining power. Their conflicts with each other, their defeats and qualified victories, are the outcome of such half-correct analyses, filled out by the addition of moral judgments.

When patriotism is accepted as a social force which simply exists and which in and of itself is neither good nor bad, neither necessarily socialistic nor capitalistic, neither Christian nor un-Christian, but an actual factor which must be reckoned with, the strategies of socialists and Christians may become more enlightened. Loyalty to family, kin, the native soil is simply present in human life. Some few individuals or groups may not be affected by it, just as some few individuals or groups may not be affected by their economic interests or by loyalty to their class. Nevertheless it is a social force which has great power. It cannot be explained as a function of the private property system. To be sure, the small owners, those who have a direct and personal relation to some bit of property, may be more patriotic than the directors of corporations with their impersonal relations, or the property-less class of employees. But patriotism is present in these groups, as the socialists of all warring countries discovered in 1914, and again in recent years. To deal with it as though it were unreal or merely hypocritical is to invite disaster.

There is no need to argue that patriotism and economic interests do not cooperate. They do. What is not evident is that one is the function of the other. For a very long time, much longer than socialists who speak of a hundred years of fascism imagine, nationalist patriotism will be a power to reckon with. It is not at all unlikely that socialism itself will enforce this patriotism and that Russia will come to a high sense of national mission as the bearer of communism, just as France and the United States developed their nationalism more strongly when they became missionary nations with the grand ideal of democracy, a class-less world, a universal brotherhood, to proclaim. Now there is no doubt that the ruling economic and political classes have allied themselves with this patriotism and made use of it to further their own ends. They did not produce it; it can, under some circumstances, become a very dangerous ally. But at all events they did not ignore it, they did not drive it into the camp of their enemy by denouncing it and its aspirations. They allied themselves with it and perverted it. A socialism which ignores patriotism or makes only grudging concessions to it will only succeed in cementing the alliance of capitalism and patriotism. Had the industrial workers of Germany been as astute as the capitalists were, they might now be in alliance with a patriotic party, directing its course into other channels than it will take under the silent guidance of the industrial barons.

What applies to the relationship of socialism and patriotism, or of class interests and national loyalty, applies equally to the relations of Christianity and patriotism. The Catholic church knows very well that it can cooperate with socialism and that it can cooperate with nationalism when occasion calls for it. In neither case does it give up its own character. Charges of hypocrisy are in place here only for those moralists who see everything in terms of black and white, for whom national patriotism is either something good or bad instead of a reality which may serve good or evil needs, or for whom the industrial workers' movement is either the prelude to the Kingdom of God or to the victory of the devil, instead of a movement which has within its potentialities for good or evil, which in and of itself is neither good nor bad but rather something to be accepted and understood as patriotism is. Nationalism may be Christian, and internationalism may be un-Christian; Gandhi's nationalism will appear to many to be more nearly Christian than the internationalism of either the international bankers or the international revolutionaries. German Protestant Christianity today finds itself in extremely uncomfortable alliance with an un-Christian nationalism partly because it had no confidence in itself as an independent power and hence did not develop its independence and seek to direct nationalism, partly because doctrinaire socialism did not realize that there were any other forces in the world save economic interests and drove religious loyalty into the arms of patriotism and capitalism. The last statement may suffice to illustrate another phase of this maladept strategy of the moralists who think in terms of good and bad men or movements only, but who, of course, always identify themselves with good men and movements. To decry Christianity as capitalistic or to praise it as socialistic, forgetting that religious loyalties have an independent root in life and that religion is a part of the whole social fabric, that it may be in alliance here with one class, there with another, now with patriotism, now with internationalism, and that it is an actual social force to be reckoned with, is to betray oneself into the false strategy which socialism followed too long in Germany and in Italy.

Christianity and socialism in America will continue to follow false strategies if they persist in this tendency to classify all movements and social realities in terms of black and white. If idealistic Christians will continue to regard national patriotism as bad and internationalism as intrinsically good they will lose their opportunity to make patriotism international in a Christian sense and internationalism patriotic in the same sense. If socialists will persist in regarding patriotism as intrinsically capitalistic they will always succeed in re-enforcing [*sic*] their enemy by driving patriotism into his camp. If they are sure that religion is bourgeois in its nature they will by their relations to it align it with their foes.

These analyses may be applied to the individual as well as to parties and movements. We may ally within ourselves our Christianity and our socialism, or our Christianity and our economic liberalism—our Christianity and our internationalism, or our faith and our patriotism. To be a Christian and a socialist is not to be merely a socialist, but neither is it evident that to be a Christian one must be a socialist; to be a Christian and a patriot is not to be merely a patriot, but neither does it appear that to be Christian one must be an internationalistic of the type which decries patriotism. Religion, class loyalties, national loyalties are strictly different things which may be associated in various ways. To attempt to reduce them to simple terms, to the antinomies of nationalism and internationalism, of the class conflict, of Christian and non-Christian, is to give up not only the attempt to analyze clearly but also all chance for an effective strategy of life.

6

Reconsidering Worldly Issues from an Orthodox Christian Standpoint

"The church is being awakened to its inner crisis by the external one in which it is involved," H. Richard Niebuhr declared in 1935, and "its continuance in the world is by no means a certainty. It knows the ways of God too well not to understand that he can and will raise up another people to carry out the mission entrusted to it if the Christian community fail him. It cannot look to the future with assurance that it carries a guarantee of immortality." His platform was *The Church Against the World*, a book he coauthored with Wilhelm Pauck, a respected University of Chicago professor who had emigrated from Germany in 1925, and Francis P. Miller, a Presbyterian layperson from Virginia's Shenandoah Valley. He recognized that a Great Depression at home and international crises abroad had laid bare the extent of the decline of mainline Protestant influence in American culture that had been deepening, but largely ignored, during the previous decade of peace and prosperity. On the horizon, moreover, there were no signs of a religious "revival." Under fire from critics within as well as outsiders, the church in Niebuhr's estimation was being driven to the point of asking, "What must we do to be saved?"[1]

Answers to this critical question were not lacking. Some, like the liberal-leaning *Christian Century*, suggested that popular perceptions of economic calamities had summoned churches to update their message by putting the evils they condemned as well as the gospel they proclaimed into more of a corporate framework.[2] Others advocated alternative economic systems such as socialism. Still others wanted to bank on President Franklin Delano Roosevelt's New Deal to preserve America's faith in its institutions. The answer Niebuhr provided in *Church Against the World* was radically different. "The question of the church," he asserted, "is not how it can measure up to the expectations of society nor what it must do to become a savior of civilization, but how it can be true to itself: that is, to its Head." As he saw it, the real threat to the church was coming not from a "changing world," but from an "unchanging God." The current state of the world and the church was bringing divine judgment to light. But at the same time, he believed this was creating a golden opportunity for Christians to seek redemption by retreating into monastic silence, by penitently examining themselves, and by returning to the truths set forth in the Scriptures.[3] The "Back to Benedict" strategy Niebuhr had first contemplated in 1925 was no longer an option. In terms of the seaside metaphor that he had used to describe the church-world paradox in 1929, he was now calling upon the church of 1935 to withdraw for the sake of its cleansing and renewal from the beaches of a world whose sands had muddied its message. Then, and perhaps

---

1. H. Richard Niebuhr, "The Question of the Church," in *The Church Against the World*, ed. H. Richard Niebuhr (Chicago: Willet, Clark and Company, 1935), 2.
2. "Why No Revival?" *The Christian Century* 52 (September 18, 1935): 1168–70.
3. Niebuhr, "The Question of the Church," 4, 12–13.

only then, would it be ready to engage the world once again and to address its issues.

For Niebuhr himself, retreating from the world meant a more careful examination of Protestantism's orthodox theological heritage. His Evangelical Synod had already bequeathed to him a hybrid Reformed-Lutheran version of it. During the 1920s, moreover, this same heritage had helped to make him as critical of the humanistic aspects of Protestant liberalism as he was of the lack of sufficient emphasis on the church's social responsibilities that he found in Karl Barth and other postwar crisis theologians. As he looked back at this time some thirty years later, Niebuhr described the 1930s as a "decisive period in the formation of basic personal convictions and in the establishment of theological formulations of those convictions," particularly with respect to God's sovereignty, human lostness, and trust in God as a miraculous gift.[4] However, his "change of mind" was more a fresh determination to give greater attention to exploring and defining orthodox features of the "cosmic faith" that he had long believed was so necessary for keeping church and world in their proper tension than it was the radical shifting of outlook to which other mainline church leaders of the Depression decade would testify.[5]

To see this, one has only to examine his 1931 Yale Alumni Lecture, "Theology in a Time of Disillusionment," which William Stacy Johnson has rightly seen fit to bring to print. As disheartening as this time was for so many, Niebuhr felt that it had inspired a renewed appreciation of divine "transcendence." The process not only identified God with the "void" left by the destruction of any faith in God's "immanence" in humankind, but became a first step in the

---

4. H. Richard Niebuhr, "Reformation: Continuing Imperative," *The Christian Century* 77 (March 2, 1960), 248–49.
5. See *The Christian Century* 56 (July 18, 1939 to September 27, 1939).

transition, best described for him by the philosopher Alfred North Whitehead, from seeing "God the void to God the enemy and from God the enemy to God the companion" as the object of one's faith. He went on to assert that getting to the point of putting faith in "God the companion" and his promise of redemption required Christians to come to the penitent conviction that the disillusioning aspects of life in their world represented not a "betrayal of our hopes," but evidence of "our betrayal of God."[6] Niebuhr would follow this same line of theological reasoning as he went on to make the orthodox doctrine of God's sovereignty his theological starting point. The *Church Against the World* bombshell that Pauck and Miller joined him in dropping was just one of many writings during this period in which he boldly stated that the societal "fissures" of the Great Depression revealed a "justice too profound to be the product of chance," because at their source was none other than "the eternal God, Creator, Judge, and Redeemer, whom the prophets and apostles heard, and saw at work, casting down and raising up."[7]

Neo-orthodoxy is the name given to the movement that included other mainline Protestants who were going down similar theological paths at the time. Like Niebuhr, they were being driven to abandon liberalism's assumptions about human nature and society in favor of a more realistic theological outlook. They also were giving fresh attention to such traditional Christian doctrines as the transcendent reality of God, original sin, and salvation based on the sacrificial death of Christ on the cross. While emphasizing divine revelation as the source of religious knowledge, however, they chose, as did Niebuhr, to continue to partake of the fruits of liberal biblical scholarship and

---

6. H. Richard Niebuhr, "Theology in a Time of Disillusionment," in *H. Richard Niebuhr: Theology, History, Culture*, ed. William Stacy Johnson (New Haven, CT: Yale University Press, 1996), 112–14.
7. Niebuhr, "The Question of the Church," 12.

to value the use of scientific and historical methodologies in the study of religion. Once he began teaching at Yale, Niebuhr became a member of the "Theological Discussion Group," a gathering of twenty-five neo-orthodox scholars summoned by Henry P. Van Dusen to meet semiannually either at Princeton University or Washington Cathedral's College of Preachers for the purpose of debating contemporary theological issues. At each two-day seminar, they discussed papers that had been circulated to all the participants in advance. Among the participants were Niebuhr's *Church Against the World* coauthors, Pauck and Miller, and other scholars such as his brother Reinhold, his Yale colleagues Robert L. Calhoun and Roland Bainton, as well as Paul Tillich, Walter M. Horton, John C. Bennett, and G. Ernest Wright.[8]

Disagreements between these representatives of the neo-orthodox movement surfaced in this setting and elsewhere. One that became public took place on the pages of *The Christian Century* and involved the Niebuhr brothers in a debate over America's response to the Japanese invasion of Manchuria in 1932. While they both deplored Japan's aggressive behavior, Richard's pox in an article entitled "The Grace of Doing Nothing" fell on pacifists and interventionists alike. In his view, both houses were self-righteously indignant, since Japan was only trying to imitate the imperialist superpowers of the West. The "inactivity" he prescribed was not that of a cynic or a self-interested opportunist. Nor did it express the exasperation of an opponent of all forms of warfare. For him, it rested "on the well-nigh obsolete faith that there is a God—a real God." Because such "faith" believed that God was at work in world events and saw him functioning as the world's Judge in the Manchurian crisis, it called forth a repentance that not only recognized and confessed the

---

8. See Samuel McCrea Cavert, "The Younger Theologians," *Religion in Life* 5 (Fall 1936): 520–31.

warped motives of every nation but also trusted that God's "mercy" was what lay on the other side of his judgment.⁹ In "Must We Do Nothing?" Reinhold agreed with his brother's assertion that in the family of nations, the "recalcitrant" one was often the creation of those nations inclined to condemn it. Yet he found Richard's "hope of attaining an ethical goal for society by purely ethical means" and "without coercion" to be an unrealistic solution to the halting of armed aggression in the Far East. "We must try to dissuade Japan from her military venture," he argued, but "use coercion to frustrate her designs" if necessary.¹⁰ Richard's response was entitled "The Only Way Into the Kingdom of God" because he believed that "self-assertion" was a worldly value; by clinging to any form of it in dealing with a nation like Japan, Reinhold was setting up a "hopeless compromise" of the "Christian method" that relied on "repentance and forgiveness" in order to attain a more just social order.¹¹

Richard's view of divine revelation is another feature of the neo-orthodox movement that this same debate between the Niebuhr brothers brings to light. As God's word, the Bible for him was not a self-contained document through which God disclosed himself once and for all through events that took place during an ancient time. Instead, the Bible pointed to a God who was taking an active role in all of human history, and it provided a lens for discerning what he might be doing at any moment. Reinhold disagreed, arguing that while it was possible to see God offering counsel to humankind through historical events, he ruled out God using immoral human forces and actions to order to bring about a better world. "Man's

---

9. H. Richard Niebuhr, "The Grace of Doing Nothing," *The Christian Century* 69 (March 23, 1932): 378–80.
10. Reinhold Niebuhr, "Must We Do Nothing?" *The Christian Century* 69 (March 30, 1932): 415–17.
11. H. Richard Niebuhr, "A Communication: The Only Way Into the Kingdom of God," *The Christian Century* 69 (April 6, 1932): 447.

reach is beyond his grasp," he quipped, "or what's a heaven for."[12] Richard ended the debate on a more hopeful note, contending that God was "always in history" as the "structure in things" and "the source of all meaning," revealing himself, even in the world's economic depressions and armed conflicts, as its enemy and redeemer, and bringing about a better future through the heaping of judgment upon self-assertive behavior.[13] Niebuhr would continue to assert this position for the rest of his career. The following articles illustrate several ways in which Niebuhr sought to apply this and other features of Christian orthodoxy, in a variety of contexts, to some of the world issues of the 1930s in order to help the church find its voice in addressing them.

---

12. Reinhold Niebuhr, "Must We Do Nothing?" 416–17.
13. H. Richard Niebuhr, "A Communication" (March 30, 1932): 447.

Greeks, Jews, and Americans in Christ

Niebuhr was already ensconced in his teaching position at Yale when he published this little-known article for the benefit of students back at Eden Seminary. Here he contended that the outlook of American Protestants resembled that of the Old Testament Hebrews in believing God to be active "in the process of history as a whole." For them, therefore, "the new world he is to bring forth is not a world beyond time but a new aeon, a new creation, a time beyond this present time, but yet a time." In the debate between the Niebuhr brothers that was taking place during the same month this article appeared in The Keryx, *it seems likely that Richard would have classified Reinhold as a "Greek." As a one who looked at history from a "Jewish" standpoint, Richard Niebuhr remained convinced, despite the criticism he received from his brother, that all of history was the realm of divine revelation, and that what God was constantly disclosing of himself as the world's Creator, Judge, and Redeemer could not be discounted in assessments of any event, including a Manchurian crisis.*

Source: *The Keryx* 22, no. 5 (March 1932): 3–4, 12.

In Christ, said Paul, there is neither Jew nor Greek: but as a Christian he was still a Jew and there have been Jews and Greeks in Christianity ever since. Jesus like Paul was a Jew and looked on God, man, and time with Jewish eyes; the writer of the Fourth Gospel was a Greek, who saw reality, mundane and divine, as a Greek must see it. Through the centuries there have been many efforts to unite the two kinds of thought and faith, but today as always the divergence becomes apparent and it may be less important to seek a synthesis than to become aware of the contrasting possibilities and to make one's decision for the one or the other mode of thought. Not that the decision can be arbitrary; for if it is true that we are born either

Aristotelians or Platonists it may be even truer that we are born Jews or Greeks and that not only a natural loyalty to our heredity but also the obligation to represent that aspect of truth which we can grasp with our historically conditioned understanding, must determine our decision.

One of the significant differences between the Jew and the Greek—perhaps the most significant one—lies in their divergent views of the theology of history. For the Jew God is always the God of Abraham, Isaac and Jacob; the God of history, past and future. He is the God of the past deliverances and of future judgments; he is the ruler of the nations, active in time. If he transcends a time it is not because he inhabits a timeless realm but because no single day, no period can contain him. Yet he is in the process of history as a whole. The new world which he is to bring forth is not a world beyond time but a new aeon, a new creation, a time beyond this present time, but yet a time. Reality is divided into periods and time itself is of the very essence of reality. Souls are not saved out of one sphere into another but out of one age into another age. In fact souls are not saved at all. It is the resurrection of the body, not the immortality of the soul, which is awaited and longed for. No less than the individual hope must the social hope be expressed in terms of time and of a single universe. For the Jew the hope was that of a Kingdom of God to be inherited by the chosen people. For the Christian Jew or Jewish Christian the hope was expressed in the Faith, "I believe in the Holy Catholic Church." That church was not this present church, not the church of this aeon, but the church of the future. It was not the sacramental institution but the fellowship of Christ's followers, of those who had accepted the redemption offered in him, the fellowship of all mankind which would bow the knee to him. It was the social church; not an empire for there was to be too much equality among its members for that; not a kingdom, for the liberty of the Christian was not compatible with a kingdom; not a commune, for it was to be too catholic, too inclusive to be a commune. Yet the holy catholic church was this-worldly, though not of this time; it was the new Jerusalem, not in heaven but coming down out of heaven. It was to be established by the returning Christ, not by his drawing of all his followers into another sphere. Judgment, revolution, natural and social catastrophes were to presage its coming, but it was coming; men were not going to go into it as by an ascent into another sphere.

The Greek and the Greek Christian live in a different world of thought. Time and eternity are two different spheres. The temporal is the transient and unreal; the eternal is the permanent, the abiding, the realm of Being. All that belongs to the temporal order is corrupted by the very transciency [*sic*] of that order; only in the universal is truth or reality to be found. God is not the God of history but the God beyond all history, beyond all time. If he enters into history it is not by way of a revelation of something that has been implicit though hidden all along, but by way of introducing something radically and wholly, qualitatively different. He inhabits eternity and his entrance into time is an unthinkable miracle. The coming of Christ is not an emergence, representing the miracle of a new event which gives meaning to all that has gone before and to all that will come after just because it is so relevant to the whole process, but it is a completely irrational miracle which only serves to reveal the unreality, lostness, nothingness, meaninglessness of the temporal order and the sole reality and goodness of the world of Being. Redemption therefore can never be redemption of the body but only the salvation of souls. Christ does not return to earth, but draws men to him in heaven. He prepares mansions for them there, he feeds them with bread from heaven, he wills that where he is there his followers may be also. The Christian's citizenship is in heaven not because Christ is to come from thence, but because he, the Christian, is to go there. And the new community, [the] object of the social hope, is not a holy catholic church realized in a new aeon but a communion of saints, the brotherhood of believers who have been rapt out of the evil world of time into the world of perfect Being.

The antithesis between the two modes of thought is not so extreme as not to provide for a considerable number of agreements. There is similarity between the ethics of the two faiths. In the Fourth Gospel and in the Johannine letters love is no less the central theme in the description of the Christian life than it is in the Synoptic Gospels and in Paul; in fact it is more of the central theme. But there is a difference. In the Greek gospel love is primarily love of the brethren and love is the very nature of God. In the Jewish gospel love is love of the neighbor and of the enemy; Jesus never defined God as love. As Father who made his sun shine on evil and on good, whose judgment upon those who offended against his little ones was terrible, he was not a Being with whom one had mystic sweet communion but one whom one obeyed, whose will one sought to share. God was not so much love as will, dynamic, forceful, inevitable and withal loyal to his children. The similarity between the two ethics, is particularly evident within the smaller social groups, within the brotherhood, between friends in Christ. The difference becomes apparent in the different attitude toward the world. Both the Jewish gospel and the Greek gospel are world-denying. But the world which the Greek gospel denies is the physical world, with its lust of the flesh, lust of the eyes and pride of life, the world through which we pass on a pilgrimage to a realm of perfection. It is morally bad, but its moral badness is mated with its temporal character. It is bad not only because it is morally bad, but also because it is transient, because it passes away. The world which the Jewish gospel denies is the world of selfishness, of self-assertion in Jewish nationalism, of trust in riches, of hatred of enemies, of narrow loyalties. It is the *present* world which is denied, not the physical world. For that physical world is itself subject to redemption; that world of bodies which shall be transformed, of nations and churches which shall be redeemed, in the real world and in it God is active.

A difference in attitudes which results from the divergence in outlook upon the world of time is revealed in the difference in the emphasis upon the present moment and the present task. For the Jewish outlook, the present is important because the kingdom of God is potential in it and because that potentiality may at any moment become actuality, not by evolution but by revolution. For the Greek view the present is depreciated because it is temporal; if it is important it derives its meaning from the fact of some incarnation of the eternal in it. The Greek faith is likely to look backward, deriving the significance of the present from the miracle of Incarnation; the Hebrew view is more likely to look forward, deriving the meaning of the now from the potential future.

Either one of these views offers us an alternative to the monistic and optimistic superstition which equated humanity with God and civilization with the Kingdom; both recognize a fundamental duality in life and history; both recognize the decisive importance of Jesus in human history. Christianity, debtor to both Greek and Jew, has sought to reconcile these kindred outlooks on reality and to form one system out of them. Augustine and Aquinas succeeded in achieving some measure of synthesis and Medieval Catholicism set forth that synthesis in life. In the Protestant synthesis the Greek received something of an advantage over the Jew while the Jew prevailed in sectarianism. We shall get nowhere today by seeking a hasty synthesis, nor by the effort to return to one of the syntheses of the past, either in the Catholic or the Protestant. The questions which are involved for us are after all not the questions of grace and the law. For both the Jewish and the Greek faiths are orientated around the idea of grace; the religion of the law belongs to a monism which is antagonistic to both these views. For the present our task is not that of seeking synthesis but of working out in our own time, in antithesis to humanism and monism, that one of these two revolutionary faiths which must be our own. The synthesis we may leave to the future.

To the writer it seems to be the task of American Christianity to develop in conformity with its heritage and character the implications of the Jewish gospel. It agrees best with that American spirit which is represented in philosophy by pragmatism and instrumentalism. John Dewey, the representative American philosopher of the past quarter of a century (who, by the way, has much in common with Barth and Brunner in their antagonism to a teleological and spiritualistic idealism), is not the antagonist but the ally of a faith based on apocalyptic Jewish thinking. The social gospel, at home in this land, needs to be delivered from its association with optimistic and idealistic humanism, but in its fundamental interests and hopes and faith it is at one with the spirit of a Jewish Christian gospel. It is this faith which comports best with that native American radicalism in political ethics which has been slumbering so long but which is yet present and awaits its resurrection. It is this faith which offers a Christian counterpart to the revolutionary program of communism, with which it has much in common as well as many disagreements. Yet it is not because such a gospel has a chance to succeed in American life, it is rather because it represents that fundamental and real insight into *the reality of God in time and of the actuality of redemption in time* which can deepen and guide American life because it is akin to that life while being immeasurably deeper, that it is recommended to us.

In Christ there is neither Jew nor Greek, neither Occidental nor Oriental, neither German nor Scotch nor American. But when we think about Christ and his meaning for us we must do so as Greeks and Jews, as Occidentals or Orientals, as Scotch or German or American. There simply is no other way; for we are what we are with a here, a now, and an I. And we may, we can trust that God who is actually directing the fortunes of history to gather us in and make us all one, if we do our duty in the here and the now, which in this particular case is that of working as hard as we can at the understanding of the implications for us of that faith by which we live.

As long as we take the God of Jesus Christ seriously, and the emergence of his meaning in Christ seriously, we shall not greatly differ from those who as Greeks seek to explicate for themselves the meaning of the gospel for them. The fundamental ideas of the gospel remain the same. For both the only way of salvation will lie through repentance; for both salvation will appear not as reward but as a gift; for both the way to redemption will lie not through evolution but through revolution; for both rebirth will appear to be the primary condition of entrance into the kingdom of God. The differences lie in the divergence of emphasis upon the social and the individual, upon the historical and the eternal. The reconciliation of these differences may be left with complete assurance to the God who works in history and they may therefore be happily regarded as reasons for co-operation rather than strife, and valued when they appear in the other just because they also represent reality.

Faith, Works, and Social Salvation

This article, which appeared in the inaugural edition of the Methodist journal Religion in Life, *shows how Niebuhr sought to probe the meaning of the orthodox Christian doctrine of salvation by God's grace apart from the good works that any human being might perform. He also seems to have been trying to assess the political choices confronting an America struggling to cope with the stresses of the Great Depression. The appeal of fascism, with its drive to organize society into an interrelated whole, appears to have worried him the most. But with respect to their shared faith in human controls and social-engineering formulas, there was a distinct resemblance between fascism, post-revolutionary communism, and the New Deal that presidential candidate Franklin Delano Roosevelt was promising the American electorate. To Niebuhr, all were guilty of seeking "social salvation" by means of their own "good works." In the election of 1932, Niebuhr probably did not vote for Herbert Hoover. Nevertheless, he saw fit to laud earlier* laissez-faire *versions of liberal democracy that chose to rely upon the engineering of the divine in history. The influence of Paul Tillich is apparent in this article; this caused Niebuhr to challenge the church to look for the "religious attitude toward life" that was at the core of any social scheme or political ideology.*

Source: *Religion in Life* 1 (Fall 1932): 426–30.

Our political and economic schemes as well as worship reflect our religious attitudes. Whether we are conscious of it or not, our most carefully considered plans in education or in church administration express our religious sense of orientation in life. The tactics of living is related to the strategy of life; if our professed strategy and our actual tactics do not agree that is an indication that our profession is not a confession. When we observe the tactical arrangements of a new movement, or of an old one, it is always important to inquire what strategy lies behind them, or what religious attitude toward life is expressed in them.

The problem of long-range planning, of rational social control and management, which now confronts the American people has such relations to a fundamental religious orientation in life. We are being told that since we have made a general mess of things, economically, religiously, politically, we must seek our salvation by reducing the complex cultural world to a pattern and by providing for the operation of its machinery as a single, interrelated whole. What is necessary, it seems, is that we impose upon our economic organization the plan of a modern efficiency-engineered factory, in which the co-operation of all factors is carefully adjusted for the purpose of gaining a certain definite result, in which rational considerations dominate the whole process of production by carefully regulating the relations of means to end.

In political life the same road to salvation is urged upon us by example or word. In Fascism and Communism the engineering principle has been applied to government. The efficient operation of the political machine requires centralized control, the subordination of the legislative to the executive function, the employment of governmental agencies as research institutions which will enable the executive to deal rationally with the raw material and produce the desired results. If Italy, Russia and Germany have adopted the scheme in practice, America is going a long way toward its acceptance in spirit. It pours scorn upon its legislature, extends its fact-finding and administrative machinery, and, despite present dissent, continues to preserve a large amount of respect for its executive engineer.

The tactics of careful planning, of the rational co-ordination of means and ends, of the exclusion of purely impulsive and traditional elements from the social processes, are evident in much of our less public life. We seek to apply their principles to the education of our children, to the management of our budgeted family finances, to the preparation of lectures and sermons, and there have been instances of their application to the manufacture of poetry and music. In a thousand ways our daily existence is modified by suspicion of the spontaneous, the organic, the non-theological, the impulsive and by reliance upon the mechanical, the rational, and the planned. Nothing in our hereditary religion is more foreign to our attitude than the advice that we take no thought for the morrow and on few have divines exercised their skill in reinterpretation more astutely and unhappily.

The economic interpretation ascribes this approach to life, in which mechanical rather than organic categories dominate, to the influence of the machine upon our habits of thought. An interpretation in terms of ideas accounts for the machine as the product of rationalism. But however we explain the origin of the approach, we cannot but discern in it the expression of a fundamentally religious attitude. The habit of social planning, of personal engineering, presupposes a certain rather definite orientation in life. It has a creed, whether it be consciously accepted or not, and the creed is a double one, containing the great negative assertion that we cannot trust nature, the social processes, history, that is, a God who works in these, and the positive affirmation that we can and must trust only our own reason, that is, the human god. The negation is quite as important as the affirmation. Fundamentally it is a religion of suspicion rather than of trust; its confidence in man's ability to master his fate is not so great as its assurance that there is no God who will work out humanity's salvation.

If the tactics of social planning rest on a doubt and a faith the older tactics of liberalism are no less the expression of a faith and a doubt. In Rousseau it was faith in nature and the natural, not the rational man; in Adam Smith it was faith in the harmony of self-interest and the social good, provided for in the nature of things and not by careful adjustment; in later liberalism it was faith in natural evolution. But it was always faith in something spontaneous, more than merely human, something which was in control of both man and his environment. If liberalism rejected governmental interference in business and religion it did so because it had confidence in the ability of more or less unrational processes to lead men to a happy issue, while it deeply suspected the adequacy of the disinterestedness and of the intelligence of any group which undertook to regulate the affairs of the commonwealth. In education it reposed a large trust in a youth's own guiding interest on the one hand and in the educational influences of free social intercourse on the other. In religion it believed with Gamaliel that truth might be trusted to win its own way. All in all liberalism was opposed to a careful engineering of life not so much because it believed in competition but because it represented an attitude of faith in the total, more or less natural processes of life, individual and social. This is a religious attitude and liberalism may be said to have been the last, if greatly attenuated, expression of a Christian confidence in the actual world and its God.

It is contended by the advocates of the engineering point of view that the approach of faith has been invalidated by experience, that particularly the faith of liberalism is responsible for the present sorry estate of civilization. Instead of reposing any confidence, therefore, in the nature of things it is necessary for us today to increase our skepticism and to fall back upon the realization that we have only ourselves and that there is no other name under heaven by which man can be saved than the name of reason. Liberals may respond that mankind's sad plight is less due to the policy of *laissez faire* than to interference with the free operation of natural factors, that tariff walls, governmental support of private interests in foreign markets, currency management, febrile efforts to stop deflations and similar efforts to control liberty must be held to account at least quite as much as the policy of freedom. They may point out that the attempt to cure our disease by a larger measure of planned control is to give an overdose of the same poison which debilitated us in the first instance—always a very doubtful expedient. Further, the liberal will question whether the method of planning is possible when the unit to which the plan is to be applied is so complex as a modern national culture and the ends to be gained so various as those which such a culture serves. A limited end, such as the economic security of a population, may indeed be projected and provision made for it, but the complexity of culture cannot be reduced to rational terms without tremendous impoverishment. Finally, it may be objected that to organize the whole of society into an interrelated organism simply increases the chances of breakdown and insures that when breakdown comes it will be thorough, involving every part. It is of no avail to point to Russia for Russia today is far from being a complex culture; its experiment will not be completed for many a decade; and for the present its people live by faith—by faith in communism as a movement enjoying cosmic support—rather than on the results of national planning.

However, the issue is not between liberalism and communism; it lies rather in the question of the religious attitudes represented by the rationalism of communism in its post-revolutionary form and by liberalism and democracy in their early, non-rational form. The former represents the doctrine of salvation by works, the latter the doctrine of salvation by faith. That liberalism is an adequate representative of the latter teaching few men are prepared to maintain today. Its inadequacy appears to be in part due to its lack of faith, to its dilution with a work philosophy, but more largely to its misplaced confidence, to its trust in human self-interest. Its failure cannot therefore be interpreted as the failure of the religious attitude of confidence in the universe and in historic processes. Ultimately the faith on which democracy rests is not a faith in democracy and the final choice before men is not the choice between communism and democracy, but the choice between a rationalistic, engineering attitude toward life and a confident, trustful adjustment to a living universe. Before we abandon that fundamental faith it behooves us to inquire whether there is not a more adequate expression of the religion of faith than liberalism offers, whether there is not an alternative to liberalism which remains true to its fundamental strategy while adopting different tactics. Have we gone so far in the Western world only to find that our whole way has led us in the wrong direction? Or did we go astray but a short distance back, whither we can return and from whence we can once more set out confidently upon our life's adventure? May not the major premise, that we are saved by faith, be right, though the minor premise, that this faith may be reposed in human nature, is wrong? May there not be in democracy, as a movement of revolt against all authoritative, expert ordering of life, a religious power which remains effective, though the peculiar form which later liberal democracy has taken be quite mistaken? Perhaps democracy, in so far as it is a political expression of faith in the God of history and of suspicion of all rationalistic, expert attempts to guide life in pre-arranged grooves, can take on other forms than the form of liberalism.

The form which suggests itself to us in these days of disillusionment and uncertainty is one which defines the object of its trust not in terms of human interest, but in terms of divine agency, and which struggles to emancipate men from the new tyrannies as effectively as the old liberalism struggled to emancipate them from the despotisms of kings and creeds. For now as before the first task of those who believe in salvation by faith and who believe that social salvation is quite as important as individual salvation is the task of liberation. If we can clear away the obstacles we may trust the force of moral health, the divine "grace" which operates in society as well as in the individual, to make its own way. Thus the task of religious democracy may be defined in terms of liberation from the two great systems of self-interestedness which have fastened themselves upon us, nationalism and capitalism. But the method of emancipation which is suggested to those who have faith in historic processes is not that of ridding themselves of these by means of an international governmental machine or of a new state-controlled industrialism. This is to place rationalism in charge and to abandon the whole religion of trust in natural processes, in God's agency. It is rather to rid themselves of these by means of non-cooperation and to await and to promote the development of a cooperative international commonwealth and of a cooperative economic order. For instead of faith in self-interest the faith of such a movement lies in the divine agency which manifests itself in cooperative life, in mutual aid, in the organic growing together of individuals and societies. We cannot believe, as did the older exponents of the social gospel, in the growth of love as an automatic process. There is evident too much of evil, too much of selfishness. Religious democracy understands that there is no road to unity save through suffering, forgiveness, repentance, restitution. But if the method of removing evil is more loving there is good reason to believe that the result will also be more love-worthy.

For those who seek their social redemption by faith rather than by works the future is by no means wholly clear. They must be content to say, "one step enough for me." They cannot blaze their trail forward with confidence that they know exactly whither it will lead them. They only know that the end is good, because it is God's end. One thing seems rather likely, that they will be forging steadfastly through the wilderness of the future after the planners and rationalizers, wearied with human stupidity, faint because of the obstacles in their road, have given up the struggle—tired radicals.

What Must We Do?

"What Must We Do?" was the first of eight sermons published in The Christian Century Pulpit *following the merger in 1934 of Niebuhr's Evangelical Synod and the German Reformed Church; Synod and German Reformed ministers each contributed four. Instead of dealing with the subject of ecumenism, Niebuhr seized this opportunity to lay out his theological interpretation of the Great Depression. Much of the New Deal rhetoric at the time called upon the American public to redouble its faith in the nation's faltering institutions. In contrast, Niebuhr contended that only a renewed faith in God was capable of stemming the crisis and clearing the way to any kind of promised land. In this sermon, he also became more specific about what repentance might involve other than simply contrition. Could a whole society be motivated to adopt an ethic of profit sharing rather than profit making? Niebuhr apparently hoped that it could. Like some of today's church leaders, he also banked this hope not so much on ecclesiastical institutions but on Christians living out their faith in God in the worldly context of their daily vocations.*

Source: *The Christian Century Pulpit* 5 (July 1934): 145–47.

And the multitudes asked him, saying, What then must we do? Luke 3:10.

And a certain ruler asked him, saying, Good teacher, what shall I do to inherit eternal life? Luke 18:18.

And he called for lights and sprang in, and, trembling for fear, fell down before Paul and Silas. And he brought them out and said, Sirs, what must I do to be saved? Acts 16:29-30.

There are times when we ask the question, "What shall we do?" because we are bored and seek escape from inactivity. There are other times when we ask it because we confront many opportunities and as free men are called upon to make a free choice. But there are also times when the question is put to us and by us with a seriousness and an intensity wholly lacking in the cases of the free man and the bored man. We live in such a time; the people of the New Testament lived in such a time; and for us as for them the question inevitably takes on the form, "What shall I do to be saved?" We know how the multitudes felt when they heard John say that the axe had been laid at the root of the tree, for the axe has been laid at the root of the tree of modern life. We know how the young man felt who came to Jesus with the question, "What must I do to inherit eternal life?" for we also have known the promise of a great opportunity and are threatened with its withdrawal.

A Sick World

We can no longer ask what we must do in order that we may achieve the ideal of a warless world. We must inquire far more desperately and seriously what must be done in order that we may be saved from the storm of war that is even now gathering upon the horizon. We can no longer ask what we must do in order that we may increase the human brotherliness and kindness. Our question now is not the question of builders of the kingdom of God on earth but the question of Cain. The blood, the pain, the misery of our brothers cries up to heaven against us. What must we do to atone for this brutal common life of ours? What must we do to be saved from continued participation in the mass murders and mass thefts of modern life? What must we do as a nation to be saved from putrefaction, from the foulness of our physical and moral disease? To look out upon our world today is to understand what Isaiah meant when looking upon his nation he exclaimed, "The whole head is sick and the whole heart is faint. From the sole of the foot even unto the head there is no soundness in it but wounds and bruises and fresh stripes." A healthy man can ask the question "What shall I do?" in one way; a sick man must ask it in an entirely different way, and we belong today among the sick.

Lost Gods

The threat against our life appears not only in the long-drawn out and ever recurrent crises which we have come in the economic and political spheres; it is present also in the loss of life's meaning for individuals and for groups. There was a time when we drew significance for our existence out of the association with the great human institutions and movements. We were part of a progressing world. Democracy, science, technology, industry, church and education, called us into their service and in their signs we were to conquer. We enlisted in great crusades. But the institutions have lost their glamour as we have discovered the stuff out of which they were made and the crusades have ended as all crusades in all the past have ended—with the crusaders in possession of a tomb. We are not ready to reject these institutions and enterprises but we do not believe in them as once we did and we cannot draw from them the sense of significant living that we once enjoyed. The gods we worshipped have shown themselves to be idols, dependent upon us for their existence. Though we continue to serve them, we worship them no longer. But having lost these gods our lives are threatened with emptiness. What must we do to be saved from utter futility?

There is yet another sense in which the question of the New Testament has become intensely real for us. Not long ago we thought that we were at the beginning of a new era. We had reason to believe it; we still have reason to believe it. But we have little reason to believe that we can make the new beginning. There are times in the life of man when he glimpses before him the prospect of a new kind of existence—happier, more peaceful, more fruitful, more energetic than anything he has known before. A new life is within his reach but he finds himself unable to lay hold of it. He might realize the promise if only he knew what to do. Not knowing what to do he follows the old familiar and unsatisfactory ways and sees his vision fade into the light of common day.

It is so in the social life. A new culture, world-wide, peaceful, happy, abundant seems within our reach even now. Never were the opportunities for newness in human life so near and so enticing. Never have the bonds of peace been so numerous, the instruments of knowledge so precise, the supplies of food so plentiful, the possibilities of freedom so abounding. A kingdom has been prepared for us, but we do not have the power to take it nor the grace to receive it.

There is that within ourselves and our common life which prevents us from being what we might be. And we cannot look upon the situation with hope, thinking that we need to take only a few more steps before we can enter upon the promised land. We cannot look upon it with patience in the knowledge that tomorrow will give us a greater opportunity. We can regard it only with the sober conviction that so far as we are concerned, so far as our nation is concerned, so far perhaps as this present civilization is concerned the opportunity is passing and may never come again. Worse than that we know that the alternative to this better life is not simply continued existence on the old basis but disaster, be it slow or sudden. What must we do to inherit this life that is being offered and being withdrawn?

The Crisis of Faith

As our questions are like the questions of the people of the New Testament so the answers which we receive are like the answers given them. The first answer which they received was a disappointing one. They asked for something to do and they were told to believe. But they were not disappointed by it in the long run and when we look deeply into the nature of our modern crisis we will not be disappointed by it either. The politicians who told us that nothing was wrong with our country save lack of confidence were right. But they were desperately wrong when they regarded this as a light thing which might easily be taken care of by a few homilies on the soundness of our institutions.

A crisis of faith is the deepest crisis that there is and it can never be overcome by a will to believe in the very things which have failed us. Nor can it be overcome successfully by the creation of new idols. For a time the idolatry of the race or the nation or the class may be able to deliver men from their futility and give them courage and strength for their tasks. But these gods are almost as transitory as the ones they have replaced and they are no less divisive and destructive in the long run. The events of our time insist that we shall not be able to find the basis of the faith by which we can live and must live save in the "I am that I am" on which we are utterly dependent for our being and our meaning. These events wring from us again the faith which no will to believe can establish, the faith in that last reality which is our creator and our slayer.

But more than that, the answer to our question "what shall we do to be saved?" directs us to Jesus Christ. It is not the love of traditional modes of thought nor the romantic flight to medieval ways of life which makes the answer "Believe on the Lord Jesus Christ" a real answer for us today. Our tragedy and our sin compel us to look again to that segment of history in which sin and tragedy and the God who brings our sin to its tragic and redeeming consequences came to fullest appearance. To believe in the Lord Jesus Christ means many things, but it means this at least, that our faith is established upon no wish nor dream but upon a very bitter reality. It does not mean to believe in a kindly spirit somewhere who may help us in our more or less pious endeavors, but it does mean that we have seen the enemy and the judge of our sin as our redeemer. There are many loud voices today shouting at us to do this and to do that in order that we may be saved. But through all the turmoil the still small voice which bids us to believe in the Lord Jesus Christ carries a conviction with it that these other voices lack. Here is the beginning of our answer. How much more it entails few of us seem prepared to say today. But we wait for the fuller answer.

The Sharing of Life

There is another New Testament reply to our question which is also a contemporary reply. John said, when the multitudes questioned him, "He that hath two coats let him impart to him that hath none; and he that hath food let him do likewise." Jesus told the rich young ruler to sell all that he had and to give to the poor. These are difficult words which the legalists with their ten per cent sharing and their fifty per cent sharing make no easier for us. But, apart from all legalistic interpretations of New Testament morality, we can well understand that we cannot be saved today unless we abandon the desperate effort to hold on to everything we have.

A little while ago we seemed to have embarked upon a new venture which promised much to our American life, but in how short a space of time have the high hopes, which many had, come to grief. Much of that result has been due to the desperate stupidity and fear with which men hold on to their possessions of wealth and prestige and power. There is no salvation for them nor for us all in the effort to conserve all the gains of the past, be they individual or social. More than that, we know that we cannot be saved even so far as our economic health is concerned unless there is a very broad division of the profits of our industry. The technique of that sharing economists and statesmen must work out. But the principle is more than economic and political. It is a part of the structure of things to which we must conform unless we are willing to be damned altogether.

We are not called upon to make sacrifices for the public welfare. Sacrifices may be made by those who have unusual merit. Nothing so noble or heroic as a sacrifice is required of us. What we must do to be saved is something as unheroic as the taking of bitter medicine by the patient who is not willing to die. Love and sharing is no noble privilege which good men are called upon to exercise in order that men may see their good works. It is the law of life which we have flouted far too long, the transgression of which has brought us well nigh to destruction.

Back into Your Vocations!

There is a third answer in the New Testament to the question "What then must we do?" Like the others it is utterly unheroic and quite disappointing to those who want to lead crusades and be messiahs. It is the answer of John to the soldiers and taxgatherers. It is the answer of Paul to his converts. In essence the answer is: Go back into your vocations; look for no great and mighty armies in which you may enlist but with repentance, with hardihood, with hope and with faith in God do your work as you never did it before. Repent of having made your vocation an opportunity for theft and violence. Know that the judgment has come upon all this. But do not think you can escape your responsibility by entering upon a crusade for the kingdom of God. This is also a part of the answer to the question of our time. Whatever be the events which will take place in the broad arena of history the work of the world must be done. And it is likely that the great events will take place in the quiet places where men and women do their own work as teachers, as statesmen, as mothers, as labor leaders, as preachers, as journalists, as engineers, as workers in a thousand fields with faith, with thorough repentance and with enspiriting hope.

Man the Sinner

Originally presented as part of a symposium on the "Christian Doctrine of Man," this article clearly substantiates Niebuhr's key role in the neo-orthodox movement of the 1930s. Like so many others, he eschewed the liberal faith in humanity, which reduced "sin" to a moral category, in favor of the orthodox Christian view of original sin as an idolatrous loyalty to other gods that every person or institution tended to exhibit. This viewpoint made his criticisms of nationalism, capitalism, and socialism all the more sweeping, and it strengthened his argument that nothing short of reconciliation to God could lead America out of the Great Depression. Interestingly, Niebuhr contended that his was an "optimistic" position because, unlike his brother Reinhold, he did not attribute sin to human nature. Doing so would undermine any doctrine of creation that upheld the goodness with which God had also endowed humanity, and it provided no hope for the redemption of the world that the "Christian revolution" might accomplish this side of heaven.

Source: *The Journal of Religion* 15 (July 1935): 272–80.

A moving passage in Waldo Frank's *Death and Birth of David Markand* describes the death of a Polish immigrant who, having dreamed the "American dream," awakened to the reality of American life when he became the victim of his friends as well as of his foes in the industrial conflict. Holding his wife's hand, caressing his daughter, he whispers over and over, "Man is bad," and so dies. A Christian theologian might have said to this Pole, "Thou art not far from the kingdom of God," for the conviction that man is bad is one of the fundamental principles of the Christian interpretation of life. That it is not the only basic dogma need not be said; that it is of essential importance and that its abandonment involves the perversion of the remainder of Christian theology and faith needs to be emphasized.

I

The importance of the doctrine of human sinfulness is evident from the consequences which flow from its acceptance. The Christian strategy of life depends as much on this principle as Marxian strategy depends on the doctrine of the class struggle. It means that in our dealing with ourselves and with our neighbors, with our societies and our neighbor societies, we deal not with morally and rationally healthy beings who may be called upon to develop ideal personalities and to build ideal commonwealths, but rather with diseased beings, who can do little or nothing that is worth while until they have recovered health and who, if they persist in acting as though they were healthy, succeed only in spreading abroad the infection of their own lives. The distinct character of the strategy which the acceptance of this conviction entails may be better understood if it is contrasted with the programs of conduct which follow from other views of evil. The common belief that evil is concentrated in certain individuals or classes—who have made bad choices or have been subjected to bad influences—leads to the restraint and the elimination of the bad by those who can regard themselves as good, and to the pursuit of ideal ends by the latter. The romantic belief that men are good and that evil resides in institutions calls for the elimination of bad institutions and the exercise of unrestrained activity by politically, economically, and ecclesiastically emancipated men. The evolutionary definition of evil, which identifies it with imperfection, with cultural lag, and the ignorance of immaturity, requires simply nurture and education as the proper treatment of the bad. But if the conviction that all men are sinners is maintained these strategies of life must be rejected; a wholly different approach will be necessary.

It may be worth while to note that though apparently the doctrine of human sinfulness is more pessimistic than the rival theories are, it is fundamentally more optimistic. The doctrine of creation is the presupposition of the doctrine of sin. The latter doctrine implies that man's fundamental nature, obscured and corrupted though it is, is perfect. His perfection as a creature, or his health, is not a far-off achievement, a more or less remote possibility which future generations may realize after infinite effort; it is rather the underlying datum of life. Well-being, joy, peace, effective activity are as near as health is to the sick man, not as remote as man is from the ape or the completed building from the blue print.

II

To say that man is a sinner is not equivalent to the statement that he is morally bad. Modern moralism has subordinated all other value categories to those of the morally good and the morally bad. It has regarded these as somehow final and not in need of further definition, while it has reduced the value categories of truth, beauty, and holiness, of intellectual, aesthetic, and religious evil to their moral "essence." Science and art have more or less successfully resisted the tyranny of moralism but religion has accepted the yoke willingly and allowed its concept of sin to be reduced to "moral guilt" as previously it allowed its concept of God to be identified with "moral perfection." It cannot be maintained that there is not an intimate relationship between the positive value categories on the one hand, the negative or disvalue categories on the other hand, but whatever that relation may be, it is evident that moral value is entitled to no pre-eminence. To make moral evil the essence of sin is to make as arbitrary a choice as when moral worth is made the essence of truth, or moral badness the essence of ugliness. The moralist forgets that he occupies a standpoint, that his evaluations are relative to that standpoint, and that the standpoint itself is of no greater finality than the standpoints of religion, science, and art.

More specifically it is to be urged against the moralistic interpretation of sin that moral judgments are relative judgments (not psychologically relative, necessarily) and that, second, the religious category of sin is not a composite term made up of a moral core and secondary accretions but a true concept which must be understood from the religious and not some other point of view. As to the first point, much may be said of the ambiguity of [the] terms "good" and "bad" as used in morality, and as evident in their application now to the object of moral choice, now to the character or conduct of the choosing agent. Nor can it be maintained that they are used in the "strictly ethical sense" only in the latter instance. In both cases, however (whether the judgment be the judge's "guilty" or "not guilty," or the agent's "right" or "wrong"), reference to a standard is implied, whether that standard be a code of laws or a table of values. This standard may be *moral,* but properly it is the standard *of* morality, presupposed by morality. If it was adopted as the result of a moral choice, that was possible only because there had previously been present in the mind of the chooser a standard by reference to which he could adopt it morally. Ultimately morality is always driven back to the acceptance of a standard which is given to it, without which morality would be impossible, but which is itself prior to all morality. The source of that standard is always religion, not morality. It depends upon what man finds to be wholly worshipful, intrinsically valuable—in other words, upon the nature of his god or gods. The "chief good" of man is not the object but the presupposition of his moral choices, and his possession of a chief good is the presupposition of all moral judgments which he or another passes upon him. To define sin in terms of morality is to ignore this fact, that morality without presuppositions is impossible, that it lacks the finality which is claimed for it. I do not mean to say that sin does not involve moral guilt; that is not the point. I do mean that the definition of sin in terms of *moral* guilt implies a mistaken conviction about the finality of morality.

In the second place, the concept of sin as a concept of the religious reason is not reducible to moral terms. Sometimes it is regarded as meaning moral guilt plus emotional overtones due to the religious feelings. [Rudolf] Otto's and [Robert R.] Marrett's brilliant psychological analysis of the sense of the holy and the negative creature-feeling or sense of impurity have indicated that even when the approach is made from the feelings, it is not an emotional-plus element with which we are dealing in religious experience, but rather a psychological state qualitatively different from the moral state. Apart, however, from the consideration of experience, it is evident that the religious reason has employed its concept of sin to connote not merely and not always moral evil, but also physical evil. It is only by eliminating from consideration all the phenomena of demon-possession that Jesus' attitude toward sin can be interpreted as a wholly moral attitude. Moreover, the practice and doctrine of forgiveness of sin (cf. the paralytic) imply a conception of sin which is not primarily moral, with emotional overtones. Furthermore, priestly practice, as again exemplified in part by modern psychiatry, indicates that the evil with which religion deals is not wholly definable in moral terms and cannot be treated with moral means.

To say then that man is a sinner does not mean exactly the same thing as to say that he is morally wicked. Nor are moral evil and religious evil to be regarded as species of a common genus of evil.

III

It is necessary now to inquire more precisely into the meaning of the concept of *sin*. Neither its definition in terms of other disvalues nor the psychological description of the sense of sin are of much help to us in this inquiry. The latter effort represents, upon the whole, the confusion of objective and subjective so typical of modern spiritualistic theology. This confusion—of sin with the sense of sin—has its practical counterpart in the aberrations of emotional, revivalistic evangelicalism with its "unrealistic" attempts to arouse the sense of sin rather than to point to the sin itself and to create a feeling of assurance rather than to point to salvation.

Various efforts have been made to define sin as sensuality or as selfishness. Such efforts are instances of the naturalistic fallacy. Selfishness and sensuality are doubtless sinful but neither flesh nor self are sinful per se. Nor is creatureliness the essence of sin. The relation of creature to creator does not involve sin; the majesty of God does not have human sinfulness for its counterpart. To be sure, the sense of man's worthlessness in contrast to the supreme worthfulness of God may be closely akin to the sense of sin. But in such experiences as Isaiah's and Job's, men would not be aware of their worthlessness—they would know only the supreme worth of the creator—were it not for the fact that prior to the experience they had tended to ascribe supreme worth to the self. The religious concept of sin always involves the idea of *disloyalty*, not of disloyalty in general, but of disloyalty to the true God, to the only trustworthy and wholly loveable reality. Sin is the failure to worship God as God. Yet it is more than the absence of loyalty to God. It is not possible for men to be simply disloyal; they are always loyal to something. Disloyalty implies a false loyalty and disloyalty to God always includes loyalty to something that is not God but which claims deity. Sin therefore is not merely a deprivation, not merely the absence of loyalty; it is wrong direction, false worship. Furthermore, loyalty to a false God implies rebellion against God. It is impossible that it should be otherwise, unless God were something less than the Creator and the essence of Being. To make a god of the self, or of the class, or of the nation, or of the phallus, or of mankind, is to organize life around one of these centers and to draw it away from its true center; hence, in a unified world, it is to wage war against God.

IV

We may return now to the first point—the Christian doctrine that man is a sinner. The statement means not that men occasionally become disloyal to God or that their disloyalty is real only in so far as they consciously choose to be disloyal; it means rather that those to whom God is wholly loyal and who are by nature wholly dependent upon him are in active rebellion against him. The moral qualification that men can be held accountable for this disloyalty only in so far as they are consciously and willingly disloyal is quite beside the point, first of all because Christianity is not primarily concerned with the question of assessing the blame but with the fact of the cure; second, because this qualification rests upon a highly dubious doctrine of freedom. The starting-point of the doctrine of sin is not man's freedom but man's dependence; freedom accounts for the fact that man can be and is disloyal, not for the fact that he ought to be loyal. At all events, the important thing for man the sinner is not that he should feel a sense of guilt but that he should see his disloyalty, his false loyalty, and the consequences. Doubtless the sense of guilt played its important role for early Protestants and for evangelicals, but it has become a barrier to the modern man's understanding of the gospel.

The statement that man is a sinner, disloyal to God and therefore involved in evil consequences of a moral, physical, and social nature may be taken by us today as a general law, perhaps in a statistical sense only. We do not begin with the facts or with our observations, which are primarily observations of ourselves; but introspection is supported by individual and social psychology and by history. We observe that men are primarily loyal to themselves, to their nations, to their pleasures, to their race, to their machines, etc. We examine their actions and their systems of morality and we can say, with greater assurance than Paul had, that they have all fallen short of the glory of God. There may be exceptions to the rule; perhaps the Marxians recognize a few exceptions to the rule of class loyalty; the rule remains as the only safe basis of conduct. The facts make the judgment inevitable that man is bad, disloyal to God, the only source of all life and all good; and that he is bound to take the consequences not because God is angry but because he is God.

V

It remains for us to try to sketch some of these consequences. The first result of disloyalty appears to be conflict within the individual and within society. It is an inevitable result, for to leave the One is to be scattered among the many. No other object is able to hold man's loyalty save that object on which he is actually dependent for life and meaning. Idolatry leads inevitably to polytheism and polytheism is conflict. It is doubtless true that some gods seem better than others, in so far as they unify men and their societies to a greater degree; thus the national god or the class god seems better than the god of self or Mammon or Venus or Bacchus. At the same time the greater gods only transfer the conflict to a broader stage and become greater demons. A second consequence is death. We are beginning again to become aware of the fact that the death of cultures is the consequence of the sin of social wholes (nationalism, capitalism, communism), and that "spiritual" death, the disintegration of the self, is the consequence of false loyalties and conflicts. The moral consequences of sin—man's inhumanity to man, cruelty to beasts, exploitation of nature, abuse of sex, greed, commercial profanization of creation and its beauty—these are no less patent.

Of particular importance for the Christian strategy of life is the consequence of man's impotence to rescue himself out of his disloyalty and rebellion, conflict, death, and vice. Moralism which makes the human free will the source of all good and evil cannot understand this impotence. Its savior is the will; every problem is solved by an appeal to the will. But there is no such thing as a free will in this sense. The will is always committed or it is no will at all. It is either committed to God or to one of the gods. "The will is as its strongest motive is." Man cannot transfer his loyalty from one of the false gods to God by exercising his will, since that will is loyal to the false god. Every effort it makes is an effort in some direction. So long as man is loyal to himself, or to his nation, or his class, or to his moral standard based upon a self-chosen highest good, his efforts to rescue himself will be determined by his loyalty. The consequence is that he involves himself more deeply in disloyalty to God. The situation is similar to the effort to bring about international peace through international war, which results only in the increase of national loyalties and the increase of war; it is similar also to the effort to bring about social justice through inter-class conflict which results in the increase of class loyalties and of social injustice. Redemption from sin is possible only by a reconciliation to God, which cannot be initiated by the disloyal creature. Man the sinner is incapable of overcoming his sin.

In conclusion, the consequence of the doctrine for Christian strategy may be more definitely pointed out than was possible at the beginning. Since man is bad, the restraint of evil—particularly of the moral evil which is the result of sin—is a necessary element in every plan for the conduct of life. "Thou shalt nots" take their place in the moral code; self-discipline and social discipline take the place of self-expression and social freedom. But three qualifications, at least, must be borne in mind in the exercise of restraint. The first is that Christian restraint is the restraint of sinners by sinners and not by the just. It is restraint exercised on the basis of a law or scale of values which the disloyal mind discerns only darkly; it is the restraint exercised by those who acknowledge their equality with the restrained, for equality in sinfulness is also equality. Whatever be the meaning of the doctrine of election it cannot be used to justify a dictatorship of the "good" over the "bad." In the second place, any restraint imposed on the basis of human sinfulness must avoid the temptation of falling into moralism; it must be medicinal rather than vindictive, conservative rather than destructive; if it uses force, which it will be loth to employ, it will use it only in this way, knowing that force cannot redeem but only prevent some external consequences of sin. In the third place, the Christian strategy of the restraint of evil must be wholly subordinated to the strategy of the reconciliation. Later Puritanism fell into the great error of giving the doctrine of sin pre-eminence over the doctrine of redemption; hence its strategy of restraint took the place of the strategy of reconciliation. But the doctrine of sin is meaningful only as it presupposes the doctrine of creation and furnishes the presupposition of the doctrine of redemption. And the use of restraint is definitely an interim measure which needs to be subordinated to the fundamental strategy of Christianity. As the communist must subordinate his interests in the amelioration of the worker's lot within the capitalist system to his interest in the revolution so the Christian must put the Christian revolution first. Where this is forgotten the result is revisionist Christianity, an abhorrent heresy.

7

Back to the Future Of Cultural Engagement

History was frequently the context in which H. Richard Niebuhr grappled with the paradox of church and world. One sees this in *The Church Against the World,* where in 1935 he asserted that the church's pattern of identification, withdrawal, and cultural reengagement had been "repeated three times in the past: in the ancient world, in the medieval, and in the modern." While his recognition of the "peculiar character" of the contemporary church and its culture prevented him from holding a purely cyclical view of the relationship, nevertheless there were enough lessons from the past to convince him that the "task of the present generation" involved "liberation of the church from its bondage to a corrupt civilization."[1] In order for the church to achieve the independence that he deemed essential for discerning how its faith in God might reshape its role in the world, it first needed to repudiate the faiths it had falsely placed in capitalist, nationalist, and humanistic ideologies. While the socialistic alliances favored by other

---

1. H. Richard Niebuhr, "Toward the Independence of the Church," in *The Church Against the World,* ed. H. Richard Niebuhr (Chicago: Willet, Clark and Company, 1935), 124.

Christian revolutionaries might appear to be a tempting alternative, he warned that "no new beginning of the church's life is possible" without a renewed "loyalty to God and to Jesus Christ."[2] In no way, however, was Niebuhr advocating a world-fleeing asceticism. On the contrary, independence for him was a strategy designed to strengthen the church's "participation in the affairs of an unconverted and unreborn world." In fact, the vision he set forth for the church included "the realization in civilization of the unity and peace of the saved children of God."[3]

To test the viability of his strategy for the church in the world of the Great Depression, Niebuhr made America's religious history his "laboratory."[4] Soon after he arrived at Yale, he began offering classes and seminars on "The Ethical Ideal of American Christianity"; in his preparation for them, he gave considerable attention to the theology of Jonathan Edwards. These efforts culminated in *The Kingdom of God in America*, published just two years after *The Church Against the World*. In his preface to this second major work, Niebuhr noted that the "sociological approach" he had used in *The Social Sources of Denominationalism* left him "dissatisfied at a number of points." While it highlighted the "particular channels" into which the American religious stream flowed, it did not "account for the force of the stream itself." Nor did it explain the Christian movement that produced institutionalized churches or consider the "unity which our faith possesses despite its variety." He had also failed to recognize "the faith which is independent, which is aggressive rather than passive, and which molds culture instead of being molded by it."[5] He said forcefully that this study had bolstered his convictions that

---

2. Ibid., 152–53.
3. Ibid., 155.
4. H. Richard Niebuhr, *The Kingdom of God in America* (New York: Harper & Row, 1937), x, hereafter cited as *Kingdom of God*.
5. Ibid., ix–x.

Christianity in any historical context needed to be viewed as a dynamic movement, expressing itself dialectically with respect to God and the world, and that in America the culture as well as Christian faith could not be "understood at all save on the basis of faith in a sovereign, living, loving God."[6]

Making such a case for the formative influence of Christianity in American culture carried a formidable challenge. Niebuhr knew he was taking direct aim at the work of leading social historians like Vernon L. Parrington. They tended to view religion much as he had in *Social Sources*, and they had succeeded in exposing the type of cultural bondage that could envelop the church in the present as much as the past. When this became the only point of view for interpreting America's religious history, however, the kingdom of God tended to become the "American kingdom of God." Instead of the "impact of the gospel upon the New World," one saw instead the "use and adaptation of the gospel by the new society for its own purposes."[7] Therefore, in *Kingdom of God* Niebuhr set out to establish a solid measure of historical support for the strategy he was proposing for the church of his own day, mired as it was in an economic crisis and facing the prospect of another world war. For one thing, he sought to recapture the "prophetic strain" in American Christianity that began with God, demanded rebirth, announced divine judgment, and looked forward to "God's salvation rather than to human victory." In addition, he drew heavily upon the philosopher Henri Bergson's distinction between religion as movement and institution, emphasizing that while institutions tended to be conservative, to yield to worldly influences, and to look to the past, they sprang from movements that were progressive and aggressive in their efforts to influence their culture, as well as future-oriented.

6. Ibid., xiii–xvi.
7. Ibid., 9.

Furthermore, he insisted that "if we are to understand American Christianity we need to take our stand within the movement," or else "we shall never see what it has seen but only the incidental results of its vision, which we shall then seek to explain as due to some strange transmutation of political and economic interest."[8]

It was no coincidence that Niebuhr chose the kingdom of God as the central theme of America's religious history. The Social Gospel movement in mainline Protestantism, as we have seen, had occupied much of his thinking in all his years of ministry in the Evangelical Synod of North America. While the movement expressed the sense of social responsibility that he believed was at the core of the Christian faith, he consistently questioned the optimistic view of human nature and of the course of Western civilization that had become its chief theological underpinning. For this reason, he was attracted to Karl Barth's efforts in Europe to put God once again at the center of all theological discourse. At the same time, he was critical of Barth because he feared that the social side of the church's gospel might get thrown out with its liberal bathwater. During the 1930s, Niebuhr had not completely resolved this issue for himself. Especially enlightening, therefore, is "The Kingdom of God and Eschatology in the Social Gospel and in Barthianism," a paper that Niebuhr prepared for his Theological Discussion Group and that remained unpublished until William Stacy Johnson included it in his anthology.[9] Here Niebuhr was ready to state that "Barth has become the legitimate heir of the Social Gospel" because of his insistence that the kingdom, when it is regarded in social as well as individual terms, is always the one "*God* establishes, has established, and will establish," and that the question this brought to light for the church was "whether we

---

8. Ibid., 10–12.
9. H. Richard Niebuhr, "The Kingdom of God and Eschatology in the Social Gospel and in Barthianism," in *H. Richard Niebuhr: Theology, History, Culture*, ed. William Stacy Johnson (New Haven, CT: Yale University Press, 1996), 117–22.

shall begin with *our* purposes or with *God's* as these are revealed, known, and believed through God's act of self-communication in Jesus Christ."[10]

In order to give this same idea an American test, the main chapters of *Kingdom of God* became Niebuhr's historical laboratory. For the sake of those who might contend that he was presenting "theology in the guise of history," he stated that his initial attempt to make the utopian version of the "kingdom on earth" (espoused by twentieth-century Social Gospelers and other champions of the "American dream") the basis for his analysis of American Christianity had failed, and that his efforts only proved adequate when seen through the lens of earlier Protestant emphases on the "sovereignty of God" and the "kingdom of Christ."[11] No better examples of Niebuhr's findings might be given than his analyses of the Great Awakenings of the eighteenth and nineteenth centuries. The first of these came into view for him as a revolution in the hearts and minds of people, inaugurating a new order that substituted liberty and love for religious regimentation and fear of God. This "kingdom of Christ," he contended, presupposed the older Puritan conviction that only the sovereign action of God could bring about this revolution in anybody's soul, and Awakeners like Jonathan Edwards asserted that it was the love of God for them that inspired and sustained their love for their neighbors. Hence, when new believers found themselves lacking in the latter, "they turned to worship, to self-examination in the presence of God, to contemplation of the cross of Christ."[12]

Niebuhr came to the same conclusion with respect to the second of America's Great Awakenings. While "humanist democrats" based their efforts to reform society on the principle of human goodness,

---

10. Ibid., 121.
11. Niebuhr, *Kingdom of God in America*, xi–xiii.
12. Ibid., 88–99.

the revivalists called for a God-given second birth that liberated people and, through Christ, enabled them to join in a revolution that included temperance, peace, and prison reform, as well as the alleviation of poverty. This new beginning for America appeared to him to be so sweeping that he called it "our national conversion."[13] In Niebuhr's estimation, those revivalists who gave more attention to the coming kingdom were of the same mind. Charles G. Finney may have thought that personal regeneration was the better way to achieve the abolition of slavery, but it was no less urgent a reforming cause for him than it was for others in the antislavery movement. When Social Gospel patriarchs like Washington Gladden and Walter Rauschenbusch burst on to the scene following the Civil War, moreover, it was upon this same evangelical foundation that they sought to build their movement.[14]

The most frequently referenced sentence in Niebuhr's *Kingdom of God* is also frequently misunderstood: "A God without wrath brought forth men without sin into a kingdom without judgment through the ministrations of a Christ without a cross."[15] With these words, he was condemning not the Social Gospel movement but what he regarded as its fatal theological transformation at the hands of its twentieth-century liberal Protestant heirs. The rehabilitation of the Social Gospel based upon the evangelical theology that had initially undergirded it was his real objective. To him, history showed that this hope was as *American* as it was *Christian*. The following writings further demonstrate Niebuhr's belief that it was with a neo-orthodox Social Gospel that the church might best reengage the world from which he was summoning it to withdraw during the 1930s.

---

13. Ibid., 99–126.
14. Ibid., 155–63.
15. Ibid., 193.

Toward the Emancipation of the Church

This article, published earlier in the same year as The Church Against the World, *is an abbreviated version of Niebuhr's major contribution to that book. It sets forth his scathing critique of the "false faith" on which he believed capitalism, nationalism, and humanism in the twentieth century had come to rely. The church's entanglement with each of them had not only caused it to compromise its own faith in God but also to lose its edge in society by becoming nothing more than "the teacher of the prevailing code of morals and the pantheon of the social gods." The article also spells out the orthodox theological moorings to which he thought the church needed to return to achieve its emancipation from these entanglements. At same time, he opposed any attempt to resolve the paradox of church and world by way of the "monism of other-worldliness" and insisted that the church must seek to renew its commitment to functioning as a "revolutionary community."*

Source: *Christendom* 1 (1935): 133–45.

The relation of the church to civilization is a varying one, and necessarily so, because each of these entities is continually changing and each is subject to corruption and to conversion. The history of the relationship is marked by periods of conflict, of alliance, and of identification. A converted church in a corrupt civilization withdraws to its upper rooms, into monasteries and conventicles; it issues forth from these in the aggressive evangelism of apostles, monks and friars, circuit riders and missionaries; it relaxes its rigorism as it discerns signs of repentance and faith; it enters into inevitable alliance with converted emperors and governors, philosophers and artists, merchants and entrepreneurs, and begins to live at peace in the culture they produce under the stimulus of their faith; when faith loses its force, as generation follows generation, discipline is relaxed, repentance grows formal, corruption enters with idolatry, and the church tied to the culture which it sponsored suffers corruption with it. Only a new withdrawal followed by a new aggression can then save the church and restore to it the salt with which to savor society. This general pattern has been repeated three times in the past: in the ancient world, in the medieval, and in the modern. It may be repeated many times in the future. Yet the interest of any generation of Christians lies in the pattern as a whole than in its own particular relation to the prevailing civilization. The character of that relation is defined not only by the peculiar character of the contemporary church and the contemporary culture but even more by the demand which the abiding gospel makes upon Christianity. The task of the present generation appears to lie in the liberation of the church from its bondage to a corrupt civilization.

I: The Captive Church

The church is in bondage to capitalism. Capitalism in its contemporary form is more than a system of ownership and distribution of economic goods. It is a faith and a way of life. It is faith in wealth as the source of all life's blessings and as the savior of man from his deepest misery. It is the doctrine that man's most important activity is the production of economic goods and that all other things are dependent upon this. On the basis of this initial idolatry it develops a morality in which economic worth becomes the standard by which to measure all other values and the economic virtues take precedence over courage, temperance, wisdom and justice, over charity, humility and fidelity. Hence nature, love, life, truth, beauty and justice are exploited or made servants of the high economic good. Everything, including the lives of workers, is made a utility, is desecrated and ultimately destroyed. Capitalism develops a discipline of its own but in the long run makes for the overthrow of all discipline since the service of its god demands the encouragement of unlimited desire for that which promises—but must fail—to satisfy the lust of the flesh and the pride of life.

The capitalist faith is not a disembodied spirit. It expresses itself in laws and social habits and transforms the whole of civilization. It fashions society into an economic organization in which production for profit becomes the central enterprise, in which the economic relations of men are regarded as their fundamental relations, in which economic privileges are most highly prized, and in which the resultant classes of men are set to struggle with one another for the economic goods. Education and government are brought under the sway of the faith. The family itself is modified by it. The structure of cities and their very architecture is influenced by this religion. So intimate is the relation between the civilization and the faith that it is difficult to participate in the former without consenting to the latter and becoming entangled in its destructive morality. It was possible for Paul's converts to eat meat which had been offered to idols without compromising with paganism. But the products which come from the altars of this modern idolatry—the dividends, the privileges, the status, the struggle—are of a sort that it is difficult to partake of them without becoming involved in the whole system of misplaced faith and perverted morality.[16]

---

16. Niebuhr's note: [The theory that modern capitalism is a system with a religious foundation and a cultural superstructure obviously runs counter to the widely accepted Marxian doctrine. It is not our intention to deny many elements in the Marxian analysis: the reality of the class struggle, the destructive self-contradiction in modern capitalism; the effect of capitalism upon government, law, the established religion. Neither are we intent upon defending the principle of private property as an adequate basis for the modern economic structure. But we are affirming that modern capitalism does not represent the inevitable product of the private property system in which early democracy and Puritanism were interested, that it has corrupted and perverted that system, making of it something which it was never intended to be nor was bound to be. We believe that the economic interpretation of history is itself a product and a statement of the economic faith and that communism is in many ways a variant form of capitalist religion.]

No antithesis could be greater than that which obtains between the gospel and capitalist faith. The church has known from the beginning that the love of money is the root of evil, that it is impossible to serve God and Mammon, that they that have riches shall hardly enter into life, that life does not consist in the abundance of things possessed, that the earth is the Lord's and that love, not self-interest, is the first law of life. Yet the church has become entangled with capitalist civilization to such an extent that it has compromised with capitalist faith and morality and become a servant of the world. So intimate have the bonds between capitalism and Protestantism become that the genealogists have suspected kinship. Some have ascribed the parentage of capitalism to Protestantism while others have seen in the latter the child of the former. But whatever may have been the relation between the modest system of private ownership which a Calvin or a Wesley allowed and the gospel they proclaimed, that which obtains between the high capitalism of the later period and the church must fall under the rule of the seventh and not of the fifth commandment, as a Hosea or a Jeremiah would have been quick to point out. The entanglement with capitalism appears in the great economic interests of the church, in its debt structure, in its dependence through endowments upon the continued dividends of capitalism, and especially, in its dependence upon the continued gifts of the privileged classes in the economic society. This entanglement has become the greater the more the church has attempted to keep pace with the development of capitalistic civilization, not without compromising with capitalist ideas of success and efficiency. At the same time evidence of religious syncretism, of the combination of Christianity with capitalist religion, has appeared. The "building of the Kingdom of God" has been confused in many a churchly pronouncement with the increase of church possessions or with the economic advancement of mankind. The church has often behaved as though the saving of civilization and particularly of capitalist civilization were its mission. It has failed to apply to the morality of that civilization the rigid standards which it did not fail to use where less powerful realities were concerned. The development may have been inevitable, nevertheless it was a fall.

The bondage of the church to nationalism has been more apparent than its bondage to capitalism, partly because nationalism is so evidently a religion, partly because it issues in the dramatic sacrifices of war—sacrifices more obvious if not more actual than those which capitalism demands and offers to its god. Nationalism is no more to be confused with the principle of nationality than capitalism is to be confused with the principle of private property. Nationalism regards the nation as the supreme value, the source of all life's meaning, as an end-in-itself and a law to itself. It seeks to persuade individuals and organization to make national might and glory their main aim in life. It even achieves a certain deliverance of men by freeing them from their bondage to self. In our modern polytheism it enters into close relationship with capitalism, though not without friction and occasional conflict and sometimes it appears to offer an alternative faith to those who have become disillusioned with wealth-worship. Since the adequacy of its god is continually called into question by the existence of other national deities, it requires the demonstration of the omnipotence of nation and breeds an unlimited lust for national power and expansion. But since the god is limited the result is conflict, war and destruction. Despite the fact that the nationalist faith becomes obviously dominant only in times of sudden or continued political crisis, it has had constant and growing influence in the west, affecting particularly government and education.

Capitalism and nationalism are variant forms of a faith which is more widespread in modern civilization than either. It is difficult to label this religion. It may be called humanism, but there is a humanism, that, far from glorifying man, reminds him of his limitations the while it loves him in his feebleness and hope. It has become fashionable to name it liberalism, but there is a liberalism which is interested in human freedom as something to be achieved rather than something to be assumed and praised. It may be called modernism, but surely one can live in the modern world, accepting its science and engaging in its work, without falling into idolatry of the modern. The rather too technical term anthropocentrism seems to be the best designation of the faith. It is marked on its negative side by the rejection not only of the symbols of the creation, the fall and the salvation of men but also of the belief in human dependence and limitation, in human wickedness and frailty, in divine forgiveness through the suffering of the innocent. Positively, it affirms the sufficiency of man. Human desire is the source of all values. The mind and the will of man are sufficient instruments of his salvation. Evil is nothing but lack of development. Revolutionary second-birth is unnecessary. Although some elements of the anthropocentric faith are always present in human society, and although it was represented at the beginning of the modern development, it is not the source but rather the product of modern civilization. Growing out of the success of science and technology in understanding and modifying some of the conditions of life it has substituted veneration of science for scientific knowledge, and glorification of human activity for its exercise. Following upon the long education in which Protestant and Catholic evangelism had brought Western men to a deep sense of their duty, this anthropocentrism glorified the moral sense of man as his natural possession and taught him that he needed no other law than the one within. Yet, as is the case of capitalism and nationalism, the faith which grew out of modern culture has modified that culture. During the last generations the anthropocentric faith has entered deeply into the structure of society and has contributed not a little to the megapolitanism and megalomania of modern life.

The compromise of the church with anthropocentrism has come almost imperceptibly in the course of its collaboration in the work of culture. It was hastened by the tenacity of Christian traditionalism, which appeared to leave churchmen with no alternative save one between worship of the letter and worship of the men who wrote the letters. Nevertheless, the compromise is a perversion of the Christian position. The more obvious expressions of the compromise have been frequent but perhaps less dangerous than the prevailing one by means of which Christianity appeared to remain true to itself while accepting the anthropocentric position. That compromise was the substitution of religion for the God of faith. Man's aspiration after God, his prayer, his worship was exalted in this syncretism into a saving power, worthy of a place alongside science and art. Religion was endowed with all the attributes of Godhead, the while its basis was found in human nature itself. The adaptation of Christianity to the anthropocentric faith appeared in other ways: in the attenuation of the conviction of sin and the necessity of rebirth, in the substitution of the human claim of immortality for the Christian hope and fear of an after-life, in the glorification of religious heroes, and in the efforts of religious men and societies to become saviors.

The captive church is the church which has become entangled with this system or these systems of worldliness. It is a church which seeks to prove its usefulness to civilization in terms of civilization's own demands. It is a church which has lost the distinctive note and the earnestness of a Christian discipline of life and has become what every religious institution tends to become—the teacher of the prevailing code of morals and the pantheon of the social gods.

How the church became entangled and a captive in this way may be understood. To blame the past for errors which have brought us to this pass is to indulge in the ancient fallacy of saying that the fathers have eaten sour grapes and the children's teeth are set on edge. The function of the present is neither praise nor blame of the past. It is rather the realization of the prevailing situation and preparation for the next task.

II: The Revolt in the Church

The realization of the dependence of the church is widespread and has led to revolt. There is revolt against the church and revolt within the church. Both of these uprisings have various aspects. The revolt against the church is in part the rebellion of those who have found in Christianity only the pure traditionalism of doctrine and symbol which have become meaningless through constant repetition without rethinking and through the consequent substitution of symbol for reality. In part it is a revulsion against the sentimentality which substituted for the ancient symbols, with the realities to which they pointed, the dubious realities of man's inner religious and moral life. In part it is the revolt of those who see in the church the willing servitor of tyrannical social institutions and classes. But these revolts against the church are not the most significant elements in the present situation, from the church's point of view. They represent desertions and attacks inspired not by loyalty to the church's own principles but rather by devotion to interests other than those of the church. Such desertions and attacks, however justified they may seem from certain points of view, serve only to weaken the church and to increase its dependence. Only a churchly revolt can lead to the church's independence.

The revolt within the church has a dual character. It is a revolt both against the "world" of contemporary civilization and against the secularized church. No other institution or society in the Western world seems to be so shot through with the spirit of rebellion against the secular system with its abuses, as is the church. No other institution seems to harbor within it so many rebels against its own present form. They are rebels who are fundamentally loyal—loyal, that is to say, to the essential institution while they protest against its corrupted form. They have no alternative religions or philosophies of life to which they might wish to flee. A few, to be sure, leave the church year by year, yet even among these loyalty is often manifest. Some of the rebels remain romanticists who try to build a "kingdom of God" with secular means. More of them are frustrated revolutionaries who hate "the world" which outrages their consciences and denies their faith but who know of no way in which they can make their rebellion effective or by which they can reconcile themselves to the situation.

Like every revolt in its early stages, the Christian revolution of today is uncertain of its ends and vague in its strategy. It seems to be a sentiment and a protest rather than a theory and a plan of action. It is a matter of feeling, in part, just because the situation remains unanalyzed. It issues therefore in many ill-tempered accusations and in blind enthusiasms. Sometimes it concentrates itself against some particular feature of the secular civilization which seems particularly representative of its character. As in all such emotional revolts there is a temptation to identify the evil with some evildoer and to make individual men—capitalists, munitions-manufacturers, dictators—responsible for the situation. Thus early Christians may have dealt with Nero and Puritans with popes. The confusion of the revolt in the church is apparent, however, not only in its emotionalism but also in its association with revolting groups outside the church. In the beginning of every uprising against prevailing customs and institutions disparate groups who share a common antagonism are likely to assume that they share a common loyalty. Such groups are united in their negations, not in their affirmations. Their positive loyalties, for the sake of which they make a common rejection, may be wholly different. The revolt in the church against the "world" and against the "world in the church" is confused today because of such associations. This confusion implies perils and temptations which may lead to disaster or to the continued captivity of the church. For if it is a frequent experience that common antagonism is confused with common loyalty, it is also well known that the allies are prone to fight among themselves because of their variant interests. One danger to the Christian revolt is that it will enter into alliance with forces whose aims and strategies are so foreign to its own that when the common victory is won—if won it can be—the revolutionary church will be left with the sad reflection that it supplied the "Fourteen Points" which gave specious sanctity to an outrageous peace and that its fruits of victory are an external prosperity based on rotting foundations or debts which cannot be paid without destroying the life of the church.

The danger of such alliance or identification is not a fancied peril. The eagerness with which some of the leaders of the Christian revolt identify the gospel with the ideals and strategies of radical political parties, whether they be proletarian or nationalistic, the efforts to amalgamate the gospel and political movements in a Christian socialism or in a Christian nationalism indicate the reality of the danger. It is not always understood by the American section of the Christian revolt that a considerable section of the so-called German Christian movement, in which the confusion of gospel and nationalism prevails, had sources in just such a reaction as its own against an individualistic, profit-loving and capitalistic civilization, and against the church in alliance with that civilization. There are many social idealists among these Germanizers of the gospel; and their fervor is essentially like that of the other idealists who equate the kingdom of God with a proletarian socialist instead of a national socialist society. The "social gospel," in so far as it is the identification of the gospel with a certain temporal order, is no recent American invention. In the history of Europe and America there have been many similar efforts which sought ideal ends, identified the church with political agencies, and succeeded in fastening upon society only some new form of power control against which the church needed again to protest and rebel. It is one thing for Christians to take a responsible part in the political life of their nation; it is another thing to identify the gospel and its antagonism to the "world" with the "worldly" antagonism of some revolting group.

The dangers and temptations which beset the Christian revolt offer no excuse for acquiescence. The danger which confronts the world in the midst of its idolatries and lusts is too real, the message of the church is too imperative, the misery of men is too actual to make quiescence possible. But the moment requires the church to stand upon its own feet, to do its own work in its own way, to carry on its revolt against "the world," not in dependence upon allies or associates, but independently. In any case the revolt in the church against secularization of life and the system of "worldliness" points the way to the declaration of its independence.

III: Toward the Independence of the Church

The declaration of the church's independence when it comes, will not begin on the negative note. A movement toward emancipation cannot become effective so long as it is only a rejection of false loyalties and entanglements. Loyalties can be recognized to be false only when a true loyalty has been discovered. Moreover, independence is not desirable for its own sake. To seek it for its own sake means to seek it for the sake of self and to substitute loyalty to a self-sufficient self for loyalty to an alien power. But the church can have no illusion of self-sufficiency.

The church's declaration of independence can begin only with the self-evident truth that it and all life are dependent upon God, that loyalty to him is the condition of life, and that to him belong the kingdom and the power and the glory. Otherwise the emancipation of the church from the world is impossible; there is no motive for it nor any meaning in it. There is no flight out of the captivity of the church save into the captivity of God. The crisis of modern mankind is like the crisis of the prophets, the crisis of the Roman Empire in the days of Augustine, and that of the medieval world in the days of the Reformation. The last appeal beyond all finite principalities and powers must soon be made. It cannot be an appeal to the rights of men, of nations or religions, but only an appeal to the right of God.

The appeal to the right of God means for the church an appeal to the right of Jesus Christ. It is an appeal not only to the grim reality of the slayer who judges and destroys the self-aggrandizing classes and nations and men. Such an appeal would be impossible and such a loyalty out of question were not men persuaded that this reality, whose ways are again evident in historic processes, is a redeeming and saving reality, and did they not come to some understanding of the manner in which he accomplishes salvation. But such persuasion and such revelation are available only through the event called Jesus Christ. If the church has no other plan for salvation to offer men than one of deliverance by force, education, idealism, or planned economy, it really has no existence as a church and needs to resolve itself into a political party or a school. But it knows of a plan of salvation which is not a plan it has devised. In its revolt it is becoming aware of the truth which it had forgotten or which it had hidden within symbols and myths. There is in the revolt something of the restlessness that comes from a buried memory which presses into consciousness. In some of its aspects it seems to be the blind effort to escape from the knowledge that the church along with the world belongs to the crucifiers rather than to the crucified. It seems to represent the desire to avert the eyes from the cross which stands in the present as in the past, and to turn attention away from ourselves to some other culprits whose sins the innocent must bear. When this memory of Jesus Christ, the crucified comes fully alive it will not come as a traditional formula or symbol, reminding men only of the past, but as the recollection of a most decisive fact in the present situation of men.

Without beginning in loyalty to God and to Jesus Christ no new beginning of the church's life is possible. But the self-evident truths and the original loyalties of the church can be recaptured and reaffirmed not only as the events in time drive men to their reaffirmation, but as the labor of thought makes intelligible and clear the vague and general perceptions we receive from life. The dependent church rejected theology or found it unintelligible because it accepted a "theology" which was not its own, a theory of life which was essentially worldly. It wanted action rather than creeds because its creed was that the action of free, intelligent men was good and that God's action was limited to the human agencies of good will. The revolters in the church have learned from history that every true work of liberation and reformation was at the same time a work of theology. They understand that the dependence of man upon God and the orientation of man's work by reference to God's work require that theology must take the place of the psychology and sociology which were the proper sciences of a Christianity which was dependent upon the spirit in man. The theory of the Christian revolution is beginning to unfold itself again as the theory of a divine determinism, of the inevitable divine judgment, and of the salvation of men by the suffering of the innocent. But whatever be the content of the theory a clear understanding of it is needed for the work of emancipation, reorganization and aggression in the Christian community.

It is evident that far more than all this is necessary. There is no easy way in which the church can divorce itself from the world. It cannot flee into asceticism nor seek refuge again in the inner life of the spirit. The road to independence and to aggression is not one which leads straight forward upon one level. How to be in the world and yet not of the world has always been the problem of the church. It is a revolutionary community in a pre-revolutionary society. Its main task always remains that of understanding, proclaiming and preparing for the divine revolution in human life. Nevertheless, there remains the necessity of participation in the affairs of an unconverted and unreborn world. Hence the church's strategy always has a dual character and the dualism is in constant danger of being resolved into the monism of other-worldliness or of this-worldliness, into a more or less quiescent expectancy of a revolution beyond time or of a mere reform program carried on in terms of the existent order. How to maintain the dualism without sacrifice of the main revolutionary interest constitutes one of the important problems of a church moving toward its independence.

Yet it is as futile as it is impossible to project at this moment the solution of problems which will arise in the future. If the future is pregnant with difficulties it is no less full of promise. The movement toward the independence of the church may lead to the development of a new missionary or evangelical movement, to the rise of an effective international Christianity, to the union of the divided parts of the church of Christ, and to the realization in civilization of the unity and peace of the saved children of one God. The fulfillment of hopes and fears cannot be anticipated. The future will vary according to the way in which we deal with the present. And in this present the next step only begins to be visible. The time seems rife for the declaration of the church's independence. Yet even that step cannot be forced; how it will come and under what leadership none can now determine. We can be sure, however, that the repentance and faith working in the rank and file of the church are the preconditions of its independence and renewal.

The Attack upon the Social Gospel

During the Great Depression, the floundering Social Gospel movement provoked some lively debates. Charles Clayton Morrison, editor of The Christian Century, *attributed the problem to the persistence of older evangelical assumptions. Once Christians let go of the illusion that faith dealt primarily with a person's inner life, he contended, their chances of Christianizing American culture were bound to increase.*[17] *Niebuhr took the opposite position. He called for the development of a "social equivalent" of the earlier evangelical approach that would rely on proclaiming the biblical faith rather than political lobbying and government legislation to reshape human hearts and lives. This strategy, he asserted in this article and elsewhere, was also more in keeping with the ways of God in history. Like Marxism, it recognized forces at work in the human narrative that were beyond human capacities.*

Source: *Religion in Life* 5 (Spring 1936): 176–81.

The question of the Social Gospel is explicitly or implicitly involved in a great deal of contemporary theological and religious discussion. To exponents of the "application of Christianity" to social problems to the new movements—neo-Protestant or Barthian, neo-Evangelical or Buchmanite and neo-Catholic or Anglo-Catholic—appear to be retreats from the battlefield of social life back to the line of individualistic and other-worldly Christianity. They believe that those who are influenced by these movements intend to give up the endeavor to influence group behavior as impossible in a world lost in sin or to devote themselves to the cultivation of a spiritual life in quietist isolation from a confusing civilization. Representatives

---

17. Charles Clayton Morrison, *The Social Gospel and the Christian Cultus* (New York: Harper & Brothers, 1933), x.

of the post-liberal movements, on the other hand, are inclined to speak of the social Gospel as though it were the epitome of all those humanistic, melioristic and anti-revolutionary tendencies in modernist religion against which they protest. They think of the Social Gospel as a message of self-help, as an optimistic faith that men can enter the kingdom of God without profound revolution, as the expression of cultural Protestantism which is more interested in civilization and its improvement than in God's judgment and love. Very important issues are at stake and it will not do to attempt a superficial synthesis of ideas which are antithetical, yet it seems to the present writer that the issues are still confused and that the debate may become more fruitful if certain distinctions are made. Above all else it seems that the issue of the objective should be distinguished from the issue of the means. The first question is whether the individual or society is the proper object of Christianity's mission; the second, whether the Church is to employ direct or indirect means.

I

The Social Gospel is characterized by the conviction that social units of every sort are the primary human realities to which the Church ought to address itself, or that, in dealing with individuals, not the isolated soul but the social individual—the citizen, class-member, race-member—should be regarded as the being who is in need of redemption. In this respect it is the heir of sociological science rather than of liberal philosophy. It rejects the doctrine of eighteenth- and nineteenth-century liberalism which proclaimed with Bentham that "the community is a fictitious body" and which regarded all societies as based upon contracts into which independent individuals entered for the sake of common interests. However true this liberalism may have been of a period in which new societies were being established, the Social Gospel has noted that it is not true of our time. Now, at least, society appears to precede the individual, to mold his character, to determine his interests, to bestow rights upon him. The individual is what he is by virtue of the place in society which he occupies; or, if this is too extreme a statement, the interaction between society and individual is such that an interpretation which always makes the individual the first term is manifestly wrong. The Social Gospel has seen sin and righteousness as characteristics of group life; it has noted that vicarious suffering is laid upon group for group rather than upon individual for individual; it has seen the problem of salvation as a social problem and it has worked for the conversion or "change" of societies rather than of individuals who, no matter how much they may be changed, yet remain bound by common social evils and participants in common social sin.

The social interest of the Social Gospel is as pertinent to our time as the individualist gospel was to the eighteenth and early nineteenth centuries. In that earlier period Christianity confronted individuals who had been emancipated from political, ecclesiastical and economic bonds, who had sometimes also—as in the case of the American frontiers—been freed from the restraint which popular mores had imposed upon them. These emancipated individuals not only became perilous to one another but were in danger of losing significance from lives which had become ends-in-themselves. The bases of a new common life needed to be laid; the individual needed to be related to a source of meaning which transcended his particular desires and his selfhood; he needed to be rescued from despair and its consequences. How well Evangelicalism (Methodism, Pietism, the American revival movement) met these problems, how splendidly it succeeded in supplying inner discipline in place of vanished external restraints, how effectively it related lives to a transcendent God, how genuinely it gave new faith, courage and zest to suppressed individuals—these facts are frequently overlooked by men who regard the whole individualistic movement as an error which might have been avoided, or who note that the Evangelical answer no longer suffices in an age which poses a different problem. But it is possible to give all due credit to the effectiveness of the individualistic gospel without maintaining that it is adequate for our day.

It is true that every person has interests, problems and responsibilities as a self which is directly related to God; no full presentation of the gospel can ever leave these out of account. Yet it seems evident that in our time the doom and the salvation, the creation, sin and redemption with which men are concerned are social rather than individual in character. The emancipated individuals of our day are the societies, the races and classes which have made themselves laws to themselves; which commit crimes against other classes, races and nations and believe they will go unpunished; which suffer injustice and suppression as groups; which are faced with the problem of their own futility and emptiness. It is in this area that the reality of sin and hell, and the necessity of salvation have become most apparent. In that sense the modern situation is more like that of the Hebrew nation in the time of the prophets than like that of eighteenth-century individuals. The question of personal salvation is important, but, as in the whole of Hebrew history, it is secondary to the question of social salvation. It is true that in this situation much can be done for men as independent individuals, and the Oxford Group movement has demonstrated something of the possibilities. But insofar as this movement deals with persons as the primary factors and tends to overlook the fact that the amount of honesty, purity and love which persons can exercise while they participate in the dishonesties, impurities and hatefulness of capitalism, nationalism and racialism is very limited, it will continue to be regarded with many reservations not only by the exponents of the Social Gospel but by all who see the problem of society as the problem of the day. But it may be that this movement will not remain as individualistic as it now appears to be, while there is nothing in either neo-Protestantism or in neo-Catholicism which is inimical to the social approach. On the contrary the exponents of these movements may claim with considerable right that their return to sixteenth- and thirteenth-century modes of thought is due precisely to the necessity of overcoming the individualism of the more recent past. After all, both Catholics and Protestants were interested in the conversion of societies, in the ordering of social life, in the fate not only of men but of humanity. It is certainly true that both neo-Protestants and neo-Catholics have a far more social conception of the Church than many even of those who represent the Social Gospel in its liberal form, for whom the Church remains too often a contract society. And both of these groups with their orthodox conceptions of original sin, of historic revelation, of general judgment and of the salvation of mankind are operating with ideas which have direct relevance to men's existence as members of mankind and its societies. Doubtless these ideas will need to be rethought, but there is nothing individualistic about them, and those who believe that in them the solution to the human problem is to be found not only can but must participate in the social direction of the Social Gospel.

II

It is at the point of the second issue that the real divergence of the day is to be sought. The Social Gospel has been directed not only toward the changing of social entities but it has largely sought to accomplish this end by indirect means, and by way of self-help. The means which it has employed are indirect from the religious point of view. It has used political and economic means to gain the end. Its exponents have sought to influence legislatures to enact laws, schools to teach attitudes, political parties to adopt programs. Or it has sought to work through the labor movement, using economic means for the purpose of changing society. It has worked for international peace by trying to influence governments to adopt treaties or by writing to congressmen with requests to vote for this or that law. Such measures are doubtless good in their place but as used by the church they represent the strategy of indirect action. They are not only efforts to get some other organization to do something about the intolerable situation but also presuppose the convictions that religion as such has no direct bearing on social life, that prophetic and Christian analysis of the situation with corresponding direct religious action are unimportant and that the analysis of society in terms of its political and economic arrangements is fundamental.

In the second place the strategy of the Social Gospel has largely been a strategy of self-salvation, or of salvation by works. It has tended to speak of social salvation as something which men could accomplish for themselves if only they adopted the right social ideal, found adequate motivation for achieving it and accepted the correct technical means. The social ideal has been regarded as the product of men's independent ethical insight, the knowledge of correct means as the product of social science, and religion has been looked to for the motivation. God, in this theory, becomes a means to an end; he is there for the sake of achieving a human ideal and he does not do this directly but only through the inspiration which he offers to those who worship him. The failure of this whole scheme of social salvation has driven many Social Gospel advocates to look for non-religious motivation in the self-interest of classes or races, in which case even the last vestige of a religious strategy has been given up.

It is against this indirect, self-help strategy, rather than against the social objective of the Social Gospel, that the major protest of the day is being made. There are significant differences, of course, between neo-Protestant and neo-Catholic movements, but they seem to agree in this; that whatever place be given to the indirect strategy the primary attack of Christianity upon the social situation or the social individual must be direct, not via governments and economic units, but via the Church or the word of God. They agree in the second place in regarding salvation, whether social or individual, as a divine process, not as something man can achieve by moralistic means.

From the neo-Protestant point of view the strategy of the Social Gospel rests upon a false analysis of the social situation, and the false strategy results from this false analysis. A true analysis will see that our social injustice and misery cannot be dealt with unless their sources in a false faith are dealt with. So long as the faith of man remains "capitalistic," that is, a faith in the security which can be given economically, so long the profit-system and the system of private property cannot be budged. So long as any sort of this-worldly security remains the object of confidence our nationalisms and mammonisms will flourish. Both just and unjust live by faith, though by different kinds of faith, and our social no less than our individual lives are an expression of these faiths. From the neo-Protestant point of view repentance for the *sins* of social life is not enough; there needs to be repentance for the *sin*, for the false faith, for the idolatry which issues in all these sins. Men will be ready for no radically new life until they have really become aware of the falsity of the faith upon which their old life is based. But an attack upon faith requires the direct action of the Church rather than indirect action.

In the second place neo-Protestantism's analysis of the situation in which social groups live runs counter to the analysis upon which the doctrine of self-salvation is based. The Social Gospel is related to the neo-Protestant movement somewhat as Utopian Socialism is related to Marxism. Utopianism also believed in the saving power of the ideal, motivated by sympathy and love of the good. Whatever the quarrels may be between "deterministic" and "synergistic" Marxians they all recognize the priority of the historic process to which the party must adjust itself; Marxian salvation at least is not self-salvation. In another sphere, with a far more profound analysis of the total situation than Marxianism offers, neo-Protestantism would base its strategy on the priority of God—not as a human ideal, or the object of worship, but as the moving force in history—who alone brings in His kingdom and to whose ways the party of the Kingdom of God on earth must adjust itself. But strangely enough the Social Gospel, when it recognizes the inadequacy of Utopianism, tends to accept Marxist rather than Christian determinism as offering the correct analysis.

The strategy toward which neo-Protestantism is feeling its way is not only the direct strategy which attacks false faith and proclaims true faith, or the strategy of action corresponding to the way of God in history as revealed in the event Jesus Christ, but for both of these reasons it is also a revolutionary strategy, which regards the death of the old life as inevitable and as necessary before a new beginning can be made.

Our interest here, however, is not that of trying to set forth the strategy of an orthodox Christianity which is thoroughly alive to the problem of the day. The development of this strategy still lies in the future. The question is rather whether such a strategy does not need to be developed. The issue between the Social Gospel and the new movements lies here, not at the point of social versus individual salvation.

The present situation may be compared to that which existed at the beginning of the eighteenth century. The rationalist effort to deal with the problem of emancipated individual life in terms of moral self-salvation and by means of indirect and melioristic action through education and reason failed. Then came the direct, revolutionary Evangelical approach based upon a theory of salvation in which—whatever the differences between Calvinists and Arminians—the adjustment of human ways to the way of God as revealed in Jesus Christ was demanded. The new movements in Christianity, it seems to the present writer, must not be interpreted as reactions to Evangelical individualism, but as efforts to discover in our own day the social equivalent of the Evangelical strategy.

Sermon Preached at the Ordination of C. Howard Hopkins

Niebuhr is remembered for his deep piety as well as his scholarship and teaching. At Yale Divinity School, he often began his classroom lectures with prayer, carefully prepared homilies for chapel services, and was frequently called upon to provide the invocation at graduation ceremonies. C. Howard Hopkins was a student whose early interest in the Social Gospel prompted further study, and in time he became one of the movement's leading historians. This ordination sermon not only provides an example of Niebuhr's piety. It also documents his unflagging commitment during the 1930s to cultural engagement on the part of the church by means of the Social Gospel. Particularly noteworthy is the connection he makes between kingdom work "on earth" and the transcendent "kingdom of heaven." We also see him at his most eloquent when he speaks of the social-gospel ministry as one of casting out "demons that inhabit the modern world."

Source: Unpublished, preached at First Baptist Church, New Haven, Connecticut, February 23, 1936.

We meet tonight for the commissioning of a fellow worker to the Christian ministry, to the task of the Christian fellowship, and it is quite fitting that we should take for the text of this occasion the story of that first commissioning of Jesus' disciples, in the tenth chapter of Matthew:

> These twelve Jesus sent forth, and commanded them, saying, Go not into the way of the Gentiles, and into any city of the Samaritans enter ye not: But go rather to the lost sheep of the house of Israel. And as ye go, preach, saying, The kingdom of heaven is at hand. Heal the sick, cleanse the lepers, raise the dead, cast out devils: freely ye have received, freely give. Provide neither gold, nor silver, nor brass in your purses. Nor scrip

for your journey, neither two coats, neither shoes, nor yet staves: for the workman is worthy of his meat.

As we read that commissioning instruction of Jesus we are reminded perhaps first of all of the great distance that lies between that day and ours, not only a matter of nineteen centuries but a matter of spirit and situation. He said to his disciples: "Go not into the way of the Gentiles, and into any city of the Samaritans enter ye not: but go rather to the lost sheep of Israel." We of the Christian church today see all the world as our parish and our workers are commissioned to go to all parts of the world, to India, to Africa—not to one little section of Palestine, not to one nation but to all nations. We say, what an insignificant occasion that was, sending out a few disciples to the lost sheep of Israel in comparison to this mighty modern Christian church which moves like a great army across the world.

And then what a great distance there is when we consider the simple message of the Kingdom of God which Jesus gave to his disciples. He said to them, "Preach, saying, the kingdom of heaven is at hand"—no more than that. Today we send out our workers and we give them a very, very complex message. They are to know something about the various sciences, particularly those which deal with human life. They are to know something about homiletics and history and about the situation of our society in the historical sequence. They are to deal with very complex individuals and they are to proclaim not only this simple word of Jesus but they are to speak of the depths of sin that are in the human soul; they are to speak of the salvation that has been wrought out by Jesus Christ; they are to deal with theories of life and death, of national and human destiny, with all sorts of difficult and complicated things.

Furthermore, that message about the kingdom of God—the kingdom of God is at hand is a message which comes out of a time in which the end of the world seemed to be, literally, at hand. Then the people honestly expected that this whole order of things was soon to perish. They expected wars and the rumors of wars; a sudden strange light in the heavens and then the coming of the Son of Man out of the clouds of heaven; the world of things was to pass away; the Kingdom of God was at hand. Now, we in the Christian church, we who have been commissioned to the ministry of Jesus Christ—we deal not with the kingdom of heaven but with the kingdoms of this earth. We do not stand before the open sky wondering about the coming of the Son of Man. We stand in buildings like this, buildings that have been built to last not only decades but perhaps for centuries. We deal with a great continuing organization, a kingdom of this world, the Christian church. We deal with the nations of this world. We know that we have a mighty function to perform, we members of Christian churches, in civilization. Our direction is not to a kingdom of heaven but to a kingdom upon earth. This we must somehow influence. Upon this we must somehow make an impression. This we must guard against error. We deal not with a passing world but with a great continuing world. How remote that message seems to our time.

When Jesus said, "heal the sick, cleanse the lepers, raise the dead, cast out devils"—was he speaking to us? I do not mean to us of the ministry alone but to all of us who are his followers in the twentieth century. "Heal the sick." We know something about comforting the sick, about offering them words of kindness and of compassion but this kingdom of God at hand meant for him a kingdom that revealed itself in power and not in word only. What shall we do with the lepers? Cleanse them? Perhaps maintain them in their places of isolation that they do not infect others. Perhaps ameliorate their condition—but cleans them? Cast out demons—is that our commission? Is that something we can do? Doesn't this all speak of a time very, very different from our own? And even the final condition: "Provide neither gold, nor silver, nor brass in your purses. Nor scrip for your journey, neither two coats, neither shoes, nor yet staves: for the workman is worthy of his meat." When we commission a disciple to a Christian church today we commission a worker in a church which has long made provision for the morrow and which will continue to make provision for years to come. We who have been members of church councils know that the providing for the morrow of gold and silver and brass is perhaps the most important part of our duty. We sit in council meetings and very occasionally we talk about the message of the kingdom of God but most of the time we talk about the provision of material things. How shall we raise adequate money for next year's budget? What shall we do to raise sufficient money to repair the church? What appeal can we make to our people in order that a bungalow may be built for this missionary or that one out in India? That is what we are concerned with and really, isn't it necessary that we be concerned with it, we ask? You who are going into the Christian ministry will discover that days and sometimes weeks and months must be devoted to the task of simply making provisions for the morrow in this wholly material way.

Yet after we have said all that and realized the distance between our church and Christianity and ministry from the church and Christianity of the disciples, we still remember that Jesus said the fundamental word and that without this all the rest of the labor he spoke about is of very little avail. Consider this matter of making provision for the morrow. Throughout the years we have tried to establish our security first of all as a church of Jesus Christ in society. And you particularly of this denomination know how that effort has been impossible of accomplishment—to establish a church by the provisions alone which we make for our security. Today we realize better than we have for along [sic] time that a church cannot be established upon the foundations which are displayed when we deal with gold, silver, brass, script, stocks and bonds, grants, laws, endowments, constitutions—none of these things give the Church of Jesus Christ any security. The church of Jesus Christ is exceedingly insecure today. The Gospel is very insecure in the world today. Over half of the members of the Christian churches live in lands in which Christianity is more or less subject to persecution and perhaps that persecution will be increased. Today we look into a morrow which offers absolutely no security, no establishment, for which we can make no provision whatever. We parents wonder about our children, remembering these last few years, whether there is any provision of material things which they may take along with them into the future. They may be able to take a bit of this and that but will it give them security in their time of stress? We realize now that we can hand them no material security and our only hope is that we may teach them the spiritual security which comes from an establishment in the Gospel or an establishment in Jesus Christ. So with the Christian church, is that not true? And you going into the Christian ministry, what are the next decades going to bring forth? Twenty years from now when you are at the very height of your ministry, or thirty or forty years, what will the church be like? You may be very sure that, like today, it will be very insecure in laws and endowments and all the rest. You may be very sure that after all, the only security lies where Jesus Christ has put it.

When one considers the area to which he sent his disciples, when one considers the people to whom he sent them, one notices also that he said the fundamental thing—"go to the lost sheep of the house of Israel." In the first place, he said "Go." The church has been a missionary church on all its great days, not a church which has simply, "Come" but a church which went out—*went out*—with a mission to those who were lost sheep. We face a world today, we are a part of the world today which is most aptly described as lost flocks of sheep. There isn't much of a message in Christianity for people who have found themselves, who are secure, who are complacent. It is a message for lost sheep, for those who wonder where this long journey of mankind in the dark is leading them, for those who are frightened sometimes as sheep are frightened and panic-stricken, for those who do not know self-confidently what it is all about but who are ready and eager to receive some guidance. Well, the world is a world of lost sheep like that, isn't it—the frightened nature of mankind today, the panic-stricken character of our national life, the way in which men run after this and that idea, the way in which they are eternally in conflict with one another because of their fears, the way in which many of them find nothing but emptiness in their lives, wondering what it is all about and what possible use it can be. All these things speak to us about the lostness of mankind and show us that Christianity is a message for these people. It is not a message for the self-righteous, the smug, the complacent who thank God that they are not like other men—it is a message for the publican and the sinner, for the lost sheep. You go out into that kind of a ministry, a ministry for those who need a shepherd, not our shepherding but the shepherding of Jesus Christ.

Above all else, the word that Jesus spoke about the kingdom of God is a word that does not belong to the distant past but that belongs to the immediate present. "Go, preach, saying the kingdom of heaven is at hand." It is a simple message, but it is the only message that the Christian church has and it will have to do. It will have to do because it is true. "The kingdom of heaven is at hand." Despite all that we have tried to say to ourselves about the kingdoms of this earth, about their security and about their glory and their longevity, we know that they rest only upon the kingdom of heaven and we know that this kingdom of heaven is verily at hand in the sense that it is beneath and above and around us all; that in it we live and move and have our being; that not for one moment could we be at all were we not supported by its everlasting foundations; that this little anthill of our civilization is surrounded and permeated by this reality that makes it what it is. We realize that the only reality comes in life when that life is related to something more lasting, something truer, something more eternal than life itself. The kingdom of heaven is at hand not only as the everlasting foundations of this world but as the threat that lies above this world. The kingdom of heaven is at hand as a result of our evil doing. We see something of the imminence of the kingdom of heaven in our crises that come upon us when we sin and stray in our economic life. We see the threat of that kingdom and the laws of God in consequence of our rationalism. We want to escape it. We would like to live as we please according to our wishes, not according to the will of God. We pray, "Thy will be done," praying that our wills may be conformed to His but we know well enough that his will will be done and that there is no escaping of that will. The kingdom of heaven is as much at hand for you and me as ever it was for those first disciples in the first century and if it is at hand it must translate itself into ever actuality in this world—in the healing of the sick, in the cleansing of the lepers, in the casting out of demons. It is not enough for the ministry to preach that the kingdom of heaven is at hand. It is not enough to console ourselves as Christians that we at least are believers and followers of Jesus Christ. No. The more we realize the truth of Christianity the more we will insist upon its realization in our life, the more we will insist this material life of ours must conform to the life of the kingdom of heaven. That is the ministry of our social gospel. It requires of us that we conform not only our separate, isolated lives to the will of God but that we conform our life with each other as neighbors to that rule of God; it requires that we cast out the demons that inhabit this modern world. For there are demons around us, the demons that are leading to destruction. The demons are those who make themselves ends in themselves. Demons are always fallen angels, creations of God who forget that they are creations of God. Such a demon is found in a nation, a nation which as a nation of God might have its life in the service of God, but willfully forgets the purpose and will of its creator. We know something about the devil of nationalism in our time. We know something about the devil of racialism in our time and we know something about the devil called Mammon in our day. The casting out of these demons remains the function of the Christian church and the more we realize how imminent the kingdom of God is, the more we will need to devote ourselves in the kingdom to [the] casting out [of] devils, the healing of the sick, the raising of the dead, the cleansing of the lepers.

Mr. Hopkins, you have been very much interested in the social gospel. You are going into the ministry with the message of the social gospel, with the message that the kingdom of God is at hand and you will recognize that whatever dangers there may be in the gospel of the kingdom of God that it is the gospel which we Christians have learned from the lips of Jesus Christ and that it is the Gospel which in our day is the only hope for the lost sheep of the house of Israel.

Niebuhr at his desk in 1950s.

Yale Divinity School.

Niebuhr portrait in the Common Room at Yale Divinity School.

PART III

Challenges of War and Peace

8

The Church and a World Again at War

Was the highly destructive conflict of nations that lasted from 1939 to 1945 actually a *second* world war? Or was it an extension of the *first* war that had engulfed the world approximately two decades earlier? During his European sabbatical in 1930, H. Richard Niebuhr had seen for himself how the draconian measures the Treaty of Versailles had imposed upon Germany were actually preparing the way for the rise of Hitler and the threat to world peace that he would soon create. In any event, the interlude between these two open conflicts had produced a profound change of attitude among Christians in America. Guilt over their endorsement of the Allied cause in 1917 moved many to become equally wholehearted in their embrace of pacifism. Several prominent Protestant leaders swore publicly that they would never support another war, and others on seminary and college campuses either signed the Oxford Oath or joined pacifist groups such as the Fellowship of Reconciliation (FOR). When the US Senate consented to the Kellogg-Briand Peace Pact in 1929, moreover, the Federal Council of Churches called for the ringing of church bells and prayers of thanksgiving throughout the nation.[1]

During the Depression decade, however, as the Japanese invasion of Manchuria was followed in short order by Italian aggression in Ethiopia, Hitler's occupation of the Rhineland, and a bloody Spanish civil war, cracks began to appear in the pacifist consensus. The division of opinion within the FOR over the merits of dogmatic pacifism led to schism; since this was a hotly debated issue among his Yale students, Niebuhr weighed in with his own perspective. Given the moral utilitarianism undergirding FOR thinking, the minority that had severed its ties with this pacifist group was, in his estimation, being more consistent than the hardline majority. While the minority was inclined to allow the use of physical violence to halt the behavior of aggressive nations, the majority deluded itself into believing that coupling verbal condemnations with economic sanctions remained a nonviolent course of action. "There are a good many men," Niebuhr pointed out, "who would prefer to die by bullets than by starvation." In Niebuhr's view, pacifism that was truly Christian recognized a "divine teleology" that made no "righteous" or "unrighteous" party exempt from God's judgment. With the aid of the cross of Jesus Christ, moreover, it clearly understood that reconciliation might involve bloodshed on the part of the innocent as well as the guilty.[2]

As the 1930s drew to close, the expansion of the Sino-Japanese War in Asia and the rolling of German armies into Poland (which shattered the accord European leaders had negotiated with Hitler at Munich) served to deepen these divisions among Christians. Bitter debates extended from pacifists to church-related groups and agencies of many types. Those that advocated neutrality found themselves

---

1. Sydney E. Ahlstrom, *A Religious History of the American People* (New Haven, CT: Yale University Press, 1972), 930.
2. H. Richard Niebuhr, "The Inconsistency of the Majority," *The World Tomorrow* 17 (January 18, 1934); 43–44.

with strange bedfellows that included Christian liberals and socialists with pacifist inclinations on the one hand and conservative Christian voices like Father Coughlin on the other, along with Charles Lindbergh, the isolationists in Congress, and everyone else who favored an "America First" position. In other instances, arguments over the merits of intervention caused good friends to part company. When the editor of *The Christian Century* came out in favor of a negotiated peace to end the war in Europe and openly attacked President Roosevelt's efforts to turn America into an "arsenal of democracy," Niebuhr's brother Reinhold chose to establish *Christianity and Crisis*, a rival periodical that reflected his conviction that the only hope for world peace and order was the halting of totalitarian aggression. To say the least, there was as much confusion in the churches as there was in American society over the best course to follow.

This period of crisis in the world as well as the church became Niebuhr's Gethsemane. He found himself following in the footsteps of Jesus during his passion to the garden where he wrestled with his Father God in prayer over his impending death. Niebuhr agonized over finding a way to lead American Christians both to seek God's will and to proclaim to themselves and to their fellow-citizens, just as Jesus had in Gethsemane's garden, "Not my will, but thine be done." Niebuhr knew that making discernment of God's will a central feature of the church's message would likely win more worldly enemies than friends. Yet he believed that this was the way by which Jesus had succeeded in overcoming the world in himself and for his followers.[3] Furthermore, he saw this challenge as a "growth" opportunity for the church to discover anew how reaffirmation of its faith in the God revealed by Jesus Christ could enable its members

---

3. H. Richard Niebuhr, "Two Lenten Meditations: 'Tired Christians' and 'Preparation for Maladjustment,'" *Yale Divinity News* 35 (March 1939): 3–4.

to see themselves and the rest of God's creation as contemporary participants in a "grand process of cosmic redemption from death and destruction to life and glory."[4]

At the same time, Niebuhr recognized how daunting a task it was to gain a hearing for such faith in the midst of a heated and highly emotional debate over America's participation in another world war. At the risk of being misunderstood, he waded into the isolationist-interventionist controversy by arguing that the religious issue at any critical moment was not about the *content* of differing potential courses of action but the *context* in which choices were made. Whether advocating intervention or nonresistance, one's motive might be egoistic (self-defensive) or nationalistic. Or it might be universalistic: ready to acknowledge one's own contributions to the conflict and willing both to assume responsibility for the well-being of all of one's neighbors (victimizers as well as victims) and to help the latter in particular get back on their feet, no matter how long it might take. To him, the church's duty was neither to take sides in the debate nor to retreat to the sidelines but to expose the faith at the heart of thinking on either side of the issue and, as he put it, "to lead men and nations to the ultimate decision, which is not the decision of war or peace but of American peace or peace of God, American war or acceptance of the judgment of God."[5]

Niebuhr's wrestling with God in order to discern his will for the church and a world at war also appears to have been a motivation for the writing of his third major work, *The Meaning of Revelation*, published in 1941. Finding the intellectual support he needed to understand *revelation* to mean "both history and God" caused him

---

4. H. Richard Niebuhr, "Life is Worth Living," *Intercollegian and Far Horizons* 57 (October 1939): 43–44.
5. H. Richard Niebuhr, "The Christian Church in the World's Crisis," *Christianity and Society* 6 (Summer 1941): 11–17.

considerable anguish, forcing him at one point to tear up his manuscript in frustration and start over. In the book, Niebuhr ended up separating *internal* from *external* ways of interpreting any historical moment. For him, the internal perspective was more normative in character than an external point of view because it reflected the values that held communities together. For the Christian community, revelation provided this perspective. It not only furnished the church with a pattern for interpreting events in every place and time but also continually called forth allegiance to the one whom Jesus regarded as Father. Hence, Niebuhr contended that what Jesus revealed of God remained a "moving thing," and every contemporary event could be viewed as part of the same drama of divine-human interaction that Jesus first brought to light through his life, death, and resurrection. Niebuhr was in no way trying to suggest that this was the only authentic view of history. Nor did he wish to devalue the findings of "external" historians. On the contrary, he believed the church could only confess to the world beyond itself what this hermeneutic was leading it to see.[6]

With the Japanese bombing of Pearl Harbor on December 7, 1941, America's involvement in World War II ceased to be an issue for debate. Pacifist ranks quickly shrank, and the number of clergy enlisting as military chaplains rapidly increased. As clergy at home went about ministering to congregations with members caught up in patriotic fervor, they tended to be more circumspect about assigning blame for the conflict and more highly committed to the achievement of a lasting peace among nations.

For Niebuhr, America's entrance into the war became a "Good Friday"; the Nazi extermination of Jewish populations and the Allied firebombing of Dresden were equally tragic features of it. Disturbing

---

6. H. Richard Niebuhr, *The Meaning of Revelation* (New York: Macmillan, 1941), 32–66.

as well were efforts on the part of Christians either to establish the "relative rightness" of the Allied cause or to separate their religion from the political expediencies of engaging in warfare. Niebuhr gave these people the name *Ditheists* because they were in effect worshiping country as much as the God of Jesus Christ.[7]

In several ways, standing beneath the cross where Jesus was crucified between two thieves helped Niebuhr make his case for the church's response to the war. For one thing, he saw God acting in the war as "vicarious sufferer" for all of the afflictions of his people and using the suffering of the innocent for the remaking of the guilty. He also concluded that since so much of the burden of suffering in this war was falling on its innocent victims, the cross negated any "just war" theory or "amoral" perspective on it.[8] At the same time, the cross served to convince him that nothing in world history lay beyond the scope of redemption. "Neither the crucified brigand nor the crucified righteous are regarded as forsaken by God and far from Paradise," he wrote in 1942. "Even should death come to them hope wraps their broken bodies in fine linen, conserving what it can, preserving on Good Friday for an Easter miracle of divine action."[9] For Niebuhr, the church's message to a nation and world once again at war involved a repentance intended to trigger in people nothing short of a "spiritual revolution." This revolution included not simply sorrow over sin, but "no excusing" of those who might consider themselves more righteous and the exacting of "no vengeance" on the part of anyone. This revolution would took place in hope and "in reliance on the continued grace of God in the midst of our ungraciousness."[10]

---

7. H. Richard Niebuhr, "War as the Judgment of God," *The Christian Century* 59 (May 13, 1942): 631.
8. H. Richard Niebuhr, "War as Crucifixion," *The Christian Century* 60 (April 28, 1943): 513.
9. Niebuhr, "War as the Judgment of God," 632–33.
10. Niebuhr, "War as Crucifixion," 515.

THE CHURCH AND A WORLD AGAIN AT WAR

As the Civil War drew to a close, a clergyman from the North is said to have written a letter to President Lincoln expressing the hope that he might now be certain that God was on their side. In reply, Lincoln stated that this did not worry him because his chief concern was that the North be on God's side.[11] The following Niebuhr writings illustrate how he, in the context of World War II, endeavored to provide the church with a similar perspective.

---

11. See Sidney E. Mead, *The Lively Experiment: The Shaping and Character of Christianity in America* (New York: Harper & Row, 1963), 74.

Two Lenten Meditations: "Tired Christians" and "Preparation for Maladjustment"

If there were a Christian season that best describes the disposition of Niebuhr as colleagues and students have remembered him, it would be Lent, with its focus on Jesus' passion. The following are two sermons he delivered during that season in 1939 at the Yale Divinity School's Marquand Chapel. Niebuhr feared that Christians might grow weary of hearing over and over again the sad news of the "agony of China" and the "crucifixion of the Jews" in Europe, allowing this to dull them into fatalistic resignation. Therefore, they needed not only to follow Jesus to the Garden of Gethsemane in order prayerfully to wrestle with God but also, upon their discovery of at least a fragment of his plan for the world, to be prepared to encounter plenty of opposition. One may suspect in reading these sermons that Niebuhr was speaking to himself as much as to the church.

Source: *Yale Divinity News* 35 (March 1939): 3–4.

"Tired Christians"

Luke 22:39-46

Were one to select and describe the ten decisive moral battles of history surely the conflict in Gethsemane would take first place among them. As military men gain knowledge of strategy from study of Hannibal's operations at Cannae, so those who seek a wisdom apt for the direction of life in its internal conflicts go back again and again to examine the strategy of Jesus in his great victory in the garden. Our present purpose is not to deal with the major points of the struggle but rather to attend to the lost engagement where Jesus' allies were defeated so that He was left alone. All the accounts agree that although the disciples had been warned to be exceedingly watchful they fell asleep. They were tired, the first gospel states; "their eyes were heavy"; but Luke says that they went to sleep for sorrow.

We all understand the weariness which can flow from sorrow. In the conflicts of the inner life there comes a time when we are tempted to go to sleep. We have fought against our pride, our self-centeredness or our desires and having been often defeated we grow very sad. We do not resign ourselves but our watchfulness diminishes and at last we are asleep. The temptation to go to sleep is even more manifest in our social conflicts. The tired radical is a familiar figure and so is the tired Christian. We have looked at the millions of unemployed for almost ten years, have thought about their sufferings, physically and spiritual, have tried to share in their agony and to alleviate it. But now we go to sleep for sorrow. We have become used to the agony of China. We were told last fall that bye and bye we would lose our sense of horror and of pity as we contemplated the crucifixion of the Jews. And we are doing so. We think we cannot stand the continued sight of suffering and sometimes say that nature has provided us with a defense against pity by allowing us to become callous or to go to sleep. Such sleep may be physical or it may be a matter of escape to a world of dreams—to the world [of] sports, or of cinema romances or of historical novels. We are very tired, we say, and must have some escape.

But Jesus seemed to think the disciples' excuse invalid, and the old church always tended to think that sleeping for sorrow was somehow a moral fault. It counted *tristitia,* or sloth, or accidy [*sic*] among the seven deadly sins. It could not be regarded as a purely physical reaction, really amoral, for both in its sources and in its consequences it had a moral character. The disciples were doubtless physically tired; their flesh revolted against further vigilance but more than a physical revolt was present. Perhaps they suffered from wounded pride, as Stonewall Jackson seems to have done when he went to sleep while

Lee was fighting at Mechanicsville. They had some right to feel wounded. They had been left out of Jesus' counsels; their advice had been rejected; had he followed Peter's injunctions the Master would never have come into such a dilemma. So Longstreet felt at Gettysburg and went to sleep for sorrow. Tired radicals and tired Christians feel that way sometimes about the social situation or about the church. Their counsel has been rejected, their advice scorned; why not go to sleep?

Tristitia may be due to our desire not to become involved. Everyone would like to be able to say, "Whatever happens, it won't touch me". [sic] We want to be Stoics who do not get too much wrapped in emotions and in the fate of others. We desire isolation, not like that of Jesus fighting his lonely battle, but like that of a spectator who wisely enjoys tragedy, comedy and farce. If the play becomes too much for us we close our eyes and go to sleep.

But the most important source of sloth is faithlessness. We look upon the agonies of men for a while with a little confidence that there is meaning in this life and a cure for its woes. But having seen the struggle continue without solution we are tempted to give up and say, "There is no sense in the whole thing. Nothing good can be done. The case is hopeless". [sic] So men go to sleep because in sleep they can forget the utter confusion. Such sleep is the consequence of loss of faith in God.

As sloth has moral sources so it has moral consequences. When the unprepared disciples were awakened by the critical event they could do nothing but run away or slash out at the soldiers with their awkward swords. Psysical [sic] sleep may be good preparation for hard and skilful work, but spiritual slumber is the worst possible preparation for meeting life's issues. Its consequences are likely to be flight and denial and betrayal and utter confusion, as in the case of the disciples.

Is there any cure for sleepiness from sorrow? Perhaps Jesus' example in Gethsemane suggests such a cure. Surely if anyone had a right to get a good night's rest before the great ordeal he had that right. But he stayed awake and he did so by wrestling with God. He did not try to subdue God to make Him do a miracle but he struggled with Him until he saw His will, His plan. Jesus refused to let God off, to say "This whole situation is so bad that God can have nothing to do with it".[same as previous] He proceeded on the assumption that there was a divine meaning in the whole sorry situation and he engaged in mental strife with God until some fragment of the divine plan was revealed. His effort was not directed toward achieving fatalistic resignation to a God who would do anyway what he had purposed to do, but rather toward understanding what God was doing in this whole affair, so that His own action might be adjusted to divine action. When he saw God's will he was ready to do his part, which was neither the part of the aggressor or of the coward.

We have many things to do in the Christian Church in these hours of world crisis, but not the least task by any means is that of wrestling with God in the faith that he has a plan and a meaning, relevant to the whole sorry and tragic situation. Such wrestling will serve at least to keep us from sloth and may prepare us for some other action in the hour of darkness than the activity of flight or of foolish sword play.

Preparation for Maladjustment

Luke 22:35-58

Luke's story about the two swords has had to bear the weight of elaborate theories and great argument. It has been thought that by this lesson Jesus was preparing his disciples for the world rulership. So Boniface VIII in the bull *Unam Sanctam* interpreted the passage to mean that both temporal and spiritual power had been committed to the church and based on it the claims of medieval Christianity to world dominion. Similar claims are sometimes made today in more subtle forms, as when Christianity is set over against communism and fascism as an alternative form of world rule. But this view of the role of the church is not only too formidable and weighty a thing to be built on the slight foundation of the story about the two swords, it is too heavy for the church itself. A Christianity which has been counselled by its Master not to rule as the Gentiles do breaks down when it is equipped with the temporal sword. Jesus surely did not want to prepare His disciples to rule in any other way than the one in which He ruled.

Again it has been said that this passage indicates that Jesus wanted to prepare his followers for self-defense. It is hard to find Biblical passages which will support that practice of coercion which we find so inescapable and apparently necessary in political life; this one seems to be a God-send after all the statements in the gospels about loving the enemy and turning the other cheek. But what an inept foundation it is for the great weight of armament which we rest upon it! The swords among twelve men! What militarist, what advocate of self-defense, would be content to equip twelve men with two swords? And perhaps, as Chrysostom suggests, they were only butcher knives at that used for the slaying and the carving of the paschal lamb. We shall need to look elsewhere for a justification of armaments, for when Jesus said, " It is enough," he could not have meant, "Two swords are sufficient for self-defense or world rule."

He said in effect, "Enough of this; you have misunderstood me again." For he was preparing His disciples neither for rule nor for defense but for hostility and age-long struggle with others and themselves. The golden days were over; no longer could they go into the villages and cities sure of a glad reception, of free meals and gracious welcome for their announcement of the kingdom. Now the once popular hero was to be numbered among transgressors and his disciples needed to make up their minds that they would be looked upon with suspicion or worse. All that Jesus seems to have meant by the counsel to buy swords was that his followers needed to prepare themselves for hostility. "Prepare" he said, "to be maladjusted."

It remains good advice for us. We want always to belong to our world and to our civilization. We are always trying to prepare ourselves to defend the church and religion against political power, against rationalism, against charges of inutility or conservatism or obscurantism. We are always tempted to get ready for the time when Christianity will be held in high honor as we think it was honored in the days of the Puritans or in medieval times. But Jesus says to us, I think, "Get ready for hostility and be prepared for continuous maladjustment. You will never be quite respectable intellectually; you will never be considered quite realistic or quite idealistic enough; you will never be thought worldly-wise enough; you will never fit in."

When one reads the letters and sermons of the Confessionalist Christians in Germany one is struck by the fact that what seems to oppress them most is not fear of concentration camps but the knowledge that they are regarded as inferior people by their contemporaries. They believe in the ancient fables; they talk about the power of the spirit, when everyone knows that blood and iron only are mighty; they are lugubrious folk in a society which believes in strength and joy; they see tragedy at the heart of life and their world wants no tragedies. What they experience in noticeable manner all Christians must expect to experience in some fashion. They are better advised if they prepare to be pilgrims and strangers and if they take maladjustment to their world as a normal thing than if they strain and protest against such maladjustment as abnormal.

Perhaps Jesus was preparing his disciples for internal maladjustment also. What incongruous characters they were with a gospel of peace on their lips and two old swords in their hands! Thomas, at least, must have smiled at himself as he thought of the picture he and his companions would present to soldiers and to Jewish patriots. What Don Quixotes modern Christians often appear to be, to themselves, as they fight against the windmills of modern industrialism and modern politics in the outmoded armor and with the old-fashioned weapons of an earlier day! How incongruous do they not seem to themselves as they try to combine a gospel of reconciliation with resistance to aggression. Perhaps Jesus was warning us all that we would never get rid of this internal maladjustment, that we would never finish with our mental strife, and that we should take for granted, rather than rebel against, the conflict within us.

At all events in that last hour Jesus was preparing himself to be numbered among the transgressors and to go into His conflict with Himself and God. And what was good enough for him must be good enough for us. We are given confidence when we recognize that it was not He who was maladjusted but rather His world, and that the worse thing He could have done would have been to seek adjustment to that world or even to His own dominant desire. Only because He was maladjusted to a maladjusted world could He say, "Let not your heart be troubled. In the world ye have tribulation, but be of good cheer. I have overcome the world."

THE CHURCH AND A WORLD AGAIN AT WAR

I Believe in the Kingdom of God

When it was requested of him, Niebuhr contributed an occasional article to the magazines of the still relatively new Evangelical and Reformed Church. This one appeared as the eighth in a series setting forth the fundamentals of the Christian faith for the benefit of its young people. The article, which provides a simply stated summary of his understanding of the kingdom of God, might also be viewed as a confession of his faith in the face of the world war that had broken out in Europe fifteen months prior to its publication. To Niebuhr "bombers over England" showed that the kingdom's coming meant experiencing crucifixion prior to there being any hope of resurrection. While this implied that he was seeing "every event that happens as coming from the hand of God," it was not his way of sanctioning nonresistance to evil. For him, active restraint of the destroyers of humanity's unity might well become the best or the only course to follow.

Source: *Youth* 4, no. 2 (January 12, 1941): 3–4.

When I say that I believe in the kingdom of God, I mean that I believe that God is king, the ruler and governor of the world he creates, sustains and redeems. I mean that behind, in and through all human empires he guides and controls all things toward the achievement of his purposes. I mean that as he is one, so all the world is one and that I am a citizen of that country whose constitution is his will and whose sovereign he is. I mean that the sufferings of the present time are not worthy to be compared with the glory which shall be revealed when he has brought his purpose to fulfillment in the lives of men. I mean that I owe my first and only loyalty to the nation of God which includes all beings.

THE PARADOX OF CHURCH AND WORLD

Negatively, such a belief in the rule of God means a lack of faith in the sovereignty of those beings which are only creatures, but claim to be ultimate and final.

Among these sovereigns there is the self. I am tempted to believe that I am the master of my fate and the captain of my soul, that I enjoy a freedom to make of myself what I please. But experience has taught me that it is a false belief. Neither my life nor my righteousness is in my power; yet they do not seem to be at the mercy of chance; there is a power that rules over them and that power I know through Jesus Christ to be God, the only adorable one.

There are the empires of this world—the Caesars of our time, the dictators and the democracies, which claim so often to be in control of themselves and of other beings. But like Assyria in the vision of Isaiah; like Pilate in the judgment of Jesus, they have no power save that which is given them from above. They are all shadows and perversions of the kingdom of God. I cannot trust them. I believe that Hitler, the modern Assyrian, and his empire will pass under the judgment of God; even that my own nation must also surrender to the eternal rule. So when I say that God is king, I mean that radical determinism and economic determinism are ultimately unreal. These are themselves determined by God. Kingdom of God means divine determinism.

It will be asked, "Does not the belief in the kingdom of God mean for you that a golden day will come to men on earth; that peace and justice will be established among us?" To this I must answer that I do in fact believe that when the rule of God has become wholly manifest, brotherhood among men will be real; that unity will be apparent; that all the hidden goodness of the divine sovereign will be a matter of sight rather than of faith.

But I must also answer that I do not expect this manifestation of divine rule this side of a great judgment upon myself and all my world. I must say to myself with Amos: "Woe unto you that desire the day of the Lord; the day of the Lord will be darkness and not light." For I am convinced that I am so little ready to participate in the kingdom of love that a painful crucifixion of my old self and the resurrection of a soul in which I can now only believe is necessary before I can enter into that kingdom.

I am convinced that our whole social world needs to undergo a transformation of the profoundest sort before it can participate in the fully realized plan of God for the world of men. That God will bring in his kingdom in its full glory is an exalting but also a sobering thought, since it reminds me that I cannot escape from the earnestness of a God who will not suffer me or my fellows to thwart his plans with our efforts to realize our own noble and ignoble wishes. The coming of God's kingdom means judgment before it means glory; it means crucifixion before resurrection; it means war and death before it means peace and life; it means pilgrimage from green pastures through the valley of the shadow to the house of the Lord.

Hard as it is to describe one's faith in the kingdom of God, it is harder to give an account of the sources of such faith. It is really not true to say that I have full faith in this rule of God. I often doubt its reality and I know that my actions indicate my scepticism day by day. There are times when I am not only tempted to the intellectual belief, but also the practical faith that "Whirl is king and has dethroned Zeus," or to the despairing conclusion that "might makes right."

I pay more attention to the bombers over England than to the ways of God. I adjust my life to human empires. Therefore it is wrong to say that I truly believe in the kingdom of God. If I did so, I would be living in another world than the one which I now inhabit. And yet I think I can say that I believe, for to this thought I must return again and again, and in this kingdom I must put my confidence in a daily renewal of repentance and faith.

Such faith is not something that I can summon up by the power of my will, but it is in a sense wrung from me. I should like to believe in myself more than in God, but experience forbids it. God makes me believe in his rule by the way in which he casts down all the idols which I erect; he makes me put my confidence in his kingdom by destroying my confidence in the empires of men. I believe in the kingdom of God, not steadily, but again and again, because I am forced to believe in it. Without that kingdom life becomes meaningless, human existence short, nasty and brutal. There are times when belief in the kingdom of God seems easy; when his goodness and his wisdom are so apparent that the faith is hailed with delight. Then it seems that I believe in the kingdom not because I must, but because I want to believe with all my heart. But in these years of the world's tragedy, it is the divine compulsion rather than this heavenly attraction which seems the more potent.

Much more can and ought to be said about the reasons for believing in the kingdom of God. Certainly there is ever present before us not only the persuasive example but also the revealing glory of that Jesus Christ who believed in the kingdom as present and to come. Yet everything comes back to the one point: God is the reason for believing in his kingdom. To believe in God, the living creator and redeemer, is to believe in his rule. He is the source as well as the end of faith. Faith, when it comes to us, is his gift.

To live in the kingdom means, I believe, to endeavor to respond with all the small strength of heart and soul one can muster to every event that happens as coming from the hand of God. It means giving up all long range plans for the future of self and society, leaving these to God, while one endeavors now to be loyal to his will. For some men such present loyalty means non-resistance to evil, no matter what may come of it; for me it means resistance to all the rebellions against the unity of the world, showing themselves in the nationalistic, racialistic and other types of idolatry. For some it means the increase of love in life; for me it means first of all restraint upon the lovelessness, the selfishness which reigns in me. But however various the responses of Christians may be, their common loyalty to the rule of God unites them. So kingdom of God means for me [a] life of gratitude for all loyal souls, and the certain hope that we shall all be one.

The Christian Church in the World's Crisis

This article appeared during the tense summer months prior to Pearl Harbor. President Roosevelt's Lend-Lease program had committed the economic power of the United States to Great Britain. His administration was also moving to embargo trade with Japan, which was expanding its war efforts into Southeast Asia. Yet most Americans remained uncertainly in the middle of the ongoing debate between isolationists and internationalists. Originally addressed to the Fellowship of Socialist Christians, a group deeply divided by this struggle, Niebuhr's article did not take either side. Instead, he concentrated on the assumptions of both sides, deftly exposing similar features of opposing points of view and specifying a new role for the church in addressing issues of foreign policy. He also argued here for the first time, as he would once America became directly involved in World War II, that the duty of Christians was to identify the "religious faith" revealed by the context in which political decisions regarding war and peace were made.

Source: *Christianity and Society* 6 (Summer 1941): 11–17.

My understanding of the duty of Christians and of the church in the world's crisis may be set forth in three general propositions:

(1) The religious issue in any particular time and place is less an issue about the specific content of actions than of the context in which each specific action is to be carried out.

(2) The important questions in the contemporary world crisis are religious questions, or questions about the context of political actions.

(3) The problem of Christians today is that of so organizing and shaping their political actions that they will express confidence in and loyalty to the Father of Jesus Christ and faith in the forgiveness of sins.

THE CHURCH AND A WORLD AGAIN AT WAR

I

The first proposition is directed against two misconceptions of the Christian life. One of these is the thought that religious faith calls for specific sorts of domestic, economic, or political action, so that Christianity as such calls for the defense of democracy, or the adoption of socialism, or the policy of isolation, or conscientious objection to participation in war, or obedience to political authority, or marriage, or celibacy, or any one of a hundred similar specific actions. The other misconceptions represent the fatal dilemma into which Christians often feel themselves to be forced when they are required to confess their Christianity either by choosing sides in some confused political struggle or by retiring from the political and social life, at least insofar as they are Christians. The latter horn of the dilemma is chosen by contemplatives, the former by activists; and some, very conscientious Christians, choose both horns by declaring a moratorium on their faith while they engage in the specific actions which their moral sense requires them to perform and to condemn.

The dilemma is a false one if actions are not considered as separate deeds, like beads strung together on a necklace, or like pebbles dropped one by one into the receptacle of the past. Actions are like words. Despite all efforts to discover the "real" meaning of a word by contemplating it long and thoughtfully, it reveals its meaning only in a sentence or paragraph in which the full intention of a speaker is made manifest. A single action apart from a total context may affect events, as an accident does, but not otherwise. It derives significance only from the context in which it stands; and the context which carries the action along, which makes it part of a total pattern, is determined by religion. Religion enters into every specific action but does not determine the rough materials to express the same contextual meaning.

A few illustrations may serve to illuminate this function of faith. A Pharisee and a publican both pray. Now prayer, considered in itself, is regarded by most religious people as a good action, but prayer in the context of the Pharisee's trust in his own goodness is a bad action, being preceded by and directed toward other actions of self-aggrandizement, while prayer in the context of the publican's faith is a work of mercy. It is wholly inadequate to require religious men to profess their faith in prayer. All men pray. The religious question is how and when and in what total context they pray or do not pray.

Another illustration may be taken from domestic life. The great alternative men have always faced in their sex life has been that of celibacy or union with a member of the other sex. But religious faith gives little answer to the question whether men ought to unite with a sex-partner or be celibate. It does affirm that whichever of these alternatives be chosen it be so chosen and so made part of a life of continuous responsibility that the act is not allowed to stand by itself but is made meaningful and effective in long devotion. What is forbidden by Christian faith is neither celibacy nor marriage, but all self-indulgence, adultery, fornication—all isolated, unformed, irresponsible acts.

Looking away from our own faith we note that every religion supplies a context, and the meaning and effect of the actions of its devotees is determined by the context. National socialism, which despite nihilistic tendencies has certain religious qualities, enjoins love of neighbor, leads to practices of mutual support, makes provision for the poor, trains youth to sacrificial service, builds for the "common" good. But the meaning and effect of these acts—on which some look with great approbation—can be understood only if their whole context, their association with military ambition, with the persecution of Jews, etc., is taken into consideration.

These illustrations suggest two affirmations about religious interest in political action and two corollaries of the general principle. The affirmations are: (1) Religious interest is directed more toward preceding and succeeding acts than toward the particular act of the moment; (2) any particular act is molded by its context.

Christianity's interest in motive is explained in many ways. Sometimes we use it to excuse ourselves from making present decisions, as when we assert that we can do no good until we have become good and that therefore our social action must wait on our personal sanctification, or our international action must be postponed until we have gained national perfection. Taken as descriptive statements the remarks of Jesus on motivation seem to mean that a visible act which stands in succession to selfish or impure, invisible acts is evil, no matter how good it appears to be in isolation. The direction of the act, be it almsgiving or prayer, is determined by the direction of the actor rather than by its intrinsic nature. For the moral agent, insistence on purity of motive does not mean that he must stop external, visible action until all his internal actions are good, but that he must strive to make his present and external act correspond to the drive and direction of those internal actions which are good or in accordance with the will of God. He endeavors to put his prayer or almsgiving in line with his neighbor-regarding or God-regarding motions of the heart rather than with his self-regarding internal actions. There is no other way of working on our motives.

Yet it is false to over-emphasize Christian interest in the antecedents of action. Christian conscience is at least equally interested in the successors of an act. For a mechanical conception of life, an act leads to determined consequences and nothing is to be done about it. For the personal conception of Judaism and Christianity, participation of the person does not end with the doing of an act. Its fundamental interest is not in any mechanical consequences of an act, beyond personal control, but in the acts which a self will perform in succession to the act of the moment. Christian ideas of recompense and responsibility, of forgiveness of sins and divine mercy, all emphasize this point. If the act performed has been sinful—as all acts are, expressing not one but many intentions—Christian faith requires the actor not to despair but to say, "By the grace of God something good may come out of this deed, if I stay with it as God stays with it, if I will trust and not despair, if I will accept my pain and remorse and the pain of the innocents I have injured." What is important is that the self follow the bad or the proud act with an act molded by penitence and faith, that it accept and work with the consequences, with the sin and pain in the self and the pain in the neighbor. It can do this insofar as it sees that God can follow the bad act with one of goodness, thinking to do good though men think to do evil. On the other hand it is important for faith that it understands how every apparently good act can lead to bad, proud successor acts which will make the effect of the whole movement evil rather than good.

Interest in the antecedents and successors of an action does not mean that faith is indifferent to the particular act. Some acts are excluded from life as being incapable, so far as man's, not God's, action is concerned, of being made significant. Some words in any language are so blasphemous that they have no place in any Christian sentence. But these are relatively few in number, while there are no words so good that they cannot be used in a wholly vulgar sentence. Apart from the question of the rare, excluded act, it is evident that an act placed in a particular context is molded and given distinctive form, even as a word in a sentence is subject—according to its position—to variations of case, tense, mood, inflection, accent. Both Pharisee and publican pray, but in the different contexts the two acts are done with a difference, apparent even in the physical form. Both Jesus and the political revolter die in martyrdom, but with a difference. The Christian conscientious objector's refusal to obey the state differs in form from the individualistic objector's; the Christian soldier does not fight as Genghis Khan does, and the Christian socialist's political campaign differs from the Stalinist's. All this does not mean that the molding of the single action is the main contribution of the context. The sentence remains more important than the word and no word justifies a speaker. Nevertheless, when two people do the same thing, it is not the same.

The two corollaries of the general proposition that the religious issue is an issue of context of actions may now be briefly stated: (1) Acts differing greatly in material content may achieve similar effects when they are placed in similar contexts; (2) acts of the same general content may achieve opposite effects in antithetical contexts. Thus a work of relief to a victim of aggression and a work of restraint on the aggressor may express the same idea and lead to the same result if the contexts of the actions are similar, while two acts of relief may express opposite intentions if one is part of a self-preservative action and the other part of a total self-denying action.

II

Our second proposition was that the important issues of our time concern the contexts in which actions are to be done rather than particular actions. I mean by this not that the great conflict is one of ideologies but rather one of faiths which are incompletely and often dishonestly represented in the ideologies.

My first illustration of this point is not the strongest one, but I believe it relevant. May it not be said that the real issue of our time in matters of property does not lie in the act of social or private ownership but in the context of such ownership? From one point of view it appears that the question of social ownership is no longer really debatable. Whatever theories are held regarding property the whole drift is toward ownership of the means of production by social groups. And the great question is whether such ownership shall stand in the context of egoistic, or of nationalistic, or of what we now like to call democratic, but which I think we ought to call universalistic socialism. Marxists operating with their stereotyped formulas see only two alternatives, private or social ownership; hence when they deal with the conflict between national socialism and their own class socialism they must interpret the former as a defense type of capitalism, based on the principle of private ownership—an interpretation that cannot hold water for a moment in view of the actual measures adopted by nationalism in socializing industry. Moreover they are unable to discern the ease with which their own kind of social ownership can be egoistic—as in bureaucratic control—or nationalistic. Again the conflict between both types of socialism and capitalism is evidently not always a conflict between social and private ownership but sometimes a struggle between nationalistic or class loyalty with universalism, that is with respect for the rights of men as members of a universal society. For in certain forms of what is vaguely called capitalism, private property does stand in the context of universalism rather than of egoism. Private ownership of the means of production by those who own property for use—as in the case of many handicrafts and to a large extent in agriculture—stands in the context of universalism more than some social ownership does. Only confusion results from exclusive attention to the mode of ownership. The question of our time is not how property is to be owned; the issue does not lie between the advocates of social and those of private ownership, but between the religions of egoism, nationalism, and universalism.

For egoism, private or public ownership will always stand in the context of private gain. What precedes it will be personal interest and what follows will be personal power. New ruling groups, more powerful than the managers of so-called private industry, will use and mold social ownership in their own egoistic context if they are not checked. For nationalism, property will be socialized or left in private hands according to the dominant interest. Universalist socialism will try to keep social ownership within the context of universal human rights and duties, and for the sake of the context allow some private property. What is not evident is that socialism, as social ownership of property, will lead to a truer universalism than private ownership has done; it may be an instrument of universalism or of nationalism or of egoistic bureaucracy. The trend of our time is toward the social ownership of the means of production, but the issue of our time is one of the context in which this ownership and any continuing private ownership are to stand.

The issue of war and peace is even more pressing than that of social or private ownership. The question is put to us in individual and social terms—whether we shall personally be non-resisters or join in coercion, whether as a nation we shall hold aloof from conflict or participate in it. These are separate though similar issues.

To take up the latter first, it must be questioned whether it is the genuine issue in our time and nation. Directly contrary actions are being urged upon us for approximately the same reasons. We are being urged to defend America by aiding Great Britain, and to defend America by abstaining from participation in so-called foreign wars. Now it is, I believe, fairly clear that whichever action is taken in the context of self-defense will be followed by another action which can stand in the same context. If we participate in war under these auspices, we shall withdraw when national interests seem no longer threatened. If we abstain from participation now in the cause of national interest, we will engage in war as soon as national interests seem genuinely imperiled. It may not make much difference in the long run which of these things we do now as long as we make national defense our cause.

The real issue of our time is between internationalism or universalism and nationalism. Whether we shall stay at peace as those who unite with other nations in acceptance of full responsibility for maintaining orderly relations in the world, in acceptance of our full share of responsibility for the rise of international anarchy, with readiness to make real sacrifice of national sovereignty, or whether we shall stay at peace as those who wish to guard at all costs their own prosperity, righteousness and independence—that is a real issue. Whether we shall participate in war as those who are responsible for the fate of small nations, who know they are accessories in the international crimes and must try to mend what they have helped to break, who know they cannot enjoy the rights conferred by order among nations without performing corresponding duties, or whether we shall participate in war irresponsibly, self-sufficiently, and self-righteously—that also is a real issue.

Whether we go to war or do not, is not a matter of indifference. But I believe that the prior question must be settled first in the mind of any agitator for participation or non-participation, and that internationalist coercionists ought to spend more time exposing nationalistic coercionists, less in assailing internationalistic pacifists, while the latter should see that they are far more closely allied with internationalist exponents of participation in war than with isolationist peace propagandists. Whatever particular action we have chosen as our moral duty, our greater duty is to make that action conform to the context of our universal or our nationalist faith. For the most part our duty begins at this point, since to a very large extent the particular action we favor seems to be less a consequence of conscious moral choice than of sentiment, training, and the pressure of events. Moreover, this is a field in which we can do our own duty instead of preaching to others what they ought to do.

It must be remembered in this connection that the larger issue is not the later issue; we cannot stay at peace nationalistically and then become internationalists; we cannot go to war nationalistically and become internationalists at a peace conference. The sentence which expresses nationalism or internationalism will modify the word, whether it be war or peace.

The personal problem of being pacifist or coercionist is very similar to the social one. Non-resistance may be an act in the context of fear for the self, physical, or moral; it may be an act in a context of love for the neighbor. What kind of non-resistance it is, what it means, and how it will become effective depends on context, or on the acts which precede and follow it. When it is the vocational non-resistance of one engaged in working for relief and for reconciliation it will stand in complete opposition to self-regarding non-resistance, whether the self which is regarded as the physical or the religious and moral self. The latter kind of non-resistance cannot reconcile, cannot reduce conflict but only encourage it by giving full sway to the brutal tendencies of men. So also, there are at least two kinds of coercionism; a soldier is not simply a soldier, a magistrate is not simply a magistrate. There is a coercionism which is self-regarding and one which puts itself under the discipline of a universal cause. The coercionism of a highwayman differs as radically from that of a soldier as the non-resistance of a coward differs from that of a Quaker.

So the real issue for any individual is not that of non-resistance or of coercionism but of the context. Or, when a man has determined what particular action he is to take he has only begun the real moral struggle; for now he must wrestle with himself and his actions to make each particular word and deed part of a continuous action which is redemptive rather than defensive.

So regarded, the strife between non-resisters and coercionists in the Christian community is not only useless; it is immoral, for in it each group tends to evade its own real moral problems, to escape its duty, and to justify itself.

III

It is evident now how the duty of the Christian church in our time must be conceived from this point of view. The duty of the church in America is to help the nation to become morally fit either to stay out or to enter into war. The unreadiness of our nation to do either is due to no lack of enthusiasm for either course. It is the unreadiness of a society which thinks in terms of self-defense—military, economic, moral—and which does not know that in history as in heaven he that seeks his own life shall lose it. It is a nation prepared on the one hand to commit the treachery of Munich, and on the other hand to wage the undeclared war which it despises when carried on by Japanese, Russians, or Germans. And much of this spiritual unreadiness of the nation to stay at peace or go to war in any constructive fashion is surely due to a church which tends on the one hand to attach a false significance to isolated acts, and on the other to dramatize itself and nation as Messianic saviour or Messianic sufferer. Hence it is a nation which is not prepared to accept its responsibility in a world that in sight and hearing as in faith is one, to acknowledge how heavily it has contributed to the erection of crosses on all the European and Asiatic Calvaries, to seek to bring forth works worthy of repentance, to act in the faith that God will not desert His thieving crucified sons any more than His thorn-crowned chosen child. It is the duty of the church to show Pilate how to be just, not how to exchange places with Him. It is the church's duty to point out the real, not the superficial issues, and to lead men and nations to the ultimate decision, which is not the decision of war or peace but of American peace or peace of God, American war or acceptance of the judgment of God.

Once more, this does not mean that Christianity is indifferent to the issues of the day. It only means that it is concerned with a solution of those issues which can have a place in the divine economy without the necessity of interminable new crucifixions.

War as the Judgment of God

This article is the first of three in The Christian Century *in which Niebuhr brought his theological perspective to bear on World War II. America's "day of infamy" at Pearl Harbor had united most of the nation around the Allied cause in Europe as well as the Pacific, and by 1942 patriotic fervor was running high. But Niebuhr took issue with any wartime set of goals and objectives designed primarily to protect America's interests. To him, the future of the entire human family depended on a more universal frame of reference. One interesting aspect of this article is the hopeful note one finds in his assessment of the war. American forces around the world at the time were on the defensive. News of any victory was sparse. Yet Niebuhr contended that to recognize "God in the war" was to live and act with "faith in resurrection."*

Source: *The Christian Century* 59 (May 13, 1942): 630–33.

It is a healthy sign that Christians of all groups are giving increasing attention to the question of God's action in this war. For too long a time we have concentrated on human action in international as in other conflicts and the disagreements among us have been at least partly due to this fact. Pacifists have approached war as an action of the lower human self—the angry, hating self—and have tried to respond to it with the action of the ideal, rational self. Coercionists have looked on war as the action of aggressive nations and have summoned men of good will to resist those of ill will.

These human actions are doubtless present in all war but Christian like Jewish interpretation of history centers in the conviction that God is at work in all events and the ethics of these monotheistic communities is determined by the principle that man's action ought always to be response to divine rather than to any finite action. Hence it is a sign of returning health when God rather than the self or the enemy is seen to be the central figure in the great tragedy of war and when the question, "What must I do?" is preceded by the question, "What is God doing?" To attend to God's action is to be on the way to that constructive understanding and constructive human reaction which the prophets initiated and Jesus set forth in its fullness.

I

To see the act of God in war is to stand where Isaiah stood when he discerned that Assyria was the rod of divine anger and where Jesus stood when he saw in the crucifixion not Pilate's or the Jews' activity but that of the Father who gave Pilate the power to crucify and whose will rather than Pilate's or Jesus' was being done.

The consequent action of Isaiah and Jesus was constructive because it was response to divine action rather than to Assyrian or Roman. It was constructive in that it built new community in the midst of tragedy, cleaned selves and society of egoism, fear and hatred, and opened up a productive future in which the tragedy was made the foundation of a new life. Had Isaiah simply attended to what the Assyrian was doing or Jesus to what the priests and Pilate were doing, it is difficult to see what constructive results could have followed had they been never so pacifist or coercionist.

The awareness of Christians that God is acting in the present conflict is still confused and uncertain; hence the reactions are confused. Doubtless much profound searching of soul, mind and Scriptures, much painful intellectual and spiritual labor are required of them, as of the Jews, if they are to learn how to act constructively or, rather, to act as those who are willing instead of unwilling servants of the active God. But something has been gained as a result of the very general recognition that God is judging the nations, the churches and all mankind in this great conflict and crucifixion. The conviction of sin, which the social gospel has brought about, and the old understanding of history, which Marxism has forced Christianity to remember, leave all Christians with a bad conscience in the presence of this struggle and with the recognition that men are reaping what they have sown.

To be sure, there are still parts of the church which think in terms of human rather than of divine judgment. For them the war is an affair of our judgment against the opponents' judgment. Such Christians tend to believe that their judgment on the enemy—both as moral evaluation and as punishment—is really God's judgment and that it is practically unnecessary to inquire what God is doing since they are executing his counsel. Happily these voices are not strong in the church. It must be conceded, of course, that the temptation to make the self the spokesman and lieutenant of the Eternal is never far from any one of us and that a more severe trial than the one we have experienced so far may lead many more of us to fall into this temptation. Still, it remains a cause for gratitude that the churches in the warring nations—on both sides—have so far not tended to confuse divine and human judgment as much as they did a generation ago. It is further a cause for thankfulness that pacifists and coercionists appear to agree on the primacy of God's judgment and its transcendence over all human judgment.

At one point this agreement in interpretation of the situation is leading to a general agreement in ethical decision. All the Christian groups seem to be resolved to exert all their powers to effect a just peace settlement—a peace which will not be based on the interpretation that only one nation is being judged or that the victors are the judges, but rather on the knowledge that all nations have fallen short of simple justice, not to speak of the glory of God. Hence it is demanded that the peace settlement recognize the necessity of sacrifice on the part of all, the limitation of national sovereignty, the

THE CHURCH AND A WORLD AGAIN AT WAR

claim of all nations to certain political and economic rights. On this the mind of the churches seems to be unified.

Beyond this point, however, there is no agreement and the continued confusion of the churches appears particularly when the question about the present rather than the future action is raised. It seems that God's judgment on the nations is not so understood as to require a present response, but only a sort of promise that we will try to be good in the future. One group appears to think that besides the action of God in judgment Christians ought to attend to the bad actions of all men who are making war and respond to the latter by refusal to participate in the conflict. Hence many pacifists desire to share in peace-making as those who stand under the judgment of God but to refrain from all participation in war because men, not God, make war.

A second group regards war as judgment of God but also as a defense of our own country against the enemies not of God so much as of our country. Hence it seeks to make a distinction between the response of the Christian to God and the response of the citizen to the enemy. As Christians, then, men do not make war, but as citizens they defend their country.

A third group makes a distinction between the absolute judgment of God to which all men must respond with penitence and the relative judgments of men to which other relative judgments must be opposed. For those who find themselves in this group the war requires the double response of contrition for common sin and of confident assertion of the relative rightness of democracy in opposition to totalitarianism.

In every case there is dualism: two actions must be responded to, the action of God and the action of the opponent. To be sure, Christians are accustomed to dualism, for their two-worldly life involves them forevermore in the crisis of time and eternity, of this aeon and the future one, of the life in the spirit and the life in the body. But the dualism of double response is an intolerable one; it makes us "double-minded men, unstable in all our ways," ditheists who have two gods, the Father of Jesus Christ and our country, or Him and Democracy, or Him and Peace. Country, Democracy and Peace are surely values of a high order, if they are under God, but as rivals of God they are betrayers of life.

Perhaps further reflection on the nature of divine judgment and on the possibilities of consistent human response to it may be of some help in resolving our confusion and helping us toward the achievement of a common Christian mind.

II

What does it mean to say that this war is a judgment of God on the nations or on all of us? It cannot mean simply that it is the action of a Being who, in primitive human fashion, executes vengeance. Since Hosea's time that interpretation has been rationally impossible. Christians in particular must be convinced by their whole gospel that judgment cannot be separated from redemption, that the harshness of God is not antagonistic to his love but subordinate to it, that divine "penology" is reconstructive and not vindictive in its nature.

The fundamental Christian assumption about divine justice may be stated in another way by saying that it is never merely punishment for sins, as though God were concerned simply to restore the balance between men by making those suffer who have inflicted suffering, but that it is always primarily punishment of sinners who are to be chastened and changed in the character which produced the sinful acts. Therefore war cannot be interpreted as hell; if it were hell we could not even be aware that God is judging us for we would be without God in war. War as judgment of God is a purgatory, not a hell.

Christians cannot interpret God's action in war as the judgment of vengeance for another and profounder reason: the pains of war do not descend primarily on the unjust but on the innocent. Wars are crucifixions. It is not the mighty, the guides and leaders of nations and churches, who suffer most in them, but the humble, little people who have had little to do with the framing of great policies. Even pacifists in jail have little reason to think of themselves as the martyrs of war when they reflect on all the children, wives and mothers, humble obedient soldiers, peasants on the land, who in the tragedy of war are made an offering for sin.

It is true also in the social sense that the greater burdens of war fall on the relatively innocent and on the weak. The nations which have suffered most in the present conflict are not those which were most responsible for the sins of commission and omission out of which this tragic demonstration of cosmic justice has issued. Czechoslovakia, Norway, the Netherlands, Belgium, Greece, China, the Philippines—these were not the conspicuous egoists, exploiters, self-satisfied and self-righteous among the countries of the earth.

This is not the place, even were the writer competent as he is not, to develop a social theory and application of the atonement. But, surely, Christians know that the justice of God is not only a redemptive justice in which suffering is used in the service of remaking but it is also vicarious in its method, so that the suffering of innocence is used for the remaking of the guilty. One cannot then speak of God acting in this war as judge of the nations without understanding that it is through the cross of Christ more than through the cross of thieves that he is acting upon mankind.

In the second place, if God is judging mankind in this war, as he is, there can be no contention before him about the relative rightness or wrongness of the various groups involved. When we are in the wrong before God we are absolutely in the wrong and no kind of relative rightness can be made the foundation of an appeal to a higher court. When Isaiah saw that Assyria was the rod of God's anger whereby Israel was chastised he also saw that Assyria was wrong before God and that the axe had no right to boast of itself "against him that heweth therewith."

This truth cuts both ways. It means that if a Hitler is seen to be the rod of God's anger he is not thereby justified, relatively or absolutely; for he does not intend what God intends, "but it is in his heart to destroy and to cut off nations not a few." It means, also, that if the United Nations are the instruments of God's judgment on Germany, Italy and Japan, they are not thereby justified, as though their intentions were relatively or absolutely right. God does not act save through finite instruments but none of the instruments can take the place of God even for a moment, either in their own view or in the view of the one who is being "punished." Whether we speak of nations or of movements, we can be as certain in our day as the prophets were in theirs that our thoughts are not his thoughts and our ways are not his ways. Hence response to the divine judgment can never mean justification of either the enemy or of the self. Insofar as justification is introduced the conviction about God's action is abandoned.

A third point about divine judgment which it seems important to recall again in our time, though it ought to be self-evident, is that it is the judgment of the one and universal God and not the judgment of a Lord of the spiritual life, or of a Lord of religious life, or of a Christian Lord over Christian life. As judgment of a redeemer it cannot be interpreted in the light of revelation, reason and experience as that of a redeemer of the spiritual, the religious or the Christian life. The redeemer is Father of all things who has created men not only in spiritual society but also in domestic, political and economic society. Hence it is impossible so to separate response to the judgment of God from politically necessary action as to make religious life an affair of repentance while political action remains essentially unrepentant, self-confident action in the defense of our values.

This is what both those groups seem to do who say that in addition to accepting divine judgment we must on the one hand defend our country and, on the other hand, defend democracy. If we do not reform our war-making as well as our peace-making, our defense of values as well as our aggression, our support of democracy as well as our opposition to totalitarianism, this means that we have excluded some part of life from the reign of God or that we have abandoned monotheism, accepting a double standard and a double deity.

III

The interpretation of God's action in this war as redemptive and vicarious, absolute and unified judgment leads to certain consequences for human action.

The first of these is the abandonment of the habit of passing judgments of our own on ourselves and on our enemies or opponents, whether these be national enemies, church enemies or enemies of our ideas. Instead of asking whether we are right people or wrong people we shall simply inquire what duty we have to perform in view of what we have done amiss and in view of what God is doing. If that duty involves, as I believe it does, resistance to those who are abusing neighbors, we shall not inquire whether our neighbors are not better people than those who are abusing them. In social life our duty frequently requires us to protect neighbors whom we dislike against the injustices of those whom we like and who on the whole seem to us to be better people than their victims are. The same principle applies in the affairs of the society of nations.

If injustice is done to totalitarian countries (as Greece was somewhat totalitarian) or communist countries or the Jewish people, the answer to our question about our duty does not depend on the answer to our question about the relative goodness of the victims and the victimizers. Nor does the answer depend on the reply to our question about our own relative goodness. Duty is duty and no man or nation has a right to excuse the self from doing the dutiful thing now because of past failures. Response to the judgment of God on men who have failed to do their duty in the past consists in the performance of present duty and not in the passing of new judgments on others because they have failed more signally in our view.

A second thing Christians under the judgment of God in war require of themselves, because he requires it of them, is the abandonment of all self-defensiveness, all self-aggrandizement, all thinking in terms of self as central. The judgment of God in this war appears to be less a judgment on past selfish acts than one on the self-centered character of nations, churches, classes and individual men; as redemptive it holds the promise of deliverance from this imprisonment in self. It is a judgment on our nation which in its actions, sentiments and omissions has demonstrated its profound preoccupation with its own prosperity, safety and righteousness, so that in its withdrawal from international political responsibilities, in its tariff, monetary and neutrality legislation, it has acted always with a single eye to its own interests rather than to those of its neighbors in the commonwealth of nations. It is a judgment on the churches which have indicated in their conduct how great their anxiety was for their own survival, their own righteousness, prestige and power.

It was apparent long ago—in the crucifixion of the Jews and China—that the Lord was laying the iniquity of us all on the backs of the innocent. Since this vicarious demonstration of our guilt did not move us we are now to be moved by a vicarious suffering which strikes nearer home. How can we respond to this judgment by persisting to think in terms of self, of defense of our country, or of our democracy, or of our religion? If we accept God's judgment on our self-centeredness we cannot respond to it by persisting in actions of self-defense and by fighting the war for the sake of protecting our selves or our values instead of for the sake of the innocent who must be delivered from the hands of the aggressor.

To carry on the war under the judgment of God is to carry it on as those who repent of their self-centeredness and who now try to forget about themselves while they concentrate on the deliverance of their neighbors. It is to wage war as those do who will not withdraw when their own interests are no longer apparently imperiled while their weaker neighbors remain in danger, who will not wash their hands of the affair if the peace is not to their liking, but who, on the contrary, accept continuous, never ending responsibility for their neighbors. It is also to wage war in such a way that a decent—a just endurable if not a just and durable—peace can come out of it.

If the war is fought with nothing but ideas of self-defense, or defense of our values, in mind, the peace will be a self-defensive peace, however much inconsistent idealists may seek to reverse the process of their own and of national thinking at that time. It must be emphasized also that for those who refuse to participate in war either by physical or spiritual action such abstention can be response to divine judgment only if it be a part of a total action in which concern for others has been given preeminence over concern for self and its values. If non-participation by individuals or by churches is self-centered, as it often is, it is as destructive in the long run as self-centered participation.

Finally, response to God's action in war is hopeful and trusting response. It never gives up the one whom we must oppose, as though he were too depraved for redemption or for restoration to full rights in the human community. It does not accept the counsel of despair in the midst of fighting, allowing vindictive measures because by "fair fighting" our cause might be lost. It trusts that if we do our duty no evil can befall us in life or in death. The response is hopeful in that it regards the time of judgment as also time of redemption and looks in the midst of tragedy for the emergence of a better order than any which has been realized before. Nothing is regarded as beyond the scope of redemption—not the political life of men, nor the economic, nor the spiritual; neither the crucified brigand nor the crucified righteous are regarded as forsaken by God and far from Paradise. Even should death come to them hope wraps their broken bodies in fine linen, conserving what it can, preparing on Good Friday for an Easter miracle of divine action.

To recognize God at work in war is to live and act with faith in resurrection. If God were not in the war life would be miserable indeed. It would mean that the cosmos had no concern with justice. But if God were in the war only as judge, man's misery would be only slightly assuaged since before the judge all are worthy of death. To see God in the war as the vicarious sufferer and redeemer, who is afflicted in all the afflictions of his people, is to find hope along with broken-heartedness in the midst of a disaster.

These are but general reflections which do not presume to say to anyone what his particular duty in response to God's judgment must be. They seek however to describe in what spirit and context Christians in varying vocations and with conflicting political convictions may meet the divine judgment and maintain fellowship with each other.

War as Crucifixion

The first of Niebuhr's wartime articles drew a barrage of criticism. For this reason, The Christian Century *allowed him to respond publicly in a second article ("Is God in the War?") to Professor Virgil C. Aldrich of the Rice Institute (now University) because his letter to the editor contained most of the objections that others were raising. One of these involved Niebuhr's view of the conflict as a form of "vicarious suffering," which Aldrich preferred to reserve for Christian martyrs. Niebuhr's response to this criticism appears to have contributed during the next year to the writing of this third article in which we catch a fuller glimpse of his theology of the cross. To him, the horrible bombings of Coventry, Cologne, and other cities demonstrated how indiscriminate modern warfare could be with respect to its victims. Nevertheless, as with the death of Jesus on the cross, this also represented for him a vicarious sacrifice through which Christians could be summoned to believe that God was bringing about a redemptive outcome for the world.*

Source: *The Christian Century* 59 (April 28, 1943): 513–15.

Man, being incurably rational, cannot act without some theory of the events in which he is participating. This truth is clearly apparent in the case of war. A blaze of unreasoning emotion may induce men to exchange a few blows but any long conflict, especially between groups, requires propaganda, which at its worst is an effort to supply a theory that will fit the emotions and at its best is an attempt to direct and restrain emotion by understanding of the situation. To be sure, theories of war in general and of any particular conflict in which we are engaged are not the only factors which influence action, but they are nevertheless important elements in any responsible behavior.

Two main theories of the nature of war are being applied to our present struggle and are influencing in various ways the responses of individuals and communities to the situation. They may be named the amoral and the moral theories. The former interprets war as a conflict of powers in which victory with its fruits belongs to the stronger and in which moral words or phrases are nothing but instruments of power by means of which emotions are aroused and men are unified. This view is held both by certain balance-of-power advocates of unlimited participation in war, so long as national self-interest is involved, and by certain pacifists who wash their hands of war because it makes no moral difference which side wins in a conflict of pure power.

Moral and Amoral Theories Inadequate

The moral view of war, on the other hand, interprets it as an event in a universe in which the laws of retribution hold sway. According to this theory war begins with a transgression of international, or natural, or human, or divine law and continues in the effort of the law's upholders to bring the offenders to justice. Those who hold this view make a distinction between unjust war—the act of transgression—and just war—the act of retribution and of defense of order. Again, both participants and non-participants in any particular war may use this theory; their differences are largely due to their estimate of this war as just or as unjust.

Both theories are inadequate and misleading, for both fail to account for all the relevant phenomena and must be abandoned at some point in practice, not because emotion is too powerful to submit to their control, but because they appear unreasonable. Since man is a self-interested being and always desires to extend his power, the amoral theory is partly true. But since man is always interested in values beyond the self and desires not only power but also the enjoyment of the good, the amoral theory is wholly inadequate. It forgets that wars are being fought by men and that human power cannot be abstracted from human rationality and morality.

Among men, might not only makes right, but the conviction of being right makes might, and it is impossible to reduce such a conviction to an emotional reaction. However much the power realists may regret the fact, it remains true that in war men do not fight simply for their own interests but make great sacrifices for distant values, for their own country, or Poland, or "democracy," or "the new order," or "the Four Freedoms." It may be said that while individuals do this in war, nations always act amorally. But this again is to deal with unreal, wholly abstract beings, since nations and their governments are human, so that the mixture of motives which is discernible in individuals is always present in groups also.

Retribution Fails

The moral view of war seems to take into account those elements which the power theory ignores, yet it also remains inadequate and is in some respects more misleading than its rival. Its failure does not necessarily lie at the point in which the power theory is interested, for it may be very much aware of men's love of power and of the necessity for taking this into account in the making of moral judgments. Its inadequacy appears rather in the impossibility of applying the whole scheme of moral judgment and retributive justice to social relations. It has often been observed that a people cannot be indicted, that the question of war-guilt which appears so easily determinable in time of conflict becomes more difficult with longer perspective, that retribution itself is impractical since the community which is to be punished cannot be excluded from the society of nations as an individual can be banished from his community by imprisonment.

The greatest difficulty of all which the moral theory faces is the fact that in war the burden of suffering does not fall on the guilty, even when the guilt is relatively determinable, but on the innocent. Retribution for the sins of a nazi party and a Hitler falls on Russian and German soldiers, on the children of Cologne and Coventry, on the Finns and the French. In order that the moral theory may be used it becomes necessary to convict all the common men, the whole opposing nation of guilt. Even if that were possible the theory does not hold since the suffering for guilt is shared by those who are on the side of "justice." Hence those who hold to the moral theory find themselves unable to follow it in practice. If they declare a present war to be just they must participate in inflicting suffering and death on the "just" with the "unjust"; if they regard a present war as unjust they must stand idly by while the "just" are being made to suffer with the "unjust."

Is War Crucifixion?

Since neither theory will do for men who want to act reasonably, on the basis of an intelligible interpretation of the facts of experience, the question arises whether there is not some other pattern than that of the survival of the fittest or that of retributive justice by means of which war may be understood and response to it guided. The question must arise for Christians whether that understanding of the nature of cosmic justice which the crucifixion of Jesus Christ discovered to men must not and may not be applied to war, as it must and may be applied to many personal events that are unintelligible save through the cross. Is war, then, crucifixion?

War is at least very much like the crucifixion. In both events there is a strange intermixture of justice and injustice on the side alike of those who regard themselves as the upholders of the right and on the side of the vanquished. Three men were crucified on Calvary, all, it appears, on more or less the same charge of insurrection. Two of them were malefactors who actually desired to overturn the established order, whether for patriotic or personal motives; yet they were not alike since one recognized the at least relative justice of his punishment while the other remained unrepentant. The third cross carried one who was innocent of the charge made against him; yet ambiguously so, since he was establishing a kingdom of a strange sort which held unknown dangers for the Roman order and the Jewish law.

Nor were the crucifiers less mixed in their justice and injustice: soldiers who did their duty in obedience to their oath, priests who acted according to their lights—though their light was darkness—a judge who failed in his duty, citizens who were devoted to the maintenance of the sacred values of Jewish culture, a mob overborne by emotion. They knew not what they did. War is like that—apparently indiscriminate in the choice of victims and of victors, whether these be thought of as individuals or as communities.

Cross Reveals God's Moral Earnestness

A second point of resemblance between war and the crucifixion is no less striking. The cross which will not yield to analysis in terms of retributive justice, will not yield either to analysis in terms of brute power. If the alternative before men were simply either that God is just in the sense that he rewards the good and punishes the guilty, or that the world is indifferent to good and evil, then the cross would be the final demonstration of God's injustice or, rather, of his non-existence. If that were the alternative then men would need to conclude that "Whirl is king and hath dethroned Zeus."

But the cross does not encourage moral indifference; it requires men to take their moral decisions with greater rather than less seriousness; it demonstrates the sublime character of real goodness;

it is a revelation, though "in a glass darkly," of the intense moral earnestness of a God who will not abandon mankind to self-destruction; it confronts us with the tragic consequences of moral failure. It does all this because it is sacrifice—the self-sacrifice of Jesus Christ for those whom he loved and God's sacrifice of his best-loved Son for the sake of the just and the unjust. War is like the cross in this respect. In its presence men must abandon their moral cynicism along with other peacetime luxuries.

We are moved in the presence of war to think more rather than less seriously of the importance of our decisions and of the evil and good possibilities of our existence. For war also is not only a great slaughter but a great sacrifice. It is the moving sacrifice of our youth for the sake of that which they love; the sacrifice by parents of their best-loved sons. In the midst of its cruelties, falsehoods and betrayals there appear sublime examples of human courage and devotion and selflessness that uplift us as we see the greatness of man revealed alongside his depravity. An almost infinite capacity for goodness is reflected in the dark glass of sinfulness. Vicarious suffering shows up dramatically the tragic issue of our wrongdoings and wrong-being in the midst of our human solidarity. War does not make for moral indifference.

The Cross Is Relevant

The analogy of war and crucifixion suggests that we are dealing with more than analogy. It indicates that the cross is relevant to the understanding of our world and to our social action in ways which neither the sacerdotal nor the moral influence theory of its meanings has made evident. Hence it directs Christians to wrestle with the problem of the cross in new ways so that new light from it may fall upon the scenes of their present social life as well as upon their personal problems and tragedies. It may well be that the meaning of the cross must become apparent to our time in new situations somewhat as the meaning of the spherical nature of the earth has become apparent in a new way to us in recent years.

The knowledge of the fact that we live on a globe has been a relatively abstract knowledge for hundreds of years. It was found significant for certain purposes, but on the whole men continued to live their daily lives on the practical assumption of the earth's flatness. All the maps translated our spherical relations into relations on a plane, and so we persisted in the thought that Europe lay to the east of us, never to the north, Asia to the west, never to the north or east. What we have known for hundreds of years we now need to learn because the old pattern of the flat earth no longer suffices even for the life of one who never leaves his continent. The existence of this nation, at least, begins to depend upon his now taking seriously a known but unappropriated knowledge. Perhaps it is like this with the cross of Christ and war and every social suffering.

What we shall find when we concern ourselves more seriously with the cross and with its meaning for our war cannot be prophesied. There is one point, however, which seems of great importance and to which all efforts to understand war through the cross must give heed. It is the point which Paul made. The crucifixion illuminated many things for him, but in particular it was the revelation of the righteousness of God which was distinct from the righteousness of the law and which, when it became apparent, showed man's righteousness to be as unrighteous as his unrighteousness.

What Kind of Universe?

Perhaps we may understand Paul's point like this: The cross of Jesus Christ is the final, convincing demonstration of the fact that the order of the universe is not one of retribution in which goodness is rewarded and evil is punished, but rather an order of graciousness wherein, as Jesus had observed, the sun is made to shine on evil and on good and the rain to descend on the just and unjust. To live in this divine order of graciousness on the basis of the assumption that reward must be merited and evil avenged is to come into conflict with the real order in things. The pattern of retributive justice simply will not work; it is like the effort to translate the global earth into the terms of a plane. To make distinctions between the just and unjust, and to employ for that purpose the standard of good works performed by them, will not work.

If men are to live at all, as souls or as communities, they must begin with the acceptance not of some standard of judgment—not even the standard of graciousness—but of an act of graciousness to which they respond graciously. The cross is not the demonstration of the fact that man has a wrong standard of judgment which he must correct or for which he must substitute a right standard of judgment by means of which to assess goodness and sinfulness, but it shows that the whole effort to assess and judge the goodness and the evil of self and others, and to reward or punish accordingly, is mistaken.

War as God's Graciousness

God's righteousness is his graciousness and his grace is not an addition to his justice; hence man's rightness does not lie in a new order of judging justice, but in the acceptance of grace and in thankful response to it. The cross does not so much reveal that God judges by other standards than men do, but that he does not judge; it does not demonstrate that men judge by the wrong standards but that their wrongness lies in trying to judge each other, instead of beginning where they can begin—with the acceptance of graciousness and response to it.

If the cross is not only a historical event but a revelation of the order of reality, then war is not only like the cross but must be a demonstration of that same order of God. How it demonstrates the disorderliness of human righteousness and unrighteousness is apparent enough. How it demonstrates the fundamental ungraciousness of both the apparently righteous and the apparently unrighteous is perhaps also clear. But that it should be the hidden demonstration of divine graciousness is hard for us to understand. The cross in ancient history is acceptable to us; the cross in "religious" history, in the history of man's relation to a purely spiritual God, is also acceptable; but the cross in our present history is a stumbling block and a folly which illustrates human sinfulness, but not divine graciousness.

Yet how the divine grace appears in the crucifixion of war may become somewhat clear when the cross of Christ is used to interpret it. Then our attention is directed to the death of the guiltless, the gracious, and the suffering of the innocent becomes a call to repentance, to a total revolution of our minds and hearts. And such a call to repentance—not to sorrow but to spiritual revolution—is an act of grace, a great recall from the road to death which we all travel together, the just and the unjust, the victors and the vanquished. Interpreted through the cross of Jesus Christ the suffering of the innocent is seen not as the suffering of temporal men but of the eternal victim "slain from the foundations of the world." If the Son of God is being crucified on many an obscure hill—then the graciousness of God, the self-giving love, is more manifest here than in all the years of peace.

It will be asked, If these suggestions, these vague gestures in the direction of the interpretation of war as crucifixion, are followed, what will be the result for action? No single answer can be given since the cross does not impose a new law on man. But one thing will be common to all actions which are based on such an understanding of war: there will be in them no effort to establish a righteousness of our own, no excusing of self because one has fallen less short of the glory of God than others; there will be no vengeance in them. They will also share one positive characteristic: they will be performed in hope, in reliance on the continued grace of God in the midst of our ungraciousness.

9

The Peacetime Church and the Threat of World Communism

Immediately following World War II, H. Richard Niebuhr became convinced that the church in the Western world had come to a critical crossroads. The flush of the Allied victories and America's return to a peacetime footing notwithstanding, Niebuhr believed that the civilization Christianity had baptized and nurtured in its infancy and then instructed and accompanied on its way to maturity in the twentieth century lay in tatters. While the war's outcome had consigned some Christians to abject physical poverty, it had deepened divisions among others. Although the power and affluence of American Christians now loomed even larger, internal anxieties and persistent fears about the future seemed to dampen their outlook. At few other times in its history had the church been more engaged in questioning itself about its adequacy and its responsibility for the ruin of a world that now seemed to threaten its future.[1]

Niebuhr had found good reasons to question America's wartime attitudes and aims. To those who might be tempted to let their patriotism turn *country* into their absolute source of value, he pointed out that this faith could only lead to division and disillusionment. More immediately, it forced one either to deny the faith claims of other nations or to become a polygamist who had chosen to marry more than one god; in other words, it created a faith relationship that was not sustainable. Faith in the God whom Jesus Christ had revealed to the entire world not only allowed for critical evaluation of an American version of democracy but it also curbed the temptation to demonize one's enemies.[2]

Niebuhr also found fault with the "Four Freedoms" (*of* speech and worship, and *from* want and fear) that President Franklin Roosevelt set forth in order to gain public support for the war. One had only to look at the sordid side of human history, he argued, to demonstrate that the "granting of freedom from physical wants" would not set people at peace with themselves and their neighbors. "Earth is not enough," he exclaimed. Extending freedom to anyone required the "disinterestedness" that only an "other-worldly" perspective was capable of generating.[3]

Another target for Niebuhr's criticism was the Federal Council of Churches, when it declared that its "first task" in the war's aftermath was to demonstrate that Christianity was the faith that could best enable all of humankind to enjoy "fullness of life." This statement, as he saw it, contained the same pragmatic logic with respect to religion that the totalitarian leaders of the recently defeated nations of

---

1. See H. Richard Niebuhr, "The Responsibility of the Church for Society," in *The Gospel, the Church, and the World,* ed. Kenneth Scott Latourette (New York: Harper & Brothers, 1946); reprinted in *"The Responsibility of the Church for Society" and Other Essays by H. Richard Niebuhr,* ed. Kristine A. Culp (Louisville: Westminster John Knox, 2008), 62–64.
2. H. Richard Niebuhr, "The Nature and Existence of God: A Protestant's View," *Motive* 4 (December 1943): 43–46.
3. H. Richard Niebuhr, "Toward a New Otherworldliness," *Theology Today* 1 (April 1944): 81–87.

Germany and Japan had employed. Christianity was being used as a means of defending America's values, of guaranteeing its prosperity, and of promising that in the process its own superiority in addressing human problems would be vindicated. Not only did history fail to support such forms of "worldly Christianity," but the biblical record—with its emphasis on "suffering service"—pointed to the contrary.[4]

How, then, might the church be *in* this postwar world without becoming *of* it? Niebuhr expressed his clearest answer to this question in "The Responsibility of the Church for Society," an article that in 1946 became a chapter in a book edited by his Yale colleague, Kenneth Scott Latourette. Acknowledging the "peculiar urgency" for the contemporary church to address this issue, he drew a distinction between being accountable *to* someone and *for* something—and framing this dichotomy theologically, between God-in-Christ and Christ-in-God. The one *to* whom Christ made his church accountable was God almighty, and because this same God was also the one "who so loved the world" that he gave it his beloved Son, Christ also made the church as responsible as he was *for* society's redemption. Niebuhr then used this same distinction to set forth his own threefold definition of the church's responsibility for society. God-in-Christ called upon the church to see itself as an *apostle*, sent to proclaim to the world that God was at the center of every aspect of its life and, like the prophets of old, to summon it to repentance for all of its idolatries. At the same time, Christ-in-God compelled the church to assume a *pastoral* role by seeking to participate in the relief of people's needs and, in priestly fashion, to alleviate the suffering brought on by injustice. By exercising both of these types of

---

4. H. Richard Niebuhr, "Utilitarian Christianity," *Christianity and Crisis* 6 (July 8, 1946): 3–5.

responsibility, the church could become a *pioneer* by first putting into practice for itself what it fervently desired to preach to the world.[5]

During these years, Niebuhr was also at work on his magnum opus, *Christ and Culture*. While it was published in 1951, the book reflected courses he had taught during the prior decade at Yale on the history and types of Christian ethics and a series of lectures he delivered in 1949 at Austin Presbyterian Theological Seminary. Moreover, in 1942 he had drafted a paper ("Types of Christian Ethics") in which he organized church-world relationships into five distinct types. In describing the church's tendency to identify itself with a prevailing civilization (Christ *of* culture) or choosing to withdraw from it (Christ *against* culture), he was clearly drawing upon a basic feature of his thinking since the 1920s. By the 1940s, however, he was ready to introduce three "mediating" church-world types: the synthesis (Christ *above* culture), the dualist (Christ and culture *in paradox*), and the conversionist (Christ *the transformer of* culture), all of which were determined to deal with the relationship between the church and the world in *both-and* rather than *either-or* terms. Another important aspect of this paper (not published until 1996) is that it gives us reason to believe that Niebuhr's chief intention in *Christ and Culture* was to provide a larger context for examining one's own type rather than a way of measuring its value or the worth of any of the other possible types. In other words, he was not purposely seeking to set up the conversionist type as the only viable paradigm for church-world relationships.[6]

---

5. Niebuhr, "The Responsibility of the Church for Society," 64–75.
6. H. Richard Niebuhr, "Types of Christian Ethics," in Glen H. Stassen, D. M. Yeager, and John Howard Yoder, *Authentic Transformation: A New Vision of Christ and Culture* (Nashville: Abingdon, 1996), 15–29. The names Niebuhr assigned to his five types in this paper were "new law" (against culture), "natural law" (of culture), "architectonic" (above culture), "oscillatory" (paradox), and "conversionist" (transformer of culture).

What the postwar context in which Niebuhr was working on *Christ and Culture* helps explain, therefore, is the process by which "Christ the transformer of culture" became his own type. First, the identification of the church with the program of National Socialism in Germany had made the "Christ of culture" type a less favorable option for him than it appeared to be in the 1920s, when he was endeavoring to help his immigrant denomination enter the American mainstream. Second, he seems to have recognized that the "Christ against culture" strategy he had advocated during the depths of the Great Depression could easily lead to an isolationism in which the churches focused their attention exclusively on spiritual matters. Third, more than anything the charge of "ditheism" that he had leveled during the war at those who sought to separate their faith in God from the pragmatic necessities of a deadly conflict between nations seems to have caused him to eliminate "Christ and culture in paradox" from his list of options. Finally, the social conservatism the "Christ above culture" type had reinforced among Roman Catholics in Europe stood out for him as one of the principal reasons their churches had failed to make a stand against Hitler and Mussolini. Hence, the 1946 article he entitled "The Church's Responsibility for Society" appears to best fit the conversionist type he went on to describe in the book for which he is perhaps still best known.

Unlike some other postwar periods in its history, America experienced a revival instead of a religious depression for more than a decade following World War II. One of the main reasons churches began to bulge at the seams was the Cold War and the threat that the spread of world communism into parts of Europe and Asia posed to the "free world." Since the Soviet Union and its communist allies were regarded as atheistic, being an active church member demonstrated one's commitment to the American way of life. It also became a means of avoiding the suspicion that Wisconsin Senator

Joseph McCarthy was stirring up with his investigations into the subversive influence of citizens who were thought to be communist sympathizers. In 1954, moreover, President Dwight Eisenhower told the American people that their government made "no sense unless it is founded on a deeply felt religious faith—and I don't care what it is." In the same year, the addition of "under God" to the Pledge of Allegiance became still another way to affirm loyalty to both God and the nation.[7]

While Niebuhr abhorred this idolatrous blending of religion and patriotism, he came to see it as an opportunity to reconsider the "deeply felt religious faith" undergirding the government the nation's founders had established. He had already begun his efforts in this regard in the 1930s with *The Kingdom of God in America,* and continued them in several subsequent scholarly presentations.[8] His thoughts on the subject amid the Cold War hysteria of the 1950s appeared in a series of lectures that were included in his book on *Radical Monotheism and Western Culture.* Here he asserted that while subject to constant assaults from various mundane centers of value, it was a monotheistic faith in Nature's God on which the basic principles of American democracy remained grounded. From the standpoint of this faith, religious liberty could not be viewed as simply a right the nation had granted to its people and their churches. On the contrary, it meant that loyalty to God, as well as one's responsibilities as a citizen of the greater human commonwealth, preceded any obligations one might have to one's own country, and that they could in fact trump them. Despite any arguments to

---

7. See Sydney E. Ahlstrom, *A Religious History of the American People* (New Haven, CT: Yale University Press, 1972), 950–54.
8. See H. Richard Niebuhr, *The Kingdom of God in America* (New York: Harper & Row, 1937), 59–65, 75–80. See also "The Relation of Christianity and Democracy" (1940) and "The Idea of Original Sin in American Culture" (1949), in *H. Richard Niebuhr: Theology, History, and Culture,* ed. William Stacy Johnson (New Haven, CT: Yale University Press, 1996), 143–58, 174–91.

THE PEACETIME CHURCH AND WORLD COMMUNISM

the contrary that reason, experience, or science might provide, the equality with which God had endowed all human beings remained the only lens through which Americans could view neighboring nations as well as themselves. This monotheistic faith, in his estimation, also served to check all attempts on the part of politicians to make the "voice of the people" the first and last word in the process of enacting legislation.[9]

The following writings illustrate several of the ways in which Niebuhr's response to the peacetime challenges that America faced following World War II, including the threat of world communism, served to sharpen insights into the church-world paradox that we also see him working out in his book *Christ and Culture*.

---

9. H. Richard Niebuhr, *Radical Monotheism and Western Culture* (New York: Harper & Brothers, 1960), 64–77.

Utilitarian Christianity

Published in the journal Niebuhr's brother Reinhold had helped to launch just prior to America's entrance into World War II, this article provides us with his perspective on the role of religion in the nation following the close of this conflict. Rhetoric depicting Christianity as a bulwark of protection against world communism consistently troubled him. The Christian faith, in his view, no matter how sincerely it was followed, did not guarantee the preservation or the enrichment of the "American way of life." He also sensed that what Americans were really trying to stave off was the decline of their own culture rather than the evils of communism. "Repentance," he maintained, "is called for not because we have chosen false means to the achievement of our ends but because our ends themselves are idolatrous."

Source: *Christianity and Crisis* 6 (July 8, 1946): 3–5.

In religion as in science there is a constant conflict between the devotees of pure endeavor after truth and the seekers after immediate, tangible results. For the latter truth is a pragmatic device by means of which men are enabled to gain satisfactions as biological and temporal rather than as rational and eternal beings. For the former truth—abstractly in the case of science, concretely in the case of religion as "The Truth"—is an intrinsic good. Devotion to it does have consequences for the biological and temporal being, but to seek it for the sake of these consequences is self-defeating. Pure science and pure faith believe that the secondary satisfactions come only by way of indirection. The secret of atomic structure is not found by those who want to win victory in war or cure diseases; the secret of the kingdom of God is not revealed to those who are anxious for their lives, for food and drink, for freedom from want and fear.

THE PEACETIME CHURCH AND WORLD COMMUNISM

In the present crisis of mankind, however, all emphasis seems to be placed on utilitarianism in both science and religion. How science is responding to the complex situation in which it finds itself is not our immediate concern here. In religion, to which we want to direct our attention, the growth of the utilitarian spirit is an alarming phenomenon. Utilitarianism seems to mark not only the attitude of the political powers that use religion for the sake of social control and transform it to suit their purposes, but also the attitude of many who oppose them. The utilitarianism of the Japanese war party in its employment of Shintoism is one thing; the pragmatism of the American military government in dealing with that Shintoism is another thing; but they are both utilitarian and pragmatic. The instrumentalism in matters of religion which characterizes Communism and National Socialism differs from the instrumentalism of the resistance movements and democracy; but in both instances we are dealing with a utilitarian use of religion in the service of non-religious ends. The utilitarianism of an individualistic period, which promised men that through faith they might gain the economic virtues and wealth, differs from the pragmatism of our social climate of opinion, in which religion is used as a means for gaining social order and prosperity; but they are both utilitarian and equally remote from the love of God for his own sake and of the individual or social neighbor in his relation to God. The use of religion for the sake of healing mental illness differs from its use in the effort to heal physical diseases; but in either case religion, the worship of God, is a means to an end.

Recently the social form of this utilitarianism has been given high sanction in an official statement made by the Federal Council of the Churches of Christ in America. Addressing the Christians in America on the subject of *The Churches and World Order*, the Council not only recommended many helpful steps which might be taken in the direction of the much desired goal of peace and order, but put its recommendations within a theological setting that is almost completely utilitarian. Doubtless there are overtones and undertones of another spirit but the major idea is a thorough social pragmatism. "Our first task," the report declares, "is to demonstrate that our Christian faith can enable all men to enjoy a fullness of life which not only equals but surpasses that which any other faith can accomplish." "Fullness of life" may mean many things; but what is meant here appears from the fact that it is something which other faiths also offer in an inferior or equal manner and that it is elsewhere declared that "our dedication ... is to the progressive realization of the dignity and worth of man in every area of life—political, economic, social and religious." It is the sort of fullness of life that will amount to "a demonstration of the practical application of our faith" and which will therefore bring into being a world "responsive to that faith." The general idea is very clear: men in our time desire some things very much—escape from suffering war and other disaster, freedom and a sense of their dignity, abundance and peace. These values they may have if they will turn to the Christian faith, if they will repent and lay hold of the sources of spiritual power that Christianity offers. The church will also benefit for the demonstration that Christianity can provide these goods will cause men to turn to it.

Similar ideas are being voiced in numerous church statements and in the writings of Christian theologians. Christianity offers an alternative to communism, it is said, as a way of organizing the economic life. Christianity, another maintains, gives us the key to the problem of justice in our time, enabling us to know what is due to every man and how to give it to him. Christianity, it is argued, shows us how we may have not only a durable but also a just peace. Christianity has the answer to all the human problems that arise in man's quest after health, peace, prosperity, justice, joy.

THE PEACETIME CHURCH AND WORLD COMMUNISM

Why there should be such a development of theological utilitarianism at any time and especially in our time we can readily understand. There is a reason in the faith itself. Its paradox of the losing and finding of life, of the addition of all other things if the kingdom of God is sought, has always tempted men to lose life for the sake of finding and to seek the divine rule for the sake of food and clothing. This temptation becomes especially acute when long cherished values are imperiled. Men beset by anxieties are likely to seek mental peace through worship since they discovered in earlier experience that it was a by-product of a devotion that had no ulterior purpose but was directed to the eternal glory. In the decline of a culture the revival of the religion which gave life to that culture is sought for the sake of staving off death, though the civilization has been a by-product of religious concern. When individual liberties are threatened men tend to cultivate the sense of duty to the transcendent for the sake of which they originally fought for those liberties. One can also easily understand why religious utilitarianism in our time should be dominantly social, since our greatest concern is for the preservation and ordering of a social life that is threatened with anarchy and since our greatest sufferings arise out of our social disorder. There is another reason for the rise of this social, religious utilitarianism—the apologetic one. Christian faith is so much faith and so little sight that its adherents are always seeking for some demonstration which will prove to themselves and others that it is true, though the demonstration is bound to be somewhat beside the point—like most miracles—proving not truth but utility, and exhibiting a power which may be that of God, but may also be that of faith itself, or of spiritual forces somewhat less than divine.

Though one can understand the reason for the rise of this Christian pragmatism it remains a dubious thing, giving birth to all sorts of skeptical questions. Will the church be able to live up to such promises? Is there any warrant in its history or in the nature of its faith for the assurance that it can if men will follow its teaching, guarantee them peace, the end of suffering, escape from disaster, the realization of human dignity and worth in politics and economics as well as in religion?

There is little basis in history for the promise that this religion sincerely followed will bring fullness of life to its adherents in the sense that theological utilitarianism intends. The Jewish people, more faithful than any similar group in the keeping of the moral laws they share with the Christians, more assiduous in the practice of repentance, more diligent in forgiveness, have indeed survived to this day and so demonstrated in a fashion the social relevance of their faith; but it would be difficult to describe the sort of existence the Jewish race has enjoyed as "fullness of life." The Christian church cannot maintain on the basis of its own record that it has made a notable contribution to the peace of the world. It has rarely if ever been at peace within itself and the wars of the nations it has most deeply influenced have equalled and surpassed in frequency and in destruction those waged by societies dominated by other faiths. It is easy to say that Christians have fought so much not because they were Christians but because they were not good Christians, but this is a dubious argument since there is no indication that men can now be more sincere in their practice of Christianity than in the past, and since Christianity makes men deeply concerned about values for the sake of which they sacrifice peace. Historically there is no ground for the assertion that faithful adherence to Christian faith reduces suffering. It leads to the alleviation of the sufferings of others, but through the operation of sympathy and compassion, of asceticism and the sense of sin to the increase of suffering among Christians.

If there is not much ground in history for the assurances of theological utilitarianism, there seems to be less ground in the structure of the faith itself. If Second Isaiah, the book of Job, and the New Testament were dropped from the constitution of the church it might be possible to maintain that the Biblical doctrine is one of prosperity as the consequence of virtue, but how shall one rhyme the ideas about the suffering service of Israel and the story of the cross with the assurance that faith leads to fullness of life? It can't be done except by means of reference to another sort of experience than is contemplated in statements about "fullness of life"; it can't be done without reference to a resurrection. On the other hand the effort to translate Christian faith into a socially useful force entails the suppression and transformation of some vital elements in it, just as the effort to make it serviceable to individualistic success in the era of early capitalism entailed the deformation of the Reformation into the sort of thing that Tawney has described for us.

All this does not mean that Christian faith has no social applications or a relevance to the crisis of our days. It does not mean that these applications and this relevance must stem from its own imperatives and not from the wishes and desires we entertain apart from the faith. It does not mean that the effort to recommend Christianity as a panacea for all the ills from which man suffers and thinks himself to suffer is erroneous and disastrous; it does not mean that Christians are not bound to seek for ways and means of alleviating these ills. It does not mean that repentance does not bear social fruits; it does mean that repentance practiced for the sake of such fruits is a bad kind of magic.

To take the last point first: Christian faith calls for a complete change of mind not because repentance is socially effective, or individually effective for that matter, but because the mind is out of harmony with reality. Repentance is called for not because we shall suffer or because civilization will perish if we do not repent, but because others are now perishing for us and because we are attacking the very son of God or God himself in our endeavor to escape suffering and to maintain our civilization at any cost. Repentance is called for not because we have chosen false means to the achievement of our ends but because our ends themselves are idolatrous. A repentance which leaves ends uncriticized and which is motivated by the desire to escape judgment in history or beyond history is a far cry away from that change of mind which the gospels present. But such radical repentance, though it is not designed to be socially relevant, may have social consequences. It may lead to that sort of disinterestedness which is able to deal with the questions of politics and economics objectively and helpfully just because it does not take them too seriously, just because it has gained a certain distance from them. It may lead to that situation in which men are able to think the new thoughts which the crisis of the times requires and which they cannot think so long as they remain bound by the passion of this-worldliness.

A Christianity that is not socially utilitarian still has social relevance because its imperatives direct it to work in society. It is imperative for such a Christian faith to remember and to realize the dignity of every man as an eternal being, in his political and economic relations as well as everywhere else, though that realization may involve the sacrifice of dignity on the part of Christians and the Christian community. Imperative Christianity does not ask whether the love of neighbor will bring forth a society in which all men will love their neighbors; it acts in hope, to be sure, but love and justice are its immediate commands and not its far-off goals. It does not condemn the abuse of atomic power because we have thereby imperiled our future but because we violated our own principles. It does not believe that social virtue will be rewarded by length of life but that "no evil can befall a good man"—or a good nation—"in life or in death."

Such a non-utilitarian faith does not undertake to show that in the Christian gospel we can find the solution to all the problems of human existence any more than we can find in the Scriptures answers to all the questions we raise about the world of nature. It does direct its followers to seek by means of all the intelligence they can muster to find out what to do to alleviate distress, to heal physical and mental disease, to order the vocations and to distribute justly the goods men produce. In consequence the social measures of such faith have nothing peculiarly Christian about them. The Christian setting in which they are conceived and practiced does not become tangibly or visually evident. There is nothing here to which one can point and say, "This is the demonstration of what Christianity can do for man." For every such measure will be only a demonstration of what disinterestedness can do, and Christians will participate with men of many other faiths in carrying them out.

In a world where the power struggle has taken precedence over every other concern, where every group is interested not only in doing good but in seeing to it that it gets credit for doing good and where good is being done for the sake of power, the church as church must surely feel called upon to go about its work with quietness and confidence, abjuring utilitarianism and the defensiveness that goes with it.

The Idea of the Covenant and American Democracy

Originally read before the American Studies section of the American Historical Association meeting in Chicago in 1953, this article was to become Niebuhr's first and only publication in Church History. *More importantly, it demonstrates his ongoing interest in identifying the theological foundations of the democratic government the nation's founders had established following the Revolutionary War. One of these, in his estimation, was the biblical notion of covenant. During the colonial era, it had helped create a society in which people sought to bind themselves together and "under God" to assume responsibility for each other and the common good. In the context of the Cold War, he was both affirming Perry Miller's earlier efforts to rehabilitate Puritan history and seeking to repudiate the tendency of contemporary Americans to fuse their religion and their patriotism, thus placing their faith in the fate of their nation rather than God.*

Source: *Church History* 23 (June 1954): 126–35.

Every effort to deal with the history of ideas is beset by hazards. Semantic traps are strewn along the way of the inquirer; such words as democracy, liberty, justice, etc., point to different concepts of varying complexes of concepts as they are used in different periods of history and by different men. The unuttered and frequently unacknowledged presuppositions of those who employ them also vary; and since meaning largely depends on context the difficulties of understanding what is meant are increased by the difficulty of ascertaining what is at the back of the minds. Our hazards are multiplied when the ideas in question are of a moral and religious sort. Then the problems of the relationship of speculative to practical reason, in Kantian terms; or, to speak with Coleridge, of the understanding and the reason, or, in the sharper but less accurate terminology of our day, of reason and emotion, present themselves. That the principles present in action and endurance are closely connected with the principles employed in understanding may be granted; but how they are connected, what the logical and psychological connections are, remains largely a puzzle. Beyond this there is the difficulty that the observer of moral and religious attitudes or decisions in the past is the man who has moral and religious attitudes of his own; he cannot reenact the past without some practical or emotional participation in its movements. Complete disinterestedness in this realm means inability to understand; but interestedness often means partisanship. We are distressed equally by the blindness of historians who deal with the seventeenth and eighteenth centuries, for instance, as if the persons they were interpreting did not believe in God, and by the partisanship of those who want to credit their party or group of believers with the major share of merit for the construction of what they regard as praiseworthy, or to exculpate them for the disapproved. With these difficulties in mind it seems foolhardy to attempt to answer such questions as those before us: To what extent did religious and specifically Christian convictions influence the development of American democracy; and, to what extent can that democracy be maintained here, or be reproduced elsewhere, without the aid of such convictions? At all events greater familiarity with historical detail and greater dogmatic certitude about the nature of Christianity or, on the other hand, greater disinterestedness combined with empathy than the present writer can muster would be necessary for the development of positive answers to these questions. Under these circumstances all that I am able to do is to suggest two hypotheses that seem, so far as my understanding goes, to fit the facts of our moral and intellectual history in democracy. Their verification or rejection, their refinement and adaptation will require wider and profounder knowledge of the history of the human mind in America than I can bring to bear.

I

The first of these two hypotheses is general; it does not apply to America only but to men, to Western men at least, in their various cultures. It reads: There is at all times a close correspondence and a dialectical relationship among the general ideas men hold about their own constitution, that of the societies and of the world in which they live; their efforts at self-control (ethics), at social construction (politics), and their attitudes toward their ultimate environment (religion) are in consequence influenced by similar ideas.

The close correspondence among ideas men hold about themselves, their societies and the world or—to use short hand, among their microcosmic, mesocosmic and macrocosmic views, or again, their psychology, sociology and metaphysics—has often been observed. But it is often affirmed also that such correspondence marks the views of ancient and medieval, not of modern men; and further, the relationship among these views is often explained as deductive or projective rather than as partaking of the nature of a dialogue. Theodore Spencer has called attention to the manner in which Shakespeare, as in medieval times, "all three domains form a single unity and are interdependent" so that "the best way to grasp any one of them is to compare it with one or both of the others." He can quote St. Thomas to good effect: "therefore let the king recognize that such is the office which he undertakes, namely that he is to be in the kingdom what the soul is in the body, and what God is in the world." For Plato the Republic was man writ large and man in his constitution was a *polis* in miniature, with reason presiding as ruler over the inferior powers of the soul. Beyond that the world as a whole with its demiurge and its form of the Good and its unorganized matter subject to the creative work and rule of the former had at least a faint resemblance to city and citizen. Democritean-Epicurean psychology, sociology and cosmology are similarly interrelated as are ethics, politics, and religion associated with them. Chance and reason are intertwined at every level of reality; and wisdom in the conduct of life will therefore be governed by this reflection, cultivating a cool detachment and a love of gentle pleasures, expecting little, unconfused by chance. The medieval pattern is like the Platonic in many respects but the hierarchical arrangement is much more emphasized. The cosmos is hierarchical: in it the whole chain of being is realized in scales of being and of value; in it the first cause operates through secondary causes; "the king and Lord of the heavens," says Thomas, "ordained from eternity this law: that the gifts of his providence should reach the lowest things by way of those that lie between." The human society with its kings, princes, feudal lords, freemen and serfs, with its popes, archbishops, bishops, priests and laity is thought to be created, and certainly the attempt is made to recreate it, along similar hierarchical lines. And man himself, in his individuality, with his soul, reason, will, habits and passions is organized in hierarchical fashion also. In the seventeenth and succeeding centuries the mechanical model in part takes the place of the hierarchical. The huge cosmos is a great machine, a grand design, similar in its execution to a gigantic clock. Man also is thought of increasingly as a kind of machine, whether materialistically or spiritualistically. He is being moved by an interior force toward pre-ordained ends, be these pleasure or self-gratification, or reproduction, or the glory of God. At the same time the effort is made to conceive society on a quasi-mechanical model, as governed by inherent iron laws. In economics this model plays a particularly significant role, but its influence can also be traced in other areas of social philosophy. In our contemporary world there seems to be real similarity among: the conception of the ultimate environment as a field of forces; the idea of political society as a grouping of powers in tension, in conflict, in polar oppositions, in alliance, in balance; and, again, the picture we have of the person as a being in whom unconscious drives, aggressions and fears, moving powers of one kind and another, are held together in more or less stable unity. There seems to be nothing peculiarly ancient, or medieval or modern about this tendency to associate the symbols and images we use for the understanding of the three spheres. To a large extent men may be unconscious of the presence in their minds of such general patterns. Only analysis that penetrates below the surface expressions reveals their presence.

There does not seem to be anything like a one to one correspondence among these images and concepts of the macrocosm, the mesocosm and the microcosm. But there is similarity. And in view of the interpenetration and interaction of the three domains it is evident that there must be some sort of similarity or accommodation if man is to reason at all about himself in his world and adjust his action to the actions upon him of society and the further environment. It has seemed to some that the reasoning which establishes this similarity or analogy among psychological, sociological and metaphysical views is a one way process, deductive or projective in character. Thus the medievalist may argue that beginning with a view of the nature of things in the gross we can descend from these ultimate principles to the more immediate realities; because the world is thus and so therefore we, as parts of the world must be thus and so in our societies and in our individual constitutions. But it is not only the medievalist who moves down from the great to the little. In modern times also we have argued down from Hegel to Darwin, from the idea of evolution through conflict as a metaphysical pattern to its use in the social realm. Again it has been thought that the movement is projective. Because we know ourselves as physical organisms we project the idea on society, thinking of it as a great body and then use the analogy further as an image of the world, the great organism. Or, when social experience is made primary, it is suggested that we project the image of our society on to the cosmos; proceeding from our idea of a human kingdom to that of a divine kingdom, or from our family patterns to a cosmic patriarchate. What is ignored in such attempts to trace the march of the human mind as though it followed a straight line is the infinitely complex pattern of our internal dialogue as it proceeds from one thing to another in a back and forth movement; using familiar patterns as hypotheses in understanding the unfamiliar; refining and changing the symbols or analogies as it discovers that they do not fit completely the new set of experiences; coming back to the original phenomena with a changed pattern and then making new discoveries there. It has been remarked that when the idea of kingship, for instance, is applied to God something is asserted not only about God but about the king and the idea of human kingship is changed by the metaphysical use of the symbol. Similarly when the idea of the machine is applied to the starry heavens something is not only asserted about the natural cosmos but new potentialities of the familiar machine are suggested; not only imagination and discovery but invention are stimulated. The use of psychology, sociology and metaphysics, in ethics, politics and religion, is inescapable. Without symbols no thought. Yet these symbols never have a simple origin; they are changed and recast as we proceed from one sphere to another and back again. Perhaps it is a consequence of this process that there is similarity among the symbols used in the various spheres of understanding and of action but never a one to one correspondence.

II

The second hypothesis I shall venture is a special application of the first one. Baldly stated it is this: One of the great common patterns that guided men in the period when American democracy was formed, that was present both in their understanding and in their action, and was used in psychology, sociology and metaphysics as in ethics, politics and religion, was the pattern of the covenant or of federal society.

It is not meant that this was the exclusive pattern in the minds of all men or exclusively present in the minds of any man. None of our symbols, save in fanaticism, is likely to be exclusively employed and there are few periods, if any, in human history when a dominant pattern of interpretation does not have its rivals. What is suggested is that a *fundamental* pattern in American minds in the seventeenth, eighteenth and early nineteenth centuries was the covenant idea, competing with the mechanical pattern and displacing the organic and hierarchical ideas.

The significance of the covenant idea for Puritan thought in the seventeenth and early eighteenth centuries has been called to our attention after a long period of neglect, by Professor Perry Miller in his *Orthodoxy in Massachusetts, the New England Mind* and *From Colony to Province*. As the religious thought of the seventeenth and eighteenth centuries is being more adequately explored other studies are beginning to contribute to our knowledge of this idea. At the same time new studies in the ideas of the Scriptures, such as [Johannes] Pedersen's *Israel* and [Walther] Eichrodt's *Theology of the Old Testament*, illuminate this aspect of that view of human life in its world which is native to the book that was more widely and thoroughly read than any other by the small and great founders of America. It is often pointed out and as frequently forgotten by those who seek to understand the minds of Englishmen and Americans in the seventeenth, eighteenth and nineteenth centuries, that in Trevelyan's words, "The effect of the continual domestic study of the book (i.e. the Bible) upon the national character, imagination and intelligence for three centuries—was greater than that of any literary movement in our annals, or any religious movement since St. Augustine." The idea of covenant had many proximate sources as it was developed in the Netherlands, in England, and in America during the seventeenth century. It had roots in Calvin; it was suggested and influenced, no doubt, by the development of contract law and of commercial companies; it was raised to special significance in religious circles by the reaction against a mechanical version of Calvinistic determinism. But its chief source in the Scriptures was available to all men and not only available but pervasively present.

If the dialectical theory of the development of the great patterns is true then the covenant idea may be thought of as something which, originating in the experience of social compacts by early Israelites, was extended to the understanding of the cosmos and, as reunderstood in its application to divine-human and divine-natural relations, was then reapplied to social life and to personal existence in society and the cosmos. In the seventeenth century there seems to be a kind of reenactment of this earlier history, though in dependence on it, with variations due to the new experiences of the time.

We may begin to define the covenant idea by noting its application to the ultimate environment, in the effort to understand the cosmic scene of human life in history. This ultimate environment, it is affirmed, is one, integrated, unified. We live neither in a world of dualistic principles at war with each other nor in a pluralistic environment of many gods or other forces. If there is chance in this world, even chance is under control, subject therefore to a kind of prediction. This unity is not to be conceived after the pattern of a logical system of thought, not as similar to a mathematical system, nor after the idea of a machine, though logical, mathematical and mechanical relations are present in it. Its unity is much more like that of human society than like that of human mind or human technique. Hence such phrases as kingdom of God, *Civitas Dei*, Divine Commonwealth are to be employed in referring to it; and when speaking of natural phenomena, the behavior of stars and gases, the political symbol of law is preferred to the symbols of automatic action.

The ultimate world, however, is not like a family, though the phrases Father and Son and children can be significantly employed with reference to certain features in it. Nor is it a company, nor a democracy in which there is a certain equality among the members. The will of the members of this society is never sovereign. They neither elect themselves into being, nor can they choose under what ultimate laws they shall live. They are the objects of action before they are its subjects. There is a thus-and-so-ness about their existence, about the conditions under which they live and die, with their bodies, given constitutions and the inescapable demands made upon them so that if the social image is to be employed at all it must be the image of an absolute kinship.

But the image of absolute despotism does not fit. There is a tie between monarch and subjects and a relationship among the subjects not compatible with the idea of absolute monarchy. The world is a peculiar kind of society in which all parts are bound to each other by *promises*. Promise or covenant is the ordering principle. There is nothing arbitrary about the king, for he is above all faithful and has bound himself to govern in accordance with purposes and the laws that he has promulgated. Though there seems to be something arbitrary about his original promulgation of the laws, there is nothing arbitrary in his administration. He does not change them because he has favorites; he is not subject to whims and caprices; his unity is like the unity of the loyal man who though he has sworn even to his own hurt does not change. Furthermore, the laws by which the king has promised to govern, in the freedom of his sovereign decision, are not unknown. Some are indeed beyond present understanding, but the processes of nature, the reason of man and the revelation of the divine will make the content of much of the fundamental law of the universe known to man. The administration of the world is reliable; the laws can be known by means of patient inquiry; their execution can be counted upon. The fundamental characteristic of the powerful One is that he is faithful, keeping his promise.

Again, this ultimate society in which men live is one in which as subjects they are invited and ultimately required to achieve the maturity of full citizenship, to accept the laws as their own, to enter into a kind of reciprocal relationship with the king and each other, engaging by promise to maintain and support a commonwealth they did not create but in whose administration they are privileged to participate. The significance of all the special covenants into which God enters with man under the fundamental covenant is this, that by their means a free and responsible citizenry is to be brought forth out of what, as a result of the great perversion, had become a mass of slaves, partly supine in the acceptance of fate, partly in insurrection against the rule they can not escape. But it is the design of the ultimate ruler and the ultimate commonwealth that the government should be not only by consent of the governed but with their participation in it.

The idea of the macrocosm as a covenant society had been derived in part from the experience of human societies of a more than "natural" sort in which men entered into relationship with each other not on the basis of feeling or of blood-kinship only but of mutual compact and promise. The covenant idea, so developed, was applied in turn to all human societies. Even when their basis was in nature, as in the case of the relationship of the sexes, they now were seen to become truly human societies only when promise or covenant was added to and transformed the natural. The question was not whether society has a natural or a contract origin but to what extent every society becomes truly human and truly a society within the cosmic society by having the moral dimension, or the covenant character, added to it. Religious society so regarded could no longer be merely a community of those who had similar interests in the supernatural or a society of those who held the same religious beliefs, though it was that. It did not become complete society until interest was disciplined by promise, obedience to external laws internalized by the oath of fealty, duties to God associated with freely accepted, promised duties to one another and, in general, belief supplemented and transformed by the will to be loyal. The covenant theory of relationships did not necessarily mean that the religious society should be made up of *individuals* without previous common relationships. But it meant that even a natural religious society did not become true church until it became a covenanted church based on promises. One must not read into the seventeenth century, for instance, the individualism that characterized the later revival periods and then regard the half-way covenant as a great distortion of original doctrine. It was probably quite in line with the original idea of covenant.

Covenant meant that political society was neither purely natural nor merely contractual, based upon common interest. Covenant was the binding together in one body politic of persons who assumed through unlimited promise responsibility to and for each other and for the common laws, under God. It was government of the people, for the people and by the people but always under God, and it was not natural birth into natural society that made one a complete member of the people but always the moral act of taking upon oneself, through promise, the responsibilities of a citizenship that bound itself in the very act of exercising its freedom. For in the covenant conception the essence of freedom does not lie in the liberty of choice among goods, but in the ability to commit oneself for the future to a cause and in the terrible liberty of being able to become a breaker of the promise, a traitor to the cause. (I use these terms in dependence on Josiah Royce who alone among American modern philosophers has seen and explored in his philosophy of loyalty the meaning of this kind of liberty and this dimension of common life.)

The view of man associated with these ideas about the world and about society was one that set his will, in the sense of his ability to commit himself by means of promise, at the center of his being. To be sure man was a rational being; he was a being with many interests; he was a happiness-seeker; but above all his distinguishing characteristic was moral. As moral man he was a being who could be trusted or ought to be trustworthy because he had given his word, pledged himself to be faithful to the cause and the fellow-servants of the cause. All the perversion which has entered into man's relationships to God and to his fellow-men through his distrust of divine faithfulness and his breaking of his own promises cannot change the fundamental fact that the moral requirement and ability of promise-keeping is central to human existence.

The conception of the covenant in the macrocosm, the mesocosm and the microcosm has been confused in the beginning and throughout subsequent history with other patterns. It was mixed in Calvin and in the Westminster Puritans and, I believe, in Jonathan Edwards with the idea of the machine. Thus ideas of *pre*determination (not ideas of election) were connected with the thought of design and of mechanical construction rather than of covenant. In Deism the mechanical image prevailed so far as the macrocosm was concerned and tended to be carried over into the political realm. From this point of view civil society was largely a self-regulating mechanism that required very little government, very little assertion of human moral freedom, since liberty to pursue one's interests was the motive spring that had been supplied while inherent laws such as those of sympathy regulated the moving parts so that harmony resulted.

On the other hand the covenant idea was confused with the idea of contract from which it had been in part derived. But contract meant something rather different from covenant. In religion it meant that God was a being who had contracted to do certain things for men in case they performed certain reciprocal duties toward him, not that he had obligated himself to maintain his realm and its laws and to liberate its citizens no matter what the cost to them or him might be. Marriage also could be regarded as a contract, entered into for the sake of gaining certain common advantages, not a covenant of unlimited commitment. Civil or political society too could be interpreted as based on limited contract into which men entered with parts of themselves, as it were, for limited purposes and which they might reject if they did not gain from it the benefits they had been promised in the contract. Contract always implies limited, covenant unlimited commitment; contract is entered into for the sake of mutual advantages; covenant implies the presence of a cause to which all advantages may need to be sacrificed. The tendency of the covenant idea to degenerate into the limited contract idea is evident in all the later religious and social history.

To what extent the covenant idea forms the chief unconscious background of American democracy as we know it, I will not venture to assess. Our democracy contains various and disparate elements in it from beginning to end. The mechanistic idea of the world and of human life with *laissez faire* as the consequent policy and freedom to pursue one's own happiness as the motive force;

the contract idea of limited obligations and of mutual aid organization—these have always been with us. But one may raise the question whether our common life could have been established, could have been maintained and whether it can endure without the presence of the conviction that we live in a world that has the moral structure of a covenant and without the presence in it of men who have achieved responsible citizenship by exercising the kind of religious freedom that appears in their taking upon themselves the obligations of unlimited loyalty, under God, to the principles of truth-telling, of justice, of loyalty to one another, of indissoluble union. Can freedom of religion be maintained on a contract basis, i.e., on the basis of tolerating one another? Or does it presuppose the presence in men of a sense of responsibility to a cause that goes beyond all limited causes and their acceptance of explicit loyalty to a community of faithfulness that is eternal and inclusive? Is freedom of speech a right that could have been maintained in society where there was no prior implicit and unlimited promise among members that they would be loyal to truth as they saw it and not bear false witness against their neighbor?

Perhaps the problem of democracy is never soluble in historical terms but only in terms of contemporary action. All the forces that have contended in our common life from the beginning are with us today and some new ones have been added. In our situation some men are making their decisions in democracy on the basis of the conception that the world at large is a field of forces, that man himself is a similar complex of powers and that social life is something that must be engineered as a system of pressures and counter-pressures. Others may be making their decisions with the conviction that a great machine is operative and seek their small freedoms within a large determinism. But the conviction that the world is fundamentally a moral society, that those who are bond [*sic*] to each other by nature and interest must bind themselves to each other by unlimited promises to be loyal to one another in common loyalty to universal principles is a conviction that is also present. Whatever the influences of Christianity on the development of American democracy have been in the past, there is no small number of men in this society today who participate in its actions, exercise their pressures, use their freedom, as those who believe that the world has this fundamental moral structure of a covenant society and that what is possible and required in the political realm is the affirmation and reaffirmation of man's responsibility as a promise-maker, promise-keeper, a covenanter in universal community. I know no way by which their influence can be measured. But they and their principles are and have been an element in our democracy. It is safe to say that without Christianity, so broadly defined, our democracy would be something quite different from what it is.

The Protestant Movement and Democracy in the United States

Subtitled "Protestantism in Relation to Democracy," the second half of this article has been selected primarily because it provides a cogent summary of Niebuhr's efforts, begun already in The Social Sources of Denominationalism, *to examine dynamic features of the paradox of church and world against the backdrop of America's form of government. To him, the freedom that democracy granted to all forms of religion was Protestantism's opponent, strengthening its tendencies to become "of the world" by way of denominational schisms and divisions, and enhancing the accommodations made by its churches to the prevailing culture and the wishes of its people. At the same time, he believed that democracy was Protestantism's ally in that it made it just as possible for churches to unite by means of mergers and reunions of disparate members of denominational families, through the creation of federations and councils of churches, or whenever voluntary associations were formed in order to address a particular social issue. In its relationship to the world, the church in a democracy could in fact remain just as "independent" as it might be tempted to become culturally "dependent." This article is also noteworthy because it was published as the postwar ascendancy of religion in America was reaching its climax. It not only reflects Niebuhr's immediate concern about the tendency of Christians amid the Cold War in the 1950s to make the American way of life the object of their faith; it furnishes a solid synopsis of his efforts to interpret the intent of democratic ideals and institutions in light of their monotheistic faith in God.*

Source: *The Shaping of American Religion (Religion in American Life* vol. 1), ed. James Ward Smith and Leland Jamison (Princeton: Princeton University Press, 1961), 47–71.

Protestantism has not proceeded on its way in isolation but only in constant interaction with other movements. Its order has been the product not only of decisions made within it, but also of pressures exercised upon it. The Reformation was accompanied by the revival of learning, the Counter-Reformation, the growth of capitalism and of nationalism; the Awakening by Enlightenment and Romanticism; the revivals by political, scientific, and industrial revolutions. Orders of belief, discipline, and worship in Lutheran, Anglican, and Reformed churches were in part imposed upon them by political powers more concerned with problems of political unity and independence than with the forgiveness of sins and righteousness of life. The churches arising out of later revivals were usually less subject to political, but more amenable to social, pressures.

In America the primary companion with which Protestantism has had to deal as friend and rival and foe has been democracy. Democracy has not been the only associate of Protestantism on its march. The great migrations from Old World to New and, within America, from east to west, from country to city, have left marks of their influence on the map of the Protestant journey. The industrial revolution, going on with accelerating tempo decade after decade, and the scientific revolution, with its critical moments for the church in the Darwinian, Freudian, and sub-atomic discoveries—these, too, have profoundly affected the Protestant course. Sometimes they have brought confusion, sometimes have led to ventures down by-ways, often have brought great defections from the ranks of Protestant churches. All these cultural movements have been interwoven, so that Protestantism as church has confronted them all as "the world." With the possible exception of science, however, it has been democracy which, among them all, has been Protestantism's most important ally and opponent. It has offered to this religion its greatest opportunities and its greatest temptations to forfeit its own soul.

Theology must leave to the historians and critics of political institutions and democratic thought the task of assessing the influence of Protestantism on democracy. It may discern certain parallels, for instance, between the line of democratic revolutions and the line of Protestant protests; between Protestant revivals and democratic liberations; between Protestant reliance on Scriptures under the government of God and democratic dependence on written constitutions under the reign of natural law; between Christian rejection of the significance of human differences in men's relation to Christ and their Creator, and the democratic doctrine of equality; between democratic suspicion of power and Protestant belief in the prevalence of original sin; between evangelical wrestling for freedom from sin and death, and democratic striving for liberty from external compulsions. It will often seem to the theological point of view that democracy is Protestantism in its secular form, that is, in the form relevant to the concerns of the present age. It becomes secularized only when this age is isolated from the age to come; when time is lived through as though unsurrounded by eternity. But when we are aware of the multiple casualties that operate in history, we content ourselves with notice of the parallels without ascribing democratic effects to religious causes. Moreover, one has reason to suspect that when Protestant theology undertakes to show how much Christianity in general and Protestantism in particular have contributed to democracy, it has already exchanged Protestant for democratic faith, has found the justification of religion in its promotion of a human temporal cause, and has confused the power of religion with the power of God. So it seems that the only question a Protestant theological critic can properly undertake to answer is the one about the effect of democracy on that Protestantism whose nature he has tried to understand from within.

By democracy we shall mean here not, in the first place, a series of doctrines or fundamental beliefs about human equality and freedom, but rather those institutions of government, those settled social habits and modes of thought that tend to prevent the absolute control of individual citizens or of groups in the American nation by any individual or communal power. In this sense democracy is not so much what the word literally means, government by the people, as, negatively, the prevention of absolute or decisive control of any part of the people by any other part. Respect for minority rights is as essential an element in its practice as consent by the minority to government by majority. Among the legal measures that tend to secure the negative purpose of democracy are the separation of the powers of government and of church and state, the restriction of governmental powers by constitution and Bill of Rights, the mutual restrictions of local, state, and federal powers, and frequent, secret elections. By democracy we mean, therefore, the ordered practice of protecting the people's liberties, the people being considered not as a unanimous whole exercising a general will, but as a community of individual selves and a community of communities. On its positive side this democracy provides for the expression of the desires and demands of individuals and groups, as well as for their cooperative action in the pursuit of common ends. It does this not only by means of legal measures and governmental arrangements that secure the right to petition and provide for representation, but by habits of association established and recognized in the mores of democratic society.

This democracy cannot easily be described by a simple phrase. It is not government of the people and by the people, since the people are not a single whole; it is not merely government by consent of the governed, since the system provides for much more active expression of will and desire than consent; neither does democracy seem to be merely a constant struggle for power among competing groups, since it provides rules under which that struggle is carried on and has cooperation no less than conflict in view. Such democracy, as known in America, cannot be defined, either, by reference to certain doctrines. Doubtless its practice presupposes certain great premises, but what they are or how they are to be formulated is often subject to dispute. The context and background of democratic practice may be stated now more in Lockean, now more in Rousseauistic, now more in Calvinistic terms, or even in semi-Hobbesian or Machiavellian fashion.

Historically, this democracy has come to expression in a series of violent and non-violent revolutions in which power that threatened the people's liberties has been checked or overthrown. The movement of democracy can scarcely be called progressive, since ever-new forces arise within and outside the nation to exert disproportionate power over the people or some of their communities. In meeting such challenges democracy, like Protestantism in this respect, develops an ordering of common life that seems largely to have pragmatic character and that shows signs of having issued out of emergencies.

A. The Increase of Protestant Disorder and Dependence

The answer to the question how democracy has affected Protestantism in the United States seems obvious. It has given the Protestant churches as well as Catholicism and every form of religion or irreligion almost complete freedom; furthermore it has allowed freedom in religious matters to every individual. The consequence seems to have been increased disorder in Protestant Christianity. Democracy, however, has also thrown Protestantism, along with every other form of faith, on its own resources, unsupported by any government. Under these circumstances Protestantism, much divided, without a long tradition, loosely related to its Old World organizations, has become a highly adaptive religion tending to forfeit its own character in adjusting itself to the wishes and felt needs of the people on whom it depends for support. It is said to have become a "Culture-Protestantism" in which all inner direction was lost as the price of conformity was paid for the sake of survival. Thus democratic freedom, it may be argued, has led Protestantism toward anarchic pluralism, and to dependence on the voice of the people rather than on the Word of God.

These fairly common observations about American Protestantism have a considerable measure of truth, and their elaboration will assist toward an understanding of the non-Catholic churches in their New World forms. But they do not constitute the whole truth and must be supplemented by the consideration of the unifying tendency in American Protestantism and of the growth under the conditions of freedom of an independent evangelical movement.

When the American religious scene is compared with that offered by other nations in Christendom, the obvious feature that strikes the eye is the multiplicity of churches in the United States. Elsewhere also, national Protestant folk- or state-church organizations are usually accompanied by dissenting groups but these, as a rule, are comparatively small and there are not many of them. Denominationalism—the system of many apparently competitive churches equally recognized by state and people—is a peculiarly American phenomenon. This denominationalism seems to be the consequence for Protestantism of that liberty in religion which American democracy has accepted and encouraged. Democratic freedom has not been the cause of multiplicity, for Catholicism has maintained its unity in the land of religious liberty, but it has supplied the conditions under which inherent tendencies toward fractionalization and division in Protestantism could have free sway.

In the first place, democracy has permitted every national form of Protestantism that had been developed in Europe to maintain itself in America. Of the more than two hundred Protestant denominations in the United States a considerable number represents the continuation in the New World of state or national churches. The Church of England, the Lutheran churches of Germany, Sweden, Norway, Denmark, Iceland; the Reformed churches of the Rhineland, the Netherlands and Scotland; the united church of Prussia—these have all survived in a nation that permitted immigrants to follow their own religious convictions and traditions. Furthermore, the dissenting churches of the Old World were placed in America on an equal footing with the successors of established churches, and under these circumstances often enjoyed a growth impossible to them under the restrictions of existence as tolerated but not approved religions. Congregationalism in the United States does not offer an unambiguous example, since it was once established in Massachusetts and Connecticut. Since its disestablishment, however, it has become a strong denomination, far outranking, when measured by usual standards, the dissenting Congregationalism of England. The Methodists, remaining relatively weak alongside the Anglican church in the country of their origin, have become the largest single Protestant organization in the United States, with a membership many times larger than that of the Protestant Episcopal Church. Baptist dissent in Europe, subject to much political and social repression, neither attracted large numbers nor achieved significantly strong organization; in America almost one third of all Protestants are Baptists, and though they are divided into many groups, their two largest associations are cohesive and influential. Alongside such dissenting denominations that in the New World have enjoyed great growth, more than a score of other European non-conformist groups have continued their existence in America. Among them one can count the Mennonites, the Society of Friends, the Moravians, Schwenkfelders, River Brethren and Plymouth Brethren, the churches of the New Jerusalem, the Associate Presbyterians, the Swedish Evangelical Mission Covenant church, and Dunkers. While migration to the United States is the antecedent cause of the presence of such groups, the promise of freedom in religion often motivated their migration, and under conditions of freedom they have flourished in a way impossible to them in situations where uniformity of religious belief was prized and enforced by social, if not political, pressures.

Democracy has not only permitted the continuance of all the old divisions of Protestantism; it has also allowed, if not encouraged, the growth of new groups. Large as the number of naturalized denominations is, it is exceeded by the number of the native-born. Most of them trace their origin to some extensive or localized revival in America such as the Second Great Awakening, out of which the Disciples of Christ and the Cumberland Presbyterian church issued, or the renewal of hope in millenarian form that produced the Adventist groups, or the Pentecostalist and Holiness movements whence came the Assemblies of God, the Church of the Nazarene, and similar groups. Their organization in separation from the older churches and their division from each other were due to many causes. Under the conditions of freedom those who felt themselves to be like-minded, to be moved by the same spirit, and who believed that the old organizations did not adequately represent what to them was all-important, tended to unite in associations for the promotion of common causes without contemplating the development of another denomination. But in time a new church developed and in the environment of freedom and religious multiplicity there was no internal or external pressure to prevent schism or enforce unity.

Geographical locality and regional culture has also contributed in the American situation toward the multiplication of native-born denominations. Groups of Protestants living in the same more or less restricted area, affected by some movement in religious conviction and emotion—including reaction against denominationalism—have tended to associate with each other and to develop common forms of thought and practice. Or Protestants previously members of one church have been divided from each other by social conflict, such as that of the Civil War, or by geographical and social distance, such as that between old and new settlements. Such groups may represent less the rapidity of the process of fission under democratic conditions than the slowness of the fusion process in a situation in which church unity is wholly dependent on motivations internal to Protestantism itself.

Again, many new forms of Protestant church life have been fashioned in democratic America by individuals. Elsewhere the individualism that seems always to be present in Protestantism has been checked by the force of the continuing Catholic tradition, by the presence of a dominant state or people's church with a widely recognized official clerical leadership. But in democracy, individuals endowed with strong personal convictions, or great personal force and attractiveness, or unusual ambition, or with all of these at once—true prophets and false ones—have enjoyed peculiar opportunities to gather bands of disciples, to set themselves up as reformers of old faith or as founders of new religions. In many instances the groups that have gathered around such leaders and eventually become denominations have been very much like the revival churches. In some the presence of economic motives suggests similarity to business enterprises; in still others a likeness to communal Utopian experiment appears.

Finally, some of the multiplicity of forms of faith and order in American Protestantism may be traced to the operation of free initiative in religious and moral enterprise. As special needs have attracted the attention of members of old churches, they have organized societies to provide religious, moral, and humanitarian services to parts of the population not under the pastoral care of existing institutions. As the Salvation Army—originating in England, to be sure—began with the effort to bring religious and moral help to neglected slums but became an organized religious body, so other groups that consider themselves to be primarily evangelistic or missionary or educational organizations have come to function as independent churches with their own membership, clergy, and common order.

The organizational pluralism that prevails in a Protestantism left free by democracy to develop in its own way seems to be matched by the pluralism of beliefs professed, hopes entertained, ways of salvation preached. Though the great mass of American Protestants continue to assert that the Scriptures are their authority, so many principles of Scriptural interpretation are used among them that diversity is the consequence. Literalism and liberalism; historical and confessionalistic interpretation; confessionalist explanation in Lutheran, Calvinist, and fundamentalist forms; mysticism and rationalism—all are represented. Officially these Protestant churches remain mostly Trinitarian in their doctrine of God, but deism and Unitarianism, immanentism and spiritualism, as well as exclusive concentration on the deity of Christ, are widely taught. Hopes of the vision of God, of His kingdom coming to earth, of brotherhood and peace, of heavenly bliss, of a millenarian reign by the returning Christ, of the progress of civilization, and of personal health and prosperity—all are promised as future gifts of God or as rewards of faithfulness in conduct and belief. Freedom in worship seems to lead to undisciplined inventiveness and formlessness. While the sermon remains the central feature in most Protestant meetings, the term "preaching" now includes not only the proclamation of the gospel and the interpretation of life in the light of Scriptural knowledge of God, man, and history, but lecturing on political, humanitarian, and literary themes, ritualistic rhapsodizing, and rote reception of holy phrases. Not only the sacraments of baptism and the Lord's Supper, but feet-washing, holy rolling and ecstatic dancing, speaking in tongues, and the handling of snakes may be found by the curious student of religious customs as he visits the meetings of groups in America that call themselves Protestant.

All such observations of the multiplicity of organizations, beliefs, and rites support the suspicion that tendencies toward schism and disorder are inherent in Protestantism, and that the conditions of freedom in democratic society have allowed them to come to full expression.

In the sixteenth century, Europe's Protestant churches, declaring their independence from Rome, became largely dependent on national states that both supported them and used them for political ends. In America, democratic political society either yielded to their desire for complete freedom or thrust independence upon them. The corollary of freedom, however, has been self-support, and the corollary of self-support seems to have been dependence, not now on government but on popular good-will. All Protestant groups, whether originally constituted as churches that include all citizens or as sects that gathered into an exclusive society only the manifestly converted, have had to become voluntary associations in the United States. Seeking to survive, thrown into competition for attention, membership, and economic support, not only with each other but with secular enterprises claiming the same resources, they appear to have adjusted themselves all too well to the wishes of the people.

Hence they have functioned among immigrant groups as conservers of the old national cultures, maintaining, for instance, the languages of motherlands and fatherlands long after their people had abandoned such usage in daily secular relations, even in their homes. Sometimes they have fostered old national loyalties long after their members had become American citizens. As churches serving prosperous classes they have presented in sermon and rite a spiritual religion only remotely relevant to the commercial, industrial enterprises in which their people for the most part were engaged—a kind of luxury faith that neither challenged the mores of secular life, nor deeply affected men's sense of their fundamental orientation in the world, but supplied them with special though mild ecstasies. Religion, like art, in this setting has been presented as something that belongs to "gracious living." Elsewhere Protestant churches have supplied to oppressed, unhappy classes, such as Negroes in garbage-strewn slums, imaginative visions of a Beulah-land to come, or enchanted them into seventh heaven by rhapsodic rites. They have sought the support of industrial workers by proclaiming a gospel that called for repentance on the part of owners and employers, pronounced blessing on the virtues of labor, and preached a crusade for a socialized economy. In rural areas they have led worshipers in adoration of virgin mother earth; in the cities they have sung the praises of man the builder, as though he were constructing the New Jerusalem. When Americans wanted above all else to remain isolated from the wars of the Old World, Protestantism was largely pacifist; when the nation was drawn into international conflict, "preachers presented arms." When people were made deeply conscious of their anxieties, churches offered them peace of mind; when they were lonely after old and new migrations, then community, fellowship, and friendship were presented as Christ's essential gifts mediated through his church.

Amidst all this adaptiveness there has been, however, a more basic adjustment of Protestantism to the spirit of American culture. In the United States, as elsewhere, the dominant religion is probably the social faith, for which society itself is the great cause to be served, and the source whence men hope to draw whatever significance they have. Democracy for this religious attitude is not a way of government; it is a way of life and a way of salvation. It is believed in, counted upon, trusted as a spirit immanent in the society, or as idea incarnated in it. The hope that accompanies this faith appears as the American dream, or as the fulfillment of Manifest Destiny, or simply as progress toward peace, prosperity, and plenty. American social religion has its sacred scriptures, its doctrines, symbols, and rites. To what extent it emerged out of Protestantism, out of other religious traditions and out of unconscious depths will long remain questionable, but in its progress and development it has been closely interwoven with Protestantism. And the latter, in many times and forms, has so adjusted itself to the American faith that it has been difficult to distinguish the one from the other. Not infrequently Protestants have defined Christian freedom in democratic terms, not as freedom from sin and death as that bondage to God which is perfect freedom, but as liberty to worship as one pleases or, better, as deliverance from political tyranny, from want, and from fear. The gospel of love that seeks out the lost and lowly, that concerns itself more for the one per cent who are sick, astray, or in prison than for the ninety-nine per cent healthily at home, is translated into the doctrine of equality. The Word of God, and the voice of the people; the hope of the kingdom of heaven, and the American dream; the forgiveness of sins, and toleration; the grace of our Lord Jesus Christ, and affable manners are confused and confounded. Such cultural Protestantism takes on many forms; fundamentalist and liberal, nationalist and internationalist types may be distinguished. But the variations are distinctly those of the social faith to which Protestantism has adjusted itself.

Thus it may well be argued that under the conditions of freedom the inherent weakness of Protestantism have become fully apparent. Protestantism in America seems to have moved from schism to schism, to have fallen prey to individualistic self-assertiveness, to have lost its character as independent church.

B. The Increase of Protestant Unity and Dynamic

While such tendencies in Protestantism in America are too evident to be denied, an interpretation that would take only them into consideration would not do justice to the ambivalent, complex phenomenon of evangelical religion in the United States. For, alongside the trend toward fractionalization, there has been in this Protestantism a countervailing movement toward unity; and alongside the tendency toward dependency on the people, there has been the constant effort to make the people fully aware of their dependence, not, indeed, on the church but on God.

The movement toward integration in American Protestantism is no less striking than the movement toward disunity. It has organizational, doctrinal, ethical, and ritual aspects, but is perhaps particularly a movement toward the attainment of a common temper, outlook, and purpose that do not need to be precisely formulated.

While democracy made it easy for successors of European national churches to continue their separate existence in the New World, it also provided conditions under which unforced union could take place between groups that, issuing from the same historic revival, had been sundered by political decisions and cultural differences. Lutherans, who in Germany were divided into many territorial churches, have come together in America. The Lutherans of Sweden, Norway, Denmark, Iceland, and Finland move slowly yet with accelerating speed toward combinations in which old political and cultural distinctions are forgotten, while the common religious heritage is maintained. Through denominational mergers and the organization of conferences, councils, and federations, Lutheranism has advanced for many a year and continues to advance toward a unity denied to it on its home continent. So also the Reformed churches of the Rhineland, the Netherlands, the Swiss cantons, and Scotland, through enacted or planned unions, close ranks that were broken by political rather than religious conflict.

A similar movement has long gone on and continues among the organizations that, though originating out of similar revivals or traditions, were separated from each other by geographical distance. The loosely knit Baptist churches, particularly subject to regional influences, have long been gathering themselves into ever larger and more inclusive associations. Churches of the North and the South, separated by political conflict but also by differences of development in different environments, and churches of the East and West, have united in the past and move more rapidly toward union as the nation itself becomes more homogeneous.

Reunions after revivals have been almost as frequent as separations during revivals and, indeed, the awakenings themselves have been integrating in their effect as well as divisive. They have rarely occurred in one denomination only, and they have brought together in new association members of previously estranged churches. They have been effective in overcoming geographic barriers that separated not only churches but regional societies. It has been noted that the Great Awakening contributed considerably to the development of a common mind in the isolated colonies of eighteenth-century America. But more significant for the church union movement was the rapprochement between Presbyterians and Congregationalists it brought about. The development of the Disciples of Christ and the

Christians, denominations that seek Christian unity, as a result of the Second Awakening, also illustrates, though somewhat ambiguously, the union movement that has been present in revivals.

The story of almost every one of the larger Protestant denominations in the United States can be read as a story of Protestant re-union quite as well as a story of division. The history of the Presbyterian church in the United States is not untypical. Beginning with the account of the founding of English, Scotch, and Scotch-Irish churches in Virginia,, Massachusetts, New York, Pennsylvania, and other colonies, it relates their organization into presbyteries and synods early in the eighteenth century, tells of the founding of new churches during the Awakening, of the subsequent rift between "old side" and "new side" groups, and of their reunion after a few years. Later chapters record: the acceptance of the Plan of Union with the Congregational churches, effective for many years; the appearance of a new strain on the family tie as Old School and New School Presbyterians take issue with each other during the Second Awakening; their reconciliation; the division between Northern and Southern Presbyterians by the war between the states; union with the Cumberland church, which had issued out of the Kentucky revival; union with the Welsh Calvinist Methodists; union with the United Presbyterian church, which was the American successor of a dissenting church in Scotland. The later story also includes accounts of participation in the founding and work of the Federal and National Council of Churches of Christ in the United States, the International Missionary Council, the Alliance of the Reformed Churches Throughout the World Holding the Presbyterian Order, and the World Council of Churches. The movement toward cooperation and organic union with the southern wing of American presbyterianism has been continuous and fruitful for several decades.

Another type of movement toward integration within denominational boundaries is illustrated by the histories of the American and Southern Baptist Conventions. Though they contain the accounts of many schisms, they report to an even greater extent the drawing together into ever more inclusive and active fellowships of independent local churches and of regional associations that had grown up in isolation from each other. Thus the stories of the denominations in America give evidence of the presence in Protestantism of a continuous movement toward unity that is no less characteristic than the tendency toward division.

That movement has its interdenominational as well as denominational forms. In the climate of democracy, free associations of Christians concerned with the prosecution of some limited ends have sprung up decade after decade. Members of Presbyterian, Congregational, Baptists, Methodists, and many other churches have united to form missionary, educational, charitable, and reform associations. The organization of colonization and anti-slavery societies of peace leagues, temperance unions, hospital associations, Sunday School unions, rescue missions, and a host of similar ventures is a unique and important element in American Protestantism. Some of these, such as the Young Men's and Young Women's Christian Associations, have become established institutions; some such as the American Board of Commissioners for Foreign Missions, have become arms of denominations; some have lost their relationship to churches and become secularized. Some of the associations have flourished during periods of crisis such as the Civil War; others have maintained themselves for decades. If order is to be found only where there is planning and central control, the multiplication of such groups will seem indicative of disorder; but if order and unity are also visible in the rise of spontaneous cooperation for the achievement of limited ends, then these associations are as representative of Protestant order and unity as the many orders and sodalities of Roman Catholicism are of the unity of the Roman church.

Another sort of integration in Protestantism has taken the form of federation. The federation may be that of whole denominations, of similar agencies of such denominations, or of local churches with varying denominational affiliations. The first type is represented by the National Council of Churches (which was preceded by the Federal Council), the National Association of Evangelicals, the National Lutheran council and the Pentecostal Fellowship; the second by the International Missionary Council, the World Council of Christian Education, and the United Christian Student Council; the third by scores of municipal, county, and state councils of churches. The development of such federations and councils is slowly giving to American Protestantism a double organization. On the one hand it is organized into denominations, for the most part national bodies, cooperating with each other through denominational offices and officials; on the other hand it is developing a geographical organization, in which local churches with various denominational affiliations combine in city and state organizations and slowly acquire agencies and offices through which to administer common concerns.

Other aspects of the tendency toward unity among Protestants come into view when one considers the growing similarity of the various groups in internal organization, religious attitudes, and action. Though many denominations distinguish themselves from others by reference to their congregational or presbyterian or episcopal polities, these terms often have more of a sentimental than descriptive value, as in actual operation the historically variant forms of government tend to approximate each other. The most evident influence leading toward agreement in this area is that of American political and social organization. Equality in voting rights, representative government, the recognition of the separate yet interdependent duties and rights of local, regional, or state and national societies, the separation of executive and legislative powers, provision for strong executive power, the multiplication of executive commissions—all these recognizable features in the changing internal order of the denominations.

While the history of religious convictions on the part of Protestants in America must take into account the continuation of the variant emphases of the more doctrinally and the more practically oriented groups, it needs also to describe changes in common outlook. The general tendency, for decades if not for centuries, has been toward disinterestedness in highly developed creedal formulations. This has been accompanied by a great emphasis on practical activity so that, from the point of view of Europe, American Protestantism seems characterized, despite all denominational variants, by its pragmatism. There is, however, another common strain in this American religion, less evident to the casual view but perhaps more significant. A strong concern for individual, personal appropriation or internalization of faith and hope and love of God and neighbor has manifested itself many times in the New World revivals and remains the great interest of churches that issued from them. Moreover it is just these churches that have grown into the strongest religious groups in America, and even the more creedal groups have been influenced by them and the revivals. Hence emphasis on personal Christian experience and commitment has become a great common denominator in American Protestant conceptions of Christian faith and life.

The consequences of these various integrating and harmonizing tendencies has been the emergence in the United States of a kind of "core Protestantism" that is still too loosely knit together to be called an American Protestant church. This core Protestantism is surrounded, here as elsewhere, by dissent, but just as the core represents an indigenous development, including the successors of old European dissenting groups as well as of old established churches, so also the dissent is largely of native and recent origin. The considerable diversity present in the central, unifying organization of interlocking activities, of interweaving interests and ideas, is probably no greater than that which is contained within ecclesiastical structures that appear to be more nearly monolithic.

In view of such considerations it can be fairly maintained that Protestantism, left free by democracy to develop in its own way, has shown as strong a bent toward unification as toward atomization, and that the process of diversification of religious conviction and action in it has been balanced by an accompanying process of integration.

The movement toward integration may, of course, be interpreted as a result of the Americanization of Protestantism, and so be regarded as offering proof of the contention that free Christianity, unregulated by an overruling ecclesiastical or political authority, tends to fall into dependence on the social culture. It seems unquestionable that the Americanization of European immigrant groups has been important in bringing their churches closer together and that the development of a national culture, erasing regional patterns of thought and behavior, has effectively promoted the association of geographically separated religious societies. The operation of social forces may nevertheless be traced in all movements toward diversification, as well as in unifying tendencies; adjustment to culture is a constant phenomenon in the history of Christianity. It would be difficult to find methods of analysis by means of which to discover whether the "core Protestantism" of the United States is more American than Lutheranism is in Europe is German, Swedish, or Norwegian; than Anglicanism is English; than Calvinism is Dutch or Scotch. The diversity and unity of Roman Catholicism, with its Spanish, Italian, Polish, Irish, Gallican, and German churches, with its historic relations to the Roman empires and Romanized culture, also show the influence of social forces on Christianity. The question about American Protestantism, then, is whether dependence on culture is unusually manifest in it, or whether the tendency in that direction is also balanced by a countervailing action.

The Americanization of Protestantism has been accompanied by its re-evangelization, and by the evangelization of the nation. The tendency to equate the gospel with the democratic social faith has been balanced by the effort to Christianize the democratic mind. The other-directedness or heteronomy of American Protestantism has been matched by self-directedness or autonomy.

Autonomy and independence are somewhat misleading terms when applied to Protestant Christianity. They designate ideas and tempers that belong in the context of democratic faith. Protestantism in all its original forms has been concerned to emphasize the direct and absolute dependence of all men and their societies on God, and only in that setting has it affirmed independence from finite powers. Its protests against churches and states have been directed less against invasions of the rights of men than against usurpations of the absolute sovereignty of God. Hence its relations to a democratic movement that begins with a dogma of inherent human rights have always been somewhat ambivalent. Though it has tended to agree with the democratic challenge of divine rights of kings or churches, it has been required to challenge every doctrine of divine right of the people. It has made common cause with the democratic claim that men had rights prior to those granted to them by any government, but it has regarded those rights as issuing only from duties prior in obligation to any duties imposed on men by governments. The right to freedom of worship for such Protestants has been based on the duty to worship God; the right to freedom in speech on the duty to speak the truth as the truth is known; the rights of conscience have been derivative, for them, from the human duty to obey God rather than men.

An "independent" Protestantism, true to its own convictions, doubtless represents other principles, such as the authority of the Scriptures, justification by faith, the duty of serving God in daily work more than in special acts of religious devotion. But in its relations to democratic culture it will show its independence vis-à-vis that culture primarily in the constancy with which it upholds the principle of divine sovereignty. It may refer first of all to Scripture or first of all to conscience as mediator of divine commandments, but in either case it affirms the immediate presence to every individual of the divine law, and it must protest against the assumption by any human authority—whether priest, preacher, magistrate, people, or popular majority—of the right to speak in the name of the absolute. It may regard the execution of the divine will as concentrated in a few critical events in history—especially in Jesus Christ and the final consummation—or it may see it pervasively present in all events; in either case it notes that all self-government is responsible to power beyond all selves and subject to overruling Providence. If Protestantism in America has lost sight of these points and accepted instead the dogmas of democratic faith, then indeed it has lost its independence; then it no longer challenges the social faith but is a passive representative of the culture.

Now, as has been noted, it is not difficult to find in the sermons and church pronouncements of Protestants many proclamations of the dogmas of democratic faith and many glorifications of the rule of "the common man," or of the beneficent effects of guidance by self-interest, or of freedom independent of responsibility. But there are few periods in history in which such themes are not overborne by vigorous and constant witness to the overruling sovereignty of God, by exposition of the divine demands and actions, by calls upon individuals and groups for obedience and repentance before the ultimate holy and gracious power.

THE PEACETIME CHURCH AND WORLD COMMUNISM

Among the occasions in American history in which the presence of such an independent Protestantism has been evident are the Edwardsean challenge to New England individualism; the Calvinistic protests against the doctrines of the French Revolution (which a Timothy Dwight found represented in Jeffersonianism, but which dissenting allies of the latter also fought vigorously); the attack made by Finney and his many associates and successors on the doctrine and practice of self-interest as the basis of the good life; the social gospel's call to repentance, directed primarily to the commercial and managing segments of the population. These, however, mark only high points in an activity of exhortation, proclamation, and education that has been constant.

Throughout American history independent Protestantism has been involved in the conflict about the context in which democratic institutions are to be used and understood. These institutions in themselves show no clear, logical relations to either the principles of "democratic faith" or to those of Christianity. They have been interpreted and employed as expressions of both. Representative government has meant delegation of the people's or a majority's authority; it has also meant the selection by the people of men they trusted to be obedient to ultimate principles of right and to be concerned about the welfare, not of constituents only, but of the whole nation—indeed of mankind. Separation of church and state has meant in one context that the state can be indifferent to religion because only individual and subjective matters are involved; in another, it has been recognized as the measure that must be taken because men's relation to God is too important a matter, too significant in consequences, for society as well as individuals, to be subjected to the short-sighted administration of political office-holders. The Bill of Rights has been interpreted within the framework of a philosophy of individualism and also in the context of the individual's obligation to a universal commonwealth. Democratic institutions in general have been set now in this context, now in that. The tactics of democracy have been employed within a grand strategy of one or the other type, and the conflict about the strategy of one or the other type, and the conflict about the strategy or the final principles to which all technical uses are subordinated has been constant in American history. In that conflict American Protestantism has not indeed been unanimously on one side of the issue, but there can be little doubt that the preponderance of its influence has been toward the side of universalism rather than of individualism, of moral obligation as prior to freedom, of representative rather than delegated government.

This has been perhaps particularly evident in connection with the interpretation and use of the Constitution—whether the fundamental law is to be interpreted as expression of a general social will subject to historic change, or as an interpretation of ultimate, natural, or divine law. Protestantism, joined later in America by Roman Catholicism, has insisted on the latter idea. Its highly Biblicistic wing has, indeed, endeavored to have the American state acknowledge the Scriptures as the written formulation of the ultimate law to which all nations are subject. The major tradition in Protestantism, as in Catholicism, has appealed to a law knowable by reason, a law of nature, which, however difficult to formulate in changeless phrases, must be constantly searched out by the people as their judges. The influence of this "cosmic constitutionalism" on American democracy in the nineteenth century was profound; it has waned in the twentieth, but Protestantism has not abandoned it. One may trace to it those practices in politics and diplomacy that political realism at home and abroad deplores as "moralistic." Yet it is not evident that it has been the source of self-righteousness more than of self-criticism.

Another area in which the presence of an independent Protestantism vis-à-vis democratic society has been manifested is that of social reform. More than in the case of state-supported or state-recognized churches, probably more than in the case of non-Protestant churches, free American Protestantism, apparently so dependent on the social culture, has functioned as the critic of that culture. Directly, or through the exercise of pressure on governments, it has undertaken to inaugurate reforms in social customs and institutions. Some church crusades against evil have been guided by narrow and trivial interpretation of divine law: none has been without opposition from within the churches themselves; all of them have been complicated by the intrusion of non-Christian interests. Nevertheless, the history of Protestant concern for social melioration—from anti-dueling agitation through anti-slavery movement to municipal reform, prohibition, and peace crusades—betokens the presence of an independent and critical spirit rather than one of compliant conformity to the social culture.

Throughout their history under the conditions of freedom, the Protestant churches in America have directed their major evangelistic efforts toward individuals. The concentration on selves in their solitariness has been in part the consequence of the Protestant view of life, in part the result of the challenge modern conditions of existence have posed to the churches. But whatever the reasons for it, concern for the religious, moral conversion and education of individuals has taken precedence in American Protestantism over interest in changing the fundamental assumptions of the common mind, the habitual actions of the whole society. The limitations imposed on Protestantism by this approach have been widely recognized in recent decades. What has not been acknowledged, and can probably never be measured, is the effectiveness of this concentration on the individual. Still, from the point of view of democratic society, it remains pertinent to ask what contribution has been made to its viability by the pervasiveness and constancy of Protestant proclamation, exhortation, admonition, call to repentance; by the prayer, preaching, and Biblical instruction that undertook to write the promises and the law of God upon the inward parts and to make men loyal and obedient citizens of an eternal, universal kingdom in the midst of all their exercise of democratic rights and duties. From the point of view of the Protestant principle it is, of course, not of fundamental importance to ask whether this work of the churches has lengthened the life of democratic society or helped to counteract the vices that attend democratic virtues. For an independent Protestantism cannot entertain a utilitarian valuation of God, of faith in Him, or of religion, as though their worth depended on the service they render to the high god of social faith—society itself, or democracy.

In themselves and in their relations, Protestantism and democracy in America present a strange picture of dynamic forces of movement and counter-movement. Not without order, the orders that are visible are those of process rather than those of status. The Protestant democrat or democratic Protestant finds the mixed picture intelligible only as he views it in the light of his fundamental faith, hope, and hunger for righteousness.

The Illusions of Power

While it was published shortly before his death in 1962, this sermon embodies Niebuhr's theological assessment of the entire postwar era of confrontation between the United States and the Soviet Union. Were American perceptions being informed by fear or by faith? To him, the threat posed by the Soviet Union was real. But God, just as he did in the Old Testament era of Israel's history, was fully capable of using an enemy who was thought to be evil as an ally to accomplish good things both at home and abroad. Hence, to regard the United States as the epitome of the "good" in the Cold War and the Soviet Union as the empire of "evil" was to follow the logic of unbelief.

Source: *The Christian Century Pulpit* 23 (April 1962): 100–103.

Isaiah 10:5-16, 24-27.

In these long years of the cold war between Christendom and communism no chapter of the Bible is more illuminating and helpful to Christian faith than Isaiah 10.

A manifold illustration results from reading it side by side with the daily newspaper. We are reminded, first of all, that our community—this Jewish-Christian society, this Christendom which often rejects the name—is encountering nothing wholly new when it finds itself assailed by alien empires. It has been through all this before, not once but many times. Before Assyria there was Egypt and afterwards there were Babylonia, Persia, Macedonia, Rome, the barbarians, Arabian and Ottoman Islam. Threatening power has stood at the gates of many another symbolic city besides Jerusalem and Berlin—Rome, Constantinople, Belgrade, Vienna. Every generation—ours not the least—tends to think that what is happening to it is without precedent. History, to be sure, does not repeat itself, but when we read Isaiah we are reminded that no trial is befalling us but such as has been common to men. Each time must meet its challenge. Every generation is put to its manifold test.

But the prophetic vision communicates more to us than that. As we follow the logic of Isaiah in his interpretation of the meaning of the threatening events which frighten his people and him, we are made aware of the difference between a beliefful [sic] and an unbelieving understanding of international conflict. In his time, as in ours, the logic of unbelief possessed the field. Its postulates are set forth in many ways, but however they are stated they imply the negative postulate—that there is no God, no world government, no universal ordering. The postulate is that the power which is the creative source of and ruler over our human history—the determiner of our destiny—is either blind in its willfulness or careless of the fate of what has come forth from it. So our interpretations of our cold war—whether offered from the pulpit or from academic chair or in the political forum, my interpretation and yours—are often interpretations addressed by unbelief to unbelief. It may be the unbelief that disguises itself as faith in some little god, some finite power, such as life itself or human reason or true religion. But behind all these idolatries there is the great unbelief in the goodness of the ultimate power which overrules both our reason and our unreason, our life and our death, our religion and irreligion; there is behind it deep distrust of the power or of the goodness of the kingdom of God. Consider from that point of view the unbelief we express in our efforts to frighten one another with visions of the extinction of human life, as though we could thwart the Almighty in his purposes if it is his intention to let us die despite our desire to live or to keep us alive despite our desire to die.

Into this conversation and debate of the unbelievers Isaiah comes with his word of God. His interpretation of what God is saying in, through, and beyond all human speech and action speaks from faith to faith. That does not mean that he speaks as a man who wholly believes in the power and goodness of God to a few men in his time who also wholly believe, but rather that out of the faith which is in him in the midst of his unbelief—with his unclean lips dwelling among a people of unclean lips—he speaks to that saving remnant of faith which is present in his ninety per cent unbelieving hearers.

Let us follow him then or rather the word of God that he speaks, the word about God and word from God that was spoken to him and reported by him as he stood with his compatriots in the presence of Assyria. It is the same word that was spoken to and by his successors in the presence of Egypt and Babylonia and Macedonia and Rome and the barbarians and Islam; the word that in various forms, yet always with essentially the same meaning, came to Jeremiah and to Jesus, to Augustine and Luther, and now is spoken to us.

First, we hear the word about God and from God in the midst of our cold war as a word addressed to our enemy: "Ah, Assyria, the rod of my anger, the staff of my fury!"; "Ah, Russia, instrument of my holy will, ax in my hand." We have no reason to believe that Assyria heard then or that Russia hears now. But Israel was meant to hear and we are meant to hear. The address to the enemy is really directed toward us to dispel our illusions—the double illusion we have about ourselves—about the goodness of our power and the power of our goodness; the double illusion also that we have about our enemy, the evil of his power and the power of his evil.

We men always tend to cherish illusions about the goodness of our power, and we fortify them by making rational comparisons between ourselves and our enemies. By standards readily available to us—in our time standards of democratic ethics or of humanitarianism or of our religion—we measure ourselves against those who oppose us. Making such comparisons it is as clear to us vis-à-vis communism as it was to Hebrews in conflict with Assyrians that with all our faults we are comparatively good. The constant warfare between life assertion and destruction, between the affirmation of all that conserves the values we cherish and the nihilism that destroys what we value, finds us fighting not only for our lives but for the maintenance of all the values to which our lives are devoted. We are often highly sophisticated about this in our day, aware of our tendency to indulge in rationalization; still, we do consider ourselves the primary instrument of human good.

So we in America, for instance, may contrast ourselves as a God-fearing people with atheistic communism; or as a people which believes in the intrinsic values of persons we compare ourselves with a nation and a movement that makes persons mere instruments of collective ends; or we set ourselves as freedom-lovers in opposition to slave-makers. Using the measures we do, we are surely right. How then can the word of God attack us in our assurance that we are the instruments of the good, that we are on God's side? It does so by bringing into view the actuality of a good will that is so much greater than our goodwill, cherishing values so much greater than ours, that comparisons between ourselves and our enemies on the basis of our standards become somewhat irrelevant. Here a power announces its presence which does not disprize us but which asserts that it uses our enemy as its instrument no less than it uses us. Who is the instrument in the hands of God? The enemy no less than ourselves, though he be an instrument of another sort than we are, as different perhaps as an ax is from a cookstove, a saw from an electric light. More significantly this word about God, the Lord of all nations, speaks to us in the midst of our illusions about the power of our goodness. There is an illusion we cherish as Israel did, as individuals, nations, religious communities of every sort at all times have done: that if we were only left alone we would realize our values and live up to our standards. It is our cry that we ought to be left in peace and not be subjected to alien pressures which prevent us from following our own proper business of living our real lives, of serving our good ends, of worshiping our God or our gods in peace. In this illusion the word of God assails us with the statement that the enemy, the instrument of divine goodness, has been sent against us a *godless* people—a people false to their own good. We need to forget, in the light of the gospel of Jesus Christ, all those notes and overtones of divine anger and human punishment which are present in Isaiah's formulation of God's word, and also all our own guilt-feelings and masochistic tendencies to appease an angry power that is trying to get even with godless men. We are dealing with the Holy One; with holy love that is not envious of man, that needs no vengeance, that does not desire the pain or destruction of his creatures, yet does insist on their healing, on their being made whole, on their becoming truly what they are in possibility.

The enemy, then, says the word of God, is the instrument in God's hands for our correction, for our restoration of ourselves to ourselves. Such correction, such restoration of ourselves to ourselves, is certainly not in the mind of the instrument—our enemy whether Assyria or Russia—but only in the mind of the one who uses it. "He does not so intend, and his mind does not so think; but it is in his mind to destroy . . ." The enemy wants to use us for his purposes, not to restore us to our purposes. But God has our correction in mind that we be truly ourselves. How shall we understand this? The ancient prophet understood it like this: every assault of the enemy means that Israel is called upon to remember its covenants, its promises. The foreign instrument is being used to call Israel back to its own fundamental character. Isaiah's whole tenth chapter is the illustration; before he refers to Assyria he pronounced his woe on those who decree iniquitous decrees, on the writers of oppression, on those who turn aside the needy from justice, rob the poor of their right, on all those who violate the covenant by means of which they have justified themselves as better than their enemies.

It appears, then, that the situation is like this: one purpose the Almighty has in using the enemy as his instrument is to make us good in accordance with our own standards of what is good. You delude yourselves, this word of faith says, when you think that if you were left in peace, not subjected to the alien pressure, your goodness would be powerful enough to realize itself in your lives. The enemy is the instrument the Almighty is using to make you good, in your own understanding of what is good. The ultimate ruler is not requiring you to conform to the enemy's ideas of goodness but to your own. The enemy is just his instrument to make you become truer to yourself.

We ask ourselves in our confrontation with our indubitable enemy today, Russia and communism, whether this word of faith is one for which we have some kind of empirical evidence. Is this the way the Almighty is working? Amidst all the mystery of his ways can this element be understood? And we must answer, there is indeed something corresponding to experience in this observation of faith. We reflect that under the pressure of our enemy we have been relentlessly pushed to keep promises which we made to ourselves and to one another in our society, to keep also the promises of our nation to other peoples. A dramatic instance is what we have been required to do under this foreign pressure in trying to overcome the deep injustice of discrimination against the Negro, an injustice by our own standards. Here there is no imposition upon us of a foreign idea. The idea is our own; the promise of equality lies at the basis of our national existence, though we have violated it from the beginning. But our goodness has been feeble. We have not had the power to be good in terms of our own standard. Left in peace we did little to live up to our own idea of goodness. Now the pressure has been exerted upon us and communism, our enemy, has been used as an instrument toward our own health. Its pressure has required us to conform to our own will for good, a will that was too feeble without pressure. So also compulsive factors made us get rid a hundred years ago of the slavery we knew to be wrong by our own standards but could not banish by the power of our goodwill. We are not whole yet. What would we do in this matter of keeping black men in a state of inequality if the pressure were relaxed? Would our goodness be powerful enough to assert itself?

There are other instances of the corrective influence of God's instrument on us. Our efforts to achieve a larger measure of social justice, by our own standard of what social justice is, during all the years since communism began to threaten us have not come forth simply out of the power of our own goodness. Further, our nation was conceived as having a mission in mankind. We came into existence as a people which did not think of itself as an isolated nation but as chosen for a purpose—to be a light in its own way to men, a light of liberation. But we began to live to ourselves, by ourselves, not as an organ of mankind but as a self-contained nation, pursuing nationally egoistic ends. Under the pressure of our enemy we have been and are being forced to become ourselves again—a nation that acknowledges its solidarity with mankind, that remembers the promise it made in its inception, to stand, for instance, for the principle that all men, not Americans only, are created free and equal. Under the pressure of that inconvenient instrument—communism—in the hands of the Almighty, we have even learned to practice some love of other enemies and have not been permitted to maintain long hatred against Japan or Germany, or even against those so-called neutrals about whom we were tempted to say that those that are not with us are against us. It is not by the power of our goodness that we have done these things, and not because we yielded to the enemy's ideas of goodness, but because the enemy has been an instrument in the hands of God to make us become more of what we promised to be, to make us measure up to our own standards.

Second, we have illusions not only about ourselves but also about the enemy just as the Hebrews had in the presence of Assyria. One of these is the illusion about the evil of his power, another about the power of his evil. By evil let us mean simply the ability to destroy what is good—the ability to kill life, to ruin the slowly built work of our culture, to destroy the ideals by which we live. Now we need make no mistake about this: that as it was in the mind of the king of Assyria to destroy not only Hebrew lives but also the Hebrew nation and Hebrew devotion to God and its covenant, so it is in the mind of the power that confronts us today to destroy our society, our western devotions to our ideals, our culture, our Jewish and Christian faith. Let us not indulge now in ideas about the real good that is in the worst of men and about the evil that is in the best. Faith in man speaks about such things and within its limits speaks truly. But we are trying to look at our situation with Isaiah from the point of view of faith in God, not with romanticists from the point of view of faith in man. What does the word about God, not about man say? The Almighty uses the destroying intentions of men to do good. The evil, destructive intentions of Assyria, Egypt, Macedonia against Israel are one thing; the constructive intentions of the Almighty who uses these as his instruments, are another. Through all the tragic story of the nations, including the story of our times, including the central, wonderfully symbolic history of the Cross of Christ, this word of God, this word about God, resounds: "You thought to do evil, but I thought to do good, to bring it about that many people should have life."

Toward the understanding of that word we can muster less evidence from history and our own experience than for the understanding of the correctional effectiveness of our adversaries. Yet this we must all have in mind today, that as a new Israel came forth out of its conflict with Assyria and Babylonia, a new Western world with Renaissance and Reformation in it came out of the conflict with Islam, so our own time is standing not only in the presence of adversaries, but of new possibilities. For instance, the emergence of a society of a more united mankind with new values, larger outlook, deeper understanding. And we cannot divorce the two things: the cold war and the promises of the day. We sense that great things may be in the making but also that we cannot make them, that we are all only instruments in the hands of the inscrutable power, a means of the all pervading creative spirit, which has greater things in mind than we can have with our intentions toward our limited goods and evils, our fear of change and our defensiveness.

What Isaiah, or better, the word of God, had to deal with, further, was Israel's illusion about the power of that will which was in the enemy to destroy. Assyria had a great sense of its power. Its king was strong in his conviction that he was sufficient to overcome all who did not submit to his will. His self-confidence was surely not weaker than a Khrushchev's. But in the long perspective of Isaiah's understanding of the power that held Assyria in its grasp, the prophet pronounced this word of God about Assyria:

> When the Lord has finished all his work on Mount Zion and on Jerusalem he will punish the arrogant boasting of the king of Assyria. . . . Shall the ax vaunt itself over against him who hews with it, or the saw magnify itself against him who wields it? . . . The Lord of hosts will send wasting sickness among his stout warriors, and under his glory a burning will be kindled, like the burning of fire.

And so it was. The pitiful remnants of Assyria remain today for archaeologists to dig out of sand and rubble.

In the sixteenth century when Ottoman power was it its height and all Europe seemed ready to fall before it, Suleiman the Magnificent prefaced a letter to the king of France with these words:

> I who am the Sultan of Sultans, the Sovereign of Sovereigns, the distributor of crowns to the monarchs of the surface of the globe, the shadow of God on earth, the Sultan and Padishah of the White Sea, the Black Sea, Rumelia, Anatolia, Caramania, Rum, Sulkadr, Diarbekr, Kurdustan, Azerbaijan, Persia, Damascus, Aleppo, Cairo, Mecca, Medina, Jerusalem, all Arabia, Yemen and other countries which my noble ancestors (may God brighten their tombs) conquered and which my august majesty has likewise conquered with my flaming sword, Sultan Sulayman Khan.

How many others have there been who regarded themselves as the waves of the future, the shadow of God, or the incarnation of inexorable laws of history of some other power. "He that sitteth in the heavens shall laugh."

The power of evil to destroy is always limited. There is a limiter who will not suffer any instrument to take the place of the one who uses it. That counts for us when we consider ourselves the shadows of God or goodness on earth. That counted for Assyria. That counts for Russia too as it sees itself the incarnation of the ultimate movement in history. But this word of God is not directed now to Russia; to speak it is not the responsibility of the interpreters of the prophets in this Western Christendom. If such interpreters are present in Russia today they will follow the same logic of faith that Western believers are asked to use. The word, however, is now addressed to us in our fearsomeness before our contemporary Assyrias and Egypts. "The Egyptians are men, and not God; and their horses are flesh, and not spirit" (Isaiah 31:3). The Russians are human, not incarnations of superhuman historical power.

We are delivered from our temptation to take our enemy as seriously as he takes himself—not when we compare our power with his own but when we think of his power in comparison with the almightiness that rules over him as well as us.

Third, what is the consequence of this reading of the story of our times in the light of the word of God? What was the consequence for Isaiah when he so read it? No supineness before the enemy, not nonresistance, surely. There are some who draw that conclusion from faith's interpretation of the story of their times. So Luther thought that since the Ottoman empire was an instrument in God's hand, therefore Europe should not resist. But he soon discovered that he had misread the word of God in Scriptures and in the story of his day. Isaiah did not draw the conclusion of nonresistance but encouraged his king and people to defend Jerusalem. But they were to do it in confidence and faith and as those who practiced a double strategy: first of all the strategy of self-reformation in accordance with their own laws and promises; secondly, the self-defense of those whose fear of Assyria was assuaged and tempered by their certainty that it had no power beyond that which the Almighty granted it for his own purposes, the assurance that in due time the Almighty would accomplish all his work for good, and then reduce the enemy to his proper size, perhaps to that of a woodshed ax or a pruning saw.

It is not the preacher's task to justify the ways of God to man. For who knows the thoughts of the Omnipresence that is above, beneath, and about us? Who can give counsel to the Almighty? His thoughts are not our thoughts, nor his ways our ways. What lies in our future? Since it is in God's hands, not ours, who can say.

But it is the duty of the preacher who interprets the prophetic and the evangelical word of God, about God, from God, to speak from faith to faith, and to say to those involved in the war of nerves, which is always our ultimate warfare: "The fear of God is the beginning of wisdom"; the fear of God is the holy fear before the one who makes us whole, who heals our diseases, who makes right our iniquities, who saves our lives from destruction. Therefore "in returning and in rest you shall be saved; in quietness and in trust shall be your strength."

10

Reclaiming the Church's Reformation Heritage

The Christian church was the environment in which H. Richard Niebuhr was most at home throughout the course of his entire life. Reared in a Midwestern parsonage, he followed his father into the ministry of the Evangelical Synod of North America. There he served faithfully, first as a pastor and then as a teacher and administrator at both Elmhurst College and Eden Seminary. Even the leave he was given to pursue his doctorate at Yale during the 1920s did not keep him from taking charge of a Congregational church in Connecticut.

This commitment set him apart from his brother Reinhold. In retrospect, Richard recalled that whereas Reinhold had assumed the responsibility of reforming their culture, the "special task" to which he felt called was the reformation of the church.[1] Scholarly achievements and academic promotions never seemed to lessen this

---

1. H. Richard Niebuhr, "Reformation: Continuing Imperative," *The Christian Century* 67 (March 2, 1960): 249.

commitment. Throughout his tenure at Yale Divinity School, he tried to instill attitudes in the hundreds of students who sat in his classes that would enrich their services to the churches where the majority of them were to become engaged in ministry.

With this devotion to the church, however, Niebuhr consistently mixed healthy doses of criticism. Pious ecclesiastical traditions, in his estimation, were no less flawed by human sinfulness than other features of a culture. Self-serving motives could distort Christian prayers as much as self-righteousness could hamper the church's witness in non-Christian cultures. Denominations were prone to identify their own organization with the true church and to view other church bodies as heterodox Christians. By substituting some "little god" for the "One beyond the many," churches were for him as guilty of idolatry as any of their individual members. In reacting to liberal theological currents, Barthians could concentrate so much on what Christ disclosed about God that they lost sight of the lordship exercised by the other members of the Trinity. In seeking to preserve the authority of the Bible, evangelical and fundamentalist groups could confuse this authority with the authority only the Bible's Author deserved to command.

Niebuhr's awareness of these and other worldly aspects of the church, which only seemed to deepen as his career progressed, may help us account for his choice of *Christ and Culture* as the title of his most enduring book. For him any portrait of "Christ," as well as all other features of a "culture," was equally subject to human corruption. But at the same time, the term "Christ" allowed him to highlight the gospel message the church was called to bring to the world's attention, and "culture" enabled him to distinguish this arena of human activity from the larger world that God had created and was intent upon redeeming.

Niebuhr believed that self-criticism on the part of the church was a key feature of its Reformation heritage. For him, the term *Protestant* stood not so much for a major branch of post-sixteenth century Christianity or a tradition to be defended against adversaries as for an ongoing process of conversion on the part of the church as well as the world from idolatry to faith. God was in fact constantly demanding of the church the same repentance to which it might, in apostolic fashion, call society or any individual human being. Like Paul Tillich, Niebuhr emphasized that this was the principle the Protestant Reformation had bequeathed to the whole Christian church.[2] In *Radical Monotheism and Western Culture*, he assigned a similar role to a "monotheistic" faith because it served to check any group seeking to invest sacred trust in the symbols of its religion and in the process to fuse reverence for these with faith in God.[3] Elsewhere he asserted that for those who agreed with him that history followed a rhythmic pattern of revival and protest against many successive "established orders," Christianity became the story of "many reformations."[4] Niebuhr disagreed with those who might see such self-criticism as an unwanted or unnecessary form of ecclesiastical negativism. For example, exposing the warped feelings of white superiority and tendencies to identify Christianity with Western culture on the part of the church's foreign missionaries, he asserted in 1951, might lead to genuine repentance. As the humanitarian efforts of Albert Schweitzer clearly demonstrated, the remorse produced over these sins could be redirected by the knowledge of God's forgiveness into "channels of restitution and help

---

2. See Paul Tillich, *The Protestant Era* (Chicago: University of Chicago Press, 1948), 192–221.
3. See H. Richard Niebuhr, *Radical Monotheism and Western Culture* (New York: Harper & Brothers, 1960), 49–63.
4. H. Richard Niebuhr, "The Protestant Movement and Democracy in the United States," in *Religion in American Life*, vol. 1, *The Shaping of American Religion*, ed. James Ward Smith and A. Leland Jamison (Princeton: Princeton University Press, 1961), 22–26.

of the injured neighbors."[5] Above all, Niebuhr felt that such self-criticism was necessary for the church to fulfill its role as pioneer in the reforming of society. Condemning nationalism, racism, or economic imperialism without repudiating the presence of these evils in the church, as he saw it, could only imply "insincerity and unbelief." By contrast, the church had a much better chance of becoming authentically visible and of reduplicating the "deed of Christ" when it chose first to set its own house in order, thus providing the model of a "world society, undivided by race, class and national interests."[6]

One reason for the seeming intensification of Niebuhr's passion for church reformation was the religious revival that was occurring in America following World War II. Church membership and attendance kept surging until 1960, and financial investments in church planting and new church construction soon reached an all-time high. Increasing enrollments were also forcing church-related colleges and seminaries to expand their facilities and faculties.[7] When he looked beneath the surface of these favorable seas, however, Niebuhr saw a number of disturbing undercurrents. Most obvious to him was that Cold War fears, rather than renewed faith in God, seemed to be fueling the uptick in church participation. At the same time, he perceived among faithful and nominal congregants, as well as their clergy, a pervasive dissatisfaction with their churches. To him, the Christian gospel's ability to address people's deepest

---

5. H. Richard Niebuhr, "An Attempt at a Theological Analysis of Missionary Motivation," *Occasional Bulletin* 14 (January 1963): 1–6. Niebuhr first prepared this paper for the Division of Foreign Missions of the National Council of Churches in April 1951.
6. H. Richard Niebuhr, "The Responsibility of the Church for Society," in *The Gospel, the Church, and the World*, ed. Kenneth Scott Latourette (New York: Harper & Brothers, 1946), reprinted in *"The Responsibility of the Church for Society" and Other Essays by H. Richard Niebuhr*, ed. Kristine A. Culp (Louisville: Westminster John Knox, 2008), 75.
7. See Sydney E. Ahlstrom, *A Religious History of the American People* (New Haven, CT: Yale University Press, 1972), 952–53.

concerns furnished a foundation for the kind of community that so many in the frequently uprooted postwar "nation of strangers" longed for. But all too often, they did not find it in the churches they had hoped would become their home.[8] Niebuhr recognized that the revival was prompting more people to ask religious questions. But for many, the traditional answers the churches were providing seemed unsatisfactory, even hollow. Others, for this same reason, did not even consider the possibility that a church would be able to meet their deepest needs. He was haunted by the thought that "the hungry sheep look up and are not fed" and declared, "Our old phrases are worn out." In order to communicate adequately "the reality of our existence before God" to the contemporary world, the Christian message must undergo a complete "resymbolization."[9]

Niebuhr's stance toward the reinvigorated ecumenical movement was similarly "protestant." The World Council of Churches, formed in Amsterdam in 1948, met in Evanston, Illinois, in 1954. Eight separate interdenominational agencies, including the Federal Council of Churches, merged in 1950 to form the National Council of Churches. Significant church unions were also being consummated, among which was the creation in 1957 of the United Church of Christ, bringing Niebuhr's Evangelical and Reformed Church into the orbit of the Congregational Christian churches. While supportive of this type of ecumenism, he felt that the movement had produced some distortions of the Christian faith. Its leaders seemed to him to give excessive attention to church structures and institutions, partly as a result of exalting the importance of their own affairs. For him, world reconciliation remained the only justifiable reason for the

---

8. H. Richard Niebuhr, "The Churches and the Body of Christ," *Friends Intelligencer* 110 (1953); reprinted in Culp, ed., 118–21.
9. Niebuhr, "Reformation: Continuing Imperative," 250–51.

existence of ecumenical institutions and the primary goal at which the church needed to aim all of its ecumenical efforts.[10]

Niebuhr was also convinced that Christian unity was chiefly a spiritual reality. It stemmed from belonging to Christ, and for this reason could be achieved only by means of the repentance and forgiveness that he inspired. To depend upon organizational methods alone was to court failure. It might even open the door to the power struggles and conflicts of conscience that tended to tear the church into so many different denominations. At the same time, he emphasized the continuing need for religious organizations. The fresh emphasis neo-orthodoxy had given to the one holy, catholic Church of Christ, he discovered, had churned up a new wave of attacks on denominationalism, causing some ecumenists to forget that the Church and the churches belonged together. Visible churches, he argued, possessed as much capacity for expressing in word and deed the true aims of the invisible Church of faith as they did of thwarting them.[11]

Taking charge of a comprehensive study of theological education in the United States and Canada, therefore, became an opportunity to reform the church that Niebuhr could not refuse. While this meant postponing the systematic treatment of his approach to Christian ethics that much of the theological world had reason to anticipate, he gladly jumped into this new project in 1954 with both feet. He may also have had a sense of returning to the reforming role he had assumed at the outset of his career as an educator in the Evangelical Synod, but this time on a much larger scale. Daniel Day Williams and James Gustafson joined his research team, and together they spent the next two years gathering information on more than a hundred

---

10. H. Richard Niebuhr, "The Seminary in the Ecumenical Age," *Theology Today* 17 (October 1960), 306–7.
11. H. Richard Niebuhr, "The Hidden Churches and the Churches of Sight," *Religion in Life* 15 (Winter 1945–1946): 115–16.

seminaries and divinity schools. Niebuhr shared his reflections on their findings in a book published in 1956 as *The Purpose of the Church and its Ministry*. His recommendations for the improvement of theological education, perhaps not surprisingly, focused on the relationship between the church and the world. Ministerial preparation, in his estimation, while it tended to be more ecumenical in tone and atmosphere, still needed to be aimed at particular forms of community service in local congregations. More importantly, he stated that he viewed the world as a "companion of the church," its enemy sometimes and its partner at other times, "often antagonist" yet "always one to be befriended," sometimes the church's "co-knower," while at other times either not knowing what the church knows or knowing what the church does not. Moreover, since God was at work in the world as much as the church, Niebuhr called for a more interdisciplinary approach to theological education; he offered "pastoral director" as a new title for persons assuming the office of pastor because it made lay congregants equally responsible for the church's ministry to the world.[12]

As the post–World War II era was drawing to a close in 1960, *The Christian Century* requested an article from Niebuhr for its "How My Mind Has Changed" series. In the article, titled "Reformation: Continuing Imperative," he wrote, "My primary concern today is still the reformation of the church. I still believe that reformation is a permanent movement, that *metanoia* is a demand made on us in historical life."[13] The following materials illustrate several of the ways in which Niebuhr, during the final years of his life, sought to bring this aspect of his own Reformation heritage to bear upon the church

---

12. H. Richard Niebuhr, *The Purpose of the Church and Its Ministry: Reflections on the Aims of Theological Education* (New York: Harper & Brothers, 1956), 9–27.
13. Niebuhr, "Reformation: Continuing Imperative," 250.

in order that it might more effectively engage the world of this period and beyond.

Evangelical and Protestant Ethics

Niebuhr freely acknowledged that the heirs of the Protestant Reformation had committed some of the same errors with which great Reformers like Martin Luther had charged medieval Catholicism. Ethically, this type of Protestantism reflected "man's unconquerable desire to defend and justify himself by his good works as well as to identify his social and political culture with God's revelation of his will." According to Niebuhr, the evangelical approach to ethics was more true to the Reformation because it called for protest against any attempt to give infinite status to anything finite or to treat something that was conditional as if it were unconditional, whether an ecclesiastical institution, a system of doctrine, or even the Bible itself. Hence, it most certainly involved the church in a continuous process of "reformation." The reader of this essay may find it confusing that Niebuhr would pit the terms evangelical and Protestant against each other until one recognizes that it was written for inclusion in a book of essays celebrating the centennial of his own Evangelical Synod's Eden Seminary.

Source: *The Heritage of the Reformation*, ed. Elmer J. F. Arndt (New York: Richard R. Smith, 1950), 211–29.

A strange duality manifests itself in every human movement. Perhaps it is the inner contradiction in man which comes to appearance in the double-minded character of political, scientific, cultural, and religious revolutions and revivals. Monarchies and tyrannies arise in protests against the rule of the strong but also as assertions of such rule. Democratic revolutions contend for the right of the people to govern themselves but also for the right of a special group—church-members or property-holders or industrial workers—to direct them. Natural science enters upon its great career under the double motto of obedience to the laws of nature and of power over its forces.

Nations and cultures come into existence as representatives of a universal cause and as exponents of particular interests; communism and Russianism, democracy and Gallicanism or Americanism, the sovereignty of law and Roman imperialism, rationalism and Hellenism accompany each other like non-identical and competitive twins. In religious history this duality and internal contradiction are also manifest. Hebraic universalism and particularism are contradictory and inseparable. Rejecting the proposition that a particular people has been chosen by the God of heaven and earth, the church asserts the same statement in a new form. Catholicism and Romanism or Catholicism and Anglicanism go hand in hand; pietism, stressing the primary importance of heart religion, concentrates attention on external behavior; theological idealism asserts the absolute dependence of man on God and the primacy of the religious consciousness.

Protestantism which from the beginning has been keenly aware of this aspect of man's misery is itself subject to the law it has discerned. Some of the ways in which this internal contradiction appears in their own history have been called to the attention of modern Protestants. Historical inquiry has illuminated the antitheses and cooperations of church and sect principles, of capitalism and Calvinism, of nationalism and the Reformation, of stateism [sic] and Lutheranism, of bibliolatry and dependence on the Word of God, of individualism and the idea of the priesthood of all believers, of legalism and liberty. Yet the illusion easily arises that while the past has been subject to the sway of original sin or that, while other men and organizations are beset by internal contradiction, we, in our own theological movement or denomination, are happily delivered from the body of this death. The Calvinist can discern the ambiguity of Lutheranism; the Lutheran sees the mote in Geneva's eye; the sectarian understands what is wrong with the churchman; the Barthian analyzes inerrantly the fallacies in Brunner; the double-mindedness of *Kultur-Protestantismus* is as plain as a pike-staff to the church-theologian, etc., etc. The great fact remains that we cannot see the beams in our own eyes, and that we can only be thankful that the Lord has constituted the church [as] a society for the mutual extraction of motes and beams.

Yet what cannot be seen in particular may be understood in general. Though each individual Christian man or group in Protestantism may be unable to discern the contradiction in himself or itself, it is possible, within limits, to understand something of the contradiction which exists in modern Protestantism as a whole. The antitheses are discernible in theology, polity and worship; but they are most evident in Protestant and Evangelical ethics.

These two terms, Protestant and Evangelical, may be used to designate the two tendencies. On the one hand we note in our answers to the question, "What shall I do?" a defensive temper which regards Protestantism as a way of life, once and for all established, which must be maintained and defended against internal and external enemies. These defensive answers in their organization we shall call the Protestant ethics. On the other hand the question may be and is answered by the simple statement, so rich in implications, "Believe in the Lord Jesus Christ and thou shalt be saved." This answer with all those implications we shall name the Evangelical ethics.

Protestant Ethics

The defensive or Protestant ethics has as many forms as Protestantism itself, yet all of them show a family resemblance. In each of them Protestant men express their pride in and their concern for the conservation of those achievements which are credited to the Reformers, however variously the nature and relative value of these achievements are defined. In each Protestants express their antagonism to destructive forces which seem to threaten those achievements and the Protestant way of life. In each there is expressed high awareness of one or the other of the negative principles of the Reformation: the doctrine of radical evil in man, the rejection of the authoritarian church, of tradition, the suspicion of reason and natural law. In each the positive content of the ethics is derived from tradition, though now from Protestant rather than medieval tradition.

One form of the defensive Protestant ethics is that which has been dubbed *Kultur-Protestantismus*. It is the social religion of a large part of Western civilization and is intimately connected with national, political, and economic ways of thought and behavior. Sometimes it is very conservative as in the case of fundamentalist groups where Protestant ethics is often identified with the prevailing mores of a static culture and with defense against all experimental types of behavior, whether in the realm of amusements, or of property-holding and union-organizing, or of ecclesiastical organization. Protestant ethics here appears as strict obedience to the traditions established in sectarian and revivalistic days on the one hand, in the days of agrarian capitalism and early democracy on the other. Dominantly an ethics of prohibitions, it seems to be founded on a deep suspicion of sinful man, especially of sinful youth and of the sinful outside "world." Its representatives live in fear of the destructive effects on the established folk-ways of communism, Catholicism and liberalism, of science and literary criticism. Avowedly biblicistic, this ethic is actually based much more on the traditions of the elders than on Scriptures, as the prominence of prohibitions against drinking, dancing, and card-playing and interest in the maintenance of rather unbiblical economic and political institutions indicate.

The extreme antithesis of this ethics seems to appear there where Protestantism is identified with socialism and even, occasionally, with communism. Here the culture with which Protestantism is allied consists of a new set of economic institutions and practices. Yet a certain identification between Protestantism and the new culture is regarded as justified by the antagonism of both to Roman Catholicism and of defensive Romanism to both.

The most prevalent kind of culture Protestantism, however, is to be found in neither of these extremes but in the great middle where the institutions of liberal, democratic, industrial, scientific culture are closely associated with the achievements of the Reformation and where the defense of such institutions with the aid of religion is the central concern. This kind of Protestantism may show more or less willingness to modify the institutions and also the religion in order that the "democratic, liberal, and Protestant way of life" may be conserved. But one thing stands out in its ethics: the utilitarian interest in promoting a faith for the sake of saving from external attack and internal decay the habits of life that have been sanctioned by tradition. That it is a pleasant tradition, that the mode of life which it enjoins is satisfying to those who follow it, that its rules serve many human values, that it enables people of differing faiths to get along with each other in nonreligious matters, that it provides for desirable reforms—all this may be quite evident. But it is also clear that this great median cultural ethics of defensive Protestantism is less interested in the transformation of life by grace than in the conservation of a kind of life once radically changed by grace or by the proclamation of a doctrine of grace.

It is remarkable how much of the current revival of interest in religion expresses itself through defensive Roman Catholicism. But Protestantism is also a beneficiary of the movement. A new interest in Puritanism is manifested by men who realize that democracy would not have arisen without the convictions of Puritanism and that without something like them it cannot be maintained. A new interest in the doctrine of God may appear in the form of concern for the foundations of modern science. Oswald Spengler called attention to the tendency in dying civilizations (we might better say in civilizations which believe that they are threatened with death) to revive the religion of the culture's creative period. Cultural Protestantism in our time seems to illustrate his thesis. Churchmen and non-churchmen now often turn to religion—what man does not?—with the idea that once upon a time this world was in a much happier state than it is now, that a fall from joy and order has taken place, that this fall was connected with the abandonment of the religion of the fathers, and that if the religion can only be reestablished all may yet be well. There may be some truth in this widespread cultural myth, though theology will point out fallacies of equating the time of man's innocency with a cultural era, such as that of the thirteenth, or of the sixteenth, or of the eighteenth century, and of identifying the fall from grace with such an historic event as the coming of the Reformation, or the Renaissance, or the Enlightenment, or the Industrial Revolution. In any case the ethics of liberal culture Protestantism is the ethics of modern culture, restored, improved, revised. Its principles are those of anti-authoritarianism, or individual religious, intellectual, and political liberty, or of the sacredness of personality. It is a Protestantism which justifies itself by calling attention to its social works and expects to be justified in the historical judgment by its continued production of socially valued effects.

The second species of Protestant ethics is made up of many families of ecclesiastical defensive moralities. In them the moral question to which answers are sought is not, "What must we do to save our culture?" but rather, "What must we do to save our church and its way of life?" It is assumed that part of the church was reformed by the Reformers and that Christianity now consists of ordered and disordered parts. Right polity, right teaching, right belief have been established, it is believed, in Protestantism or in the particular variety of Protestantism in question. Sex life and the family, at least in principle, have been rightly ordered since the aberrations of medieval monasticism have been eliminated; a Christian doctrine of vocation has been substituted for a false one; right relations of church and state have been established. Such defensive morality may be more liberal, seeking some changes in the traditional Protestant ways of life or more conservative, resisting all changes. But in either case the emphasis is on the maintenance of tradition, though the tradition which the Reformers rejected is also rejected and the one that began with them is affirmed. So it is a characteristic of contemporary Protestant scholarship that it seeks in the writings of its Fathers—of Luther, Calvin, Wesley, Edwards—sanctions for the ethical decisions it needs to make in social life with the same avidity and inventiveness that Roman Catholic scholars employ in the exegesis of Thomas Aquinas or Jewish rabbis in the analysis of the Torah.

Defensive Protestantism, of course, appears not only in these social forms but also in highly individualized fashion. It has often been pointed out that the revolt against legalism which characterized the Reformation issued in a new kind of legalism, that is, in a new manifestation of the old spirit of rigorous obedience to laws, accompanied by the fears of punishment and the hopes of reward which mark such moralty [sic]. Where this spirit obtains, whether in Judaism or in Christianity, whether in Roman Catholicism or in Protestantism, morality has a defensive character. Man seeks to justify himself by his works; he wrestles with the problem of making God friendly toward him; he lives in fear of the divine righteousness; his activities are accompanied neither by confidence in God nor by thankfulness but by distrust of the divine good will and by the feeling that the Lord is a hard taskmaster. Men who have been nurtured in Protestantism find it hard to deny that such an attitude is widely prevalent in it or that it is not nurtured by the very manner in which Protestant doctrine is transmitted from generation to generation. The narrow and fearsome spirit which characterized the second generation of Puritans in America and was represented by Cotton Mather manifests itself in one way or another is every group. In one case, indeed, it may appear as a meticulous concern for correct religious belief, in another case as fearsome respect for taboos in eating and drinking—especially drinking, in still a third as careful suppression of every angry or self-regarding thought. But whether it is more concerned with spiritual or with carnal sin, with perfection in conduct or perfection in belief, it is always the same spirit of negative and self-conscious morality. It is not wholly an accident or a mistake that in popular literature Protestants are more frequently chosen than Catholics to exemplify this narrow, self-defensive and uncreative morality. It is doubtless fallacious to seek for the sources of this perversion of the gospel in the Protestant formulations of the Christian creed or the Reformed doctrine of the Christain [sic] life, since moral decision and personal, religious relations are not based on conceptual propositions, whatever the service these may render the life of practical reason. Sin is not correlated with doctrines about sin; it does not abound more nor is it diminished where doctrines or sin abound. It is only remarkable that Protestantism itself illustrates the prevalence of that human moral orientation which it tends to associate in peculiar fashion with Roman Catholic doctrine and polity; and that it makes evident in its own history and actions man's unconquerable desire to defend and justify himself by his good works as well as to identify his social or personal culture with God's revelation of his will.

Evangelical Ethics

If only defensive and self-justifying morality had appeared in the Reformation that event would have little Christian significance, whatever political or cultural meaning it might have. If only defensiveness in ethics characterized its historic successors Christian faith today would turn away from their churches and rites to find its wellsprings elsewhere as once it turned away from defensive medieval religion. Of course, the Reformation contained negative and defensive elements. Its exponents were sometimes more aware of human sin than of divine grace, more conscious of the pope's errors in granting indulgence than of the truth in Christ's forgiveness, more afraid of earthly enemies than confident of heavenly friendship. But it was also and perhaps dominantly the expression of an affirmative and joyful, a positive and creative Christian life. However much the motives of a life according to man were mixed up in it with the motives of citizenship in the City of God, the latter were gloriously present. These gave the sixteenth century movement élan and power whenever in later days the spirit rather than the letter of the Reformation has been manifest among its "children after the flesh" these motives have again been evident, however mixed with defensiveness and fearful self-justification. We have called the positive movement and orientation of the Christian life Evangelical ethics, using a term which the Reformers themselves preferred to such words as Protestant or Reformed. The name, of course, is a matter of relative indifference so long as the thing itself is adequately located and described.

Evangelical ethics cannot be located, as a self-justifying temper always seeks to do, by looking for it in the self and one's own community, or in any isolated person or group. We cannot fix it by looking for it in Luther rather than in Calvin or in Calvin rather than in Luther, in sectarian rather than in ecclesiastical Protestantism or vice versa. To be sure we are more aware of its presence when we read Isaiah than when we study Leviticus, when we identify ourselves with Paul than when we do so with the author of II Peter, and when we look at God and ourselves with the aid of Calvin than when we do so under the guidance of Cotton Mather. But the spirit of Evangelical ethics is not discernible in men; it exists only in the relations of men to God and of God to men. It is as erroneous to look for it in men or churches as it is fallacious to look for manifestations of magnetism in steel fittings in the absence of a magnet.

The chief descriptive statement which can be made about this Evangelical ethics is that it is the mode of life which issues out of a positive relation to God, as that relation is established by, through, and with Jesus Christ. It is *theocentric* ethics. It is the ethics which accompanies a dominant orientation of the self and the community toward the action of God. This is the grand idea which pervades the utterances of a Luther and a Calvin and which is symbolized by such phrases as "The Sovereignty of God" and "Justification by Faith," which is set forth in many variations in the *Sermon on Good Works* and in the *Institutes*. As the prophets call upon Israelites to drop their preoccupation with the maneuvers of their mundane enemies and with their own religious activities to turn their eyes to the workings of the living God, so the Reformers out of their own experience of mighty deeds of God proclaim, "We are not our own: therefore let us as far as possible forget ourselves and all things that are ours; we are God's; to him therefore let us live and die."

The distinction of this dynamically theocentric spirit in ethics from some of its specious surrogates will help make its character more evident. Because God is not known in his might and favor without the aid of a fallible authority it is easy to substitute pedagogical authority for the reality to which it directs attention. In Roman

Catholicism that temptation had resulted in concentration on the church so that Roman Catholic ethics tended to become the morality of those who were always oriented toward the church, listening to its commandments in the first place, and watching its deeds as the most important in the world. The Reformers were assured that the authority of the Bible was a corrective to this tendency and that the Bible could always be counted on to point away from itself to the God-in-Christ and Christ-in-God to whom it bore witness. Yet sometimes they themselves and more frequently their successors looked away from the living God to whom the Bible pointed and oriented themselves toward the Bible itself. The consequence was then a new legalism in which the question was no longer, "What doth the Lord require of thee?" but, "What does the Bible demand?" A God-centered ethics, however, looks with the Bible and through the Bible to the Lord of the Scriptures.[14] Similar reflections about the Spirit who leads men to God-in-Christ and Christ-in-God apply to the spiritualistic and subjectivistic perversion of Evangelical ethics, to the confusions of the authority of religious experience and of conscience with the God to whom they bear witness. Evangelical ethics, however, is not oriented toward the inner spirit or conscience but toward the transcendant [sic] God revealing himself in mighty acts—above all in the mighty act of Jesus Christ.

God-centered ethics is partly definable also by noting its differences from those orientations of life in which the center of attention is occupied by the negative counterparts of theocentrism. The acknowledgement that God saves us by his grace has as its

14. Niebuhr's note: [It may be that Evangelical thought in our time is more appreciative of the fallible authority of the church because it has recognized in consequence of the post-Reformation development both that there is fallibility in the Scriptures and that human fallibility can substitute the Bible for the God of the Bible almost as easily as it can put the church in place of the Lord of the church. At all events the tendency of modern Evangelical thought is to recognize the necessity and the fallibility of both these authorities and the idolatrous penchant of man to substitute any fallible authority for God.]

negative counterpart the conviction that we do not save ourselves from moral and spiritual death by our works. An ethics, however, which takes the latter conviction as its starting point will differ widely and radically from one which begins with the former. It will be an ethics of despair rather than of hope, a negatively humanistic rather than a positively theistic ethics. And it cannot but fall into a new defensiveness, though what will now be defended will not be man's righteousness but perhaps physical life or wealth or a recognizedly [*sic*] temporal and sinful culture. Again, the negative counterpart of the realization that God is holy is the realization that men are all profane and that they fall short of his glory in everything they do. But an ethics which starts with the realization of human ingloriousness, profaneness and sinfulness and in which men keep their eyes centered on the sin which stains all human acts will be profoundly different from the ethics of the glory of God. Evangelical ethics is God-centered, not sin-centered. When our fundamental orientation in life is that of persons who live vis à vis our own sinful selves rather than vis à vis God, the spirit of Evangelical ethics takes flight no less surely than when we live in the contemplation of our own righteousness.

It is, secondly, characteristic of Evangelical ethics that it is the mode of life which issues out of *faith in God*. Faith and God, as Luther often pointed out, belong together. And he made it equally clear that faith and ethics belong together. In Evangelical ethics faith is not a virtue which can be added to other moral excellencies. It is rather the root and ground of all man's free actions. The direction of a man's loyalty and trust gives direction to every act he performs, so that if he speaks with the tongues of men and of angels and sells all his goods to feed the poor but has not faith in God, these acts not only profit him nothing but are destructive of self and of others. The conduct of life issues out of the central faith, not as conclusions are drawn from premises but as fruit derives from trees. Men are so created that they cannot and do not live without faith. They must trust in a god, such as their own reason, or civilization, or one of the many other idols to which they look for salvation from meaningless existence. Hence the great ethical question is always the question of faith, "In what does man trust?" Moral reasoning always builds on the explicit or implicit answer given to this prior question. A mode of life that is not founded on faith in God is necessarily founded on some other faith. There is no faithless ethics. Moreover, it is clear to us in the Evangelical situation that God, the Lord of heaven and earth, the One we deal with in all our dealings, is never absent from us as we make our choices and guide our conduct in the directions given by our loyalties to idols. We can take no neutral attitude toward God. In our very acts of trust in idols we affirm our distrust of God; in our choices of good under the guidance of our loyalty to the self we reject the divine claim to our loyalty. There is no atheistic morality; it is either theistic or anti-theistic. If we do not trust God we distrust him, however much we may seek to hide this fact from ourselves by pretending to ignore him.

The recognition of this deep connection between conduct and faith is mated then with the understanding that reformation of faith is the reformation of life and that the great work of Christ for moral beings is his work as the renewer and transformer of faith. He redeems us by reconciling us to God, by winning us out of our distrust and fear of the Holy One, by drawing us away from our despairing trust in idols and in self. Faith in God is the gift of God through Jesus Christ and with that faith all things are given, including the transformation of human conduct.

Evangelical ethics is not, or course, the result of these insights but the result of faith itself. When statements about faith are substituted for faith in God, only perverted forms of Evangelical ethics can result, for then belief is substituted for trust and loyalty. When that takes place, as has often occurred and will often occur, our real trust is directed not toward God but toward a system of truths on which we depend for salvation from sin and death. A related perversion of Evangelical ethics issues in antinomianism rather than in legalism. This seems to happen when faith is separated from its divine object of trust. Then we say to ourselves that we are saved by faith rather than that God alone saves us and allow ourselves to do whatever we can do with confidence rather than those things which we can do with trust in God, the Father of Jesus Christ, and in loyalty to Christ. We are sometimes encouraged in this perversion of faith-ethics by our habit of reducing our fundamental principles to a kind of shorthand. For the statement that God saves us by faith we substitute the proposition that we are saved by faith and with the aid of this device theocentric ethics may become fido-centric ethics. So also for the commandment that we ought to love God and our neighbor we often substitute the statement that love is the law of life and so both indicate and encourage the substitution of a love-centered morality for a God-centered one. But Evangelical ethics is not an ethics of faith; it is the ethics of that *faith in God* which is given by, in, and through Jesus Christ.

Such God-centered, faith-founded ethics is, in the third place an ethics of *freedom*. Freedom is not a third and accidental attribute but belongs with God and faith as faith and God belong together. Where faith in God is present the self is free from concern for itself. It has not achieved freedom from concern for itself. It has not achieved freedom from self-concern, but has been set free by God through the gift of faith in him. It is able to accept itself as the forgiven self and as one which will continually be forgiven by God, not as though we did not take the self's sin seriously but as though he were determined to make it good and right, to redeem it from every physical and spiritual disease by whatever mild or harsh medicines and surgery are necessary. In the contemplation of Christ the mind moved by the spirit of repentance discovers at one an the same time how bound the moral self is to itself and how great was the freedom of Jesus Christ in this respect. Then, with the repentance and faith given through him, the divine possibility appears, that man can and will be free from self-concern as Christ was free.

With freedom from slavery to the self goes freedom from bondage to the physical and cultural values without which we think that we cannot live. How strict that bondage is, how heavily its chains lie on every thought and aspiration of men the whole history of our common and personal moral life indicates. Because the Jews had to cling to their culture with its values as the only reality that gave significance to their own existence they rejected Jesus Christ; and for the same reasons we who call ourselves Christians reject him over and over again. We cannot believe that if we will seek the kingdom of God and its righteousness all other things necessary to us will be given in free abundance. Do we not know what is necessary and do we not know that these things do not come to us without anxious thought? Hence we compromise the ethics of the gospel with the ethics of culture in many and devious ways. But with the gift of faith in God the possibility of freedom from this bondage arises into view as a promise that will be redeemed and is being redeemed. It does happen, not merely in visions of an eschatological future but in moments when eternity breaks into time that by faith God enables men to say, "Let goods and kindred go, this mortal life also, the body they may kill; God's truth abideth still; His Kingdom is forever." It is in such moments that the Evangelical ethics appears as a mode of life in freedom which, though impossible to man, is being made possible by God.

Another aspect of this freedom is release from bondage to the law. So long as the direct relation to God called faith does not exist or so long as the direct relation to him is one of distrust, we are necessarily under the authority of moral traditions, of churches, and states. They require us to do those things which, in their more or less fallible recognition of the nature of reality, are known to be necessary if we are to survive as men in communities. They must prohibit those deeds which arise out of our deep distrust of that reality and of one another. The direct encounter with God, the recognition on our own part of his omnipotence and goodness changes the bondage to men and their laws into a bondage to God. With that change there comes a great conversion of the power, spirit and content of the law. The law which is known to be God's, not one ascribed to him by men, has a force that compels our obedience. Known, moreover, as the demand of the One who is wholly good toward us, it takes on the character of counsel while bondage turns into the freedom of sonship. And again the content of the law known as law of God undergoes a metamorphosis; what was important becomes unimportant, what was insignificant becomes great. How these things can be, Paul and the Reformers have described over and over again. But the truth of what they have said only becomes apparent to us when we find ourselves in the Evangelical situation, while everything they have said is twisted into something different when we are defensive and self-justifying.

The freedom of the Evangelical mode of life is not only a freedom *from* but also a freedom *to*. How it is a freedom to love the neighbor Luther has wonderfully described. How it sets men free to deal creatively with the social and personal situations that confront them and to respond with inventiveness and artistry to the challenges they meet needs to be set forth more fully than has yet been done in either Catholic or Reformed theologies. In the thought of the Eastern church, as partly represented by Berdyaev, something of this dimension of Evangelical morality has been suggested though in connection with a dubious metaphysics of freedom. The free creativity of a faith-in-God morality can be illustrated by the works of a Paul and of many a lesser Christian, but its analysis in theology remains incomplete. Creative morality is not bound by rule, though it knows all the rules. It does not meet the changing situations of life with the repetition of acts found good in the past, but with deeds that fit the immediate situation, recognized as a situation in the kingdom of God. Taught by faith in the creating God, it discerns beauty and glory where these had been hidden to the distrustful eye and in the Master's workshop produces moral works of art. The tragic element is doubtless always in them since they are the works of forgiven sinners in a world of sin and forgiveness. Nevertheless they are creative and new.

Finally, the evangelical mode of life may be described as *momentary* in character. It is not a life that plans far ahead to insure the future, whether in heaven or on earth. It knows that God ties the present and the future together and that no provision for the morrow is necessary to the life which he redeems. Because the future is in the hands of Love therefore man is free to do the right thing now, that is, to love his neighbor. Because God is Lord of the present no less than of the future therefore the temporally insignificant deed may have more eternity in it than the one designed to outlast the years. Evangelical ethics does not underscore the melancholy wisdom of the world that all our pomp is to be reduced to ashes or that "the best-laid plans of mice and men gang aft a-gley." It sets this wisdom in the positive context of the affirmation that what has been done to the least of the brothers has been done unto him and that one day in the Lord's sight may be a thousand years. This "momentariness" which gets its meaning only from the presence of the eternal God who is Lord of both present and future is always offensive to our calculating human reason. Yet its apparent recklessness is deeply wise in the context of faith-knowledge.

Karl Barth has remarked that Luther wrote beautifully about Christian liberty—far too beautifully. It is easy to write too enthusiastically about the Evangelical ethics, as though the divine possibility for man had become a human possibility through the Incarnation and even through the Reformation. But it is also easy to write too skeptically about it, as though divine possibility were only a future event and as though God were not redeeming his promises and realizing his possibilities in this present world. The faith of the disciples remains smaller than a mustard seed and they remove no mountains; but it is not non-existent and sometimes they cast out demons by the power of God. The freedom to which Christ sets them free is used as the occasion for the new bondage; but cribbed and confined as they are in themselves, sometimes they do free deeds and perform acts of liberation. The rule of God does not appear in their works so that men can say, "Lo, here it is." But sometimes it appears in lightning flashes that illuminate the dark scene of self-justifying, defensive human life and give evidence of the energy waiting to be received and pressing into human existence.

The ethics of the Reformation with its duality of works-righteousness and faith-righteousness, of self-righteousness and righteousness in God, of life in the world of sin and life in the world of forgiveness is a testimony to the fact that the Christian lives between the times and between the worlds. But it is only the Evangelical element in that ethics that makes it Christian. Take that away and all that is left is an ethics of North European civilization, or of capitalism, or of democracy, or, perhaps, of socialism, or of that amorphous social religion called Protestantism.

Issues Between Catholics and Protestants

Niebuhr looked on the ecumenical movement that was sweeping the American church scene following World War II with a discriminating eye. In this instance, we see him protesting the idolatrous faith in the nation that was prompting political leaders in the name of "tolerance" to call on American Catholics and Protestants to form a united religious front against communism. Also apparent in this article is the emphasis he placed on ecumenism as a spiritual undertaking. Catholics and Protestants could only be drawn into a closer relationship if they looked at each other from the standpoint of charity rather than fear. At the same time, holding fast to the truth that divided them could produce a form of "creative conflict" that might be of benefit to all of Christendom as well as to each of their denominational families.

Source: *Religion in Life* 23 (Spring 1954): 199–205.

Too many discussions of Protestant-Catholic relations are carried on as though the great issues that divide or unite the confessions were primarily political or cultural. The attitude of Roman Catholicism toward democratic institutions, the effectiveness of Protestantism as an agency for the preservation of civil liberties, the need for unity among all Christians in common opposition to Communism—these and like matters are debated. In this context, also, pleas for mutual toleration are made, that the national life may not be divided and political issues may remain unconfused by religious loyalties.

Both genuine Catholic and genuine Protestant Christians cannot but feel very uneasy about this way of dealing with their problem. Neither group, however dear to them their culture and nations are, can accept as a presupposition of the whole Catholic-Protestant argument the proposition that these are the primary goods or the first objects of loyalty. For neither is toleration for the sake of maintaining political harmony the greatest of the virtues, however commendable and desirable it is in all matters that are subject to compromise. They cannot help but find occasion for humor in the tolerance of men who brook no heresies or schisms in the political realm while they constantly urge tolerance on those who are concerned "merely" with matters of religion, who condemn religious while they carry on political inquisitions. Such people look on the wars of religion in the past as though they were great follies, but regard wars for political principles as tragic necessities.

The faith that forms the common background of Catholics and Protestants and which at the same time divides them, insofar as it requires different actions from each, is, after all, a faith in nothing human but in the kingdom of God. The virtue that they seek to exercise in their relations with each other, insofar as they are Catholic and Protestant *Christians*, is not tolerance but charity. The confession of faith both groups repeat is not an oath of allegiance to a national flag (they live in many countries) but the *Credo;* and their common prayer is not "God bless America" but "Thy kingdom come, Thy will be done on earth as it is in heaven." That in America as elsewhere they pray for their country and seek to discharge faithfully their civil responsibilities is evident enough; but it is certain that neither Protestantism nor Catholicism is a variant form of the religion of nationalism, and that neither has defined the preservation of democracy or any other form of government as the chief end of man. This is not to say that there are not members in both groups who are not primarily nationalists or primarily devotees of the religion of democracy or of some other human institution; but neither group as such, whether we think of it historically, geographically or credally, can be defined by reference to such aberrations.

I

When we begin—as Protestants now—to reflect upon the problem of our relations to Roman Catholics as a problem in the kingdom of God rather than in Western civilization or something of that sort, we soon discover that we are united to our apparent opponents by the very principle that also divides us, namely, by a common loyalty to the kingdom of God, or to the reign of Jesus Christ. We are required by our acknowledgement of the reality of that realm and of our duty to it to honor them as those who believe in and are loyal to the same cause. Yet we note that we are required by the specific demand that this kingdom makes upon us to contend with them, insofar as we are convinced that their understanding of the duties of citizenship contains great fallacies as a result of a certain confusion of the kingdom of God with the church. We must contend with them; for that is our duty in obedience to God as we understand this obedience—saying to them, "We must obey God rather than man" even though the man be representative of the church. Yet at the same time we recognize them as bound to us and we to them in a common life, as we are not bound to those who make the culture or the nation the supreme object of loyalty.

We may press the analogy of politics a little further; our attitude toward Roman Catholics in the kingdom of God seems to be something like the attitude of a great political party in a modern nation towards an opposing party. There may be a certain bitterness in this relation, because great issues are at stake, but there is no avoiding the recognition that the opposing group is part of the same commonwealth and, despite all charges of treason that are leveled against each other, the recognition is present that there is probably as much loyalty to the commonwealth in the opposition party as in our own. For Catholics and Protestants, however, the homeland is always the Divine Commonwealth.

Insofar, then, as we try to think and deal with our fellow-Christians within this context of the kingdom of God, two attitudes seem required of us in our relations with each other—the attitudes of charity and of creative conflict.

We are bound in the context of the kingdom of God to look upon Roman Catholicism with charity rather than with tolerance. Tolerance, as usually understood, is too weak a virtue for this situation. It is passive rather than active; it does not affirm the other's value but simply accepts it. The charity that is required and possible in this context is not the product of pleasant good will but rather of the experience of Divine Grace. It will appear, therefore, as gratitude for the good gifts that have been given to us through our neighbor, in this case our neighbor church. No Protestant looking at Roman Catholicism in the context of grace will be able to escape a sense of profound thankfulness to God for the values that have been mediated to him through this great Church.

He will think perhaps first of all of the Christian heritage that he has received from the ancient and medieval Catholic Church—of the liturgy, the theology, the discipline on which he with his fellow Christians continues to be dependent in his personal and in the common life. Though as Protestant he has placed the Bible far above tradition, yet he has found that he needs tradition as an illuminator of the Scriptures and so as a guide to faith and practice. However he may need to protest against any exaltation of tradition above the Scriptures, yet he continues to use the prayers, the ceremonies, the symbols, the art and many of the forms of organization that the pre-Reformation church developed. As he uses these gifts he will ask himself the question whether he would not have dissipated this heritage had not Roman Catholicism with its guardianship of these treasures been the constant companion of his Protestantism through the centuries. When he remembers what Protestantism in certain periods of extreme fervor did in the way of destroying the traditional heritage, he will be inclined to think that he owes the preservation of many of these gifts not to his own Protestant fathers but to the Roman Catholic Church.

Protestantism again must feel gratitude to God for the fact that he has given Roman Catholicism to it as its companion to prevent it from falling into anarchism. In the polarity of freedom and order, Protestantism has always tended to this side of freedom. This has been part of its mission and vocation, to preach and practice the liberty of the Christian man. But the emphasis carries hazards with it: had Protestantism not been subject to due pressure of the great unified, ordered Catholic Church, it could easily have fallen into an even greater particularism and atomism than marks its present existence. Not only the example of unity in Roman Catholicism but the competition that this church has offered to its Christian rival in the West has contributed to the maintenance of those elements of unity and order that are present in Protestantism.

The Protestant, when his mind is illuminated by some charity, also notes that Roman Catholic theology, with its great stability, has at times maintained Christian truths close to the heart of Protestantism with greater effectiveness than Protestantism itself. There have been periods in history when the Roman Church has known, better than many of us who are outside of it, how important the truth of "justification by faith" is. When Protestantism, or parts of it, tended in the direction of humanism, it was Roman Catholicism which maintained the principle of the sovereignty of God. Sometimes it was this Roman Church, more than the Protestant, that resisted human authority when this conflicted with the authority of the word of God.

The Protestant who regards Roman Catholicism in the light of charity sees other characteristics in it than the man who approaches it with fear. Fearsomeness sees the Roman Church as a great monolithic, authoritarian structure, threatening the life of diversified evangelicalism and of pluralistic society. But love notes that this structure is by no means so centralized, unified, and militant as anxiety pictures it to be. There is a rich diversity in that Catholicism, a grand variety in the unity. Augustinianism is mated with Aristotelianism in its thought; its theology does not come to rest in a static system but is engaged in continual dialectic; the piety of mysticism softens and enriches the piety of fideism; among Gothic structures, physical and intellectual, highly modern edifices make their appearance. There are stresses and strains, also, in this apparently single-minded movement—stresses that are good not only for those who seem to stand in its way but for the Catholic Church itself. The historic polarities of the great Church and monastic protests against its secularism, between clergy and laity, between higher and lower clergy, have their counterparts in the modern organization. The orders correct and criticize each other; anticlericalism in the movement itself is a counterpoise to clericalism. Catholic anti-Protestantism is subject to Catholic protests by those who are above all Catholic Christians.

In light of charity the Protestant sees a Roman Catholicism that he does not need to fear. He finds within that movement itself men and groups that are as deeply concerned about what seem to him to be the paramount interests as he is himself. Fearful Protestantism, seeing universal sinfulness, discovers in the apparent opponent only the desire for power and a threat to its own existence; believing Protestantism, aware of universal grace, marks the presence in the opponent of inner restraints upon the desire for power and discovers helpfulness rather than danger. It notes with appreciation how in history popes have tried to restrain extremist political persecutors of Protestantism, or vice versa; how Catholic laity have contended for religious freedom.

All human reality is, of course, mixed but there are always present in it not only those aspects which fear discerns but also those features that charity discovers, and fear is blinder than love is. So the Protestant, regarding Roman Catholicism in the kingdom of God, says to himself that Catholicism is present by the will of God and that it is not the divine desire that Protestantism should alone represent Christian faith. He notes that Catholicism is doing tasks which Protestantism does not and probably cannot perform; that its presence is of benefit to the Protestant churches themselves, as well as mankind at large.

II

Nevertheless the conflict remains. Protestantism continues to protest against the Roman Catholic version of the faith; it is subject to Catholic attacks upon its existence. In trying to regard this situation from the point of view of the common life in the kingdom of God, the Protestant recognizes that the vocation which he needs to carry out involves him in conflict with Roman Catholicism. He does not exist as a Protestant for the sake of that conflict; to be a Protestant is not to be an anti-Catholic; he exists and his communities have their being for the sake of pointing to the positive work of God as the only Savior and Justifier. Yet this witness involves him in antagonisms with those who seem to have another vocation, who seem to him to point more to the means of grace than to grace itself, to church than to the church's cause.

Protest against deification of anything finite leads to protest against what he must regard as a divinization of the Church; to be sure, in our time, it must lead even more to protest against the divinization of the nation, but the earlier protest also remains in force. He protests against Mariolatry and the worship of the saints, though he is even more profoundly concerned to affirm and practice the sole worship of God. It is his vocation to criticize the confusion of the faith with certain philosophical and social ideas of the past though, positively, it is even more his vocation to understand and to confess what he believes. In this situation he will always find himself in a certain conflict with Roman Catholicism; but insofar as the positive element in his vocation is in the forefront of his mind, and insofar as he is aware of other challenges to Christian faith than the one he sees in Catholicism, the conflict can be for him and his opponent a creative rather than a destructive one. On the positive side there remains great unity present among those who are divided by the secondary, though important, issues.

Protestantism, true to its past and its principle, will be less concerned to maintain political freedom of religion than it will be to exercise its duty of worshipping freely and of proclaiming its faith boldly. It did not receive religious freedom as a grant from the state, but exercised that freedom in carrying out its duty to God before any state conceded the right. Should the time come when Protestants do not exercise this freedom except when political and ecclesiastical powers permit them to do so, Protestantism will have vanished in reality, whatever vestigial remnants of a past Protestantism may remain. In America the state did not grant religious freedom to its citizens; it recognized that the right to religious freedom belongs to man as man, as citizens of the universal society, and that a state's interference with that liberty is transgression. This recognition was dependent upon the actual exercise of religious freedom and of religious responsibility by Christians during days when the state was intolerant; they had won religious freedom despite the state, not through it or because of it.

In its exercise of free religion Protestantism will doubtless always be in a certain conflict with the Roman Catholic Church since the latter believes that there can be only one "true religion," while Protestantism as such knows little about one "true religion" and is concerned with devotion to the one true God. But whatever perils Protestantism may encounter in this conflict, these will ultimately arise out of its own failures of conviction rather than out of the convictions of its opponent.

III

If we look at Protestant–Roman Catholic relations in this way it may seem to us, also, that we Protestants may be making a contribution to Roman Catholicism, and that it, in its own way, may be able to look upon us also with Christian charity while it engages with us in creative conflict. Perhaps it is part of our function as Protestants, in the present as in the past, to contribute something to the development of the church in the world by stimulating Roman Catholicism to build up and reform its own structure as well as by advancing our movement. Certain Roman Catholic theologians have remarked that Reformation was a great event in the life of the Catholic as well as in the life of the Protestant church, that the old Church was thoroughly reformed while a Reformed Church was being founded. It is apparent, also, that Roman Catholicism is very different in spirit and action in those countries where a strong Protestantism acts as its critic and more or less friendly ally than in regions where it exists alone. So it may be that Protestant missions in South America, in Italy and Spain, will contribute more to Christianity by leading to the self-criticism of the Catholic Church in those areas than they will be able to contribute directly by building up great Protestant movements there.

If we approach Protestant-Roman Catholic relations in this mood—one of thanksgiving and of confidence that the conflict is meaningful—we shall also look forward to the future with the hope that at some time the great division in Christendom will be overcome, though as Protestants we will not be able, for the sake of unity, to abandon those principles which tend to our exclusion from the Catholic Church. For the preservation of the church's unity is a less important duty to our conscience than the proclamation of "grace alone."

Why Restudy Theological Education?

Clamor for change marked the postwar climate in American education, and there was just as much dissatisfaction with the status quo that pervaded seminaries and theological schools. Hence, the American Association of Theological Schools in 1954 asked Niebuhr to conduct a thorough study of theological education in the United States and Canada. In this article, he presented his reasons for undertaking the project. For him, it was the Protestant principle that compelled Christians in every age to assess their deeds in repentance and with hope, and the trending of society toward secularization and the church toward ecumenism in the 1950s made it all the more imperative for this kind of study to take place. His longstanding appreciation of the paradoxical features of church-world relationships becomes apparent as well in his vision of the church as both a "fellowship of faith" and the "seed-plot of a new humanity." When seen in this way, he declared, "the church becomes the preacher and the pastor to society while the ministry becomes the leadership of a ministering church."

Source: *The Christian Century* 71 (April 28, 1954): 516–17.

The question whether theological education should be restudied has been raised frequently in recent years; as often as it has been raised it has been answered in the affirmative. Since Mark May and William Adams Brown issued the voluminous study of education for the ministry in 1934 various denominations have made new inquiries into their own work in this area. The Presbyterian Church, U.S., made a survey of its colleges and theological seminaries in 1942. The Northern Baptist Convention sponsored a survey by Hugh Hartshorne and associates in 1944–45. The Methodist Church followed in 1946 with a study of its own institutions by John L. Seaton. A special inquiry into the education of the ministers of the

Universalist and Unitarian churches is now under way, and the Disciples of Christ have very recently held a conference dealing with this subject. The Presbyterian Church, U.S.A., and the Methodist Church have just organized committees for a new examination of theological education in their denominational schools. In addition to all this many individual seminaries have undertaken in the years since the close of World War II to make more or less comprehensive studies of the effectiveness of their work and have frequently reorganized curricula, methods of teaching, admissions policies, and so on, in consequence of their findings.

The study of theological education in the United States and Canada that the American Association of Theological Schools has now set in motion is therefore only the most recent among many similar ventures. In this situation it may be able to serve a double purpose. On the one hand, this study may be able to draw together into a cooperative and hence mutually constructive enterprise the various special inquiries, since schools and denominations are frequently isolated from each other as they carry on their research, and hence do not adequately profit from each other's experiences, observations, analyses and insights. On the other hand, the enterprise may be able to represent the interests in theological education of the larger church or of the Christian people in this American sector of world Christendom.

Concern Widespread

However that may be, it is evident that wide-scale concern for theological education and its improvement is a characteristic element in contemporary church life. There are doubtless many reasons why this concern has arisen. In part the churches and the schools reflect the same interest which is evident in America and perhaps Western society in general. Since the end of the war education has been the subject of much reflection and there has been much searching of souls among college administrators, teachers and others responsible for the training of youth. Many of our large universities have projected more or less radical reorganizations of the teaching program; books on the problem of the university continue to come from the press; teacher training programs are being subjected to new and critical study; professional schools of every sort are surveying and reorganizing their work.

It is, of course, true that the restlessness indicated is in part characteristic of the general movement of mind in our Western world. Since the days of the Reformation, but particularly since the beginning of the 19th century, the questioning of tradition has become traditional. We have not been content to do things as they have always been done; respect for the fathers' methodologies is not great in any sphere of our culture. But there are also more particular reasons in our time for this widespread concern for education. In part its source is to be sought in the society's and the educators' dissatisfaction with present processes. In part fear of the future is responsible for the new ferment.

Discontent with Educational Results

There is dissatisfaction in the schools as faculties regard some of the apparent results of the work that they have been doing. Sometimes when they observe the narrowness of view that is characteristic of some of the leaders of social institutions they question whether these could have gained very much from their years in college and secondary schools. More specifically, they are worried about the effects of the specialization that has been a characteristic feature of modern education. In professional schools in particular—such as the engineering, medical and law schools—the question is raised whether specialized training without a broad humanistic background and without accompanying education in morals and "values" can be adequate. At the same time the pressure for a type of education that will prepare men for specialized professional work in society continues to be very great. The problem of relating specialized knowledge or skills with moral and philosophical and religious understanding is an acute one.

There is another source of dissatisfaction. The conviction is widespread that the critical attitude towards tradition in the Western world has resulted in an anti-traditionalism that has cut contemporary culture loose from its roots so that it is in danger of withering. How to bring education into contact again with the living tradition of the long past out of which modern science, literature and political life have grown is the question many educators are asking. In consequence of the inquiries, many have undertaken to reintroduce into the curriculum of the modern school the study of the classics of the past and have shown a real concern for the introduction of the great religious tradition as well as of the political and philosophical bases of Western civilization.

It is not only dissatisfaction with contemporary education that is responsible for the concern. The educator in the nature of the case needs to look ahead for almost a generation. He has before him young people who will not become leaders of society until twenty or thirty years have elapsed. Consciously or unconsciously he tends to think of the challenges they will need to face in that relatively distant future and to take seriously his responsibility of preparing them to meet them. But he does not know what these problems will be. This future seems to him to be both hazardous and hopeful. The speed with which the conditions change under which men are living is constantly accelerating.

Trying to Pierce the Future

What the consequences of the scientific and industrial revolution will be in political and human terms can hardly be foreseen, yet it seems evident that the youth of today will need to meet problems different in character and in scope, more pregnant with danger and great possibility, than have been even those great issues that the present generation has been required to face. Every responsible education is therefore seriously engaged in answering the question as to what he can do for these young people who must be helped to answer problems not yet raised.

Theological education participates in this general movement but it does so in a rather special way. It is an education that Christians seek to carry on and therefore it is not characterized by that same reliance on the educational process itself that is present in so much of the secular society. There the question how folk are to be prepared for the future tends to be answered by reference to knowledge rather than to faith. But those who are responsible for theological education have no less of a sense of their duty. They may not be as frenetic in the search for educational answers to questions of life and death, but the feeling of obligation to do the very best they can as educators is not diminished by the recognition that unless "the Lord builds the house they labor in vain that build it" and that "the foolishness of God is wiser" than the plans of the educated. Though they are undergirded by their faith in the providence of God, they are at the same time subject perhaps to an even deeper dissatisfaction with the results of their own efforts than are the secular-minded. The dissatisfaction of ministers, church boards, theological schools and others with what they have done and are doing in theological education necessarily has something of the character of repentance and change of mind.

Dissatisfaction Felt by Theological Faculties

The dissatisfaction of theological educators like those of other teachers are [sic] also specific. They are concerned about the question of specialized versus general education. In some respects, to be sure, the problem in theology is the reverse problem to the one encountered in specialized secular education. In many schools at least, theological education has doubtless helped students to arrive at broad views and a general orientation in life but has given them inadequate professional training; criticisms of the schools on this point are constant. The many specialized forms of the ministry in the city and rural churches, in college communities and in the so-called foreign fields, demand a specific training that has often not been given. The demand for more professional training arises also in connection with the responsibility of the minister not only for preaching but for pastoral counseling, church administration, youth work, leadership in social policy formulations and like matters.

However, the opposite problem also comes to appearance in the schools that prepare men for the ministry. In some of them the multiplication of specialized courses has developed to such an extent that the question of "integration" is a serious one. To the old curriculum with its emphasis upon Bible, history, theology and homiletics there have been added many more or less highly specialized courses in religious education, social ethics, social problems and policy, psychology of religion and psychology of counseling, rural sociology, rural church work, industrial relations, race relations, student work, religious leadership in colleges, religion in the arts, and so on and on. Hence the problem arises how all this work is to be brought into a single focus and how men shall be prepared to become ministers of the church rather than "professionals." The suggestion that the period of time to be devoted to theological study be lengthened from three to four years is being widely made and considered. Perhaps it is a partial answer to the problems that have been raised; perhaps it is an evasion of the real question.

Contact with a Living Past

In a very special way the church needs to deal with the question of the relationship to the past, though theological education never separated itself so sharply from the great tradition as secular education did. Nevertheless, it also frequently tended to move from Scriptures to the contemporary scene without participating in that long dialogue with the Scriptures which marked the centuries between the first and the twentieth. Today there is in the church as a whole a growing interest in resuming contact with a living past. The newer movements in the development of church worship as well as in theology give evidence of this interest.

Beyond all this, the church itself has risen into view as a great historical community. If on the one hand it no longer appears simply as an evangelistic church seeking to save individual souls—though this also it must do—on the other hand it also appears as something other than a social agency whose mission in society might be comparable to that of the political organization or the school. It appears as a great community, a "body of Christ," a fellowship of faith, the seed-plot of a new humanity. And when the church is so understood and so valued, then the ministry of the church is also seen in a new perspective. It is no longer a profession like law, medicine and teaching, though it shares some of the characteristics of these professions. Its service to the society outside the church is conceived in terms of the church itself; now the church becomes the preacher and the pastor to society while the ministry becomes the leadership of a ministering church.

It is this new perspective on the church which is partly responsible for the concern of its leaders with theological education. Pastors, mission boards, bishops, lay leaders and many others are looking to the seminaries not for final answers to the questions they raise about the nature of this church, about its mission and organization, but nevertheless they rightly expect from them some guidance and great activity in reflection. The schools are to a certain extent focal points of the church's life and work.

In all of this the sense of the critical future is present. New possibilities and new problems arise for the church as it faces the unknown years ahead. How shall the church, how shall the ministry of the future, help human beings to meet hopefully and constructively, in repentance and in faith, the great problems that lie ahead? How shall the church in its ministry communicate its gospel to the people of a strange culture? The problem is not merely that of preaching to Chinese or to Indians but that of communicating to the people of the secularized culture, present in all regions of the earth. There are signs of a religious hunger in folk who have been long alienated from God and Christ as the church has proclaimed them. There are certainly signs that the relevance of faith to human existence is being more widely understood.

How the church is to meet this contemporary and future challenge is a question in the minds of many. The need for examining its proclamation and its total work, of maintaining the great tradition while being highly critical of the "traditions of men," including its own, becomes increasingly acute.

There is a closely related problem: how shall the contemporary churches prepare men through education for work in the great world church? The ecumenical movement, most manifest to us in its original form, is much wider and deeper than appears in the efforts to achieve such organization. It is a movement of the spirit and of the mind. It appears in the growing unity of the church in the spirit as well as the forms of its worship. It appears in the increasing recognition of the values in the theologies and ethical activities of other denominations than one's own. In the nature of the case no ministry today can be as exclusively denominational as was that of a generation ago. Yet the special heritage of each Christian order must also be safeguarded, lest the great church be impoverished.

These are only some of the reasons, or suggestions of reasons, for the restudy of theological education. Such reexamination, with the reorganization attendant on it, is something that the churches living in repentance and hope are always required to do. The call to do it now is particularly strong.

Theology—Not Queen But Servant

This article is the published version of Niebuhr's address to a convocation held in the summer of 1954 at the University of Chicago's Rockefeller Chapel, where he also was given an honorary degree. With the meeting of the World Council of Churches taking place at the time on the other side of town, he appears to have seen this moment as an opportunity to set forth a version his own longstanding commitment to world ecumenism rather than just the churchly expressions of unity and cooperation. In this address, he provides an eloquent definition of the "theological idea of a university." This definition explores various dimensions of the "servant" role of theology in bringing together a multitude of diverse, and sometimes conflicting, areas of study on the campus of an institution of higher education into relationships of "mutual limitation" and "mutual service," not only with each other, but as partners with the nation and its churches in working for the common good of the universal family of humankind.

Source: *The Journal of Religion* 35 (January 1955): 1–5.

We celebrate today the close of a term at the University of Chicago while a great congress of churchmen and theologians is meeting in the neighborhood under the auspices of the World Council of Churches. This university long concerned with the reinvigoration and reorganization of learning is honoring theology in the persons of some of its representatives and has invited a teacher of theology to give the convocation address. In such circumstances it seems appropriate to consider the place of our ancient discipline in the hierarchy, or the republic, or the anarchy, of human studies.

There are some who see only anarchy in what was once, they believe, a universe of science. They look with nostalgia toward a mythical golden age when stable order prevailed in intellectual society. Then, they think, academic lions and lambs lived in peace under the benign government of Queen Theology; and all the faculties—of schools as of men—worked together for good. In that beautifully ordered hierarchy of learning and instruction, first things always came first; the intellectual virtues were properly exalted above moral or civil excellence; and in cultivation of those virtues ultimate values—the grand old trinity of the beautiful, the good, and the true—were given rightful precedence over the merely empirical, the natural, and historical as proper objects of contemplation.

Something very important is often forgotten by the devotees of that myth. In the spotted reality of the medieval world it was not theology that governed the universities but rather the empirical church; just as it was not metaphysics but the city state that dominated the thought of Greece and as it is not natural science but the nation-state and economic utilitarianism that tend to control intellectual life today. It is also forgotten that theology no less than other human inquiries was in servitude then and that when the great emancipation took place, theology, no less than humanistic studies and natural science, participated in the revolt. It did not abdicate a rule it never held; it pointed rather to a sovereignty that no human institution—whether a church or a state or a science—could usurp without inviting catastrophe.

The modern university developed amid the complex interactions of Renaissance, Reformation, and nationalism; of natural science, religious awakenings, modern technology, and popular government. In that confused history, theology sometimes played only a minor role; sometimes it became the servant of other human sovereigns—of states using churches and schools for the sake of achieving national conformity, of popular opinion trying to speak with the voice of God. Servant to these, it sometimes functioned for them as taskmaster and censor of other studies. But whenever it returned to its proper loyalty and achieved its own freedom to serve only its Lord, it also contributed to the liberation of its fellow-sciences from servitude to finite dominion. The other side of the picture is this: whenever some pretender to absolute sovereignty has arisen, it was usually theology that he sought, first of all, to buy or cudgel into servitude and, failing that, to eradicate. Never the queen, theology has always had to choose whom it would serve and in what service to find freedom.

Today it sometimes seems to us as if in the various human communities—the intellectual as well as the political and religious—no choice is left to us save the one between a complete pluralism and an absolute, though artificial, monism. On the one hand, we can continue, it appears, in the direction of what, theologically regarded, is a proliferating polytheism; on the other hand, we are asked to submit for the sake of order and peace to some overlordship, whether this be exercised in the name of a nation or cause whose security is valued beyond all other goods, or of a movement that promises to deliver man from evil by five easy five-year stages. Polytheism is as real in reputedly irreligious modern society as it ever was, though now the gods go by the name of "values" or "powers." In our religious zeal we serve truth for truth's sake only, health for health's sake, life for life's sake, man for man's sake, nation for nation's sake. These many objects of devotion are further pluralized into many kinds of truth, many incomparable, existing individual men, many nations, many lives irreverent toward one another. The greater the fragmentation, the greater is the peril—and the attractiveness—of some monistic organization of study as of devotion. Ought we not to organize our polytheism into an idolatrous pantheon governed by the most attractive value or the most dynamic power of the moment?

The radically monotheistic theology that played a part in earlier reformations of churches, nations, and universities points, I believe, to another alternative. To be sure, as a theology of protest against the assumption of sovereignty by any finite power or against the presumption of any human voice to speak the ultimate word, it seems to invite pluralism and fragmentation in schools, churches, and nations. But the protest is only the negative side of the positive conviction which such theology seeks to demonstrate. This is the conviction that there is an ultimate word, a Word of God, that there is a universal Sovereignty, or, better, that the Universal Power is good; it is the conviction that man when he is right in any way—right in inquiry, right in thought, right in conduct, right in belief—is right by faith, right by virtue of his reliance upon and his loyalty to the last Word and Universal Sovereign. Such theology does not undertake to be the science of God, for it knows that the Transcendent Universal is known or acknowledged only in acts of universal loyalty and in transcending confidence, precedent to all inquiry and action. Loyalty and confidence of that sort, it knows, are not demonstrated more in so-called "religious" acts than in so-called "secular" activities. Hence it calls attention to the way in which every individual, group, and institution are [sic] directly related to the Transcendent whether positively in trust and loyalty or negatively in distrust and disloyalty.

The part that these convictions have played in the political field in the development of what we call "democracy" has again become the subject of considerable discussion. What does it mean to a state that it is "under God"—without absolute sovereignty, directly responsible to the Transcendent, one institution among many with similar responsibilities to the same One; having citizens who are, first of all, citizens of another, prior, and universal Commonwealth? The alternative to pluralistic democracy, in which every man is a king or every minority or majority group the court of last resort, is not a dictatorship of an individual or a class or of the national will, but a democracy in which loyalty to the universal Commonwealth and its constitution is maintained, though no single human power or institution—including the church or the people—can represent that Great Republic or do anything except point to it and to try to be loyal to it.

Perhaps the theological idea of a university is as little realized anywhere in the world today as is the radically monotheistic idea of democracy. But as the latter is an ingredient in the life of many nations, so the former seems to be hiddenly present in the activities many intellectual societies. At least it seems so to the theologian. He finds many colleagues in the university who will not or cannot speak his language in whom the essential elements of what he calls life in faith are present. They practice, without confessing, a universal loyalty; they count upon the victory of universal truth and justice; they exercise a constant repentance, a *metanoia*, in self-examination and the search for disinterestedness; their scientific humility seems to have a religious quality. But whatever be the present situation, it seems worth while that we should examine some of the main features of the idea of such a university.

It is, in the first place, a university which takes it [*sic*] place alongside church and state and other communities or institutions without subordination to any one of these. It is as directly responsible to the Transcendent in the performance of its particular duties of study and teaching as they are in their administration of the laws or in their preaching and worship. It is under obligation to try to understand what is true for all men everywhere in the universal community and to communicate the truths it understands without bearing false witness against any neighbor, whatever be their loyalties or privileges. Located in a nation, it is not of the nation but of the universe, part of a culture, it can but try to transcend the outlook of that culture.

Further, this theological idea of a university is the thought of a community of learning which is undergirded by the confidence that the nature of things is such that bias, deceit, and falsehood, issuing from individual and social self-interestedness, cannot in any long run—in the final judgment, so to speak—triumph over honesty and rigorous self-discipline in study and communication.

Again, it is the idea of a university in which the intellectual virtues neither assume priority over the moral goods of character nor assert their independence, but where the intellect is directed toward the universal in an intellectual confidence in the unity of all truths in him, an intellectual hope of salvation from error and falsehood as well as from ignorance. As universities, churches, and states exist alongside one another in mutual service and mutual limitation—interacting communities in one great commonwealth—so the intellectual activities are carried on in constant interaction with civil and moral activities and with the religious exercise of prayer and confession. There have been times, indeed, when theology has undertaken to substitute for the old aristocratic idea of the supremacy of the intellectual virtues a romantic exaltation of the life of feeling or a nominalist, pragmatic assertion of the priority of will. But under the discipline of its own fundamental convictions it has again rejected these new hierarchies, acknowledging that the problem is not whether heart or mind or strength should be supreme but whether each should be directed toward the Universal and Transcendent or perverted toward the particular and exclusive. And this seems to be in accord with experience, for the battles of the intellect for freedom are directed less against sentimentalism and willfulness than against the pettiness of mind and intellectual dogmatism, as the problem of the will is not so much the problem of maintaining itself against reason as of learning to say, "Not my will be done, but Thine." It is a poor theology that makes human reason the image and representative of

God, but the theology that puts feeling, albeit a religious feeling, or moral will above reason in the service and similitude of God is no less idolatrous.

In a university in which the radically monotheistic idea comes to expression, the various departments, schools, and methods are related to one another in mutual service, including the service of mutual limitation and creative conflict. The theology of radical monotheism knows that the Second Commandment is implicit in and equal to the First. If the first requirement of every man in every action is loyalty to the Universal and Transcendent, its corollary is loyalty to all other being emanating from and proceeding toward that Beginning and End of all. A kind of equalitarianism must prevail, therefore, in the universal society, not only among individual men, communities, and cultures but among the orders of being. Matter and spirit, mind and body, nature and supernature, proceed from the one source and are found together in one community in which there is no high or low, no chain of being, but in which each kind of being is entitled to reverence, understanding, and service, while it, in turn, is servant to the rest. And as all beings are bound together in mutual dependence, so the students of their natures and their relations are necessarily united in interdependent service.

There is another element in the equalitarianism of such a university. In it the common recognition is present that pretension to deity is universal among men, that in one way or another we all try to play god. Preachers and priests and theologians want to be theocrats, but so in their own way do the guardians of other traditions and the seekers after another knowledge. Economic interpretations of the self and naturalistic explanations of the way all things came into existence take their place alongside ecclesiastical orthodoxies. Where this is known and acknowledged, where it is understood and confessed—with irony and humor—that all of us are involved in this pretentiousness, there limitation and criticism by one another, even occasional humiliation, are not resented but reluctantly welcomed as a kind of mutual service. Creative conflict prevents such a university from being too beautifully ordered to be alive.

In a university controlled by such a faith, theology can by no means be queen. In so far as it is theology based on confidence in God and on loyalty to the Universal Community, radically monotheistic rather than polytheistic in character, it can only ask for a place of service. It enters into the company of faith sciences and studies, not to be ministered unto, but to minster. To be sure, it scorns the role of sycophant, for it has its own responsibility and freedom under God. It looks with distaste on the kinds of activities that call themselves theology but which, instead of being concerned with man's relation to God, are efforts at the self-justification of human religion, whether in the presence of the community of natural science or of a society intent on the achievement of security or peace of mind. It knows itself to be, first of all, a servant of God. It does not presume to believe that because it is concerned with the knowledge of God, it is therefore pre eminently his servant. On the contrary, it realizes that its temptations to try to be more than servant are perhaps greater than those of other studies. But in the service of God it is also the servant of its fellow servants. It is servant of the church, seeking to serve the faith that the church, when it is really church, tries to express in word and deed. Theology is not automatically church any more than literary criticism is necessarily literature or logic wisdom. Its function is service to the church, by means of the criticism of religion and of the effort to help the church understand what it believes. The theology which is servant to the church under God is also a servant of the university and of political society, since not only the church is in the Kingdom of God and since faith exists and does its work not only in the church. Within the university, theology does not undertake to render service with the freedom of the uncommitted; but this is not less a loss of freedom, since the wholly uncommitted are free only to serve themselves. It cannot seek truth for its own sake, but only for the sake of the divine glory—truth as reflection of the nature of being itself. Insofar as it does that, seeking truth not for the sake of the church's glory or in order to glorify anything at all except the Transcendent Source and End of all things, its work in the university will not be less free than that of other inquiries. It ought to be the freest of all. As a fellow servant of truth in this sense, theology takes its place in the university alongside other inquiries, never separated from them, never dependent upon them, never isolating itself with them from the totality of the common life which is the universe.

Sometimes, indeed, our faith grows very dim. Is not this world a "pluriverse" in which a scattered human race wanders aimlessly, fights fruitlessly, moves toward nothing? But then the gift of faith returns; confidence is resurrected, as Chesterton puts it, the flag of the world is unfurled. In such moments theology is reborn; then we re-establish and reorganize our universities; we call our scattered churches together and summon our states to abandon their fears and to maintain the unity of mankind. In such hours theology takes queenly pride in her handmaiden's role.

Martin Luther and the Renewal of Human Confidence

This lecture, which Niebuhr gave at a relatively small Lutheran university in the Midwest, illustrates another way in which he sought to reclaim the church's Reformation heritage. At the time, there was still ample evidence of a religious revival in America. But to Niebuhr, it looked more like the critical point to which the medieval church had come when Martin Luther burst onto the scene. Just as it had in the sixteenth century, the church, with its reliance on dated doctrinal formulations, was again giving people familiar with the evil unleashed by war and facing a future marked by scientific innovation more reasons for doubt than faith. Luther stood out in his time because on the basis of his own faith journey he offered something "new" derived directly from the word of God. Niebuhr did not venture to say whether the contemporary church, as it moved into its own future, would be able to inspire a similar "renewal of human confidence." But the example of Luther gave him a measure of hope.

Source: Unpublished lecture given on March 18, 1959, at Valparaiso University in commemoration of its one-hundredth anniversary.

You have done me a high honor in inviting me to celebrate with you the centennial of the founding of Valparaiso University and to lead you for a little while in your reflections on the past and future of a school that is devoted to the service of God and fellow men in the spirit or with the mind of Martin Luther. But now that I am about to discharge the task expected of me I am aware that the honor has tempted me to accept a responsibility I am poorly endowed to perform. I do not belong by long association to that closer community of Luther's followers which mediates to its members his religious convictions, spiritual experiences and relations to reality. Nor on the other hand have I been presented with the opportunity or challenge to take part intensively in that different and often profound work of scholarship which has made Luther its object in recent times. The layman in this field is astonished and overwhelmed by the fecundity, the seriousness, the painstaking of an intellectual and religious devotion which, with the aid of ninety volumes or so of Luther's writings is producing many times that number of new studies of the heart, mind, experiences, intentions and effects of the great Reformer. The scholars who turn to this mine to extract from it new gold or precious stones belong to many religious organizations; though mostly Lutheran themselves, there are Calvinists and Methodists and Roman Catholics and Friends and men of no institutional religious connection at all among them. Mostly they are probably theologians, but among them one finds also lawyers and literati, psychologists and many historians of culture of one of its aspects from language to music to power politics. This company overawes me. Far from being able to speak for them, I am not even able to understand them during much of that brief time I spend in their company. So I cannot speak to those of you who are Lutherans and Luther-scholars as one who by training and concern has learned to deal discriminatingly with the profound issues that occupy you. Since I cannot take your ground so far as you are Lutherans or Luther-scholars I must ask you to take my ground with me for this brief hour. It is the ground of one who as a Protestant Christian of a perhaps rather nondescript sort is deeply concerned about the condition of man in our time, and as a scholar equally nondescript and unspecialized, looks to the past to discern there the broad outlines of those great movements which have imparted to men—not less beset by doubts than we are—new force and courage for life's strange journey. These are movements which have given us direction and impetus; hence movements to be carried forward in our day. They are also movements that tend to come to a stop; they issue in institutions and modes of thought which become all too familiar to us and lead us to think that we live in a world in which all great possibilities have been realized. We can therefore always think of them in a double way; either they are great creative and revelatory periods whose inventions and revelations we must conserve, or they are prophetic and paradigmatic movements which show forth the kind of renewal we may expect and prepare for in our own future. Among such movements the Reformation is one of the greatest; it takes a secondary place in our history only to the nodal point in our whole human time—the coming of Jesus Christ—and perhaps to that earlier, preliminary junction point in our history when new life came into the world with the prophets and their contemporaries. I propose to you that we look at Martin Luther and the Reformation and at ourselves from the second point of view, with gratitude for the past to be sure, but even more with hope for the future.

1. The Newness in the Reformation

On one thing all the interpreters of Martin Luther seem to be agreed. He brought a marvelous newness, freshness and openness into our human existence. They seem agreed further on the fact that he was not so much the immediate source as the mediate instrument and channel of that newness of life. But when they deal with his relation to the old, to the heritage he had received and the Christian faith of which he was the heir, they seem to differ more in their interpretations. So do they also when they begin to describe the content and the sources of that newness of life of which he was the fullest, the overflowing channel in his time. These differences, of course, are not necessarily contradictions. We call the rare, gigantic figures that are given to us human beings now again as bone of our bone and flesh of our flesh yet as towering over the rest of us by such names as geniuses and heroes and prophets. But they fit into no categories; not even into a common category save that of greatness; their work is so manifold, their effects on life so many that they must be described in many ways, from many points of view. Yet of course we discern differences of importance and value in the manifold interpretations; though the most myopic may contain moments of truth, there are those which do greater justice to the subject.

What then was the newness that through Martin Luther came into our history and what were its sources? There are those who like Metzdee in some of his utterances see the newness mostly as one of human vitality and its source in a kind of biological élan vital of which Luther was a channel. Here life in all its urgency, in its revolt against the conventions that keep it in strait jackets, asserts itself in primitive power. And, of course, it is true that Luther impresses one as a man of super-abundant vitality, endowed with life force, with exuberant energy despite the many ailments of body and perhaps psyche to which he was subject. It seems true also that in consequence of his work human energies, including physical energies, that had long been held leashed were given freedom. But when we think of his work and its effects in the spirits and minds of men, individually and in their societies, we shall not be long tempted to say—this was the important new thing and this the source of power—pure physical vitality. Strange psychosomatic creatures that we are such vitality is often doubtless an accompaniment, perhaps even a consequence of some of our resurrections from sleep or death, but indefinable and diffuse as it is, reference to its presence explains little or nothing.

It is pointed out by others that Luther was the German man in whom the new self consciousness, the new aspirations, the new language and politics of the German people found their focus and their generative point. The nationalist interpretation of Martin

Luther's person and work has had a long history which culminated in recent generations in the travesties of a Hitlerian, Rosenbergian "Deutsch-Christeutum" [sic] for which Luther's German Bible was almost a new creation, inspired by the German spirit that chose him as its instrument for the revelation of a German God destined to take the place of a Hebraic Jehovah. Apart from such caricatures there is, of course, more than a grain of truth in the idea that one of the new things which came into being through the Reformer's instrumentation was a German language, a German people, a German culture. But other nations also are indebted to that movement of which he was the foremost representative. All northern Europe and—because of later developments—North America also can celebrate the day at Wittenberg when Luther first challenged Rome as the symbolic beginning of liberation from the authority of the mind, the language and the law of southern, Latin Christendom. But to describe the newness of life that came into history with the Reformation as the new birth of national freedom and the rise of new nations is to put into the center of the interpretation something which belongs somewhat in the periphery. That was indeed a part of the newness of life that followed from the inspirations and struggles of the early sixteenth century; the maturation of independent nations and the release of popular energies are inseparably connected with the other generations and regenerations that then took place, but neither in the intention nor in the results of the Reformer's work can they be given the central place, except perhaps by nationalists who have no other final term than nation to use in understanding, explaining or valuing human affairs. For this movement affected existence more extensively and more intensively than in its national confines and forms.

We may then direct our attention to the newness which it brought into Western culture in its more spiritual aspects. The great achievement of Luther, says that discriminating and subtle historian Wilhelm Dilthey, lies in the fact that he represented and expressed in the religious and moral life, and then by consequence in political and social life in general that individualism and that inwardness of personal existence for which the great objective and communal systems of belief and moral rule had left little room. For faith as obedience to the doctrines of the great church he substituted the heart's assurance of God's mercy; for morality as conformity to the requirements of a system of laws he brought into his own and others' experience the personal morality of the sensitive conscience obligated beyond all human rules to their ultimate source. "Luther divorced completely," writes Dilthey, "the religious process from the objective imagery (Bildlicheit) of dogmatic thinking and the regimented externalities of the church" (Ges. Schir. [*Gesammelte Schriften*] II – 53 et. seq.). In him the movement toward inwardness and personalism in religion and ethics that had begun in Francis of Assissi [sic] and in Mysticism came to its fruition. And when this happened in Luther it happened in the German nation and in European culture, for in the lonely monk and lonelier hero at Worms and loneliest soul struggling with great temptations the emerging new individual recognized himself; with that aid he discovered himself; this kind of life he re-enacted in himself. The newness which came into the world—at least into the Western world—with Luther was the newness of a new personal inwardness, of an intensely subjective life on the part of religious-moral man. Religion now came to be what man does with his solitariness; morality what he does on the hidden stage where the law in the members and the law in the mind carry on their struggle. The new individual is not a mystic separating himself from the world and sense; he takes his place rather in the world of tangible creatures, of political, economic and ecclesiastical affairs, he is no subjectivist for whom the not-self is a projection from the self. In his own inwardness he meets always an Other, but the other is not the social system of beliefs, dogmas, rules. The Other also is a self who challenges the human self to self identification and responsibility, who gives to the lonely yet social man freedom from social bondage but also liberty from fear about his own fate. I have gone beyond Dilthey and also fallen short of him in my effort to describe the newness that came into cultural, religious, moral Western civilization with Luther and his companions in the Reformation, for I have wanted to emphasize the particular point that this great movement did indeed bring forth something new in the style of life. It will not do to describe pre-Reformation man as collective man, as other-directed man, as dependent man and post-Reformation man as individual, autonomous and theonomous, free man. The lines cannot be drawn so clearly. But it seems very true that with Luther and partly through him there came into our historic human existence a new self understanding of the individual and a new ethos of personal existence. In the later course this individualism expressed itself and developed or degenerated in scores of admirable and also despicable forms—in economic atomism and laissez faire, in political liberalism and license, in varieties of religious subjectivism from Spener to Kierkegaard to Feuerbach. To those who see its bad fruits only the new individualism was a great departure from the desirable standard of human existence. To those of us who cannot quarrel with history but rejoice in the new creations that rise in it out of the eternal fountain of being, this emergence of a new sense and a new reality of individual existence is an object of wonder, however much we mourn over that sin in man which brings corruption to all that is good. Still, as we acknowledge the historic truth that such interpretations as Dilthey's contain, we raise the question in ourselves; Was this individualism of the Reformation the important point in its creative and recreative action? Was it the important point for Luther; is it the important point for us as we ask what can we now derive from him in our present hour of need?

The Roman Catholic historian Joseph Lortz is more aware than many a Protestant of the freshness, the newness of Luther's reformation. There is about it, as we look at it with his eyes, something of the character of a summer day's clear sunrise hour, of an April morning.

> "The ultimate secret of Luther's effectiveness," he writes, "is in his own vitality. . . . Life is present only there where there is something that has not been worn out, something new. But everything that belongs to the world of creatures must wither. And to this belongs even the form in which God's Word proclaims to us God's never aging revelation. In this situation the church must ever and again realize the word: 'Behold I make all things new.' Now there can be no doubt that the Christendom of late medievalism had become very old in this sense. Its formulae had been used in an unheard of measure and so had been used up; or otherwise they were new but not derived from the Word of God itself, distilled rather out of other previously derived formulae; they were strangely distant from the heart of the Bible and of the liturgy, strangely complicated, necessarily sterile. Luther sensed this in a measure beyond that of anyone around him. . . . The secret of his success was that he brought through this sterile, antiquated, atomized conceptual language and forced his way to the sources of a new proclamation. He made things new. He spoke a new language." (from Bornkamm, p. 349)

We can try to describe this kind of newness that Luther brought in another though not better way. We human beings grasp and represent all reality that presents itself to us or comes within our reach with the aid of analogies, metaphors, ideas and images. And our social custom is such on the one hand, our laziness or stupor such on the other hand that after a while we never grasp the reality afresh but always see in it the form or image originally used. We even tend to substitute the idea or image for the real. Thus having encountered in the past men from the Orient and having called them "yellow men" or "slant-eyed" men we tend not only to see each individual as a simple specimen of a genus so that all Chinese look alike to us; but we also have in mind a picture of the genus that we do not correct. We do not see an Oriental man but our mind's eye picture, our stereotype of what we once upon a time long ago decided an Oriental looked like. As we all recognize, this common observation about ourselves applies to the whole range of our experiences. We live to a large extent in our world as in a kind of art gallery containing pictures painted by those who freshly and personally grasped and re-enacted what they encountered; it is more like a room plastered with bad copies of copies of copies of such original paintings. We need only to think of the faded images that are in our minds when we use such words as *truth*, or *spirit*, or *idea*, when we employ the great Biblical words and phrases such as kingdom of God, redemption, judgment, grace and salvation.

The point that Lortz makes and which others have made before him is not the simple one that Luther translated a Hebrew and Greek Bible into the common German tongue, or that he Germanized the Latin man, or that he took the well-known theological theory of man's justification by faith and made it meaningful by using common illustrations and common words to communicate theological subtleties—as young students of theology today sometimes speak of the difficulty of translating their theology into homiletic language. The point is very different. It is that Luther wrestled for himself and by himself in direct encounter with those realities to which Biblical and theological words refer. He knew about conscience not because the doctors had taught him what synteresis and syneidesis meant; he knew about the wrath of God not from commentaries on the prophets; he had met Jesus Christ somewhat as Paul himself had met him, though not by way of vision or in mystic solitude; he knew grace and forgiveness with the knowledge of acquaintance, not with the knowledge about these experiences his teachers had mediated to him. Always with the Bible as his companion, his interpreter, the herald of God's Word, yet in direct relation to that Word, in direct experience of wrath and mercy, judgment and forgiveness he forged a new language, new terms, new metaphors to set forth the real. He could translate the Bible into hard, gripping German not only or even primarily because he knew Hebrew and Greek but because he knew the faith and the love, the hiddenness and revealedness of God, the cross and resurrection to which Hebrew and Greek sentences referred. So with Luther Western man's symbolism and language, the means with which he approaches and grasps and understands his God, his sin and his salvation became new. The newness was not that of new wineskins containing old wine, but of new wineskins for new wine, albeit the wine was the product of grapes long cultivated.

The newness which Luther and the Reformation brought into our historic existence in this respect centered in man's immediate relation to God and Jesus Christ, but it was not confined to that sphere. It may be difficult to trace the relations of the Reformation to the new art which, by means of color and form and sound, gave men new symbols with which to see and understand the meaning of the human face and of nature's various objects. But there seems to be a kinship as has often been pointed out between Luther and his reforming companions on the one hand, Duerer and Cranach and Rembrandt on the other. The point again, however, is not so much that the Reformation was allied with a renewal in art; it is rather that the new art was both means to and expression of a new human encounter with the world. Perhaps the situation is similar when we think of the new science that flourished in the wake of the Reformation. Historians usually relate it more closely to the Renaissance and to humanism than to the Reformation. Yet it has been observed that despite all tendencies to conflict on specific points of teaching about the natural world, the spirit of the new science was much like the spirit of the Reformation. It cast off the old formulae, the outworn patterns of interpretation which confined the mind to stereotyped visions of the natural world and to conventional patterns of their interpretation. It forged new symbols after direct meetings with the given phenomena of nature; it saw connections and relations to which minds dominated by old formulae had not been open.

When we consider the Reformation from this point of view as a great revolution in our symbolic, interpretive life the sense for the newness that was in it and issued from it increases. It was much more than a restoration of a system of religious doctrine and an ethos that had been corrupted by time. It was something rather different from the re-establishment of an ecclesiastical organization that had been ruined by the weather of centuries, the vandalism of unconverted powers, the neglect of complacent custodians. Its relation to the early church seems like that of the 8th century prophets to the Israel of Moses and Joshua's day. In Luther as in Isaiah the prophecy was fulfilled: "Remember ye not the former things, neither consider the things of old. Behold, I will do a new thing; now shall it spring forth." (Is. 43:18, 19)

2. The Newness of Faith

The newness and freshness that came into the religious-moral life of the West and hence into the rest of culture is only described, it is not accounted for when it is understood and interpreted as a revolution in the symbolic, interpretative life of the Western Mind. Perhaps it cannot be accounted for. There is something as miraculous as spring itself, as the birth of a new person, about the major turning points in human history; or better—there is something about them like the effusion of the Spirit which comes and goes like the wind about whose whence and whither we remain ignorant. But we may make the attempt to locate with somewhat greater precision the point at which new life, new understanding, new moral sensitivity, new organization of social existence, had its beginnings. That point so far as I can see was in the moment of faith, of confidence, of assurance in Martin Luther's soul and in the spirit of the people of his time. At bottom, in its origins the newness that came with Luther was a newness in man's confidence; what was formed and reformed in the Reformation was faith in being, confidence in reality, assurance of God's good will. and out of this flowed forth—speaking in human terms only—the rest of that renewal which is the mark of the movement. As I try to interpret Luther and the Reformation in this way I am aware that the words and forms of thought I am using are derived not only from his day but from ours and that in interpreting him I am perhaps more intent on understanding our times than his. Yet I trust I will not do him a real injustice since the understanding of human faith and its effects in life that I have derived, I believe, from him in this sense at least that he remains *the* teacher who points out to us in and with the aid of Scriptures what this thing *faith* is in our lives.

When now we speak of faith as we have in mind in the first place not a system of beliefs about God and men—necessary as it is to formulate and express our understanding of our total environment and our relations to it in such beliefs. What we mean by it is what Luther always meant in the first place—confidence, assurance, trust. By such confidence men live and without it life comes to a stop. Ultimately the question of human confidence or trust is always a question of confidence in the ground, the source, the nature of total and central being itself, that is of confidence in the last power, trust in God.

But as Luther so often pointed out, faith as such and God go together. What the heart clings to, what it relies upon, that is its God.

And for most men, most of the time the object of trust on which they rely to give worth to personal life and all its works is the social reality in which they seem to live and move and have their being. They have confidence in it as an on-going movement in which their own lives are secured against futility and worthlessness by being made part of this larger, enduring whole. They accept its ethos, its morals, and its beliefs as the true law and true belief on which they can depend. Hence they live in confidence, go about their work with assurance, accept the disciplines of this social life without rebellion, contribute even with enthusiasm to its glory. In this confidence in our community we accept it not as meaningful in itself, or as the last power with which we have to deal, but as representative of the ultimate power. Its beliefs—whether as the religious beliefs of medievalism or as the naturalistic beliefs of modern civilization or as the metaphysical beliefs of a Greek city—are accepted as truth; its laws are reverenced as emanating not from itself but from the nature of Being itself, from God. And indeed it is true that at some time in the past each such society formed its convictions about the true and the right, the just and the beautiful in some critical moment of encounter with reality.

When this ordinary confidence of men in their society as enduring, as representative of the real nature of things, as divine and representative of the divine fails, then life tends to come to a stop. Then issue the questions about the worthwhileness of human endeavor, about the meaningfulness of moral striving, about the value of maintaining by infinite labor the social institutions and organizations. In speaking of the failure of confidence in this fashion I am evidently using the words and experiences of our day rather than those of the Reformation. We speak of meaninglessness and of futility, of nothingness and chance where the men of that time spoke of death and hell, of the wrath of God and his capricious will.

Doubtless their choice of symbols was wiser than ours. But I believe that there is a fundamental likeness between the failure of assurance about the goodness and meaningfulness of human existence of which we are now aware.

The newness of assurance, of confidence in God and so of confident living which marks the life of Martin Luther and of the Reformation began negatively in a great and spreading doubt, with an eroding process of distrust. The faith by which men had lived, the confidence they had in church and law and the system of beliefs and in their whole structured world was deeply shaken. It was shaken by the revelation of the inconsistencies and hypocrisies of institutions that were not what they seemed or claimed to be, by the great distance that opened between the image they had or presented themselves and their appearance in actual behavior. The holiness of the church and the unity of the Empire became ideals that had no relation to what men experienced in direct relation to them. The social faith was shaken also by the coming into view of actualities and powers, by the experience of forces and realities that did not fit into the established systems of belief and ordered conduct. The rediscovery of ancient learning and classic art, the discovery of America, the new recovery of the Bible—these acted upon many, less as exhilarating prospects of new worlds into which man might enter than as ominous portents of a familiar world falling into ruins. By no act of will, not by a resolution like Descartes to doubt the wisdom of the ancients but by necessity, Luther became the representative disbeliever, the great distruster of his time. The faith of the fathers in church, in the great intellectual structure of beliefs, in the moral laws of the society was destroyed in him by no wilfulness of unbelief but by what he saw and witnessed and in his singular honesty had to acknowledge. The new confidence that was born in him was conceived in the doubt, distrust, in a soul left empty as it were by the failure of that social truth by which his fathers had lived.

The distrust of previous objects of faith went deeper than that. When a man loses confidence in the fixed structures of the social life as enduring and trustworthy, as reliable sources of meaning and as fit objects of at least mediate devotion, they tend to turn to themselves. In stoic fashion they turn to the reason that is in them, to the moral law in their conscience, or to the human spirit which has manifested its power in the past. This is what the humanists in their own way did in the days of the Reformation. In them faith robbed of its objects of trust in the social world sought something on which to rely in the creative powers of mind and in the free will of the moral self. In his own highly personal way Luther also took that road only to discover that his will examined under the microscope of Scriptures was neither free nor good. Many a modern sees in Luther a believer who substituted the conscience and inner religious experience, even faith itself, for the objective social structures of the medieval world on which man could now rely. But this is to misunderstand thoroughly the man and the moment who found in human inwardness the foundation on which they could build. There was a deep distrust in Luther of human reason and of human will as powers that could save men from destruction, from the hell of conflict and of alienation, in the self, in the society, in the world, in the relation of man to God. And this distrust also was not willful; it was not based on a determination to rely on, to believe first of all in something else. It issued out of agonizing experience with himself and in himself as he saw himself and knew himself in the mirror of the Scriptures.

The distrust, the suspicion of the finite objects of faith as representative of real power, as able to save his and any life and all life from nothingness, meaninglessness or worse—from continuation in everlasting conflict and an endless movement of disintegration—found their goal in the great distrust, the great questioning of the reliability, the goodness, the faithfulness of the ultimate power on which all being is absolutely dependent, whence all things come into existence, whither they all return. God might be defined by Luther as whatever object faith relies upon and the heart clings to. But when all the images of God, and all representatives of God became objects of his deep distrust, he stood in the presence of God beyond all Gods, of the power that in cosmic wrath negates the idols and little gods that are not gods. And the God beyond all Gods appeared to him in no wise as the kind Father who love[s] but as dark and inimical power—as God of wrath and destruction. Faith in Luther made no easy transfer from childhood God or church God to Bible God. For the God of the Bible who was the God of being appeared in the Bible as in experiences as the hidden Deus absconditus, known in his wrath but not as a God of faith. Now doubt had reached its deepest point. There was no further God for faith, for human trust to seek, no ground on which to stand.

Luther's wrestle with the final problem of human faith, his Jacob-like wrestle with God himself was resolved in the strange manner in which it had been resolved over and over again in our history—by the coming into his view of the darkest fact of all—the crucifixion of Jesus Christ—and by its illuminating, lightful sequels—resurrection and session at the right hand of power. Now the great reconciliation took place, how God of wrath became God of grace, how confidence was established not in any human or finite power, not in church or even in Bible but in God himself no one has ever made wholly clear in the case of Luther any more than in the case of Paul, or of the early church or of all the others in whose lives such struggles of unbelief, despair and faith have been re-enacted. We have our theological and our psychological theories. But they seem as far removed from the actuality of life in distrust and faith, before wrath and mercy, as fleshless, bloodless battle-maps in history books are distant from the actualities of Gettysburg or Okinawa. The struggle of faith and despair, the reconciliation of God and man, the victory of a faith that relies on the last, the ultimate power of being, the crucifixion and the resurrection of the self with Christ are enacted in the living self. And there is an almost impenetrable mystery at the heart of every great renewal of faith in a man such as Martin Luther. But one thing seems clear: confidence such as came to birth in him, confidence, joyful assurance in the marvelous good will, the glorious mercy at the source and center of all being is not established until the hardest, the most difficult barriers to faith have been encountered, have been thrust upon men—as they are in the cross, in the wrath of God falling upon the very best that man can offer in the way of obedience, in the way of faithfulness, in the way of brotherly love.

In the sweep of human history I must think then of Martin Luther not so much as restorer of true doctrine, or as a reconstructer of a church threatened with utter ruin, or as true interpreter of previously misinterpreted Scripture. To all this he doubtless also made his great contributions. But I must see him first of all as the soul in whom new confidence in God was born, through whom the gift of faith—not in a God who may or may not exist but in the power and source of being itself—was given once again by the mediation of the pioneer and perfecter of faith, Jesus Christ. And I believe that all the other newness which came with the Reformation—the new vitality, the new social existences and institutions, the new inwardness of individual life, the new symbolic structures by which man learned to understand himself, nature and his destiny—that all this other newness was rooted in the new confidence, the new trust and the glad affirmation of life and all being that accompanied it. I cannot verify this thesis with the aid of extensive and profound scholarship.

Take it. I can only beg, as one poor draughtsman's effort to sketch his personal portrait of a hero of faith.

3. Conclusion

It may be that we stand near to another nodal movement in human history. Modern man has come to live by faith in the structures of social life, the systems of beliefs, the moral codes and standards that gave concretion to the personal convictions and experiences of the Reformation. He has conceived confidence in the doctrine and institutions that expressed the faith in God given at that time. Many a man to be sure, in the course of the Protestant centuries and in our time has indeed re-enacted or been forced to reproduce the very wrestle of the soul with the God of wrath and grace that Luther enacted as the father of the Protestant faith. But to a large extent it seems true that as in all periods of the past a social faith has largely taken the place of the faith that is directed immediately to God beyond all gods. The Kierkegaards may protest all they want to against the kind of trust we put in our institutions, our doctrines, our ways of life as impersonal men who share a kind of common mind, a common faith which has small intensity because it is so secure, because it is anchored in such nearby, familiar things as doctrines and churches and very well known Bibles—so well known that they are taken for granted. Despite such protests against Protestantism we tend to put our trust in it. Or otherwise we live in a more political confidence in the value, the endurance, the meaningfulness of national life, or of Western civilization, of its systems of belief, of its more or less well-ordered ways of behavior in which we play our part and have our personal meaning.

There is no use in crying out against this fact; there is no justice in accusing our fellowmen of leading inauthentic existences. There is something authentic and right in all conservatism. There is a grace and providence of God apparent in the manner in which he preserves the past for us and makes us preservers of the past. Even the Reformation was not all newness of life. It maintained or was made the instrument of conserving a large part of its own past.

But despite the prevalence of social faith, in which God is mediated to us in the symbols and the doctrines of the church, in which we rely on social laws believed ultimately to be founded on his will, it has long been apparent that some great cracks are running through our structure. No century is like another but there is something in our time that reminds us of the fifteenth rather than of the sixteenth century. The glad confidence we once had in our civilizations, in our Christendom, in our nations has been deeply shaken. It has been shaken by the great distance that has opened up between our images of ourselves and our actuality in behavior. We have become distrustful in religion itself [and] of our human religion, but vainly seek to separate with Barth true revelation from Christian religion. The new developments in science do not so much open up to us vistas of the future into which we would gladly move forward as threaten the stability of the world-picture to which we have become accustomed.

To a greater extent than was true in late medievalism the formulae and symbols we have used with which to grasp reality, to understand ourselves and God and Jesus Christ have been worn out, have become often as characterless as coins that have passed through too many hands.

Meantime also the power of evil has become so manifest in our world that it has become easier for many a modern to believe in the reality of devils or demonic powers than in gracious forces and ministries. But there is no need to multiply testimony to the presence among men today of a deep distrust of existence; it is saddest when it appears in the form of boredom, most agonizing when it comes as despair. The temper manifests itself in our whole society; it invades the churches which try to erect dogmatic defenses against it. But sometimes the very dogmatism of the system seems to indicate the presence of the foe—distrust, suspicion, despair of life, belief in the infinite distance of God from our common human scene.

In this situation our attitude to Martin Luther and the Reformation may be a twofold one. On the one hand we shall try to reappropriate the truth of that old struggle of man with God, of that new appearance of the cross at the heart of life and of the great reconciler. But on the other hand we shall look forward with hope to the renewal not of the fruits of faith but of faith itself. Such a renewal will not come without travail; no youth will, knowing what is involved, offer himself easily to become its prophet. It will not come by design or any human will. Yet as we look at our past human story, at Isaiah and Paul and Martin Luther and many another, our confidence in their God and Savior will at least take the form of trust that he will renew our trust. Not as lonely individuals only, but as members one of another. Behold, says the Lord, I will do a new thing.

Epilogue: Niebuhr and Post-Church America

The year that Stanley Hauerwas and Will Willimon chose to mark as the end of Christendom came shortly after H. Richard Niebuhr's sudden death of a heart attack on July 5, 1962. To them, the opening of the Fox Theater on Sundays in 1963, and the jettisoning of other such blue laws in places like Greenville, South Carolina, signaled the closing in America of the long era of privilege and influence the church in the West had enjoyed, in one form or another, since the days of the Roman Emperor Constantine.[1] Several adjectives are used to describe this shifting of the American religious landscape, including *post-Constantinian*, *post-Christendom*, and *post-church*.

The year the new era actually began is difficult to pin down. Moreover, its trajectory is far from uniform. In *American Grace*, Robert Putnam and David Campbell have aptly called the transition a "shock" followed by "two aftershocks." The initial shock was the social revolution of the 1960s. The post–World War II revival of religion had already passed its peak when the civil-rights marches, the women's liberation movement, radically new attitudes toward sex, and mounting opposition to the Vietnam War rocked the American

---

1. Stanley Hauerwas and William H. Willimon, *Resident Aliens: Life in the Christian Colony* (Nashville: Abingdon, 1989), 15–19.

scene. By the time the 1970s dawned, the once-flourishing mainline churches had shifted into reverse, and most of these denominations experienced declining memberships. Masking the full impact of this first "aftershock," however, was the conservative Christian reaction to the social upheavals of the previous decade. It soon swelled the ranks of more conservative evangelical churches with persons desiring to uphold traditional forms of personal morality. It also helped to birth the influential Religious Right in American politics. The second "aftershock" of the 1990s came as more of a jolt to the prevailing religious equilibrium. This time, members of a new generation of Americans were finding churches too closely identified with conservative mores and politics, and many of those who were brought up in one of them began to leave in droves. Classified as "nones" (no religious identity), their numbers steadily increased with the arrival of each new year.[2] By the time the twenty-first century arrived, Christian churches of all types had awakened, at least to some degree, to the fact that the world of America was no longer their oyster.

Characteristics of Post-Church America

The literature on post-church America is extensive and continues to grow in volume. However, much of it tends of emphasize a number of common themes. First, a significant change in people's religious habits has become discernible in almost every community. Those who are old enough to have grown up in a 1950s or early '60s neighborhood remember knowing where most families on the block went to church. Unchurched neighbors stood out. Today, churchgoing neighbors are the exception; they are the ones to who tend to stand out.

---

2. Robert D. Putnam and David E. Campbell, *American Grace: How Religion Divides and Unites Us* (New York: Simon & Schuster, 2010), 91–133.

Second, the influence of the church on the world around it has steadily eroded. It is not only theaters and shops of many kinds that are now open on Sundays; athletic events and programs for school-age children are also routinely scheduled during the prime hours of the Christian Sabbath. Grief over the church's loss of privilege is often expressed as outrage over the removal of the crèche from the courthouse lawn at Christmas, the banning of prayers once delivered by a member of the local clergy association at the opening of city council meetings, and the removal of Christian holidays from public-school calendars. For many Christians, the tables appear to have been turned. The unchurched members of the community who were once the outsiders now seem to hold the reins of power, and churchgoers who were once the insiders in the community are now on the outside looking in. To the contemporary church, a once-friendly world often feels like a hostile environment.

Third, while belief in God and interest in the spiritual side of life remain very high among Americans, participation in church-related events continues to decline. While there is considerable variation in the statistics that measure regular worship attendance, the arrows all point in a downward direction, to as low as several percentage points less than one-fifth of the total population. Regardless of whether it ever was, the church is now not at the center of the spiritual lives of most Americans.

Fourth, America's religious tapestry has become more pluralistic than ever. Major versions of people's faith now include not simply Catholic and Protestant Christianity, along with Judaism, but also Islam, Buddhism, Hinduism, and other world religions. Finding ways to relate to these religious newcomers, many of whom are immigrants, has become a formidable challenge for Christians and their churches in the new century.

Fifth, the social and political polarization of the American people that is reflected in the governing bodies and leaders whom they elect to serve them is often just as evident in the churches to which they may belong. In congregations that explicitly or implicitly endorse a conservative or a liberal social agenda, persons of the opposite persuasion soon sense that they do not really belong. In the face of a divided congregation, clergy frequently feel forced to remain silent about the hot-button social issues such as abortion, gay marriage, or climate change.

Finally, the authors of this body of literature tend to be not altogether pessimistic about this shift in American religious life. On the contrary, they see it as an opportunity for the birth of a more authentic and vital form of Christianity to take place. When contrasted with the global South, where Christianity is rapidly growing, North America takes on the appearance in their eyes of a mission field that is exceedingly ripe for harvest. The reaping of this harvest has become the chief objective of the various remedies they have proposed for the twenty-first-century church.[3]

How Churches Are Perceived in Post-Church America

Two books, based upon Barna Group research of eighteen- to twenty-nine-year-old Americans conducted by David Kinnaman, are particularly illuminating for churches seeking to gain a firmer footing in this new century. Both books provide a mirror into which churches can look in order to gain a better sense of how they are perceived, not only explicitly by a majority of the members of the rising mosaic or millennial generation but also implicitly by many

---

3. See, for example, Loren B. Mead, *The Once and Future Church: Reinventing the Congregation for a New Mission Frontier* (Washington, DC: The Alban Institute, 1991); Reggie McNeal, *The Present Future: Six Tough Questions for the Church* (San Francisco: Jossey-Bass, 2003); and *Missional Renaissance: Changing the Scorecard for the Church* (San Francisco: Jossey-Bass, 2009); David T. Olson, *The American Church in Crisis* (Grand Rapids: Zondervan, 2008).

others who are dissatisfied with or alienated from organized forms of Christianity. The first book, *UnChristian*, which Kinnaman coauthored with Gabe Lyons in 2007, draws attention to persons outside the church who have tended to perceive Christians, among other things, as hypocritical, judgmental, too political, and out of touch with reality. These survey respondents have also detected in Christians an undercurrent of arrogance and moral superiority that makes them more interested in being right than in listening to persons with other points of view, and for this reason unwilling to engage in genuine dialogue. As one of them put it, "Most people I meet assume that *Christian* means very conservative, entrenched in their thinking, antigay, antichoice, angry, violent, illogical, empire builders; they want to convert everyone, and they generally cannot live peacefully with anyone who doesn't believe what they believe."[4]

Kinnaman's second book, published in 2011 and entitled *You Lost Me*, summarizes the results of his extensive polling and interviews of millennials who were reared in the church but then found reason to "drop out." He found that these "insiders," estimated to be 59 percent of those in this age group who grew up in the church, are not all alike in terms of their attitudes toward the church. While some have slowly faded to the margins of their congregations, others have renounced their memberships or even "deconverted." Still others have wanted to pursue God-honoring lives but have found the church to be just as overprotective, shallow, opposed to modern science, sexually repressive, exclusive, or intolerant of anyone entertaining doubt about their faith as the other "lost" members of their generation.[5]

---

4. David Kinnaman and Gabe Lyons, *UnChristian: What a New Generation Really Thinks About Christianity . . . and Why It Matters* (Grand Rapids: Baker, 2008), 26.
5. David Kinnaman, *You Lost Me: Why Young Christians Are Leaving Church . . . and Rethinking Faith* (Grand Rapids: Baker, 2011), 19–198.

The aim of both of these books was not so much to tear down the churches of Christendom as to help them find ways to reinvent themselves in a post-church world. Kinnaman has in fact pointed to those in the emerging generation as the ones that might best lead the way. Their "great struggle," he writes, "is learning how to live faithfully in a new context, to be in the world but not of the world." As this "tension" manifests itself for them, the rest of the church ought to be ready to provide support and encouragement rather than criticism or rejection.[6] While Kinnaman did not mention H. Richard Niebuhr, he has highlighted the same question Niebuhr sought to address throughout his adult years: "How can we live in- but-not-of lives in the world that surrounds us? In a culture skeptical of every kind of earthly authority, where information is dirt cheap and where institutions and leaders so often disappoint, *we need God-given wisdom*."[7]

Niebuhr's Contributions to Post-Church America

Can Niebuhr offer any of this *"God-given wisdom"* to the twenty-first-century church in North America? Despite the efforts of critics to consign his Christ-and-culture paradigm to the realm of church-era antiquity, there appears to be a growing consensus among religious scholars that Niebuhr's work remains as relevant as it ever was, and that he deserves a prominent seat at the table of post-church conversations. Timothy Beach-Verhey, for example, argues that Niebuhr offers corrective insights regarding assumptions about American culture and Christian churches that are as applicable in the twenty-first century as they were in his own time, and that in some ways he appears to be "more at home" in a post-church age. William Werpehowski, moreover, lauds Niebuhr's legacy and asserts

6. Ibid., 11–12.
7. Ibid., 210.

that he remains a valuable conversation partner in the broader field of Christian ethics. Even critics like Glen H. Stassen and D. A. Carson, who find fault with particular aspects of it, still grant to Niebuhr's Christ-and-culture paradigm a measure of ongoing usefulness in a postmodern, global, and increasingly pluralistic religious environment.[8] In my estimation, there is probably even more relevant Niebuhr wisdom than this collection of his writings, designed as it is to illustrate the ways in which he wrestled with the paradox of church and world, could ever hope to communicate. But here are some features that stand out.

The World as a Sphere of God's Activity

First, Niebuhr may help today's church recognize that the world outside of itself is also the sphere of God's creative and redemptive activity. By refusing to draw sharp lines between the sacred and profane realms, he seems to have shared the conviction of his Lutheran contemporary Dietrich Bonhoeffer, who asserted in his posthumously published *Ethics*, "There are not two realities, but *only one reality*, and that is God's reality revealed in Christ in the reality of the world. Partaking in Christ, we stand at the same time in the reality of God and in the reality of the world."[9] To see this, one has only to examine Niebuhr's interpretation of the orthodox Christian doctrine of the Trinity. He contended that within the Godhead, the Son not only participated in the world's creation, but was sent by the Father to redeem the world in its entirety. The life,

---

8. Timothy A. Beach-Verhey, *Robust Liberalism: H. Richard Niebuhr and the Ethics of American Public Life* (Waco, TX: Baylor University Press, 2011), 5–6; William Werpehowski, *American Protestant Ethics and the Legacy of H. Richard Niebuhr* (Washington, DC: Georgetown University Press, 2002), 1–13; Glen H. Stassen, "Preface," in *Authentic Transformation: A New Vision of Christ and Culture* (Nashville: Abingdon, 1996), 9–13; D. A. Carson, *Christ and Culture Revisited* (Grand Rapids: Eerdmans, 2008), 4–30.
9. Dietrich Bonhoeffer, *Ethics*, Dietrich Bonhoeffer Works vol. 6, ed. Wayne Witson Floyd, Jr. (Minneapolis: Fortress Press, 2005), 58.

death, and resurrection of Jesus were events that took place during an ancient period in history and then became part of the biblical record that remained an essential and enduring feature of the church's life. At the same time, through the Holy Spirit, who proceeds out into the world from the Son as well as the Father, all of history as well as every present or future moment also becomes a platform for divine revelation.[10] Therefore, Niebuhr always pondered what God was doing in and through world events, whether it was the Manchurian crisis over which he publicly crossed swords with his brother Reinhold, the economic woes of the Great Depression, the tragic human toll of World War II, or the Cold War and the threat of communism. If God did not rule the entire world, none of it would exist, he reasoned, and if he did not hear prayers for the coming of his kingdom, it long ago would have become nothing more than a "den of robbers." Hence, for him "every moment and period" is "an eschatological present," because in each of them we are "dealing with God."[11]

Niebuhr thus appears to provide a strategy for the contemporary church in North America to connect with those for whom the space in which it has traditionally gathered, primarily for worship and other activities, is no longer as central as it was for prior generations. For many people today, other spaces, such as their neighborhood, local coffee shop, public school auxiliary, voluntary community service organization, or online social media platform, have replaced the often well-appointed church building complete with services dispensed by professionals for those who come through the doors. Engaging such people, Niebuhr might advise, involves the recognition that God is at work in the world through various other agents and agencies

---

10. H. Richard Niebuhr, "The Doctrine of the Trinity and the Unity of the Church," *Theology Today* 3 (October 1946): 371–84.
11. H. Richard Niebuhr, *Christ and Culture* (New York: Harper & Row, 1951), 228–29.

of the culture besides the church, and that what makes the church unique is that it consists of a people who recognize and confess Jesus Christ as the One sent by the Father for the sake of the world's redemption. Therefore, rather than approaching those who come together in these other spaces from the standpoint of superiority, as if it is church members who possess a patent on Jesus Christ and on what God promises to the world through him, the better strategy for the church to follow may be one of *accompaniment*, of meeting people outside its walls on their turf and of joining forces with them, wherever the opportunity presents itself, as coworkers in God's work of preservation and redemption in a world where every member of the human family—churchgoers as well as persons for whom a weekend worship hour is currently not a feature of their spiritual life—is called to be a participant.

The Human Experience of Faith

Second, Niebuhr's own life experience and response to a "religious depression" that began in America during the decade following World War I and deepened with the economic collapse of the 1930s may serve as a useful example for the twenty-first-century church as it struggles to rediscover its voice in a culture that has marginalized its influence and relegated religion to the private sphere. The starting point to which he directed the church of his day was the universal human experience of faith. To him, faith was not the exclusive property of religion. Nor did it involve an assent to a certain intellectual set of propositions about God, oneself, and the world. On the contrary, the type of faith common to every human being, including the self-proclaimed atheist, consisted of whatever served as the object of one's devotion, whatever one relied upon to make life worth living, or whatever gave it real meaning and purpose. In this regard, he cited a version of Martin Luther's statement that since "trust and faith of the heart alone make both God and idol," then whatever "thy heart clings to ... and relies upon, that is properly thy God." Time and again, Niebuhr liked to point out that there were many gods in which people placed their faith. They were not only personal, including self, family, or home, but such "Olympian" deities as nations, sociopolitical ideologies, free market or planned economies, ecclesiastical institutions, or a particular civilization's pursuit of progress through science and the arts. Yet sooner or later, all of these gods lost their luster, failed to deliver what they promised, or even turned out to be a source of division in and among those who had placed their faith and trust in them. Niebuhr was convinced that these moments of truth, when the faith people were prone to place in these gods was exposed as false, were the first step in the process of their coming to faith in God. In any age or culture, such moments forced people to search for something else surrounding them and yet beyond their world. While this "something" might appear to be nothing more than a void, or to wear the countenance of the mortal enemy or the terrifying judge of humankind, it set the stage for the next crucial step toward making Almighty God the object of one's faith. At this tipping point in the process Niebuhr pointed to the place in the Old Testament Scriptures where Job cried out, "Though he slay me yet will I trust him" (Job 13:15), because he believed it provided a vivid description of conversion. It not only enabled one to embrace God as a faithful companion and trustworthy friend on life's journey; it also led to a reordering of one's direction and purpose in life. Niebuhr called it a revolution of the *mind*, because all sacred or profane knowledge now could be openly scrutinized, and of the *heart* because the love it created for other forms of life erased any boundaries that separated friends from enemies.[12]

---

12. See, for example, H. Richard Niebuhr, "The Nature and Existence of God: A Protestant View" *Motive* 4 (December 1943): 13–15, 43–46.

EPILOGUE: NIEBUHR AND POST-CHURCH AMERICA

The role of the church, as Niebuhr saw it, was to testify to the world of the Christian experience of coming to such faith in God. The drama of Jesus Christ's life, death, and resurrection provided the script. At the cross to which this obedient Son of God was nailed and on which he experienced the deepest feelings of abandonment, one came face-to-face with the slayer of all other gods and the stark reality of divine judgment upon those who falsely place their faith in them. By witnessing this agony and death of Christ at the cross, however, one also came to believe that reconciliation with God had occurred through this event, and that redemption was the chief objective of his plan for the world. For Niebuhr, since this was the path God chose to take in the course of all human events, it was the only one for the church to follow. It continually called forth repentance in and among Christians, and he often described it as the painful process of renouncing, just as God had through the cross of his Son, the false gods that had mistakenly become the object of trust. It also resulted in an equally revolutionary change of mind and heart, a new life patterned after the same selfless love for God and for all of one's neighbors in his creation that his Son Jesus had demonstrated during his life on earth.[13]

Niebuhr's lifelong experience in the church demonstrates that testifying to the world about such faith in God presents more of a challenge in practice than it does in theory. When the Great Depression laid bare the faith that Western Christendom had falsely placed in capitalist, nationalist, and humanistic ideologies, he called upon the church to take a stand *against the world*. In order to ground its message once again in the faith in God to which Jesus Christ had testified, he felt it needed to step back and penitently repudiate these cultural entanglements.

---

13. See, for example, H. Richard Niebuhr, "What Then Must We Do?" *The Christian Century Pulpit* 5 (July 1934): 145–47.

However, Niebuhr would not be inclined to lend his support to post-church advocates of cultural separatism as the only way for the church to remain true to its calling in today's American culture. For one thing, he never intended withdrawal to be anything but a temporary strategy that was occasioned by the church having become too closely identified with the world. He was also keenly aware, on the basis of his own experience and his knowledge of their history, that ecclesiastical institutions were as corruptible as those in the secular world. For this reason, the church could not really hope to become a corps of "resident aliens." In fact, the church's need to make itself the focus of its criticism and seek ongoing reformation forms a major theme in the writings included in the third section of this book. In addition, Niebuhr would probably suggest that a church seeking to build a culture counter to, or as a replacement for, the prevailing one around it might be tempted to become too self-regarding, to make itself the object of its faith, and thus to demonstrate the kind of defensiveness he believed was a telltale symptom of an idolatrous relationship. Furthermore, because Niebuhr saw the world, and not just the church, as the realm of divine activity, no feature of it could remain exempt from transformation. Hence, he would encourage today's church to keep scanning the terrain of the culture into which its Lord continues send it, looking for key moments and opportunities to shoulder the mantle of the prophet and to expose those gods in which its people have falsely placed their trust, and then setting forth courses of action that faith in God might be calling cultural institutions and the church to join hands in pursuing. And finally, in view of the inevitable rebuke the church might receive from those outside as well as within it for overstepping its boundaries and trying to make Christianity the established religion of the culture, he would be likely to point to the universal human experience of faith and, on this basis of this language, call upon the church to communicate its message of revolution.

Beach-Verhey makes a solid case that Niebuhr can contribute to a sorely needed redefinition of the church's role in a polarized political environment. He finds the current tendency to fuse Christianity with the socially conservative or liberal agendas of America's major political parties just as deplorable as Hauerwas and Willimon did in the late 1980s. In addition, he flags postmodern iterations of the social contract theory of government because they allow no role for religion whatsoever in the public square. In a democracy, this leaves the people and their leaders to their own devices in the process of governing the nation. Like Niebuhr, Beach-Verhey sees the world of post-church America, which frequently criticizes Christians for being "too political," as the church's friend, calling the church to repentance for substituting a particular version of the American dream for its own gospel message.[14] During his lifetime as an observer of the American political scene, Niebuhr constantly warned the church against this temptation to form alliances with political causes, movements, and organizations. One of the more eloquent of these passages appeared as early as 1935, and a version of it has been included in this collection. "In the beginning of every uprising against prevailing customs and institutions disparate groups who share a common antagonism are likely to assume that they share a common loyalty," he wrote. "Such groups are united in their negations, not their affirmations. Their positive loyalties, for the sake of which they make a common rejection, may be wholly different." The danger for a church, he went on to point out, was that the "aims and strategies" of their political allies might be "so foreign to its own that when the common victory is won—if it can be

---

14. Beach-Verhey, *Robust Liberalism*, 4–5.

won—the revolutionary church will be left with the sad reflection that it supplied the 'Fourteen Points' which gave specious sanctity to an outrageous peace and that its fruits are an external prosperity based on rotting foundations or debts which cannot be paid without destroying the life of the church."[15]

As a possible solution to the political polarization that has created a fault line that runs through twenty-first-century American churches and their culture, Beach-Verhey, in his book *Robust Liberalism*, calls for a reexamination of the "theocentric covenant" that undergirds the nation's Christian and democratic traditions. In support of his hope of making this idea the one that holds Americans with differing political points of view together while they are living in an increasingly pluralistic society, he effectively explicates some of Niebuhr's writings on the subject (one of which, "The Idea of the Covenant and American Democracy," I purposely selected for this book). Beach-Verhey clearly demonstrates how Niebuhr's recognition of the transcendent perspective this idea furnishes for all citizens of America's democracy, as it was first envisioned by founders like James Madison, keeps their attention focused on a set of values that are universal in scope. It also makes them, as well as the leaders they elect to office, accountable for their actions not just to themselves, but to God and to their neighbors in the entire human family.[16]

Niebuhr did not tend to highlight the phrase "under God" that was added to the Pledge of Allegiance during the 1950s, but I see it as the essence of the counsel he would offer to churches seeking to maintain their independence in addressing issues over which there is, and continues to be, considerable political division and acrimony. Instead of taking one side or another on a divisive issue in the political arena, Niebuhr tended to encourage the church to address the faith,

---

15. H. Richard Niebuhr, "The Emancipation of the Church," *Christendom* 1 (1935): 141.
16. Beach-Verhey, *Robust Liberalism*, 179–87.

or "religious attitude toward life," that informed the positions being taken on the issue. Hence he could excoriate socialists, fascists, and New Deal liberals alike as they sought to create plans and programs designed to lift society out of the depths of the Great Depression. To him, all of them were operating as if God were dead. Despite the fact that the modern world had become both more complex and unpredictable, they chose to place their faith in their own rationality and to depend upon human engineering schemes. Was it any wonder that so many of their efforts often came to naught? Conversely, the living God in whom Christians put their faith required a death of the old for a new birth to take place, and it inspired self-sacrifice rather than self-interest, cooperation instead of class warfare.[17]

Moreover, in the fiercely contested foreign-policy debate during the years prior to Pearl Harbor, Niebuhr sided with neither the interventionists nor the isolationists. Instead, he advised Christians and non-Christian groups on both sides of the issue to take a closer look at the *context* rather than the specific *content* of the choices they were trying to make. Did that context bring to light a faith that was egoistic or nationalistic in character, or was the faith it revealed universalistic enough to be concerned about everyone involved in the conflict?[18]

After World War II, when America found itself in the throes of the Cold War, Niebuhr continued to offer this approach to political issues as a model for the church. Today's church might do well to consider returning to this approach as it seeks to address important public policies in the areas of immigration, LGBTQI discrimination, health care, and the environment, in a twenty-first-century culture that is politically polarized, and at times paralyzed.

17. See H. Richard Niebuhr, "Faith, Works, and Social Salvation," *Religion in Life* 1 (Fall 1932): 426–30.
18. See H. Richard Niebuhr, "The Christian Church and the World's Crisis," *Christianity and Society* 6 (Summer 1941): 11–17.

The Fruits of Repentance

Third, Niebuhr offers an equally sage perspective for a culture in which the church's younger generations are often turned off by the hypocritical and self-serving attitudes of professing Christians, and in many instances have turned away from any type of organized religion. Starting with *The Social Sources of Denominationalism*, his own running list of un-Christian behavior on the part of churches in America became as long as that of any of the other critics of his day. In addition to the secularism and sectarianism with which he found fault throughout his career, there were two other ecclesiastical sins he highlighted following World War II. The first of these was proselytism: "We have wanted men to become as we are because we are Christians, and have confused the imitation of ourselves with the imitation of Christ," he asserted in 1948. "Hence also we have carried into non-Christian countries divisions relevant to our culture, but alien to theirs." The other sin was unbelief. As he saw it, the church could act as if the risen Christ was still in his grave, believing instead "that it is we who must give others His orders," thus arrogating to itself "the right to rule His Church for him."[19]

At the same time, Niebuhr insisted that community remained an essential feature of faith in God. To him, Christians recognized this whenever they professed their allegiance to the "one, holy, catholic Church." This statement made everyone else whom Jesus Christ had revealed to be the objects of God's faithfulness one's sisters and brothers. This community also transcended the boundaries of time and space. It not only projected Christians into the future, when God promised to completely restore all of his broken creation, but also transported them backward into the past, where the words and deeds

---

19. H. Richard Niebuhr, "The Disorder of Man in the Church of God," in *"The Responsibility of the Church for Society" and Other Essays by H. Richard Niebuhr*, ed. Kristine A. Culp (Louisville: Westminster John Knox, 2008), 42–44.

of sainted forebears in the faith could again come to life for them. Christians also knew that without the interpretive role performed by the "community of faith," chiefly through the medium of the Scriptures, their own experiences of God would most likely be confusing and prone to error. While he admitted that people longed for this community of faith but did not find it in churches, Niebuhr took the position that there was still an indispensable connection between the two. Without churches, this community could not even exist, he argued, "anymore than the personal self without mind and without body."[20] He underscored this assertion most plainly in an article in which he was reacting to the heavy emphasis neo-orthodox theologians were placing on the eternal reality of the "Church" by rhetorically asking, "How can the family be for us part of the Church if its life does not begin in and accompany the life of the churches? How shall friendship give us assurance of the presence of the Church if it does not possess the symbols and common language of the churches? How shall we build and serve the Church without the prayers, works, and services of churches?" Christians, he responded, "do not know how to aspire after membership in the Church without joining the churches nor how to build the holy Catholic society, the universal fellowship of reconciliation, without increasing, reforming, supporting, and even defending those contradictory organizations—our religious institutions, these Western counterparts of Shintoist and Hindu cults."[21]

Therefore, if Niebuhr were to address the churches from which members of Kinnaman's lost generation and others have felt alienated, and in some cases grown to despise, he would probably encourage them to adopt an eschatological perspective and to give

---

20. H. Richard Niebuhr, *Faith on Earth: An Inquiry Into the Structure of Human Faith* (New Haven, CT: Yale University Press, 1989), 112–18.
21. H. Richard Niebuhr, "The Hidden Church and the Churches of Sight," *Religion in Life* 15 (Winter 1945–1946): 115–16.

attention to those places and activities in their midst where signs of a "community of faith" were the most apparent. At the same time, he would discourage all disclaimers or defensiveness of any kind and instead issue a clear call for repentance. He might also warn today's churches not to make this a utilitarian exercise, engaging in self-examination and confession of their failures so that they might regain their lost position of privilege. On the contrary, he was convinced that repentance could produce in churches the same fruits it did in the lives of individual members: renewal of faith in God and the change of mind and behavior that always accompanied it. In the process, the eyes of persons outside the churches would also stand a better chance of being opened to the existential reality of the "one, holy, catholic Church" as God's gift to their world.

Confessional, Not Apologetic

Finally, twenty-first-century North American Christians may find Niebuhr to be a guide worth consulting as they seek to deal with the significant demographic changes in the religious makeup of their culture as well as the world beyond it. As greater numbers of Muslims, Buddhists, or Hindus move into their neighborhoods and erect mosques and temples, the religious context in which they find themselves operating is no longer strictly inter-Christian, or even Judeo-Christian, but increasingly *interfaith*.

Niebuhr clearly believed that there was a witness the church had to share with the world. "I am a Christian," he confessed, "because my relation to God has been, so far as I can see, deeply conditioned by the presence of Jesus Christ in my history and in our history." He also stated that for him Christ was "the one who lived and died and rose again" for the sake of bringing God to other persons and other persons to God, and of reconciling them to "each other and their world."[22] Given the universality of the human faith experience as well as the unbounded scope of divine activity, however, he refused to make the claim that God worked in the world exclusively through Christ. Non-Christians, in some cases, could also be informed by a genuine faith in the divine reality, show a deep love and respect for all of life, and possess an abiding hope for their future. Especially when it came to humanitarian efforts, they sometimes succeeded in putting Christians to shame. Niebuhr resisted the idea of turning all theology into Christology and, on the basis of this, making the church out to be a "special group" with a God and destiny apart from the rest of humanity. It thus undoubtedly seemed puzzling to many in his own neo-orthodox camp that Niebuhr would choose to attack the Christomonism that Karl Barth, in particular, was expounding. In his estimation, though, this Barthian trend of the 1950s was erecting the very kind of walls that Christ had come to break down, denying the "society of universal being" that he had called his church to become.[23]

Hence, the approach that Niebuhr would advocate for a church residing in a culture that has become more distinctively interfaith in its religious composition would be *confessional* rather than *apologetic*. He would tell us that a deeper appreciation of one's own Christian faith, and a better understanding of Islam or any other world religion at our doorstep, is more likely to be achieved through mutual respect and open dialogue rather than heated verbal exchanges or isolationist strategies.

On the global scene, moreover, the balance of the Christian population in the twenty-first century has shifted from North to South. The rapid growth of Christianity in Africa, Asia, and Latin America, coupled with its decline in the northern hemisphere, means that there are now more Jesus followers living there than in Europe,

---

22. H. Richard Niebuhr, *The Responsible Self: An Essay in Christian Moral Philosophy* (New York: Harper & Row, 1963), 43–44.
23. H. Richard Niebuhr, *Radical Monotheism and Western Culture* (New York: Harper & Brothers, 1960), 59–60.

the United States, and Canada. As a result of this shift, the mix of voices in the worldwide chorus of the Christian church has become more diverse than at any other point in history. Niebuhr could help us in this situation by reminding us that pluralism is a fact of life in theology as much as any other human endeavor. God is an absolute reality and not the figment of one's imagination, but theology is always expressed in terms that are relative to a time period and a cultural context. In the hands of liberal theologians like Ernst Troeltsch and Adolf von Harnack, "historical relativism" became a weapon in the war of liberating Protestantism from its bondage to the past. Niebuhr, however, perceived that the opposite had in fact occurred. Scripture scholars had come to a greater awareness than ever of the life and times of the people depicted on the pages of the biblical text. Historical studies were showcasing the similarities as well as the variant features of problems facing the church in every age. In general, church fathers and leaders down through the centuries were becoming household names. As a result, representatives from the church's past were being brought into its present context to serve as the church's "counselors" and as "fellow-inquirers." Niebuhr saw this creating for the church a "community of interpreters." Because of the relativity of their time-bound cultural experiences, none in this community possessed the absolute truth or the only answer to any question. All of them, however, had something to contribute to the conversation, but only as everyone looked beyond themselves in order to discern what God at the present moment in time, based on his revelation in Christ, was doing to them and through them. What Niebuhr envisioned was the birth of a "*living* tradition," one "free from slavish dependence on the views of others because with them we are directed toward that which is viewed, yet bound for our own sake to their companionship in a community of interpretation as well as in a community of faith."[24]

EPILOGUE: NIEBUHR AND POST-CHURCH AMERICA

As Christianity trends demographically in the direction of the global South, Africans, Asians, and Latin Americans will no doubt continue to bring to the table elements of their own unique traditions and cultural backgrounds. As conversation ensues among all who are seated there, this catholic vision may prove to be one of Niebuhr's most enduring gifts to the church.

Signs of Niebuhr's Living Tradition

Signs of the living tradition that Niebuhr envisioned in his day are beginning to appear in post-church America and offer a better future for Christians seeking to engage this culture. For instance, following his work with David Kinnaman on their bestselling *UnChristian,* Gabe Lyons went on to publish *The Next Christians.* Subtitled "How a New Generation Is Restoring the Faith," the book calls those who are leading the way "restorers" because their faith has enabled them to see themselves as partners with God to infuse the broken world around them with a greater measure of beauty, grace, love, and justice.

Three examples stand out. First, as the result of a hospital declining admission, one person, along with friends, cared for a neighbor in need of detox for five days. Second, another person gave up the comfort and safety of home to go off to Rwanda to help investigate the genocide of 800,000 people. Still another used photography to create a book with pictures that show how the world ought to be in contrast to what is often perceived to be the case.

Lyons also sets forth a typology similar to the one that Niebuhr produced for the church of his day. He distinguishes the restorers from Christian separatists, who view the world as their opponent, and from cultural Christians who seek to blend into the world around them. Lyons states that these restorers have let the full biblical

---

24. H. Richard Niebuhr, "The Gift of Catholic Vision," *Theology Today* 4 (January 1948): 507–21.

tradition of creation, fall, redemption, and restoration become the narrative for their own lives at every present moment and in all of their relationships. In this regard, they would appear to fit squarely into the Christ-and-culture type that Niebuhr chose to designate as *conversionist*. Furthermore, Lyons asserts that as they honor their callings in the world, restorers tend to remain grounded in the Scriptures and other spiritual disciplines, to consciously create a community to support them, and in the process to succeed in filling yet another void in their often-impersonal world.[25]

The Hope of Glory

Over a half century prior to *The Next Christians*, Niebuhr climbed the steps to the high pulpit in the chapel of Duke University on Sunday, February 3, 1957, to preach a sermon called "The Hope of Glory" to the assembled churchgoers. He chose as his text the words of St. Paul in Romans 8:18 (KJV): "For I reckon that the sufferings of this present time are not worthy to be compared with the glory which shall be revealed in us." As he often did in other sermons, Niebuhr began by distinguishing this "hope of glory" from the hope of achieving prosperity, security, longevity, or heavenly immortality rather than eternal punishment. Instead, he depicted the hope of glory as encompassing all of culture and nature. It was "the hope of God," of "participating with God in ultimate goodness and unity," which could only be received with gratitude as a gift from God. He proceeded to reference a variety of places in the realm of culture that not only brought out the longing for such hope but also revealed courageous suffering on the part of some who were seeking to overcome evil in themselves and in others, as well as an

---

25. Gabe Lyons, *The Next Christians: How a New Generation Is Restoring the Faith* (New York: Doubleday, 2010).

admirable endurance given to others as the only real answer to their daily prayers.

Addressing those assembled before him, Niebuhr asked whether they felt the hope of glory had been taken away from them or if they had put it away. Pointing first to the American dream, which promised a new world where a new life could be lived, he stated that it was being exchanged too easily for the joy of immediate prosperity and instantaneous glamour. Likewise, the contemporary church, in his estimation, had found it too convenient to put aside this hope in order to glorify itself and its past, or else to employ it as an instrument for saving itself and condemning others. But Niebuhr went on to assert that despite the evidence to the contrary in the church and world of the twentieth century, he still found this hope motivating people in both realms—especially in those in every calling and profession who were resisting the temptation for immediate glory for themselves and instead patiently choosing to carry out their responsibilities as if they were laboring for eternity.

One can only imagine that if he were invited to preach this sermon in our time, Niebuhr might also cite Lyons's new generation of twenty-first-century Christians as another prime example of such hope. Then he would indeed be transcending himself, his categories, and even the ones we might design in order to illuminate the paradox of church and world. And just as he did in moving toward the conclusion of his message in 1957, he might also turn to us today and say, "Thank God for the hope of glory."[26]

---

26. H. Richard Niebuhr, "The Hope of Glory" (February 3, 1957), Digital Collections, Duke University Libraries, Durham, NC.

Index of Names and Subjects

Ahlstrom, Sydney, 128
Aldrich, Virgil C., 347
Alexander, Samuel, 124
American dream, 265
Ames, Edward Scribner, 117
Amos (Old Testament prophet), 6, 92, 160, 321
Anabaptists, xv, 104, 160
Anglicanism, 104, 406, 434
Anthropocentrism, 201, 272–3
Aquinas, Thomas, 230, 374–75, 439
Aristotelianism, 227, 456
Arminianism, 290
Augsburg Confession, 4, 98, 179, 184
Augustine, Saint, 76–77, 230, 278, 379, 415

Bainton, Roland, 223

Barnes, Harry Elmer, 107; *The Twilight of Christianity,* 107
Barth, Karl, 89, 113, 119, 121, 140, 165, 179, 198, 221, 231, 264, 450, 497, 517; Barth's theology, 89, 119, 121, 140, 170, 198–99, 221, 231, 264, 450, 497, 517
Barthianism, 121, 170, 198–99, 264, 282, 426, 434, 517
Barton, Bruce, 128; *The Man Nobody Knows,* 128
Baur, Ferdinand Christian, 108
Baumgarten, Otto, 16
Beach-Verhey, Timothy, 504, 511–12; *Robust Liberalism,* 512
Berdyaev, Nikolai, 448
Bergson, Henri, 123, 263; concepts of *movement* and *institution,* 263
Benedict, Saint, 93–95

Bennett, John C., 223
Bentham, Jeremy, 283
Berkeley, George, 107, 115
Biblicism, xxi, 436; see also biblicism
Bibliolatry, 38, 434; see also biblicism
Boehm, Hans, 45
Bolshevism, 117, 178
Bonhoeffer, Dietrich, 187, 505
Boniface VIII, Pope, 315
Bornkamm, Gunther, 486
Brown, William, 113
Brown, William Adams, 461
Browning, Robert, 115
Bruening, Heinrich, 183
Brunner, Emil, 231, 435
Bryan, William Jennings, 35, 82

Calhoun, Robert L., 223
Calvin, John, 34, 76–77, 87, 102, 127, 270, 379, 383, 391, 439, 441–42
Calvinism, 54, 87, 290, 379, 391, 406, 409, 434, 480
Campbell, David, 499; *American Grace*, 499, 500n2
Capitalism, 87, 145, 153, 180, 188, 206–11, 216–17, 239, 249, 257, 267–68, 270–72, 285, 330, 369, 388, 434, 436, 450
Carson, D. A., xx–xxi, 505
Catholic Churches, Roman, 82, 98, 142, 179, 183–85, 216, 361, 395, 440, 443, 480; see also Catholicism, Roman and Neo-Catholicism
Catholicism, Roman, 16, 82, 98, 103, 143, 145, 183–85, 230, 272, 286, 391–92, 404, 406, 410, 433–34, 436–37, 439, 443, 451–60; see also Catholic Churches, Roman and Neo-Catholicism
Chesterton, E. K., 478
Chicago, University of, 7, 219, 470
Christ and Culture, xiii, xiv–xxi, xxiii–iv, 37, 90, 360–61, 363, 426, 504–5; of culture/worldly type, xiii, 360–61; against culture/separatist type, xiii, 360–61; above culture/synthesis type, xiii, 360–61; in paradox/dualist type, xiii, 360–61; transformer of culture/conversionist type, xiii, xv, xx, 360–61

INDEX OF NAMES AND SUBJECTS

Christian Century, 73, 91, 98, 107, 178, 198, 206, 220, 223, 282, 307, 336, 347, 431
Christian Century Pulpit, 241
Christianity and Crisis, 307
Chrystal, William, 6
Chrysostom, John, 316
Church Against the World, The, 213, 219, 220, 222–23, 261, 267
Church History, 372
Church (type religious group), 85, 89, 98, 100
Coe, George Albert, 22
Cold War, 361–62, 372, 387, 413–15, 421, 428, 506, 513
Coleridge, Samuel Taylor, 75, 372
Communism, 40, 153, 158, 180, 188, 190, 193–94, 206–7, 209–12, 216, 231, 233, 237, 269n16, 316, 357, 361, 364, 365, 413, 415, 416, 419, 436, 451; see also Russian Communism
Congregational Christian Churches, 129, 429
Conrad, Joseph, 115
Constantine, (Roman Emperor), 499
Conwell, Russell H., 128; *Acres of Diamonds,* 128
Coolidge, Calvin, 127

Coughlin, Father Charles, 182
Coulter, Stanley, 123
Council of Trent, 98
Counter-Reformation (Roman Catholic), 388
Cranach, Lucas the Elder, 488
Crisis theology, 113, 140, 149, 157, 165, 179
Culp, Kristine A., xxiv; *"The Responsibility of the Church For Society" and Other Essays by H. Richard Niebuhr,* xxiv

Darby, John Nelson, 36
Darrow, Clarence, 35
Darwin, Charles, 376; see also Darwinism
Darwinism, 36, 388; see also Darwin, Charles
Dawes Plan, 188
Deism, 118, 383, 396
Democracy, 22, 40, 114, 135, 216, 233, 237–39, 243, 260n16, 307, 325, 339, 343, 345, 349, 358, 362, 365, 372–86, 387–96, 399, 410, 412, 434, 436, 450, 473–74, 511–12; see also Democracy, American
Democracy, American, 362, 372–86, 392, 410, 512; see also Democracy

Denominationalism, 86, 101, 141, 153, 392, 395, 430
Descartes, Rene, 115, 492
Dewey, John, 231
Dilthey, Wilhelm, 484–85
Diognetus, Epistle to, xi
Don Quixote, 318
Driesch, Hans, 123
Duerer, Albrecht, 488
Durkheim, Emile, 108, 117
Dwight, Timothy, 409

Ecumenical movement, 128, 429, 451, 468; see also Ecumenism; Stockholm conference (1925), 128, 198; Lausanne conference (1927), 128, 201–2; Jerusalem conference (1928), 202; institutional mergers and cooperation, 128, 400–406
Ecumenism, 130, 140, 429, 451, 461, 470; see also Ecumenical Movement
Eddington, A. S., 123–24
Eddy, Sherwood, 191
Eden Theological Seminary, 3, 4, 5, 9, 11, 26, 34–35, 39, 85, 133, 157, 165, 174, 177–78, 226, 425, 433
Edwards, Jonathan, xiii, 6, 262, 265, 383, 409, 439

Eichrodt, Walther, 378
Eisenhower, Dwight D., 362
Ellwood, Charles A., 60
Elmhurst College, 3, 4, 5, 7, 26, 31, 34, 38, 173, 425; service conference, (1927), 34, 88
Engels, Friedrich, 207
Evangelical and Reformed church, 129, 319, 429
Evangelical Herald, 34, 86, 178, 183, 187, 191; *Der Friedensbote*, 178
Evangelical Synod of North America, xiv, xxi, xxiv, 3–8, 11, 14, 26, 28–30, 32, 34, 37, 38, 44, 54, 63, 86, 88, 91, 107, 113, 128–29, 131–32, 140, 157, 179, 191, 221, 241, 264, 425, 430, 433
Evangelicalism, American, 4, 37, 80, 254–55, 284, 404, 456

Fascism, 178, 188–89, 215, 233, 234, 316
Federal Council of Churches, 34, 128, 306, 358, 429
Fehrenbach, Constantin, 183
Fellowship of Reconciliation (FOR), 154, 213, 305–6, 515
Fellowship of Socialist Christians, 324

Feuerbach, Ludwig, 108, 116, 485
Finney, Charles G., 45, 266, 409
Fox, George, 155
Francis, Saint, 154–55, 219, 484
Frank, Waldo, 249; *Death and Birth of David Markand,* 249
French Revolution, 44, 50, 59, 74, 115, 207, 409
Fundamentalism, 35, 37, 80–84, 165, 167, 169, 201
Fundamentalist-Modernist controversy, 36

Gamaliel (New Testament character), 236
Gandhi, Mahatma, 217
Gladden, Washington, 34, 200, 266
Graham, Billy, 80
Gogarten, Friedrich, 170
Great Depression, xxiv, 181, 182, 206, 219, 222, 233, 241, 249, 262, 282, 361, 506, 509, 513
Gustafson, James, xix–xxi, 430

Haeckel, Ernst, 123
Handy, Robert T., 127
Hannibal, 312
Harding, Warren G., 33
Hardy, Thomas, 115
Harnack, Adolf von, 38, 518

Hartshorne, Hugh, 461
Hauerwas, Stanley, xv–xvi, xx–xxi, xxiv, 499, 511; *Resident Aliens: Life in the Christian Colony,* xv
Hegel, Georg Wilhelm Friedrich, 108, 116, 376
Heidelberg Catechism, 4
Higher criticism, 36, 38
Hitler, Adolf, 178–79, 187–89, 191, 213, 305–6, 320, 342, 350, 361, 483
Hobhouse, Leonard Trelawny, 123, 163
Hodge, Archibald, 36
Hoover, Herbert, 181, 233
Hopkins, C. Howard, 291, 298
Hopkins, Mark, 6
Horton, Walter M., 223
Hosea (Old Testament prophet), 270, 340
Humanism, 157, 158, 160, 165, 201, 209, 231, 267, 271–72, 455, 488
Hume, David, 107, 115

Industrial Revolution, 60–61, 209, 388, 438, 465
Inerrancy (biblical), 36, 38, 80, 82
Innere Mission (Home Mission), 4

527

Isaiah (Old Testament prophet), 18, 92, 160, 242, 254, 320, 337, 342, 369, 413–14, 417, 420, 421, 423, 442, 489, 498
Isolationist-interventionist debate, 306–7, 324, 513
Ivan the Terrible, 195

Jackson, Stonewall, 313
James, Henry, 115
James, William, 108, 111, 122
Jeremiah (Old Testament prophet), 270, 415
Jesus, xi–xii, xv, 15, 16–17, 23–25, 27, 37, 46, 52, 55–56, 59, 62–64, 69, 75, 77, 78, 80–81, 88, 90, 91–92, 121–22, 128, 162, 165, 169–70, 200, 202, 226, 229, 230, 232, 242, 245–46, 253, 262, 265, 278–79, 289–90, 291–98, 306, 307, 309, 310, 312–18, 320, 322, 324, 327, 329, 337, 340, 347, 350, 352, 353–55, 358, 399, 408, 415, 417, 435, 442, 443, 445–47, 453, 481, 487, 488, 494, 495, 497, 506–7, 509, 514, 516, 517
Job (Old Testament character), 19, 254, 369, 508

John, Gospel of, xi–xii; Fourth Gospel, 226
Johnson, William Stacy, xxiv, 221, 264; *H. Richard Niebuhr: Theology, History and Culture*, 12
Judaism, 161, 327
Just war theory, 310, 348

Kant, Immanuel, 107–8, 115, 119, 158, 160, 163, 372
Keller, Adolf, 146n9
Kellogg-Briand Peace Pact (1929), 305
Keryx, xxii, 9, 11, 39, 40, 43, 133, 165, 226
Khan, Genghis, 329
Khrushchev, Nikita, 421
Kierkegaard, Soren, 485, 496
Kingdom of God, 13, 22, 34, 42, 45, 47, 52, 54–58, 62, 64, 71, 75, 78, 90, 91, 118, 129, 139, 149–50, 153, 156, 166, 198, 204, 216, 224, 227, 230, 232, 242, 247, 249, 263, 264, 270, 275, 276, 283, 289, 292–94, 296, 298, 319–23, 364, 367, 380, 414, 447, 449, 452–54, 457, 477, 487

Kingdom of God in America, The, xii, xxii, 89, 262, 263, 265, 266, 362

Kinnaman, David, 502–4, 515, 519; *Unchristian,* 503; *You Lost Me,* 503

Ku Klux Klan, 84

Kultur-Protestantism, 435, 436

Kuno [Cuno], Wilhelm, 183

Kutter, Hermann, 168

Labor movement, 33, 44–53

Latourette, Kenneth Scott, 359

Lee, Robert E., 312

Levy-Bruhl, Lucien, 108, 117

Liberalism, 218, 222, 235–38, 272, 283, 436, 485

Liberal Christianity 87, 107, 130, 131, 165–70, 221, 396

Lincoln, Abraham, 311

Locke, John, 119; Lockean thought, 391

Longstreet, James, 314

Lortz, Joseph, 486–88

Luke, Saint, xi, 75, 241, 312, 315

Luther, Martin, 4, 45, 50–52, 74–77, 415, 423, 433, 439, 441–42, 448, 450, 479–98, 507

Lutheranism, xiv, 4, 16, 29, 54, 78, 98, 104, 163, 179, 184–85, 204, 221, 388, 396, 406, 434, 480

Lutheran churches, 29, 34, 82, 102, 117, 129, 196, 202, 393, 400–401, 404

Lyons, Gabe, 503, 519; *Unchristian,* 503; *The Next Christians,* 519

Machen, J. Gresham, 36; *Christianity and Liberalism,* 36

Macintosh, D. C., 88, 112, 113, 119–21

Madison, James, 512

Manchurian crisis, 223, 226, 506

Manrodt, Manfred, 37

Marrett, Robert R., 253

Marsden, George, xviii, xix, xxi

Marty, Martin, xix, xxi

Marx, Karl, 180, 207

Marxism, 128, 160, 181, 188, 206, 250, 256, 269n16, 282, 288–89, 330, 338

McCarthy, Joseph, 362

Mather, Cotton, 440, 442

Mathews, Shailer, 88; *The Faith of Modernism,* 88

May, Mark, 461

Meaning of Revelation, The, 308–9

Metzdee, 482

Micah (Old Testament prophet), 160

Miller, Francis P., 219, 222, 223

529

Miller, Perry, 372, 378
Modernism, 83, 87, 201, 272
Monasticism, 92–97, 137, 439
Morrison, Charles Clayton, 282
Mueller, Alfred Dedo, 179, 203
Mussolini, Benito, 190, 361
Mysticism, 93–94, 100, 109, 157, 161, 396, 456, 484

National Council of Churches, 402, 404, 429,
National Socialism, 190, 326, 330, 361, 365; see also Nazi party
Nationalism, 34, 50, 52, 86, 93, 103, 137, 141, 145–46, 147–48, 152, 190, 213–18, 229, 239, 249, 257, 267, 271, 272, 276, 285, 288, 298, 330–33, 388, 428, 434, 452, 471
Nazi party, 179, 187, 213, 350; see also National Socialism
Neo-Catholicism, 286
Neo-Orthodoxy, 222, 430; see also Neo-Protestantism
Neo-Protestantism, 286, 288, 289
Nero, 275
New Deal, 182, 220, 233, 241, 513
Niebuhr, Gustav, 3, 4, 5, 35
Niebuhr, H. Richard, xii–xiv, xvii–xviii, xx–xxiii; family, church background, education, 3–6, 9, 11, 34–35, 38, 54, 73; career in the Evangelical Synod, 6–8, 14, 26, 34, 37–38, 39, 44, 54, 86, 88, 91, 129–30; European sabbatical, 177–81, 183–95; Yale career, 177, 181, 262, 291, 306, 312, 426, 430–31, 461; relationship to Reinhold Niebuhr, 3, 5–7, 26, 34–35, 191, 223–25, 249, 364, 425, 506; theme of repentance, 46, 155–56, 167, 169–70, 241, 247, 281, 288, 321, 334, 343, 355, 364, 369–70, 447, 469, 474, 509, 514–16; theology of the cross, 52–53, 278–79, 306, 312, 319, 321, 335, 337, 341–46, 347–56, 420; view of history as revelatory, 224–25, 226–32, 308–9, 336–37, 505–6; Christianity as "revolution," 258–59, 279, 310, 355, 508
Niebuhr, Lydia Hosto, 3
Niebuhr, Reinhold, 3, 5, 6, 7, 26, 34, 35, 172, 182, 191, 223–25, 226, 249, 307, 364, 425, 506
Niebuhr, Richard R., 181
Niebuhr, Walter, 6–7

Otto, Rudolf, 119, 253
Oxford movement, 285

INDEX OF NAMES AND SUBJECTS

Pacifism, 48, 137, 305–6
Parrington, Vernon L., 263
Pauck, Wilhelm, 219, 222, 223
Paul, Saint, 15, 16, 22, 24, 45, 54, 75, 78, 103, 154, 162, 226, 229, 241, 247, 256, 269, 353, 442, 448, 487, 494, 498, 520
Pedersen, Johannes, 378
Pentecostalism, 104, 394, 404
Peter, New Testament apostle, 314
Pilate, Pontius, New Testament character, 320, 334, 337
Plato, 163, 374
Platonic, 375
Platonists, 227
Porter, Frank C., 38
Post-Constantinian church, 13, 522
Pragmatism, 108, 111, 117, 231, 365–67, 405
Press, Samuel D., 5, 35, 172, 178
Prohibition, 63, 128, 182, 411
Prussian Union, 4
Purpose of the Church and its Ministry, The, 37, 431
Psychology of religion, 107–11, 157, 466
Puritanism, xiii, 50, 163, 258, 265, 275, 317, 372, 378, 383, 437, 440
Putnam, Robert, 499; *American Grace*, 499

Quakers (Friends), 138, 155, 160, 394, 480

Radical Monotheism and Western Culture, 362, 427
Rauschenbusch, Walter, 34, 200, 266
Realism, 119–20, 410; see also Religious realism
Red Scare, 117
Reformation, Protestant, 15, 45, 47, 54, 59, 74, 75, 149, 150, 159, 185, 206, 208, 209, 278, 279, 369, 388, 421, 425, 427, 431, 433, 434, 436–39, 441, 450, 459, 463, 471, 479, 481, 483, 485–86, 488–90, 491, 492, 493, 495, 496, 497, 498
Reformed Church, German, 4, 241, 393
Relativism, xx, 163, 199, 518
Religion in Life, 233, 282, 451
Religious freedom, 385, 457–58
Religious realism, 198, 203–5; see also Realism

Rembrandt van Rijn, 488
Ritschl, Albrecht, 20, 38
Roosevelt, Franklin Delano, 220, 233, 307, 324, 358; *Four Freedoms,* 349, 358
Rousseau, Jean-Jacques, 235; Rousseauistic thought 391
Royce, Josiah, 383
Russell, Bertrand, 67
Russian Communism, 96, 159, 418, 434; see also Communism
Russian Orthodox Church, 102, 180
Russian Revolution, 115, 180, 209

Sect (type religious group), 85, 89–90, 98, 100–101, 138, 154–55, 160, 434
Sermon on the Mount, 24, 49, 54, 62
Schiller, Friedrich, 123
Schleiermacher, Friedrich, 20, 107, 108, 111, 116, 117
Schweitzer, Albert, 427
Scopes Trial (1925), 35, 80, 81
Seaton, John L., 461
Secularism, 76, 155, 209–12, 213, 456, 514
Seeberg, Reinhold, 184
Sidgwick, Henry, 163
Smith, Adam, 236

Smith, Gerarld L. K., 182
Smith, Timothy, xiv
Social Gospel, 34, 44, 54–55, 63, 64, 71, 78, 91–92, 94, 117, 128, 132, 149-50, 165–70, 198, 200, 201, 205, 231, 239, 264, 265, 266, 276, 282–90, 291, 297, 298, 338, 409
Social Sources of Denominationalism, The, xii, xxii, 37, 44, 85–86, 87, 89, 128, 130, 140, 177, 262, 263, 387, 514
Socialism, 44, 50, 128, 146, 152, 158, 160, 185, 213–18, 220, 249, 288, 325, 326, 330-31, 436, 450; Christian socialism, 166–67, 170, 204, 276
Soviet Union, 177, 180, 191, 361, 413; Soviet experiment, 180, 191
Spencer, Theodore, 374
Spener, Philipp, 485
Spengler, Oswald, 438
Stalin, Joseph, 191; Stalinism, 181, 329
Stoicism, 314
Stassen, Glen H., xvii–xviii, xxi, 505
Strauss, David Friedrich, 108, 116
Suleiman the Magnificent, 422

Synoptic Gospels, 17, 76, 229

Tawney, R. H., 208
Tennyson, Alfred Lord, 115
Tertullian, xi
Theological Discussion Group, 223, 264
Theology Today, 358, 430, 506, 519
Thomas (New Testament apostle), 317
Thompson, Francis, 115
Thompson, J. A., 123
Tillich, Paul, 179–80, 198, 203, 204, 223, 233, 427; *The Religious Situation*, 180
Trevelyan, George M., 379
Troeltsch, Ernst, xiv, 38, 73, 85, 89, 98, 100, 168, 184, 518; *The Social Teaching of the Christian Churches*, 85
Tyler, Wat, 45

Union Theological Seminary, New York, 7
United Brethren in Christ, 129
United Church in America, 129
United Church of Christ, 129, 429
Utilitarianism, 306, 365, 367–68, 371, 471

Valparaiso University, 479

Van Dusen, Henry P., 223
Versailles, Treaty of, 7, 178, 183, 188–89, 305

Walnut Park Evangelical Church, 4
Warfield, Benjamin B., 36
Washington University, St. Louis, 7, 39
Weber, Max, 87, 103, 208
Wesley, John, 30, 76–77, 104, 270, 439
Westminster Confession, 98
Whitehead, Alfred North, 124, 222
Wieman, Henry Nelson, 120–21
Williams, Daniel Day, 430
Willimon, William, xv–xvi, xx–xxi, xxiv, 499, 511; *Resident Aliens: Life in the Christian Colony*, xv
Wilson, Woodrow, 7; *Fourteen Points*, 276, 512
Winrod, Gerald, 182
Wirth, Joseph, 183
World Council of Churches, 402, 429, 470
World Tomorrow, The, 157, 213
World War I, 5, 7, 9, 38, 80, 83, 86, 113, 114, 119, 127, 178, 213, 507

World War II, xv, xvii, xxiv, 309,
    311, 319, 324, 336, 357, 361,
    363, 364, 428, 431, 451, 462,
    499, 506, 513, 514
Wright, G. Ernest, 223
Wycliff, John, 45

Yale Divinity School, xxii, 4, 182,
    291, 300–301, 312, 426

Yale University, 177
Yeager, D. M., xvii
Yoder, John Howard, xv–xviii, xx,
    xxi
Young Plan, 188

Zeus, 321, 351
Zwingli, Ulrich, 74

www.ingramcontent.com/pod-product-compliance
Lightning Source LLC
Chambersburg PA
CBHW071144070526
44584CB00019B/2647